Marx, Engels, and Marxisms

Series Editors
Marcello Musto
York University
Toronto, ON, Canada

Terrell Carver
University of Bristol
Bristol, UK

D1449389

The Marx renaissance is underway on a global scale. Wherever the critique of capitalism re-emerges, there is an intellectual and political demand for new, critical engagements with Marxism. The peer-reviewed series Marx, Engels and Marxisms (edited by Marcello Musto & Terrell Carver, with Babak Amini and Kohei Saito as Assistant Editors) publishes monographs, edited volumes, critical editions, reprints of old texts, as well as translations of books already published in other languages. Our volumes come from a wide range of political perspectives, subject matters, academic disciplines and geographical areas, producing an eclectic and informative collection that appeals to a diverse and international audience. Our main areas of focus include: the oeuvre of Marx and Engels, Marxist authors and traditions of the 19th and 20th centuries, labour and social movements, Marxist analyses of contemporary issues, and reception of Marxism in the world.

More information about this series at
http://www.palgrave.com/gp/series/14812

Shaibal Gupta • Marcello Musto
Babak Amini
Editors

Karl Marx's Life, Ideas, and Influences

A Critical Examination on the Bicentenary

palgrave
macmillan

Editors
Shaibal Gupta
Asian Development Research Institute
Patna, Bihar, India

Babak Amini
London School of Economics
London, UK

Marcello Musto
Department of Sociology
York University
Toronto, ON, Canada

ISSN 2524-7123   ISSN 2524-7131   (electronic)
Marx, Engels, and Marxisms
ISBN 978-3-030-24817-8   ISBN 978-3-030-24815-4   (eBook)
https://doi.org/10.1007/978-3-030-24815-4

This Palgrave Macmillan imprint is published by the registered company Springer Nature Switzerland AG.
The registered company address is: Gewerbestrasse 11, 6330 Cham, Switzerland

SERIES FOREWORD

THE MARX REVIVAL

The Marx renaissance is under way on a global scale. Whether the puzzle is the economic boom in China or the economic bust in 'the West', there is no doubt that Marx appears regularly in the media nowadays as a guru, and not a threat, as he used to be. The literature dealing with Marxism, which all but dried up twenty-five years ago, is reviving in the global context. Academic and popular journals and even newspapers and online journalism are increasingly open to contributions on Marxism, just as there are now many international conferences, university courses and seminars on related themes. In all parts of the world, leading daily and weekly papers are featuring the contemporary relevance of Marx's thought. From Latin America to Europe, and wherever the critique to capitalism is re-emerging, there is an intellectual and political demand for a new critical encounter with Marxism.

TYPES OF PUBLICATIONS

This series brings together reflections on Marx, Engels and Marxisms from perspectives that are varied in terms of political outlook, geographical base, academic methodologies and subject-matter, thus challenging many preconceptions as to what 'Marxist' thought can be like, as opposed to what it has been. The series will appeal internationally to intellectual communities that are increasingly interested in rediscovering the most powerful critical analysis of capitalism: Marxism. The series editors will ensure that authors and editors in the series are producing overall an eclectic and stimulating yet synoptic and informative vision that will draw a very wide and diverse audience. This series will embrace a much wider range of scholarly interests and academic approaches than any previous "family" of books in the area.

This innovative series will present monographs, edited volumes and critical editions, including translations, to Anglophone readers. The books in this series will work through three main categories:

Studies on Marx and Engels
The series will include titles focusing on the *oeuvre* of Marx and Engels which utilize the scholarly achievements of the on-going *Marx-Engels Gesamtausgabe*, a project that has strongly revivified the research on these two authors in the past decade.

Critical Studies on Marxisms
These volumes will awaken readers to the overarching issues and world-changing encounters that shelter within the broad categorization 'Marxist'. Particular attention will be given to authors such as Gramsci and Benjamin, who are very popular and widely translated nowadays all over the world, but also to authors who are less known in the English-speaking countries, such as Mariátegui.

Reception Studies and Marxist National Traditions
Political projects have necessarily required oversimplifications in the twentieth century, and Marx and Engels have found themselves 'made over' numerous times and in quite contradictory ways. Taking a national perspective on 'reception' will be a global revelation and the volumes of this series will enable the worldwide Anglophone community to understand the variety of intellectual and political traditions through which Marx and Engels have been received in local contexts.

Toronto, Canada   Marcello Musto
Bristol, UK   Terrell Carver

Titles Published

1. Terrell Carver & Daniel Blank, *A Political History of the Editions of Marx and Engels's "German Ideology" Manuscripts*, 2014.
2. Terrell Carver & Daniel Blank, *Marx and Engels's "German Ideology" Manuscripts: Presentation and Analysis of the "Feuerbach chapter"*, 2014.
3. Alfonso Maurizio Iacono, *The History and Theory of Fetishism*, 2015.
4. Paresh Chattopadhyay, *Marx's Associated Mode of Production: A Critique of Marxism*, 2016.
5. Domenico Losurdo, *Class Struggle: A Political and Philosophical History*, 2016.
6. Frederick Harry Pitts, *Critiquing Capitalism Today: New Ways to Read Marx*, 2017.
7. Ranabir Samaddar, *Karl Marx and the Postcolonial Age*, 2017.
8. George Comninel, *Alienation and Emancipation in the Work of Karl Marx*, 2018.
9. Jean-Numa Ducange & Razmig Keucheyan (Eds.), *The End of the Democratic State: Nicos Poulantzas, a Marxism for the 21st Century*, 2018.
10. Robert Ware, *Marx on Emancipation and the Socialist Transition: Retrieving Marx for the Future*, 2018.
11. Xavier LaFrance & Charles Post (Eds.), *Case Studies in the Origins of Capitalism*, 2018.
12. John Gregson, *Marxism, Ethics, and Politics: The Work of Alasdair MacIntyre*, 2018.
13. Vladimir Puzone & Luis Felipe Miguel (Eds.), *The Brazilian Left in the 21st Century: Conflict and Conciliation in Peripheral Capitalism*, 2019.
14. James Muldoon & Gaard Kets (Eds.), *The German Revolution and Political Theory*, 2019.
15. Gustavo Moura de Cavalcanti Mello & Mauricio de Souza Sabadini (Eds.), *Financial Speculation and Fictitious Profits: A Marxist Analysis*, 2019.
16. Michael Brie, *Lenin—Dialectics of Revolution and Metaphysics of Domination*, 2019.
17. August H. Nimtz, *Marxism versus Liberalism: Comparative Real Time Political Analysis*, 2019.
18. Gustavo Moura de Cavalcanti Mello & Mauricio de Souza Sabadini (Eds.), *Financial Speculation and Fictitious Profits: A Marxist Analysis*.
19. Michael Brie, *Rediscovering Lenin: Dialectics of Revolution and Metaphysics of Domination*.
20. August H. Nimtz, *Marxism versus Liberalism: Comparative Real-Time Political Analysis*.

Titles Forthcoming

Igor Shoikhedbrod, *Revisiting Marx's Critique of Liberalism: Rethinking Justice, Legality, and Rights.*

Juan Pablo Rodríguez, *Resisting Neoliberal Capitalism in Chile: The Possibility of Social Critique.*

Alfonso Maurizio Iacono, *The Bourgeois and the Savage: A Marxian Critique of the Image of the Isolated Individual in Defoe, Turgot and Smith.*

Antonio Oliva, Ivan Novara & Angel Oliva, *Marx and Contemporary Critical Theory: The Philosophy of Real Abstraction.*

Jean-Numa Ducange, *Jules Guesde: The Birth of Socialism and Marxism in France.*

Spencer A. Leonard, *Marx, the India Question, and the Crisis of Cosmopolitanism.*

Kevin B. Anderson, Kieran Durkin & Heather Brown, *Raya Dunayevskaya's Intersectional Marxism: Race, Gender, and the Dialectics of Liberation.*

Kaan Kangal, *Friedrich Engels and the Dialectics of Nature.*

Vesa Oittinen, *Marx's Russian Dimension.*

Victor Wallis, *Socialist Practice: Histories and Theories.*

Giuseppe Vacca, *Alternative Modernities: Antonio Gramsci's Twentieth Century.*

Marcello Mustè, *Marxism and Philosophy of Praxis: An Italian Perspective from Labriola to Gramsci.*

PREFACE

Capitalism was ushered into Europe when the First Industrial Revolution began in about 1760. Since then, global material production has increased manifold. But this has simultaneously resulted in skewed development. Some people have become ultra-rich, while others remain poor and devastated. Marx wrote about the unfolding of economic and social script since the French Revolution. Not only did he interpret the world the way it was, but he also provided a strategy to change it. If an author's eternal youth consists in his capacity to keep stimulating new ideas, then it may be said that Marx has without question remained young in the past 200 years. Thus, even after two centuries, Marx is still relevant.

Marx was born when the First Industrial Revolution was over. When he died, the Second Industrial Revolution was in full swing. He could not see the ultimate face of the Industrial Revolution manifesting as "assembly line production". Most of his formulations were around these two industrial revolutions. Marx left many of his most famous texts incomplete. Volumes II and III of *Capital* were posthumously edited by Engels, while the *Economic and Philosophic Manuscripts of 1844*, *The German Ideology* and *Grundrisse*—all of them non-conceived for publication—appeared almost one century after they were written. Recently, the resumed publication of the *Marx-Engels-Gesamtausgabe* (MEGA²), the new historical-critical edition of his complete works, has been helping scholars around the world for an overall reassessment of Marx's *oeuvre*. Many new materials show us an author very different from the one that numerous critics or self-styled followers presented for such a long time. For example, they reveal an author who extended his examination of the contradictions of capitalist society beyond the conflict between capital and labour to other domains. In the lesser-known period of his life, Marx also devoted a lot of his time to the study of non-European issues. Moreover, contrary to interpretations that equate Marx's conception of socialism with the development of productive forces, some manuscripts demonstrated that ecological concerns figured in his work.

Amongst the biggest authors of political and economic thought, Marx is the one whose profile has changed the most in recent years. Some manuscripts highlighted that he was widely interested in several other topics that people often ignore when they talk about him. Among them, there are the potential of technology, the search for collective forms of ownership not related to state control, and the need for individual freedom in contemporary society: all fundamental issues of our times. The renewal in the interpretation of Marx's thought is a phenomenon destined to continue. He is not at all an author about whom everything has already been said or written, despite frequent claims to the contrary. Many sides of Marx remain to be explored.

Marxism is not as alive today as it was in the past. Aside from the Soviet Union and the Eastern Bloc, most of the anti-colonial struggles across the world in the last century were anchored around Marxian doctrine. At one point of time, "actually existing socialism" countries covered nearly one-third of the world. Yet the changed political landscape also contributed to the present Marx revival. The fall of the Berlin Wall liberated him from the chains of an ideology that had little to do with his conception of society. The implosion of the Soviet Union helped to free Marx from the role of figurehead for a state apparatus. At the same time, to relegate Marx to the position of an embalmed classic, suitable only for academia, would be a serious mistake.

Returning to Marx is still indispensable to understand the logic and dynamics of capitalism. While billionaires have mushroomed around the globe, the recent Inequality Index, Global Hunger Index or Human Development Index all tell dismal stories about the other side of the world. Starvation is still a diabolic reality. At the same time, there is a continuous move to fetter the workers, instead of ensuring their welfare. Moreover, Marx's work is also a very useful tool that provides a rigorous examination addressing why previous socio-economical experiments to replace capitalism with another mode of production failed. Economic crises, profound inequalities that exist in our society—in particular between the Global North and South—and the dramatic environmental issues of our time have urged several scholars and politicians to reopen the debate on the future of capitalism and the need for an alternative.

This volume contains the proceedings of the five-day international conference, *Karl Marx's Life, Ideas, Influences: A Critical Examination on the Bicentenary*. This event, held at Asian Development Research Institution (Patna, India), from 16 to 20 June 2018, was amongst the largest international conferences in the world convened to celebrate the 200th anniversary of Marx's birth. It included the participation of 53 scholars, from all continents and 17 countries.

The Bicentenary conference on Marx in Patna in 2018 was a follow-up to the conference on Marx, 50 years ago, in a small subdivisional town of Begusarai in Bihar (India) in 1967, to celebrate the 150th anniversary of his birth. The canvas of the Begusarai conference was limited to "Marx and India"; in contrast, the canvas of the Patna conference was much wider geographically as well as thematically. In the Patna conference, it was not Marx alone who was remembered; there were 38 dedicated memorial lectures in the memory of philosophers, economists, academics and political figures, such as Friedrich Engels, Rudolf Hilferding, György Lukács, Kozo Uno, E. M. S. Namboodripad, Puran Chand Joshi and Frantz Fanon, who had either influenced him or were influenced by him.

This book contains a selection of 16 papers that were presented at the conference, divided into two parts: "On the Critique of Politics" and "On the Critique of Political Economy". Part I begins with an essay by Miguel Vedda which offers an interpretation of Marx as an essayist and one of the founding figures of the modern critic-Intellectual. By comparing Heinrich Heine and Marx, the chapter highlights the authenticity of Marx's role as a critic-Intellectual beyond the Hegelian concept of "torn conscience" as a politically engaged orientation towards the world with the purpose of understanding and transforming it. The next chapter by Marcello Musto argues that Marx's idea of socialism was profoundly different from State socialism and reformism that emerged in the German Social Democratic Party and that became hegemonic after the foundation of the Second International. Marx's vision of a revolutionary transition from capitalism is what Kohei Saito's chapter probes into. It sees Marx's theory of revolution as an attempt to overcome the modern dualism of the state and civil society through a dialectic understanding of the "separation" and "unity" of the economic and the political under capitalism. The chapter uses this framework to propose a critique of post-Marxist theorists. Michael Brie's chapter elaborates on Marx's theoretical-methodological approach as consisting of a new mode of critique that is both dialectical and emancipatory. The chapter exemplifies the maturation of this mode of critique in *Capital* in which the dramatic exploration of the exploitive dynamics of capital also reveals pathways that point to elements for the formation of a new society. Peter Hudis's chapter delves deeper into how Marx's critique of political economy always already contains an emancipatory vision of a post-capitalist society. The chapter by Peter Beilharz audits some of the new innovations in scholarships on Marx in the Anglophone world that drive the Marx revival in recent years. Babak Amini's chapter traces the genesis of the notion of "workers' control", defined in contrast to a vision of a communist society based on state or party control, in Marx and Marxists from the Paris Commune up to the February Revolution in Russia. Another example of such an innovative reading of Marx is exhibited in Andrew J. Douglas's chapter, which considers Martin Luther King Jr.'s call for a "revolution of values" through the lens of a theory of value production and circulation within global (racial) capitalism, the foundations of which can be traced to Marx's critique of political economy. Part I closes with a chapter by Paula Rauhala which presents the (dis)continuities in the interpretations of *Capital* in Germany between the 100th and 150th anniversaries of its publication by contextualizing these receptions in the historical contexts within which they emerged. The chapter therefore argues that any new readings of *Capital* must put the specificity of the present historical conjecture at the centre of their interpretive framework—a task that requires historicization of the past receptions of *Capital*.

Jan Toporowski opens Part II of the book by exploring Marx's critique of the classical theory of interest, as articulated by David Ricardo. The chapter argues that in a purely capitalist economy, interest is a simple transfer of capitalists' monetary resource. Therefore, interest does not require a surplus of production over costs and is independent of the rate of profit. Ramaa Vasudevan takes a philosophical view of Marx's theory of money (including credit money) and argues that it reflects both his materialist conception of history and dialectic method of analysis. Samuel Hollander seeks to replace the view of Marx as a "revolutionary" who embraced a violent overthrow of capitalism with an evolutionary one. He argues that Marx's evolutionism extends not only to his understanding of advanced capitalism but also to his vision of the transition beyond it. Tian Yu Cao analyses the possibility of a non-statist model of socialism guided by Marx's ideas of establishing a socialized economy through the struggle of the working classes. It offers a framework of socializing economic activities based on the Marxian notion of association of free and equal producers which still leaves room for various forms of embedded market transactions. Ajit Sinha's chapter locates the root of Marx's problem of relating values to prices and surplus values to profits in his analysis of labour time in a capitalist economy. The chapter further argues that Piero Sraffa was able to overcome these problems by liberating Marx from his metaphysics of "human labour". Cynthia Lucas Hewitt empirically examines the validity of Marx's understanding of the monopolizing tendency of capital amidst capitalist market expansion at a global scale by analysing the IMF Financial Access Survey Data. It also analyses the particular challenges that the rise of China has introduced within the capitalist world system and the possibilities for African peripheries with communal principles in a period of core system collapse. In the last chapter of the book, Muhammad Ali Jan and Barbara Harriss-White critically examine the extent to which Marx's conceptions regarding the dynamics of transition from pre-capitalist to capitalist societies are applicable to understand the scale and persistence of petty commodity production in India.

These contributions all come together to give a sense of new directions in the scholarship around Marx. What they make clear is that the ideas of Marx continue to engage the intellect, imagination and conscience of human minds across the world from perspectives that are understandably very diverse. Thus, during the bicentenary of the great philosopher, it is certainly an apt moment not just to remember him, but also to rethink and interrogate all that is sourced to him, both academically and politically.

Patna, India   Shaibal Gupta
Toronto, ON, Canada   Marcello Musto
London, UK   Babak Amini

CONTENTS

Notes on Contributors

Babak Amini is a PhD Candidate in Sociology at the London School of Economics. He is the editor of *The Radical Left in Europe in the Age of Austerity* (2016) and the co-editor of *Routledge Handbook of Marx's Capital: A Global History of Translation* (forthcoming).

Peter Beilharz is Professor of Critical Theory at Sichuan University, China, and Professor of Culture and Society at Curtin University, Australia. He is the author of *Socialism and Modernity* (2009), *Circling Marx* (forthcoming), *Alastair Davison—Gramsci in Australia* (forthcoming) and *Working with Zygmunt Bauman* (forthcoming).

Michael Brie is a senior fellow at the Institute for Critical Social Analysis of the Rosa Luxemburg Stiftung, Berlin, Germany. He is the author of *Lenin neu entdecken. Zur Dialektik der Revolution und Metaphysik der Herrschaft* (2017) and *Luxemburg neu entdecken. Freiheit für den Feind* (2019). He is the editor of *Karl Polanyi in Dialogue. A Socialist Thinker of Our Times* (2017) and co-editor of *Karl Polanyi's Vision of a Socialist Transformation* (2018).

Tian Yu Cao is Professor of Philosophy at Boston University, USA. He is the author of *Power and Rationality: Marxism and Liberalism in the World History* (2016). He is the editor of *Labor's Property Rights and the China Model* (2006), *The Social Democratic Trends in China's Contemporary Reform* (2008), *Culture and Social Transformations in Reform Era China*

(2010) and *Culture and Social Transformations—Theoretical Framework and Chinese Context* (2014).

Andrew J. Douglas is Associate Professor of Political Science at Morehouse College, Atlanta, GA, USA. He is the author of *In the Spirit of Critique: Thinking Politically in the Dialectical Tradition* (2013) and *W. E. B. Du Bois and the Critique of the Competitive Society* (2019).

Shaibal Gupta is the founding Member Secretary of Asian Development Research Institute in Patna, India. He is the author of *Idea of the Hindi Heartland* (2014) and *Idea of Bihar* (2013). He is the co-editor of *Resurrection of the State—A Saga of Bihar: Essays in Memory of Papiya Ghosh* (2013).

Barbara Harriss-White is Emeritus Professor of Development Studies at Oxford University, UK. She is the author of *Rural Commercial Capital: Agricultural Markets in West Bengal* (2008) and *Dalits and Adivasis in India's Business Economy* (2014). She is the editor of *The Comparative Political Economy of Development: Africa and South Asia* (2010), *Mapping India's Capitalism: Old and New Regions* (2015), *Middle India and Urban-Rural Development: Four Decades of Change* (2016) and *The Wild East: Criminal Political Economies in South Asia* (2019).

Cynthia Lucas Hewitt is Associate Professor of Sociology and Faculty of the Sustainability Minor and the African American Studies Program at Morehouse College, Atlanta, GA, USA. She is the author of *The Nana Ohemaas ("Queen Mothers") of Ghana and Good Governance in Africa* (forthcoming).

Samuel Hollander is an Officer in the Order of Canada and University Professor Emeritus at the University of Toronto, Canada. Among his recent publications are *The Economics of Karl Marx: Analysis and Application* (2008), *Friedrich Engels and Marxian Political Economy* (2011), *John Stuart Mill: Political Economist* (2015) and *A History of Utilitarian Ethics: Studies in Individual Motivation and Distributive Justice, 1700–1875* (2019).

Peter Hudis is Professor of Philosophy and Humanities at Oakton Community College, Illinois, USA. His most recent works are *Marx's Concept of the Alternative to Capitalism* (2012) and *Frantz Fanon, Philosopher of the Barricades* (2015). He is the co-editor of *The Rosa*

Luxemburg Reader (2004) and *The Letters of Rosa Luxemburg* (2011). He currently serves as general editor of *The Complete Works of Rosa Luxemburg*.

Muhammad Ali Jan is a junior research fellow at Wolfson College, University of Oxford, UK.

Marcello Musto is Associate Professor of Sociological Theory at York University in Toronto, Canada. He is the author of *Another Marx: Early Manuscripts to the International* (2018) and *The Last Years of Karl Marx: An Intellectual Biography* (forthcoming). He is the editor of *Karl Marx's Grundrisse: Foundations of the Critique of Political Economy 150 Years Later* (2008), *Marx for Today* (2012) and *Workers Unite! The International 150 Years Later* (2014); and the co-editor of *Routledge Handbook of Marx's Capital: A Global History of Translation* (forthcoming).

Paula Rauhala is a doctoral researcher at Tampere University, Finland.

Kohei Saito is Associate Professor of Political Economy at Osaka City University in Osaka, Japan. He is the author of *Karl Marx's Ecosocialism: Capital, Nature and the Unfinished Critique of Political Economy* (2017). He is the co-editor of *Marx-Engels-Gesamtausgabe*, vol. IV/18, *Exzerpte und Notizen: Februar 1864 bis Oktober 1868, November 1869, März, April, Juni 1870, Dezember 1872* (with Teinosuke Otani and Timm Graßmann, De Gruyter, 2019).

Ajit Sinha is Professor of Economics at Azim Premji University, Bengaluru, India. He is the author of *Theories of Value from Adam Smith to Piero Sraffa* (2010), *A Revolution in Economic Theory: The Economics of Piero Sraffa* (2016) and *Essays on Theories of Value in the Classical Tradition* (2019). He is the editor of *A Reflection on a Revolution in Economic Theory* (forthcoming).

Jan Toporowski is Professor of Economics and Finance at SOAS University of London, UK. He is the author of *Why the World Economy Needs a Financial Crash and Other Critical Essays on Finance and Financial Economics* (2010), *Michał Kalecki: An Intellectual Biography Volume I, Rendezvous in Cambridge 1899–1939* (2013) and *Michał Kalecki: An Intellectual Biography, Volume II: By Intellect Alone 1939–1970* (2018).

Ramaa Vasudevan is an associate professor at the Department of Economics, Colorado State University, USA. She is the author of *Things Fall Apart: From the Crash of 2008 to the Great Slump* (2013).

Miguel Vedda is a Full Professor of German Literature at the University of Buenos Aires, Argentina, and Principal Investigator of the National Scientific and Technical Research Council (CONICET). His recent publications include *Siegfried Kracauer: Un pensador más allá de las fronteras* (2010), *Urbane Beobachtungen: Walter Benjamin und die neuen Städte* (2010), *La irrealidad de la desesperación: Estudios sobre Siegfried Kracauer y Walter Benjamin* (2011), *Walter Benjamin: Experiência histórica e imagens dialéticas* (2015) and *Leer a Goethe* (2015).

LIST OF FIGURES

LIST OF TABLES

Marx's Prescient Theory of Centralization of Capital: Crises and an Nkrumahist Response

PART I

On the Critique of Politics

Heinrich Heine and Marx As Essayists: On the Genesis and the Function of the Critic-Intellectuals

Miguel Vedda

I. On Genesis and Functions of the Intellectuals

These reflections could begin by referring to the words with which the Latin American Marxist thinker José Carlos Mariátegui defines his particular thought and writing style at the beginning of his most famous work: "None [of these essays] is finished; they never will be as long as I live and think and have something to add to what I have written, lived and thought. […] I am not an impartial, objective critic. […] I am far removed from the academic techniques of the university".[1] He commends the heuristic and aesthetic value of *what is provisional* against that systematic philosophy which attempts to conceal every trace of the bond with the living experience, under the pretention of conclusion and closure. Georges Sorel, one of Mariátegui's

---

[1] José Carlos Mariátegui, *Seven Interpretive Essays on Peruvian Reality*, trans. Marjory Urquidi (Texas: Texas University Press, 1971), 12.

M. Vedda (✉)
University of Buenos Aires, Buenos Aires, Argentina

Scientific and Technical Research Council (CONICET), Buenos Aires, Argentina

© The Author(s) 2019
S. Gupta et al. (eds.), *Karl Marx's Life, Ideas, and Influences*, Marx, Engels, and Marxisms, https://doi.org/10.1007/978-3-030-24815-4_1

3

most celebrated models, shows a similar disposition in his methodological considerations. In the letter to Daniel Halévy which precedes *Reflections on violence*, the French thinker writes back to those who have objected to him for abiding by writing style conventions and making readers uncomfortable due to the untidiness of his expositions. Sorel smugly introduces himself not as a professor or as a science reporter, but as an autodidact who publicly exhibits the notebooks that have fuelled his own learning. He is not as interested in registering knowledge as he is in deleting the ideas imposed on him; hence his method: "I put before my readers the product of a mental effort which is endeavoring to break through the constraints of what has previously been constructed for common use and which seeks to discover what is personal. [...] I readily skip the points of transition because they nearly always fall into the category of commonplaces".[2] You can say that ideas such as Mariátegui's and Sorel's take us back to a particular historical and philosophical context—the irrationalism of the beginning of the twentieth century, whose most negative features we do not have to (nor can we) mention. But we do not intend to pinpoint the conditions in which these ideas are born; what we mean to point out today is the absence of positions such as the aforementioned and, because of that, their validity.

What the foregoing authors highlight is the *exploratory* dimension of Marxism, that which has been its method since the hour of its birth and for each of its leading representatives. What is involved here is to promote, in revolutionary thinking, an openness and a ductility which are not the product of intellectual laziness; instead, they result from the proximity to experience, from the attention to each of its realities and latencies and, at the same time, from the rejection of dogmas and received ideas. This position evinces the *elective affinity* between dialectical materialism and the tradition of essayism, not only as a genre but also, and more importantly, as a method of enquiry and even as an ethical and political stance towards the world. The word used by Montaigne to refer to the tradition that he himself starts, points at the direction we are discussing. The term suggests that this type of writing is characterized by experimentation in a double sense: on the one hand, it aims to be just a test, an experiment, an exploration; on the other hand, its proximity to the concrete experience distinguishes it from the dogmatic abstraction of the treatise. The essayist, from

---

[2] Georges Sorel, *Reflections on Violence*, ed. Jeremy Jennings (Cambridge: Cambridge University Press, 1991), 328.

the beginnings of the genre, is someone who only considers true those judgements which he has formed out of his own experience or, at any rate, those which match such experience. The scepticism towards received ideas accounts for the development of a writing which, as Friedrich explains in relation to Montaigne, "is not a subsequent addition to a finished result, rather, it is an accompanying process of capturing his own process of change".[3] The interest in the path, rather than the goal, is the expression of a thought that escapes what is definitive and that appears to manifest itself in the same moment in which it is wrought, as we have commented in relation to Mariátegui.

The topic is relevant for us today because it helps, above all, to define the possibilities and the limits of Marxism in Latin America. The revolutionary thought in "Nuestra América" (Our America) was not directed *mainly* towards the composition of systematic and comprehensive works, due to the material conditions and the dominant traditions of thought, as well as the institutional precariousness and the unstable conditions in which Latin American intellectuals had to live. It managed, though, to turn necessity into virtue, which explains the broad and fruitful production of essays by Latin American Marxism. This *corpus* gathers, amongst its outstanding representatives, not only "classic" writers such as Mariátegui, Aníbal Ponce, Ernesto Guevara and Caio Prado Júnior, but also more contemporary figures such as Carlos Nelson Coutinho, Antônio Candido, David Viñas, León Rozitchner and Roberto Schwarz, to mention just a few important names, some arbitrariness notwithstanding. A second reason for the relevance of essay writing in Latin America is related to a central question of our times: the problem of the genesis, the history, the functions and the vanishing of the figure of the critic-Intellectual. In the third place, the previously mentioned affinity between essayism and Marxism is a *fundamental* feature in Marx's work and the tradition of thought and praxis he has started. Forsaking this essayist perspective has had devastating effects on historical materialism.

Let's start with the second point. A question that has remained unexplored is to what extent the genesis of the modern critic-Intellectual developed in the Paris of the Restoration period. One of the first outlines of that model—if not the first one—emerges in the context of the dispute between Ludwig Börne and Heinrich Heine, about what Enzensberger

[3] Hugo Friedrich, *Montaigne*, trans. Dawn Eng (Berkeley: University of California Press, 1991), 328.

wrote: "[It] is possibly the controversy with the greatest consequences for German literature. Their debate lasts one hundred and fifty years and no ending in sight".[4] The essay "Ludwig Börne: A Memorial" (1840) is one of the first and most challenging attempts to define the peculiarities and the function of the modern intellectual. This figure is defined in contrast with the model embodied by the author of *Dramaturgical Pages*. The book about Börne was thought of as a *livre maudit* when it appeared. Heine's hostility towards the essayist from Frankfurt earned him much scathing criticism from those who only perceived the *argumentum ad hominem* but failed to reach the core of the book, which partly focused on the confrontation between two intellectual models and two kinds of political praxis. In the German-speaking intellectual stage, there was a noteworthy exception: Marx. At the beginning of April 1846, he wrote to Heine about the "Börne debate" as follows:

> A few days ago a short lampoon against you happened to fall into my hands—posthumous letters of Börne's. I should never have held him to be so dull, petty and inept as it is possible to read here in black and white. [...] I shall be writing a detailed review of your book on Börne for a German periodical. A more clumsy treatment than that suffered by this book at the hands of these Christian-Teutonic jackasses would be hard to find in any period of literature, and yet there's no lack of clumsiness in period of Germany.[5]

The revision of the Heine/Börne controversy is one of Marx's invaluable yet unfulfilled projects. Part of what we will hereby say aims at clarifying where the affinity between the revolutionary philosopher and the radical poet may lie. The first aspect worth mentioning may be Heine's inflamed essayism. In the context of the debates with the untimely Jacobin Börne, Heine expressed his conviction that the only reasonable option for the modern intellectual could not mean embracing a doctrinaire *Weltanschauung* which had already resolved all theoretical problems and should therefore be simply spread and applied by his advocates. Instead, it should be an exploratory practice for which there are no predetermined paths or goals. Located *between the fronts*, the intellectual cannot find shelter in the aestheticist withdrawal or in the comfort of a political doctrine, but rather in a search deprived of certainties,

---

[4] Hans Magnus Enzensberger, "EditorischeNotiz," in *Ludwig Börne und Heinrich Heine. Ein deutsches Zerwürfnis*, ed. H. M. Enzensberger (Leipzig: Reclam, 1989), 385; when not otherwise stated, the translations are mine.

[5] Karl Marx, *Capital*, vol. III, in MECW (New York: International Publishers, 1998), 38.

which represents the only and genuine commitment to the wretched of the earth. The typical tearing of Modernity demands that the intellectuals should forsake their dogmatic certainties and uncertainties typical of the *torn consciousness*. In the *Pictures of Travel*, Heine alluded to the meaning of this homology between the fragmentation of the world and the inner fragmentation of the writer's mood:

> Ah dear reader, if you would complain of morbidness and want of harmony and division, then as well complain that the world itself is divided. For, as the heart of the poet is the central point of the world, it must, in times like these, be miserably divided and torn. He who boasts that his heart has remained whole, confesses that he has only a prosaic out-of-the-way corner-heart. But the great world-wound passed through my own heart, and on that account I know that the great Gods have highly blessed me above many others, and held me to be worthy of a poet-martyrdom.[6]

Such an attitude allowed "torn" Heine to become the *Urform* of a central figure of Modernity: that of the critic-Intellectual. It is known that for Sartre the birth date of the modern intellectual is the last third of the nineteenth century, in the context of the agitation around the Dreyfus affair. However, Gerhard Höhn well pointed out that "before '*les* intellectuels' manifest themselves, there were already individual intellectuals"[7] and that the Paris of the Restoration had already offered the favourable grounds for their emergence.[8] The fact that, according to Sartre, the tearing (*déchirure*) is a defining feature of the intellectual endorses Höhn's proposal, especially if it is considered to what extent Heine felt torn apart between the meticulous task of writing and the necessity to surpass the limits of his own *métier* to commit to the reality of his time. It is telling that not only was Heine the target of the conservative offensive due to his political radicalism, but he was also questioned by the revolutionaries who found his respect for artistic perfection unacceptable. But Heine was also pestered for not making his criticism serve *one* political party and for preserving his

---

[6] Heinrich Heine, *Pictures of Travel*, trans. Charles Godfrey Leland, 8th revised ed. (Philadelphia: Schaefer & Koradi, 1879), 312.

[7] Gerhard Höhn, *Heine-Handbuch. Zeit, Person, Werk* (Stuttgart: Metzler, 1987), 67.

[8] "Without having had to do a change of place, but with a clear chronological postponement, Paris 1832 and not Paris 1898 can be identified as the authentic hour of birth of the modern intellectual—with the 'contestation permanente' of the old German society and with the radical criticism of French modern society; with, in short, the *Preface* and the *French Conditions* as documentary act" (Ibid., 31).

autonomy in terms of an independent intellectual.[9] Heine anticipated one of the dilemmas that the critic-Intellectual faced throughout the twentieth century: the difficulty and the necessity to keep the independent individual's lucid stance and to affirm, nonetheless, a commitment to social reality. Heine thus embodies the attempt to represent the role of the intellectual who takes the risk of choosing their own ways forward by delineating his own paths. It is not by chance that the German poet questioned the paralysing effect of the orthodoxies. Less enthusiastic than his republican or conservative contemporaries, he feels attracted by scepticism; better still, he feels dragged by a swinging movement between certainty and doubt, action and thought, *pathos* and satire. Each of these extremes dialectically contributes to relativize the abuses that the other may carry with it. This problematic appears in the *Börne* book as an alternation between the revolutionary ebb and flow, or between the zeal of empathy and the cold critical distance. Unable to examine the essential dialectics of the movement of history, Börne is carried away in one direction or the other by the movements produced on the surface of the agitated social life.

Heine introduces his rival as a subject imprisoned in the present, incapable of looking beyond the closest visual field, in keeping with Börne's own identification with the model of the *Zeitschriftsteller* (the writer for reviews). The description of the character suggests, at the beginning, some shallowness and a rush that will become his constituent elements: Börne comes into the room where Heine is reading and begins to walk to and fro *looking for, precisely, a newspaper.* Years later, when Heine meets him again in Paris, he notices that the writer has kept his interest in fleeting phenomena, though the previous joviality has been replaced by resentment and bigotry:

> His skipping from one topic to another no longer arose from a mad mood but from a moody madness, and was probably to be ascribed to the variety of newspapers with which Börne at that time occupied himself day and night. In the middle of one of his terroristic expectorations, he suddenly reached for one of the daily papers that lay strewn in front of him in great heaps.[10]

---

[9] According to Laube, Heine has made the following comment to him in the course of a conversation: "how can you expect [...] that I should renounce to all that for the sake of the wisdom of your party! I do not belong to any party, or only- he finished with a laugh—to *my* party" (H. M. Enzensberger, ed., *Ludwig Börne und Heinrich Heine. Ein deutsches Zerwürfnis*, 109).

[10] Heinrich Heine, *Ludwig Börne: A Memorial*, trans. Jeffrey L. Sammons (New York: Camden House, 2006), 53.

Börne's unexpected "jumping from a morose mood into a gay one"[11] provides further evidence for the fact that the essayist is a subject who swings between opposite positions, carried by zigzagging times. Börne, however, ignores it and believes that he remains invariable and that it is others who swing. The strategy which evinces Börne's behaviour as *childish* aims at highlighting the infantile feature of voluntarism: according to Heine, this is an aesthetic or "political *Sturm und Drang*", which should be followed by a "mature" reflection, guided not so much by subjective enthusiasm rather than by a definition of one's own perspectives of action based on a survey of the historical reality. This mode of reflection makes it possible to relativize both activist optimism and depression into despondency and melancholy, which tend to afflict the utopian when history does not satisfy his whims.

Subjectivism hinders Börne's sober enquiry into historical reality and imposes limits on him at the level of artistic production: confined to the confines of his environment, he disregards both the thoughtful consideration of the object he is to shape and the technical means he is to use. Fascination with the present paralyses the critic, who "had his eye only on the present day, and the objects that occupied him all lay within his immediate horizon. He spoke about the book that he just read, the event that had just happened, Rothschild, whose house he passed every day".[12] Once again, this attraction to what is close at hand appears as a feature of Börne's political or artistic personality. This short-sightedness leads to a paradox: the subjectivist who wants to shape the world according to his own will is also the clay which adopts the multiple shapes external influences impose on him. In this regard, Heine states:

> The objects with which Börne accidentally came into contact not only gave his mind immediate occupation but also had a direct effect on his mental mood, and his good or bad humor stood in direct connection to their alternation. Like the sea from passing clouds, Börne's soul took on its respective coloration from the objects he encountered on his way.[13]

This malleability is a key to understanding Börne's behaviour after the July Revolution—his inflammation at the minor variation of the political climate and his tendency to allow agitators to invoke him and manipulate

[11] Ibid., 73.
[12] Ibid., 8–9.
[13] Ibid., 13.

him like an effigy or a puppet in order to carry out their projects. It is as if Börne's extremely impressionable character, which has allowed him to grasp the smallest variations of his contemporary reality, has also condemned him to a permanent swing and, eventually, to a shipwreck. Imagery related to the sea and the seafarer pervade Heine's essay. In his letters from Helgoland, the sea is the image of history. Its ebb and flow depend on laws which will be understood only by those who can think of those movements free of hasty hopes and fears. As far as the sailor is concerned, Börne is the reckless captain who exposes himself to the danger of a shipwreck: haunted by the urgencies of the present, he lacks the freedom to tackle what is beyond the current moment. Heine describes Börne's shipwreck as inevitable and confesses to being incapable of reaching out his hand: "I could not grasp it; I could not abandon the precious cargo, the sacred treasures entrusted to me, to certain destruction. I carried on board my ship the gods of the future".[14]

The restriction to current sociopolitical circumstances is connected with an activism that made Börne more and more vulnerable to the optimism of the will. The experimental essay writing of his early work started to give way to an instrumental concept of literature. For him, the aesthetic dimension remains behind the rhetorical will to transmit contents and convince the reader—a concept in which doctrinaire features increasingly prevail. This literary asceticism is coupled with that Nazarene austerity which relates Börne to both the Jacobinism in Robespierre's fashion and the Christian mysticism of Lamennais. We know that among the distinctive identity traits of the Jacobin ideology there are the postponement of economic differentiations and the endowment of politics with exaggerated importance.[15] In keeping with this, Börne bestows less interest and importance on material circumstances than he does on political institutions, contrary to Heine. According to Hohendahl:

> After the disappointing experience of the 1830 Revolution, Heine's interest moves onto economic problems, whereas Börne sticks to the model of the French Revolution in 1789. It is not by chance that, from 1833 onwards, Börne should be again concerned with the French Revolution and that he

[14] Ibid., 25.
[15] Leo Löwenthal, *Das bürgerliche Bewußtsein in der Literatur* (Frankfurt/M: Suhrkamp, 1990), 435.

submits historical bibliography to critical revision. Studying the French Revolution is for Börne the path towards a model of a radical German revolution.[16]

It is faith in the validity of Jacobin moralism that leads Börne to exert violence on history, by trying to impose a possibility which is not present in it. Unlike Börne, Heine believes that the possibilities of political intervention can only be found *within the historical process*. In order to discover them, it is necessary to look into the tendencies of the present that point to the future. These conditions cannot be artificially created. Trying to impose a historical change without paying attention to reality will only lead to catastrophe. In his essay about *Don Quixote* (1836), Heine refers to the risks of a political practice of such nature; voluntarism is presented as a greater insanity than that of the hidalgo, who expected to revive a past long expired:

> Alas! I have found since that it is just as fruitless a form of folly to try to bring the future too soon into the present, if in such an attack on the ponderous interest of the day one has only a very sorry jade, very rotten armour and a body itself in as bad repair. The wise shake their sagacious heads as much at one as at the other kind of Quixotism.[17]

In his *Börne*, Heine directs his criticism to those revolutionaries who can only administer radical treatments whose effect is a steeper decline and, in general, to those who want to produce a revolution without paying attention to historical conditions. At the end of chapter IV, there appears an allegory of the revolution in the image of golden chains which hold the Messiah down, since "without these fetters the Messiah, when he sometimes loses patience, would otherwise suddenly hurry down and undertake the work of salvation too soon, in the wrong hour".[18] The idea is to prevent a rush which would exert violence upon history from thwarting the messianic liberation from all forms of oppression; hence the appeal for

---

[16] Peter Uwe Hohendahl, "Kosmopolitischer Patriotismus. Ludwig Börne und die Identität Deutschlands," in *'Die Kunst—eine Tochter der Zeit'. Neue Studien zu Ludwig Börne*, ed. Inge Rippmann and Wolfgang Labuhn (Bielefeld: Aisthesis, 1988), 183.

[17] Heinrich Heine, "On Cervantes and the Don Quixote," in *Bloom's Literary Themes: The Grotesque*, ed. Blake Hobby (New York: Infobase Publishing, 2009), 51.

[18] Heine, *Ludwig Börne*, 103.

human emancipation to not be thwarted due to voluntarist zeal: "Oh, despair not, handsome Messiah, who wants not only to save Israel, as the superstitious Jews think, but all of suffering mankind! Oh, do not break your golden chains! Oh, keep him bound for a time so that he does not come too soon, the saving king of the world!"[19] The doctrinaires tend to believe that if historical and material facts do not match their own obsessions, so much worse for the facts. This accounts for Börne's stubbornness to introduce himself as an internally unitary personality, rooted in convictions which can be encoded into fixed dogmas and spread as such. This also explains his anger at Heine's reluctance to ossify himself in a monolithic intellectual sedentarism. In his first sketch of *Ludwig Börne*, Heine thus defines his stance towards Jacobinist voluntarism and towards the reactionaries:

> We, the others, who are neither Jacobins nor Jesuits, want to keep the lie as long as possible, since we cannot justify ourselves by means of the firmness of our convictions. Many times we have doubts about ourselves. Any mental draft moves our thoughts, roots in a sandy soil of school wisdom, as reeds in the water. We do not find happiness in our beliefs; we would find less happiness in martyrdom.[20]

Whereas Börne suffers from sclerotic moralism, Heine—as already said—swings between *pathos* and satire. The latter intends to reveal contemporary reality as a comedy and hints at dismantling all empathic identification with reality, every attempt to endow it with tragic seriousness and *grandeur*. From this perspective, the controversy between Börne and Heine reminds us of the opposition between the *noble consciousness* and the *base consciousness*, as it is developed in the *Phenomenology of Spirit*, from an analysis of *Neveu de Rameau*, by Diderot. We can recall that Hegel's conclusion is that the indecorous nephew is more in keeping with modern times than the advocates of an uncorrupted morality. The bohemian is the representative figure of a world in which wealth means everything, in which the spirit feels like a pilgrim on earth and in which there exist the "absolute and universal inversion and alienation of the actual world and of

---

[19] Ibid., 104.
[20] Heinrich Heine, "Erster Entwurf zu *Ludwig Börne. Eine Denkschrift*," in *Ludwig Börne und Heinrich Heine. Ein deutsches Zerwürfnis*, ed. H. M. Enzensberger (Leipzig: Reclam, 1989), 99.

thought".[21] In these conditions, the noble consciousness means depravity and hypocrisy, while the base consciousness reaches a paradoxical probity: "The language of this disrupted consciousness is, however, the perfect language and the authentic existent Spirit of this entire world of culture",[22] in contrast with the apparently noble and essentially base language of hypocrisy. Jean Hyppolite remarks that, in this passage of the treatise,

> [t]he bohemian strips the veil off a world and a social system which have lost their substantiveness, a world whose moments lack all stability. The consciousness of this loss transforms action into a stage comedy and pure intentions into hypocrisy. Ambition and the desire for money, the wish to master power, these are the truth of this comedy.[23]

The torn consciousness sarcastically speaks the language of economy, whereas the noble consciousness keeps on using the language of an anachronistic moralism. This explains why Rameau, in Hegel's view, not only embodies a historical period but also symbolizes progress in the light of the philosopher's conservative perspective.[24] Marx acknowledged the depth of this analysis and in a letter to Engels on April 15, 1869, he referred to both the importance of the novel and the comments of Hegel.

II. THE METHOD OF ESSAYISM IN KARL MARX

So far, we have barely talked about Marx. Nevertheless, the foregoing comments hint at him since he is one of the most outstanding figures in that first generation of critic-Intellectuals who made use of the essay as an eminent form. Marx is, in fact, one of the major nineteenth-century German essayists. This does not mean that the German revolutionary was not a great philosopher or a brilliant scientist; we simply highlight, on the

[21] Georg Wilhelm Friedrich Hegel, *Phenomenology of the Spirit*, trans. A. V. Miller (Oxford, New York, Toronto, and Melbourne: Oxford University Press, 1977), 316.

[22] Ibid.

[23] Jean Hyppolite, *Genesis and Structure of Hegel's Phenomenology of Spirit*, trans. Samuel Cherniak and John Heckman (Evanston, IL: Northwestern University Press, 1974), 412.

[24] "The consciousness that is aware of its disruption and openly declares it, derides existence and the universal confusion, and derides its own self as well; it is at the same time the fading, but still audible, sound of all this confusion. This vanity of all reality and every definite Notion, vanity which knows itself to be such, is the double reflection of the real world into itself: once in *this particular self* of consciousness *qua* particular, and again in the pure *universality* of consciousness, or in thought" (Hegel, *Phenomenology of the Spirit*, 319–20).

one hand, that among Marx's talents there was *also* his capacity to write essays argumentatively acute, aesthetically remarkable and stirring. On the other hand, as we have anticipated, *essayism* is for him a methodology and, further, a way of relating to the world. It is suggestive that one of the first and major attempts to understand these questions was born in Latin America. We are making reference to the study by Ludovico Silva; the Venezuelan thinker discovers in Marx a technique we have identified as a feature of the essay as a form—the development of a type of writing that is not closed beforehand but seems to form itself at the very moment of writing:

> It is typical for great thinkers who are at the same time great stylists to present their work not as the result of previous thoughts, but as *the process or the very act of thinking.* The reader thus attends an uninterrupted birth and profits from it since, instead of being forced to digest hardened thoughts, he is moved to think, to rethink, to recreate the very act of theoretical discoveries.[25]

As an essayist, Marx was capable of using a multiplicity of styles and registers. In all of them excels his resolution to break with pre-established forms. *Manifesto of the Communist Party* offers a typical example. As it is known, the first version written by Engels—*The Principles of Communism*—was composed as a catechism articulated upon questions and answers, as it was usual in his time. The *Manifesto,* whose writing only corresponds to Marx, abides by the demand Engels issued on November 23–24, 1847 ("Give a little thought to the Confession of Faith. I think we would do best to abandon the catechetical form").[26] The text thus rids itself of a tradition of scholastic socialism in a brilliant way. The style, the aesthetic and rhetorical structure of the *Manifesto,* the rich imagery, the effective use of satire and irony are such defining features of this *essay* as the demands it puts forward to the reading public of its time. Readers do not find a set of conclusive answers but an invitation to delve, like explorers, into *terra incognita.* Marx's obsession to learn from reality is an authentic essayistic gesture. It would be worth highlighting in Marx, as Lukács has done in Balzac, his scrupulous attention to "the structure of objective reality whose wealth we can never adequately grasp and reflect with our ever all

---

[25] Ludovico Silva, *El estilo literario de Marx,* 2nd ed. (Mexico: Siglo XXI, 1975), 6.
[26] Marx, *Capital,* vol. III, 149.

too abstract, all too rigid, all too direct, all too unilateral thinking".[27] The struggle against prevailing idealism, especially in the 1840s, is a fight against the logicist attempts to exert violence upon reality by subduing it to *a priori* rigid moulds, instead of paying attention to its complex and varied dialectics. What annoys Marx, above all, is Bruno Bauer's, Széliga's or Proudhon's obstinate expectation for the natural and social world to be kind enough to adapt themselves to their abstract schemes inspired by Hegel.

This attention is related to Marx's unwavering hatred against everything that is petrified. One of the most prominent expressions of such hatred in the *Manifesto* is the acclaimed passage which celebrates the outbreak of the bourgeois era, in spite of its ill-fated aspects, because in that period "[a]ll fixed, fast-frozen relations, with their train of ancient and venerable prejudices and opinions, are swept away, all new-formed ones become antiquated before they can ossify. All that is solid melts into air, all that is holy is profaned".[28] Just like Heine, Marx wanted to rescue Germany from the inertia during the Restoration period. Apart from these specific circumstances, his attitude describes the philosopher's fundamental stance. In addition, liberating historical reality from the spell that captivates it is valid, according to Marx, in so far as this liberation does not mean imposing on such reality a course of action which is alien to it. This liberation means paying scrupulous attention to the latent elements in the core of reality. Young Marx refers to this in his well-known statement: "these petrified relations must [be] force[d] to dance by singing their own tune to them".[29] Marx's basic idea is that the transformation of the world does not call for the imposition of an external idea, but the liberation of the potentialities that remain locked in the world. Unknowingly, Walter Benjamin recovers this principle in the thesis *On the Concept of History* when he celebrates Saint-Simon's conception of labour which, "far from exploiting nature, would help her give birth to the creations that now lie dormant in her womb".[30] The essence of this method can be summarized in Michelangelo's

[27] György Lukács, "Balzac: Lost Illusions," in *Studies in European Realism*, trans. Edith Bone (New York: Grosset & Dunlap, 1964), 58.
[28] Karl Marx and Friedrich Engels, *Manifesto of the Communist Party*, in MECW (New York: International Publishers, 1976), 6: 514.
[29] Karl Marx, "A Contribution to the Critique of Hegel's 'Philosophy of Right'. Introduction," in MECW (New York: International Publishers, 1975), 3: 178.
[30] Walter Benjamin, "On the Concept of History," in *Selected Writings. Vol. 4*, trans. Edmund Jephcott et al. (Cambridge, MA and London: The Belknap Press of Harvard University Press, 2002), 394.

verses, which Lukács took pleasure in paraphrasing: "The greatest sculptor can no thought conceive/That doth not lie deep buried in stone".[31]

In very different periods, Marx frequently condemns subjective violence, harshly questioned by Heine as well in relation to Börne and his followers and contested by the allegory of the chained Messiah. It is present in his literary discussions. In his analysis of *Mystères de Paris*, Marx finds it annoying how the author manipulates his materials instead of examining their latencies. Sue is carried away by the temptation to reduce his characters to automata, subservient to the author's abstract conceptions. His novel gains some vitality when its characters manage not to subdue to the author's spiritualist ethics. Along these lines, Lukács states that a great writer's learning from reality is expressed as long as he "locks himself with his characters; he lives life according to their own rules of movement—not his desires; he learns from them, he accepts their destiny".[32] This criticism against aesthetic voluntarism also plays a major role in the "*Sickingen*-Debate", since it establishes a relation with the concept of the theorist and the revolutionary leader. What Marx and Engels deplore in Lassalle's writing is, on the one hand, the fact that he is driven by his subjective idealism and reduces his characters to mere spokespersons of their *Zeitgeist*. On the other hand, Lassalle deems the revolution a process which unfolds mainly in the revolutionary leader's mind; the corruption of the revolutions is that of the leader's thought, who becomes a *Realpolitiker*. Subjectivism prevents Lassalle (as a writer, as a revolutionary leader) from examining historical reality, to learn from reality. Against the manipulative artistic praxis which as such ruins the object and hinders the development of the creator's *essential forces*, Marx introduces that activity through which "man knows how to produce in accordance with the standard of every species, and knows how to apply everywhere the inherent standard to the object. Man, therefore, also forms things in accordance with the laws of beauty".[33]

It is conspicuous how close these positions are to Heine's in his controversy with Börne, Ludwig; as conspicuous as the distance Marx stays at from those intellectuals who stick to the surface of social life without

[31] Michelangelo Buonarotti, *The Sonnets*, trans. S. Elizabeth Hall (London: Kegan Paul, Trench, Trübner & Co., Ltd., 1905), 99.

[32] György Lukács, *Moskauer Schriften. Zur Literaturtheorie und Literaturpolitik 1934–1940*, ed. Frank Benseler (Frankfurt/M: Sendler, 1981), 133.

[33] Karl Marx, "Economic and Philosophic Manuscripts of 1844," in MECW (New York: International Publishers, 1975), 3: 277.

examining its laws. Marx was aware of the fact that the downside of the phenomenological closeness to the world of the nineteenth-century essayist's own life was the danger of remaining attached to immediacy, to the hectic surface of appearances. Marx shared with Hegel the conviction that it is necessary to focus on *die Ruhe des Wesens*—the calm of the essence, that is, the principles that lie on the base of apparent phenomena and are, thus, less visible. As we have seen, Heine addresses his criticism towards *Zeitschriftsteller* such as Börne, and his shallow perspective. The search for what is essential behind the shaken circumstances is a feature that characterizes Marx and distinguishes Heine from his contemporaries' perpetual swing between extreme optimism and extreme hopelessness; let's remember once again his criticism against Börne. Old Lukács has well contrasted young Marx's dispositions with Ruge's pessimism, with the "Hölderlin-Stimmung" of the desperate intellectuals of the *Vormärz*. In his 1925 study about Lassalle's letters, Lukács already referred to the depressions, which sometimes "reached such an intensity that he wished to withdraw completely from the movement. It cannot be decided, of course, to what an extent such wishes would have been translated in action. [...] What we *can* say is that Marx, Bebel and Lenin (to pick out three completely different personalities of the opposite type) never knew such moods at all".[34]

Marx's objectivity is in keeping with a feature that has essentially distinguished all the great essayists: the resistance to accept worshipped authorities and received ideas without questioning them. The word *critique*, which is present in so many titles of Marx's work, defines his stance as regards his preceding traditions. Unlike many of his young fellows, Marx never was a Young Hegelian. This also accounts for his relationship with Feuerbach or with the political economists. His attitude is different from Engels', who was much more prone to a receptive attitude towards other thinkers and who, when young, blindly worshipped Ludwig Börne. In his well-known essay "Of the Education of Children", Montaigne expressed his desire to turn essay writing into the base of the education of men:

I had a private interview at Pisa with an honest man, but so great an Aristotelian, that his general thesis was: "That the touchstone and standard of all solid imaginations, and of all truths, was their conformity to the doctrine

---

[34] György Lukács, "The New Edition of Lassalle's Letters," in *Tactics and Ethics. Political Writings 1919–1929*, trans. Michael McColgan, ed. Rodney Livingstone (New York, etc.: Harper & Row, 1972), 161.

of Aristotle; that all besides was vain and chimerical; for that he had seen all, and said all". [...]

Let the tutor make his pupil thoroughly sift everything he reads, and lodge nothing in his fancy upon mere authority. Let the principles of Aristotle be no more principles to him than those of the Stoics or Epicureans, only let this diversity of opinions be laid before him; he will himself choose, if he be able; if not, he will remain in doubt: "Che non men the saver, dub-biar m'aggrata" ["I love to doubt, as well as to know"—Dante, Inferno, xi. 93]. For, if he embrace the opinions of Xenophon and Plato, by his own discourse, they will no longer be theirs, but his. He that follows another, follows nothing, finds nothing, nay, does not seek for anything.[35]

Undoubtedly, Marx would have endorsed these propositions, which are vividly embodied in his writings: for him, truth did not lie in the writing of a thinker, but in the free exploration of a living reality. One could not imagine a starker contrast than that between the founder of Marxism and many of his so-called disciples. We started this article with an allusion to a Latin American thinker; we will finish by referring to another one: in his aforementioned study about Marx's literary style, Silva highlights that in the core of the attack to Proudhon there lies the conviction that such work is no more than an attempt to subdue history to Hegelian categories. According to Marx, the mistake Proudhon made is the same "grave mis-take that inspectors-philosophers in Marxism make today. They behave as the Pretorian Guard in relation to the 'three laws of dialectics' and turn Marx into the most frenzied Hegelian idealist. [...] For Marx, dialectics was not a logic[al] method strictly speaking; it was a historical method. For a method to be formally correct, emptiness is its first condition; but Marx was fully interested in history, its multiple concretion".[36] There might not be a more appropriate way to describe Marx's essayism.

BIBLIOGRAPHY

Benjamin, Walter. "On the Concept of History." In *Selected Writings. Vol. 4*, trans-lated by Edmund Jephcott et al., 389–411. Cambridge, MA and London: The Belknap Press of Harvard University Press, 2002.

Buonarotti, Michelangelo. *The Sonnets*. Translated by S. Elizabeth Hall. London: Kegan Paul, Trench, Trübner & Co., Ltd., 1905.

---

[35] Michel de Montaigne, *Essays*, trans. Peter Coste (London: C. Baldwin, 1981), 169–70.
[36] Silva, *El estilo literario de Marx*, 40.

Enzensberger, Hans Magnus. "Editorische Notiz". In *Ludwig Börne und Heinrich Heine. Ein deutsches Zerwürfnis*, edited by H. M. Enzensberger, 385–88. Leipzig: Reclam, 1989.

Friedrich, Hugo. *Montaigne*. Translated by Dawn Eng. Edited by Philippe Desan. Berkeley: University of California Press, 1991.

Hegel, Georg Wilhelm Friedrich. *Phenomenology of the Spirit*. Translated by A. V. Miller. Oxford, New York, Toronto, and Melbourne: Oxford University Press, 1977.

Heine, Heinrich. *Pictures of Travel*. Translated by Charles Godfrey Leland. 8th revised edition. Philadelphia: Schaefer and Koradi, 1879.

Heine, Heinrich. "Erster Entwurf zu *Ludwig Börne. Eine Denkschrift*." In *Ludwig Börne und Heinrich Heine. Ein deutsches Zerwürfnis*, edited by H. M. Enzensberger, 98–102. Leipzig: Reclam, 1989.

Heine, Heinrich. *Ludwig Börne: A Memorial*. Translated by Jeffrey L. Sammons. New York: Camden House, 2006.

Heine, Heinrich. "On Cervantes and the Don Quixote." In *Bloom's Literary Themes: The Grotesque*, edited by Blake Hobby, 49–56. New York: Infobase Publishing, 2009.

Höhn, Gerhard. *Heine-Handbuch. Zeit, Person, Werk*. Stuttgart: Metzler, 1987.

Hohendahl, Peter Uwe. "Kosmopolitischer Patriotismus. Ludwig Börne und die Identität Deutschlands." In *'Die Kunst—eine Tochter der Zeit'. Neue Studien zu Ludwig Börne*, edited by Inge Rippmann and Wolfgang Labuhn, 170–200. Bielefeld: Aisthesis, 1988.

Hyppolite, Jean. *Genesis and Structure of Hegel's Phenomenology of Spirit*. Translated by Samuel Cherniak and John Heckman. Evanston, IL: Northwestern University Press, 1974.

Löwenthal, Leo. *Das bürgerliche Bewußtsein in der Literatur*. Frankfurt/M: Suhrkamp, 1990.

Lukács, György. "Balzac: Lost Illusions." In *Studies in European Realism*, translated by Edith Bone, 44–64. New York: Grosset and Dunlap, 1964.

Lukács, György. "The New Edition of Lassalle's Letters." In *Tactics and Ethics. Political Writings 1919–1929*, translated by Michael McColgan, edited and introduced by Rodney Livingstone, 146–71. New York: Harper & Row, 1972.

Lukács, György. *Moskauer Schriften. Zur Literaturtheorie und Literaturpolitik 1934–1940*. Edited by Frank Benseler. Frankfurt/M: Sendler, 1981.

Mariátegui, José Carlos. *Seven Interpretive Essays on Peruvian Reality*. Translated by Marjory Urquidi. Texas: Texas University Press, 1971.

Marx, Karl. "A Contribution to the Critique of Hegel's 'Philosophy of Right'. Introduction." In MECW. Vol. 3. 175–87. New York: International Publishers, 1975a.

Marx, Karl. "Economic and Philosophic Manuscripts of 1844." In MECW. Vol. 3. 229–347. New York: International Publishers, 1975b.

Marx, Karl. *Capital.* Vol. III. In MECW. Vol. 37. London and New York: International Publishers, 1998.

Marx, Karl and Frederick Engels. *Manifesto of the Communist Party.* In MECW. Vol. 6. 477–519. New York: International Publishers, 1976.

Montaigne, Michel de. *Essays.* Translated by Peter Coste. London: C. Baldwin, 1981.

Silva, Ludovico. *El estilo literario de Marx.* 2nd edition. Mexico: Siglo XXI, 1975.

Sorel, Georges. *Reflections on Violence.* Edited by Jeremy Jennings. Cambridge: Cambridge University Press, 1991.

Marx's Critique of German Social Democracy: From the International to the Political Struggles of the 1870s

Marcello Musto

I. The Limited Participation of the Germans in the International Working Men's Association

The workers' organizations that founded the International Working Men's Association in 1864 were something of a motley. The central driving forces were British trade unionism and the mutualists, long dominant in France but strong also in Belgium and French-speaking Switzerland. Alongside these two components, there were the communists, grouped around the figure of Karl Marx, elements that had nothing to do with the socialist tradition, such as the followers of Giuseppe Mazzini, and some groups of French, Belgian and Swiss workers who joined the International with a variety of confused theories, some of a utopian inspiration. The General Association of German Workers—the party led by followers of Ferdinand Lassalle—never affiliated to the International but orbited around it. This organization was hostile to trade unionism and conceived of political action in rigidly national terms.

M. Musto (✉)
Department of Sociology, York University, Toronto, ON, Canada

© The Author(s) 2019
S. Gupta et al. (eds.), *Karl Marx's Life, Ideas, and Influences*, Marx,
Engels, and Marxisms, https://doi.org/10.1007/978-3-030-24815-4_2

21

In 1865, the International expanded in Europe and established its first important nuclei in Belgium and French-speaking Switzerland. The Prussian Combination Laws, which prevented German political associations from having regular contacts with organizations in other countries, meant that the International was unable to open sections in what was then the German Confederation. The General Association of German Workers—the first workers' party in history,[1] founded in 1863 and led by Lassalle's disciple Johann Baptist von Schweitzer—followed a line of ambivalent dialogue with Otto von Bismarck and showed little or no interest in the International during the early years of its existence. It was an indifference shared by Wilhelm Liebknecht, despite his political proximity to Marx. Johann Philipp Becker tried to find a way around these difficulties through the Geneva-based "Group of German-speaking Sections".

While Liebknecht did not understand the centrality of the international dimension for the struggle of the workers' movement, Marx also had deep theoretical and political differences with von Schweitzer. In February 1865 he wrote to the latter that "the aid of the Royal Prussian government for co-operative societies", which the Lassalleans welcomed, was "worthless as an economic measure, whilst, at the same time, it serve[d] to extend the system of tutelage, corrupt part of the working class and emasculate the movement". Marx went on to reject any possibility of an alliance between the workers and the monarchy:

> Just as the bourgeois party in Prussia discredited itself and brought about its present wretched situation by seriously believing that with the "New Era" the government had fallen into its lap by the grace of the Prince Regent, so the workers' party will discredit itself even more if it imagines that the Bismarck era or any other Prussian era will make the golden apples just drop into its mouth, by grace of the king. It is beyond all question that Lassalle's ill-starred illusion that a Prussian government might intervene with socialist measures will be crowned with disappointment. The logic of circumstances will tell. But the honour of the workers' party requires that it reject such illusions, even before their hollowness is punctured by experience. The working class is revolutionary or it is nothing.[2]

---

[1] At this time, the German party had about 5000 members.

[2] Karl Marx to Johann Baptist von Schweitzer, 13 February 1865, quoted in Karl Marx, "Marx to Engels, 18 February 1865," in MECW (New York: International Publishers, 1987), 42: 96.

The critique of state socialism was a common theme in Marx's political reflections during that period. A few days after the letter to Schweitzer, he suggested to Engels that the position of the Lassalleans in Germany was akin to the "alliance of the 'proletariat' with the 'government' against the 'liberal bourgeoisie'" which the two of them had firmly opposed in 1847.[3]

Marx's critique to the policy of German social democracy continued in 1866. In the *Instructions for Delegates of the Provisional General Council*, prepared for the Geneva congress, Marx underlined the basic function of trade unions against which not only the mutualists but also certain followers of Robert Owen in Britain and of Lassalle in Germany had taken a stand. Lassalle advocated the concept of an "iron law of wages", which held that efforts to increase wages were futile and a distraction for workers from the primary task of assuming political power in the state. Marx wrote:

> This activity of the Trades' Unions is not only legitimate, it is necessary. It cannot be dispensed with so long as the present system of production lasts. On the contrary, it must be generalized by the formation and the combination of Trades' Unions throughout all countries. On the other hand, unconsciously to themselves, the Trades' Unions were forming centres of organization of the working class, as the mediaeval municipalities and communes did for the middle class. If the Trades' Unions are required for the guerrilla fights between capital and labour, they are still more important as organized agencies for superseding the very system of wages labour and capital rule.

In the same document, Marx did not spare the existing unions his criticism. For they were "too exclusively bent upon the local and immediate struggles with capital [and had] not yet fully understood their power of acting against the system of wages slavery itself. They therefore kept too much aloof from general social and political movements".[4]

In September 1868, Marx returned to the question of state socialism. In a letter to Engels, he suggested that what von Schweitzer had described the previous month in Hamburg at the congress of the General Association of German Workers as the "summa of Lassalle's discoveries"—that is, state credit for the foundation of productive associations—was "literally copied

---

[3] Karl Marx, "Marx to Engels, 18 February 1865," in MECW (New York: International Publishers, 1987), 42: 97.
[4] Karl Marx, "Resolutions of the Geneva Congress (1866)," in *Workers Unite! The International after 150 Years*, ed. Marcello Musto (London: Bloomsbury, 2014), 86.

from the programme of French Catholic socialism", inspired by Philip Buchez, which went back to "the days of Louis-Philippe".[5]

Instead, strong opposition to the government would have been good for the social struggle: "The most essential thing for the German working class is that it should cease to agitate by permission of the high government authorities. Such a bureaucratically schooled race must undergo a complete course of 'self help'."[6]

In a letter to Schweitzer, Marx set out at greater length his differences with the Lassallean tendency. The first question was his opposition to the strategy of "state aid versus self-help", which Buchez, the leader of Catholic socialism, had used against the genuine workers' movement in France, and on the basis of which Lassalle himself had later made "concessions to the Prussian monarchy, to Prussian reaction (the feudal party) and even to the clericals". For Marx, it was essential that the workers' struggle should be free and independent. "The main thing is to teach [the worker] to walk by himself", especially in Germany, where "he is regulated bureaucratically from childhood onwards" and believes in the authority of superiors.

The other significant area of disagreement was the theoretical and political rigidity of Lassalle and his followers. Marx criticized the comrade with whom he had been in touch for many years, on the grounds that "like everyone who claims to have in his pocket a panacea for the sufferings of the masses, [Lassalle] gave his agitation, from the very start, a religious, sectarian character", and, being the founder of a sect, "he denied all natural connection with the earlier movement, both in Germany and abroad". Lassalle was guilty of the same error as Proudhon—that of "not seeking the real basis of his agitation in the actual elements of the class movement, but of wishing, instead, to prescribe for that movement a course determined by a certain doctrinaire recipe". For Marx, any "sect seeks its raison d'être and its *point d'honneur* not in what it has in common with the class

[5] Karl Marx, "Marx to Engels, 19 September 1868," in MECW (New York: International Publishers, 1988), 43: 105.

[6] Karl Marx, "Marx to Engels, 26 September 1868," ibid., 115. Although he declined an invitation to the Hamburg congress, Marx nevertheless found some signs of progress. To Engels he remarked: "I was glad to see that the starting points of any 'serious' workers' movement—agitation for complete political freedom, regulation of the working day and international co-operation of the working class—were emphasised in their programme for the congress. [...] [I]n other words, I congratulated them on having abandoned Lassalle's programme", Karl Marx, "Marx to Friedrich Engels, 26 August 1868," ibid., 89–90.

movement, but in the particular shibboleth distinguishing it from that movement".[7] His opposition to that kind of politics could not have been clearer.[8]

In the fight against state socialism, Marx also took issue with Liebknecht. After one of his speeches in the Reichstag in summer 1869, Marx commented to Engels: "The brute believes in the future 'state of democracy'! Secretly that means sometimes constitutional England, sometimes the bourgeois United States, sometimes wretched Switzerland. He has no conception of revolutionary politics."[9]

What disappointed Marx most was that in the North German Confederation, despite the existence of two political organizations of the workers' movement—the Lassallean General Association of German Workers and the Marxist Social Democratic Workers' Party of Germany— there was little enthusiasm for the International and few requests to affiliate to it. During its first three years, German militants virtually ignored its existence, fearing persecution at the hands of the authorities. The weak internationalism of the Germans ultimately weighed more heavily than any legal aspects, however, and declined still further when the movement became more preoccupied with internal matters.[10]

The unification of Germany in 1871 confirmed the onset of a new age in which the nation state would be the central form of political, legal and territorial identity. This placed a question mark over any supranational body that required its members to surrender a sizeable share of their political leadership. At the same time, the growing differences between national movements and organizations made it extremely difficult for the General Council of the International to produce a political synthesis capable of satisfying the demands of all. Anyway, after the end of the International, in September 1872,[11] Marx continued to criticize the path of German Social Democracy any time he had a chance.

---

[7] Karl Marx, "Marx to Johann Baptist von Schweitzer, 13 October 1868," ibid., 133–5. The actual letter has been lost, but fortunately Marx preserved his draft.

[8] Cf. also Marcello Musto, *Another Marx: Early Writings to the International* (London: Bloomsbury, 2018), esp. chapters 7, 8 and 9.

[9] Karl Marx, "Marx to Engels, 10 August 1869," in MECW (New York: International Publishers, 1988), 43: 343.

[10] Cf. Jacques Freymond, ed., *Études et documents sur la Première Internationale en Suisse* (Geneva: Droz, 1964), x.

[11] Cf. Marcello Musto, "Introduction," in *Workers Unite!*, esp. 42–51.

II. Against the "Gotha Programme" and the Social Democratic Deviation

At the end of 1874, Marx learned from the papers that the General Association of German Workers, founded by Ferdinand Lassalle, and the Social Democratic Workers' Party, linked to Marx, intended to unite into a single political force. Marx and Engels were not consulted about the merits of the project, and it was only in March that they received the draft programme of the new party.[12] Engels then wrote to August Bebel that he could not "forgive his not having told us a single word about the whole business",[13] and he warned that he and Marx could "never give [their] allegiance to a new party" set up on the basis of Lassallean state socialism.[14] Despite this sharp declaration, the leaders who had been active in building what would become the Socialist Workers' Party of Germany (SAPD) did not change their positions.

Marx therefore felt obliged to write a long critique of the draft programme for the unification congress to be held on 22 May 1875 in the city of Gotha. In the letter accompanying his text, he recognized that "every step of real movement is more important than a dozen programmes".[15] But in the case of "programmes of principles", they had to be written with great care, since they set "benchmarks for all the world to … gauge how far the party [has] progressed".[16] In the *Critique of the Gotha Programme* (1875), Marx inveighed against the numerous imprecisions and mistakes in the new manifesto drafted in Germany. For example, in criticizing the concept of "fair distribution", he asked polemically: "Do not the bourgeois assert that present-day distribution is 'fair'? And is it not, in fact, the only 'fair' distribution on the basis of the present-day mode of production?"[17] In his view, the political demand to be inserted into the programme was not Lassalle's "undiminished proceeds of labour"[18] for every worker, but the transformation of the mode of production. Marx

---

[12] Frederick Engels, "Engels to August Bebel, 18–28 March 1875," in MECW (New York: International Publishers, 1991), 60.

[13] Ibid., 66.

[14] Ibid., 64.

[15] Karl Marx, "Marx to Wilhelm Bracke, 5 May 1875," in MECW (New York: International Publishers, 1991), 70.

[16] Ibid.

[17] Karl Marx, *Critique of the Gotha Programme*, in MECW (New York: International Publishers, 1989), 24, 84.

[18] Ibid.

explained, with his customary rigour, that Lassalle "did not know what wages were". Following bourgeois economists, he "took the appearance for the essence of the matter". Marx explained:

> Wages are not what they appear to be, namely the value, or price, of labour, but only a masked form for the value, or price, of labour power. Thereby the whole bourgeois conception of wages hitherto, as well as all the criticism hitherto directed against this conception, was thrown overboard once for all and it was made clear that the wage-worker has permission to work for his own subsistence, that is, to live only insofar as he works for a certain time gratis for the capitalist (and hence also for the latter's co-consumers of surplus value); that the whole capitalist system of production turns on increasing this gratis labour by extending the working day or by developing productivity, that is, increasing the intensity of labour power, etc.; that, consequently, the system of wage labour is a system of slavery, and indeed of a slavery which becomes more severe in proportion as the social productive forces of labour develop, whether the worker receives better or worse payment.[19]

Another controversial point concerned the role of the state. Marx maintained that capitalism could be overthrown only through the "revolutionary transformation of society". The Lassalleans held that "socialist organization of the total labour arises from the state aid that the state gives to the producers' co-operative societies which the state, not the worker, calls into being".[20] For Marx, however, "cooperative societies [were] of value only insofar as they [were] the independent creations of the workers and not protégés either of governments or of the bourgeois"[21]; the idea "that with state loans one can build a new society just as well as a new railway" was typical of Lassalle's theoretical ambiguities.[22]

All in all, Marx observed that the political manifesto for the fusion congress showed that socialist ideas were having a hard time penetrating the German workers' organizations. In keeping with his early convictions,[23] he

[19] Ibid., 92.
[20] Ibid., 93.
[21] Ibid., 94.
[22] Ibid., 93.
[23] See Karl Marx, "Contribution to the Critique of Hegel's Philosophy of Law," in MECW (New York: International Publishers, 1975), 3, where he writes, concerning "the antithesis of state and civil society", that "the state does not reside in, but outside civil society" (ibid., 49). "In democracy, the state as particular is merely particular. The French have recently

emphasized that it was wrong on their part to treat "the state as an independent entity that possesses its own intellectual, ethical and libertarian bases", instead of "treating existing society as ... the basis of the existing state".[24] By contrast, Wilhelm Liebknecht and other German socialist leaders defended their tactical decision to compromise on the programme, on the grounds that this was necessary to achieve a unified party.[25] Once again, Marx had to face up to the great difference between choices made in Berlin and in London; he had already remarked on it in relation to the scant involvement of German organizations in the International Working Men's Association.[26]

During the spring of 1875, Marx continued working on the studies he needed for some outstanding sections of *Capital*. At the same time, he reworked parts of Johann Most's popular compilation of extracts from Volume I, with a view to the printing of a second edition.[27] Between mid-May

interpreted this as meaning that in true democracy the state is annihilated. This is correct insofar as the political state ... no longer passes for the whole" (ibid., 30).

[24] Marx, *Critique of the Gotha Programme*, 94.

[25] In the calmer waters of 1877, Engels returned to the argument in a letter to Liebknecht: "The moral and intellectual decline of the party dates from the unification and could have been avoided had a little more caution and intelligence been shown at the time" (Frederick Engels "Engels to Wilhelm Liebknecht, 31 July 1877," in MECW (New York: International Publishers, 1991), 45, 257). Years later, Liebknecht recalled that "Marx, who could not survey the condition of things from abroad as well as we in Germany, would not hear of such concessions." And he claimed: "That I did not make a wrong calculation in this respect has been brilliantly demonstrated by the consequences and the successes." In McLellan, *Karl Marx: Interviews and Recollections* (New York: Barnes & Noble, 1981), 48.

[26] After the printing of the programme ratified at Gotha, Engels noted that "not a single critical text" appeared in "the bourgeois press". Had there been one, it might have noted "the contradictions and economic howlers ... and exposed ... [the] party to the most dreadful ridicule. Instead of that the jackasses on the bourgeois papers have taken this programme perfectly seriously, reading into it what isn't there and interpreting it communistically". He went on to stress that "the workers [were] apparently doing the same" and that this had "made it possible for Marx and himself not to disassociate [themselves] publicly from the programme" (Frederick Engels, "Engels to August Bebel, 12 October 1875," in MECW (New York: International Publishers, 1991), 45: 98). Marx's *Critique of the Gotha Programme* was published only in 1891, the year in which the Erfurt programme, much closer to his own principles, was adopted. Cf. Boris Nicolaevsky and Otto Maenchen Helfen, *Karl Marx— Man and Fighter* (London: Methuen, 1936), 376, who argued: "The split, which Marx regarded as inevitable, [did not] occur. The Party remained united, and in 1891, at Erfurt, adopted a pure Marxist programme."

[27] Johann Most, *Kapital und Arbeit: Ein Populärer Auszug aus "Das Kapital" von Karl Marx* (Chemnitz: G. Rübner, n.d. [1873]). The second edition came out in 1876.

and mid-August, he composed another manuscript for Volume III, "The Relationship between Rate of Surplus-Value and Rate of Profit Developed Mathematically" (1875),[28] and in September he was animated once again by the desire to progress as much as possible in his writing of *Capital*, Volume II.

In the early months of 1876, having received new books and publications with statistics about Russia, Marx engaged in further systematic research into the social-economic changes taking place there. His study, in 1870, of *The Situation of the Working Class in Russia* (1869)—a work by the economist and sociologist Vassilii Vassilievich Bervi, known by the pen name N. Flerovsky—had also given him the political motivation to delve deeper into the reality of the country.[29] Marx's reading in the mid-1870s also included a little book entitled *Revolutionary Conservatism* (1875) by the Slavophile thinkers Yuri Samarin and Fyodor Dmitriev, and several volumes of the *Proceedings of the Tributary Commission* from 1872 to 1873.

During this period, there were significantly less social struggles and Marx, whenever his health allowed, dedicated himself to new theoretical questions. He took the opportunity to expand his range of interests to areas he had little explored before. In the spring, he turned his attention to physiology, both botanical and human. In addition, he planned to read new books on subjects of major interest such as agronomy, landownership and credit, again after he had finished his studies for the completion of *Capital*.

From the middle of March, Marx returned to his research on forms of collective property. Among the texts he summarized by the end of the year were the very important *History of the Village Order in Germany* (1865–66) by the historian and statesman Georg Ludwig von Maurer, an *Essay on the History of Landownership in Spain* (1873) by the lawyer and minister Francisco de Cárdenas Espejo, and *Common Abodes of the South Slavs* (1859) by the writer and politician Ognjeslav Utješenović.

His new research endeavours were interrupted by the summer break, which his physical problems had made a necessity rather than a diversion. Also, in the autumn of 1876, Marx suffered from several complicated health

---

[28] Karl Marx, "Mehrwertrate und Profitrate mathematisch behandelt," in MEGA² (Berlin: Dietz, 2003), II/14: 19–150.

[29] In a letter dated 12 February 1870, Marx wrote to Engels that Flerovsky's "book shows incontestably that the present conditions in Russia are no longer tenable, that the emancipation of the serfs of course only hastened the process of disintegration, and that fearful social revolution is at the door", Karl Marx, "Marx to Engels, 12 February 1870," in MECW (New York: International Publishers, 1988), 43: 429–30.

issues. Despite these tribulations and the constant work pressure from many sides, Marx made a major effort to find a publisher for the German version of *Histoire de la Commune de 1871* (1876) by the French journalist and Communard Prosper-Olivier Lissagaray.[30] Between September and the end of 1877, he invested time and energy in revising the translation of what he called "the first authentic history of the Commune".[31]

III. POLITICAL BATTLES AT AN INTERNATIONAL LEVEL

Despite adversities and poor health, Marx continued to follow all the major political and economic events attentively and critically, attempting to envisage the new scenarios to which they might give rise and how these would affect struggles for the emancipation of the working class.

At the beginning of 1877, Jenny von Westphalen communicated to Sorge that her husband was "deeply in the Eastern question and highly elated by the firm, honest bearing of the sons of Mohammed vis-à-vis all the Christian humbugs and hypocritical atrocity mongers".[32] In April, Tsar Alexander II declared war on Turkey in pursuit of his expansionist aims, using the pretext of the rebellions against Constantinople by Christians living in the European territories of the Ottoman Empire.

Marx had already been active against the British Liberals' support for Russia: between February and March, together with the journalist Maltman Barry, he had written three short articles—"Mr. Gladstone and Russian Intrigue", "Mr. Gladstone" and "The Great Agitator Unmasked"—which were printed in Barry's name in *The Whitehall Review* and *Vanity Fair* (and later in various local English, Scottish and Irish papers).[33] Marx

[30] For a recent edition in English, see Prosper Olivier Lissagaray, *History of the Paris Commune of 1871* (St. Petersburg, FL: Red and Black Publishers, 2007).

[31] Karl Marx, "Marx to Wilhelm Bracke, 23 September 1876," in MECW (New York: International Publishers, 1991), 45: 149. The English translation was done by Eleanor, who at the time, against her father's wishes, was emotionally attached to the French revolutionary.

[32] Jenny Marx, "Jenny Marx to Friedrich Adolph Sorge, 20 or 21 January 1877," ibid., 45: 447. The main reference was to the British Liberal Prime Minister William Gladstone, author of the highly successful pamphlet *The Bulgarian Horrors and the Question of the East* (London: William Ridgway, 1876), who, like "all the freemen and stillmen and merrymen", had depicted the Russians as "civilizers" (ibid.).

[33] See Maximilien Rubel, *Bibliographie des œuvres de Karl Marx* (Paris: Rivière, 1956), 193. Also, of interest here are two letters to Liebknecht (4 and 11 February 1878), composed in the form of articles, which the Social Democrat leader eventually published in an appendix to the second edition of his pamphlet *Zur orientalischen Frage oder Soll Europa kosakisch werden?* (Leipzig: Commissions, 1878).

reported to Engels that many papers had "shied away" and that the deputy editor of *Vanity Fair* feared a "libel action".[34] To Sorge, he wrote with satisfaction that "English parliamentarians in the Commons and the Lords ... would throw up their hands in horror if they knew that it was the Red Terror Doctor, as they call me, who had been their *souffleur* during the oriental crisis."[35]

Marx was critical of Bracke, however, since in his view "the workers' press concern[ed] itself too little with the oriental question, forgetting that the government's politics gamble wantonly with the lives and money of the people".[36] With excessive optimism, he wrote to Sorge: "That crisis marks a new turning-point in European history." He thought that Russia had "long been on the verge of an upheaval" and hoped that the Turks might "advance the explosion ... through the blows they have dealt ... to the Russian army and Russian finances". "This time", he concluded, "the revolution will begin in the East, hitherto the impregnable bastion and reserve army of counter-revolution".[37] Engels reiterated this conviction to the editor of the Italian paper *La Plebe*, Enrico Bignami: "Once Russia has been spurred to revolution, the whole face of Europe will change. Until now, Old Russia has been the great army of European reaction. It acted as such in 1789, in 1805, in 1815, in 1830 and in 1848. Once this army is destroyed—we shall see!"[38]

When it became clear in February 1878 that the Russians had been victorious, Marx regretted the fact in a letter to Liebknecht, repeating that defeat would not only have "greatly expedited social revolution in Russia" but also brought about "radical change throughout Europe".[39] Nevertheless, buoyed up by his confident expectations at the time, he predicted to the English Chartist and publicist Thomas Allsop that there would soon be a "succession of wars, which w[ould] precipitate the Social

---

[34] Karl Marx, "Marx to Engels, 7 March 1877," in MECW (New York: International Publishers, 1991), 45: 209.

[35] Karl Marx, "Marx to Friedrich Adolph Sorge, 27 September 1877," ibid., 277–8.

[36] Karl Marx, "Marx to Wilhelm Bracke, 21 April 1877," ibid., 223.

[37] Marx, "Marx to Friedrich Adolph Sorge, 27 September 1877," 278.

[38] Frederick Engels, "Letter to Enrico Bignami on the General Elections of 1877, 12 January 1878," in Marx and Engels, *Lettere 1874–1879* (Milano: Lotta Comunista, 2006), p. 247. This letter was lost and the only parts we know are the ones included by Bignami in an article he published on *La Plebe* on 22 January 1878.

[39] Karl Marx, "Marx to Wilhelm Liebknecht, 4 February 1878," in MECW (New York: International Publishers, 1991), 45: 296.

Crisis and engulf all the so-called Powers, those sham-powers, victors and vanquished—to make room for a European Social Revolution".[40] In a letter he sent to Engels in September, the horizon was similar: "Nothing Russia and Prussia … can now do on the international stage can have other than pernicious consequences for their regime, nor can it delay the latter's downfall, but only expedite its violent end."[41]

From time to time, Marx had to concern himself again with the International Working Men's Association, in order to defend its name and to recall the esteem that its political line still enjoyed. In July 1878, in answer to George Howell—an old member of the organization who had become a reformist trade-unionist—Marx pointed out in an article for *The Secular Chronicle* that what had gained the International "a worldwide reputation and a place in the history of mankind" was not "the size of its finances", as Howell had slanderously argued, but "the strength of its intellect and its abundant energy".[42]

Marx also continued to trust in developments on the other side of the Atlantic. In July 1877, he noted in a letter to Engels "the first outbreak against the associated capital oligarchy that has arisen since the Civil War"; it would "of course, be suppressed", but it might "well provide a point of departure for a serious workers' party in the United States".[43] Britain, on the other hand, was a country about which the two friends no longer had any illusions. In February 1878, Marx wrote to Liebknecht that "the English working class had gradually become ever more demoralized, as a result of the period of corruption after 1848, and finally reached the stage of being no more than an appendage of the great Liberal Party, i.e., of its oppressors, the capitalists".[44] In a letter to Eduard Bernstein, Engels was even more realistic: "A genuine workers' movement in the continental sense is non-existent here"; there might still be strikes, "victorious or otherwise", but "the working class makes no progress whatsoever" as a result of them.[45]

---

[40] Karl Marx, "Marx to Thomas Allsop, 4 February 1878," ibid., 299.

[41] Karl Marx, "Marx to Engels, 24 September 1878," ibid., 332.

[42] Karl Marx, "Mr. George Howell's History of the International Working-Men's Association," in MEGA² (Berlin: Dietz, 1985), I/25: 157.

[43] Karl Marx, "Marx to Engels, 25 July 1877," in MECW (New York: International Publishers, 1991), 45: 251.

[44] Karl Marx, "Marx to Wilhelm Liebknecht, 11 February 1878," ibid., 299.

[45] Frederick Engels, "Engels to Eduard Bernstein, 17 June 1879," ibid., 361.

IV. The Critique of "Armchair Socialism"

Marx never lost sight of the main political developments in Germany. After the major tensions surrounding the Gotha congress had passed, he continued his attempts to orient the Socialist Workers' Party of Germany in an anti-capitalist direction. However, other tendencies were developing that would create fresh occasions of conflict. From 1874 Eugen Dühring, an economics professor at Berlin University, began to receive significant attention from Party intellectuals. Articles in support of his positions appeared in *Der Volksstaat* (The People's State), which had been the organ of the Social Democratic Workers' Party of Germany. Therefore, having been asked by Liebknecht to get involved, and having listened to Marx's view that it was necessary "to criticize Dühring without any compunction",[46] Engels decided to write a full-scale critique of the German positivist. This task, which extended from late 1876 until July 1878, ended in the book *Anti-Dühring* (1877–78), whose publication was preceded by excerpts in the columns of *Vorwärts* [Forward], the daily paper of the Socialist Workers' Party of Germany born out of the Gotha fusion congress.[47]

Marx played an active part in the *Anti-Dühring* project: in the winter of 1877, he wrote the key chapter "On 'Critical History'", both on Engels's behalf and in his own name, conceiving it as a response to attacks contained in Dühring's *Critical History of Political Economy and Socialism* (1871). Marx shows that "by value Herr Dühring understands five totally different and directly contradictory things, and, therefore, to put it at its best, himself does not know what he wants". Moreover, in the German economist's book, the "'natural laws of all economics', ushered in with such pomp, prove to be merely universally familiar, and often not even properly understood, platitudes of the worst description".[48] The "sole explanation" he gives of "economic facts" is that "they are the result of

---

[46] Karl Marx, "Marx to Engels, 25 May 1876," ibid., 119.

[47] On the importance of this text, see Karl Kautsky, "Einleitung," in *Friedrich Engels' Briefwechsel mit Karl Kautsky*, ed. Benedikt Kautsky (Vienna: Danubia, 1955), 4, where the German Party theorist recalls that no book did more to advance his understanding of socialism. H.-J. Steinberg, showed that "both Bernstein, who studied *Anti-Dühring* in 1879, and Kautsky, who did the same in 1880, became 'Marxists' through reading that book," in *Sozialismus und Deutsche Sozialdemokratie* (Hannover: Verlag für Literatur und Zeitgeschehen, 1967), 23.

[48] Frederick Engels, *Anti-Dühring*, in MECW (New York: International Publishers, 1987), 25: 242.

'force', a term with which the philistine of all nations has for thousands of years consoled himself for everything unpleasant that happens to him, and which leaves us just where we were".[49] For Marx, Dühring does not try to "investigate the origin and effects of this force", and, when compelled to elucidate the capitalist exploitation of labour, he "first represents it in a general way as based on taxes and price surcharges" à la Proudhon, then "explains it in detail by means of Marx's theory of surplus-labour". The result is totally implausible: "two totally contradictory modes of outlook, ... cop[ied] down without taking his breath".[50]

In the elections of January 1877, the Socialist Workers' Party of Germany won nearly half a million votes, raising its share above 9 per cent. But despite this success, the state of the party continued to trouble Marx. Writing to the German doctor Ferdinand Fleckles, he ridiculed the "short pamphlet" entitled *The Quintessence of Socialism* (1879) of sociologist Albert Schäffle as "fantastic, truly Swabian ... picture of the future socialist millennium as ... the kingdom come of your cosy petty bourgeois".[51] In this context, when asked by the journalist Franz Wiede to take a prominent role in founding a new review, Marx commented to Engels: "It would certainly be very nice if a really scientific socialist periodical were to appear. This would provide an opportunity for criticism and counter-criticism in which theoretical points could be discussed by us and the total ignorance of professors and university lecturers exposed, thereby simultaneously disabusing the minds of the general public."[52] In the end, however, he had to accept that the shortcomings of its contributors would have precluded "the prime requirement in all criticism": that

---

[49] Ibid.

[50] Ibid.

[51] Karl Marx, "Marx to Ferdinand Fleckles, 21 January 1877," in MECW (New York: International Publishers, 1991), 45: 190. Few years later, in a letter to Karl Kautsky, Engels wrote of the numerous inaccuracies and misunderstandings that the German economist Albert Schäffle and other "armchair socialists [*Kathedersozialisten*]" displayed in relation to Marx's work: "to refute, for example, all the monstrous twaddle which Schäffle alone has assembled in his many fat tomes is, in my opinion, a sheer waste of time. It would fill a fair-sized book were one merely to attempt to put right all the misquotations from *Capital* inserted by these gentlemen between inverted commas". He concluded in peremptory fashion: "They should first learn to read and copy before demanding to have their questions answered", Frederick Engels, "Engels to Karl Kautsky, 1 February 1881," in MECW (New York: International Publishers, 1992), 46: 56.

[52] Karl Marx, "Marx to Friedrich Engels, 18 July 1877," in MECW (New York: International Publishers, 1991), 45: 242.

is, "ruthlessness".[53] Marx also directed sharp comments against *Zukunft* [Future], deriding its "endeavour to substitute ideological catch-phrases such as 'justice', etc., for materialist knowledge [and ...] to peddle phantasms of the future structure of society".[54]

In October, Marx complained to Sorge of a "corrupt spirit" spreading in the party, "not so much among the masses as among the leaders".[55] The agreement with the Lassalleans had "led to further compromise with other waverers". In particular, Marx had no time for "a whole swarm of immature undergraduates and over-wise graduates who want[ed] to give socialism a 'higher, idealistic' orientation". They thought they could substitute for its "materialist basis" (which "calls for serious, objective study if one is to operate thereon") a "modern mythology with its goddesses of Justice, Liberty, Equality and Fraternity".[56]

What lay behind these criticisms was never feelings of jealousy or rivalry. Marx wrote to the journalist and parliamentarian Wilhelm Blos that he did not "care a straw for popularity", reminding him that "such was [his] aversion to the personality cult that at the time of the International, when plagued by numerous moves ... to accord [him] public honour, [he] never allowed one of them to enter the domain of publicity", nor "ever repli[ed] to them, save with an occasional snub". This attitude had sustained him ever since the political commitments of his youth, so that when the Communist League was born in 1847, he and Engels had joined "only on condition that anything conducive to a superstitious belief in authority be eliminated from the Rules".[57] His only concern had been, and continued to be, that the nascent workers' organizations

---

[53] Ibid. Engels was certainly in agreement with Marx about this. As he put it in a letter to the zoologist Oscar Schmidt, "ruthless criticism ... alone does justice to free science, and ... any man of science must welcome [it], even when applied to himself". Frederick Engels, "Engels to Oscar Schmidt, 19 July 1878," ibid., 314.

[54] Karl Marx, "Marx to Wilhelm Bracke, 23 October 1877," ibid., 285.

[55] Karl Marx, "Marx to Friedrich Adolph Sorge, 19 October 1877," ibid., 283. Steinberg had convincingly demonstrated the theoretical eclecticism among German Party activists at the time. "If we take the mass of members and leaders," he wrote, "their socialist conceptions may be described as an 'average socialism' composed of various elements. The view of Marx and Engels that the Party's 'shortcomings' and theoretical ignorance and insecurity were the negative consequence of the 1875 compromise was only an expression of the Londoners' warnings about members coming out of the General Association of German Workers," Steinberg, *Sozialismus und Deutsche Sozialdemokratie*, 19.

[56] Marx, "Marx to Friedrich Adolph Sorge, 19 October 1877," 283.

[57] Karl Marx, "Marx to Wilhelm Blos, 10 November 1877," ibid., 288.

should not blur their anti-capitalism and—in the manner of the British labour movement—adopt a moderate, pro-bourgeois line.[58]

A major event in the late 1870s was the attempted assassination of Kaiser Wilhelm I by the anarchist Karl Nobiling in June 1878. Marx's reactions were later recorded by Kovalevsky: "I happened to be in Marx's library when he got news of [the] unsuccessful attempt. ... [His] reaction was to curse the terrorist, explaining that only one thing could be expected from his attempt to accelerate the course of events, namely, new persecutions of the socialists."[59] That was precisely what ensued, as Bismarck used the pretext to introduce the Anti-Socialist Laws and get them adopted by the Reichstag in October. Marx commented to Engels: "Outlawing has, from time immemorial, been an infallible means of making anti-government movements 'illegal' and protecting the government from the law—'legality kills us'."[60] The debate in parliament took place in mid-September, and Bracke sent Marx the stenographic record of the Reichstag sessions and a copy of the draft legislation. Marx planned to write a critical article for the British press[61] and began to compile extracts and notes for that purpose. In a few pages, he outlined the difference between the mass Socialist Workers' Party of Germany and the anarchists: the former constituted "the genuine historical movement of the working class; the other ... a phantom of a dead-end youth intent on making history, [which] merely shows how the ideas of French socialism are caricatured in the declassed

---

[58] Two years later, Engels wrote in similar vein to Bebel: "You know that Marx and I have voluntarily conducted the defence of the party against its opponents abroad throughout the party's existence, and that we have never asked anything of the party in return, save that it should not be untrue to itself." Using diplomatic language, he tried to get comrades in Germany to understand that, although his and Marx's "criticism might be displeasing to some", it might be advantageous to the party to have "the presence abroad of a couple of men who, uninfluenced by confusing local conditions and the minutiae of the struggle, compare from time to time what has been said and what has been done with the theoretical tenets valid for any modern proletarian movement", Frederick Engels, "Engels to August Bebel, 14 November 1879," ibid., 420–1.

[59] McLellan, *Karl Marx—Interviews and Recollections*, 131.

[60] Karl Marx, "Marx to Engels, 17 September 1877," in MECW (New York: International Publishers, 1991), 45: 322. Marx wrote the final clause in French—*la légalité nous tue*—harking back to the words used by Odilon Barrot, briefly prime minister in 1848–49 under Louis Bonaparte, in a speech he gave to the Constituent Assembly in January 1849 that defended the outlawing of "extremist" political forces.

[61] Marx, "Marx to Engels, 24 September 1878," 332.

men of the upper classes".[62] In rebutting the argument of the Prussian interior minister, August Eulenburg, that the workers' aims were violent, he made his position quite clear:

> The objective [is] the emancipation of the working class and the revolution (transformation) of society implicit therein. An historical development can remain "peaceful" only for so long as its progress is not forcibly obstructed by those wielding social power at the time. If in England, for instance, or the United States, the working class were to gain a majority in Parliament or Congress, they could, by lawful means, rid themselves of such laws and institutions as impeded their development. [...] However, the "peaceful" movement might be transformed into a "forcible" one by resistance on the part of those interested in restoring the former state of affairs; if (as in the American Civil War and French Revolution) they are put down by force, it is as rebels against "lawful" force.[63]

For Marx, then, the government was "seeking to suppress by force a development it dislike[d] but could not lawfully attack". That, necessarily, was "the prelude to violent revolution"—"an old story which yet remains eternally true", he added, quoting Heinrich Heine (1797–1856).[64]

In a letter to Sorge from September 1879, Marx described the new tendencies emerging in the German party. He stressed that people like the publisher Karl Höchberg, "nonentities in theory and nincompoops in practice", were "seeking to draw the teeth of socialism (which they have rehashed in accordance with academic formulae) and of the Party in particular".[65] Their aim was "to enlighten the workers, ... to provide them, out of their confused and superficial knowledge, with educative elements" and, above all, "to make the party 'respectable' in the eyes of the philistines". They were, he concluded, "poor counter-revolutionary windbags".[66] With subtle humour, he suggested that Bismarck had "done a lot of good not to himself, but us", by imposing selective silence in Germany and allowing such windbags "a chance of making themselves plainly heard".

---

[62] Karl Marx, "The Parliamentary Debate on the Anti-Socialist Laws (Outline of an Article)," in MECW (New York: International Publishers, 1989), 24: 247.

[63] Ibid., 248.

[64] Ibid., 249.

[65] Karl Marx, "Marx to Friedrich Adolph Sorge, 19 September 1879," ibid., 413.

[66] Ibid.

In a French police report from London, an agent claimed that, "following the death of Lassalle, Marx [had become] the undisputed leader of the German revolutionaries. If the socialist deputies in Germany [were] the official leaders, the divisional commanders, Marx [was] the chief of the general staff. He devised the battle plans and watch[ed] over their implementation".[67] In reality, Marx's criticisms of the party often went unheeded, and from his study in London he observed "the depths" to which "parliamentary representatives" had "already been brought by parliamentarism".[68]

Another polemical focus was the question of who should edit the new journal of the Socialist Workers' Party of Germany, *Der Sozialdemokrat* [The Social Democrat], publication of which began in Zurich in September 1879. Marx and Engels, disagreeing with the proposed stance of the paper, felt obliged to send another letter (drafted by Engels) to Bebel, Liebknecht and Bracke. In this "Circular Letter" (1879), as it became known, they denounced the growing consensus in the party behind the positions of Höchberg, the main source of finance for the undertaking. He had recently published an article in the *Jahrbuch für Sozialwissenschaft und Sozialpolitik* [Annals for Social Science and Social Policy], a reformist journal under his direction, in which he called for a return to the Lassallean spirit. In his view, the Lassalleans had given birth to a political movement open "not only [to] the workers but all honest democrats, in the van of which [should] march the independent representatives of science and all men imbued with a true love of mankind".[69]

For Marx, all these were views he had firmly rejected since his early years and the *Manifesto of the Communist Party* (1848). The "Circular Letter" underlined the dangers of one of Höchberg's statements: "In short, the working class is incapable of emancipating itself by its own efforts. In order to do so it must place itself under the direction of 'educated and propertied' bourgeois who alone have 'the time and the opportunity' to become conversant with what is good for the workers." In the view of this "representative of the petty bourgeoisie", then, the bourgeoisie was "not to be combated—not on your life—but won over by vigorous propaganda".[70] Even the decision to defend the Paris Commune had

[67] Enzensberger, *Gespräche mit Marx und Engels*, 490.
[68] Marx, "Marx to F. Sorge, 19 September 1879," 413.
[69] Karl Marx and Frederick Engels, "Marx and Engels to August Bebel, Wilhelm Liebknecht and Wilhelm Bracke ("Circular Letter"), 17–18 September 1879," in MECW (New York: International Publishers, 1991), 45: 402.
[70] Ibid., 403.

allegedly "put off people otherwise well-disposed towards" the workers' movement. In conclusion, Engels and Marx noted with alarm that Höchberg's objective was to make "the overthrow of the capitalist order ... unattainably remote" and "utterly irrelevant to present political practice". One could therefore "conciliate, compromise, philanthropize to one's heart's content. The same thing applie[d] to the class struggle between proletariat and bourgeoisie."[71] The disagreement was total.

Marx's tenacious opposition to what he called the "armchair socialist riff-raff"[72] was akin to his view of those who confined themselves to empty rhetoric, however concealed beneath radical language. Following the launch of the journal *Freiheit* [Freedom], he explained to Sorge that he had reproached its editors not for being "too revolutionary" but for having "no revolutionary content" and "merely indulg[ing] in revolutionary jargon".[73] In his view, both these positions, though stemming from very different political tendencies, were no danger to the existing system and ultimately made its survival possible.

Marx's idea of socialism was very different from State socialism and reformism that emerged in the German Social Democratic Party and that became hegemonic after the foundation of the Second International. The Marx revival under way today will be much more effective if Marx's writings are re-examined for an understanding not only of how capitalism works but also of the failure of socialist experiences until today. It goes without saying that we cannot today simply rely on what Marx wrote a century and a half ago. Nor should we lightly discount the content and clarity of his analyses or fail to take up the critical weapons he offered for fresh thinking about an alternative society to capitalism.

BIBLIOGRAPHY

Engels, Frederick. "Anti-Dühring." In MECW. Vol. 25, 5–309. New York: International Publishers, 1987a.

Engels, Frederick. "On the Socialist Movement in Germany, France, the United States and Russia." In MECW. Vol. 24, 203–6. New York: International Publishers, 1987b.

---

[71] Ibid., 406.

[72] Marx, "Marx to Sorge, 19 September 1879," 412.

[73] Ibid., 411. Cf. Frederick Engels to Johann Philipp Becker, 10 April 1880," in MECW (New York: International Publishers, 1992), 46: 7: "*Freiheit* [wants] to become, by hook or by crook, the most revolutionary paper in the world, but this cannot be achieved simply by repeating the word 'revolution' in every line."

Engels, Frederick. "Letter to Enrico Bignami on the General Elections of 1877." In Marx and Engels, *Lettere 1874–1879*, 246–8. Milano: Lotta Comunista, 2006.

Enzensberger, Hans Magnus. *Gespräche mit Marx und Engels*. Frankfurt: Insel Verlag, 1973.

Freymond, Jacques. *Études et documents sur la Première Internationale en Suisse*. Geneva: Droz, 1964.

Gladstone, William. *The Bulgarian Horrors and the Question of the East*. London: William Ridgway, 1876.

Kautsky, Karl. "Einleitung." In *Friedrich Engels' Briefwechsel mit Karl Kautsky*, edited by Benedikt Kautsky, 1–55. Vienna: Danubia, 1955.

Liebknecht, Wilhelm. *Zur orientalischen Frage oder Soll Europa kosakisch werden?* Leipzig: Commissions, 1878.

Lissagaray, Prosper Olivier. *History of the Paris Commune of 1871*. St. Petersburg, FL: Red and Black Publishers, 2007.

Marx, Karl. "Contribution to the Critique of Hegel's Philosophy of Law." In MECW. Vol. 3, 3–129. New York: International Publishers, 1975.

Marx, Karl. "Mr. George Howell's History of the International Working-Men's Association." In MEGA². Vol. I/25, 157. Berlin: Dietz, 1985.

Marx, Karl. *Critique of the Gotha Programme*. In MECW. Vol. 24, 81–99. New York: International Publishers, 1987a.

Marx, Karl. "The Parliamentary Debate on the Anti-Socialist Laws (Outline of an Article)." In MECW. Vol. 24, 240–50. New York: International Publishers, 1987b.

Marx, Karl. "Mehrwertrate und Profitrate mathematisch behandelt." In MEGA². Vol. II/14, 19–150. Berlin: Dietz, 2003.

Marx, Karl. "Resolutions of the Geneva Congress (1866)." In *Workers Unite! The International after 150 Years*, edited by Marcello Musto, 83–8. London: Bloomsbury, 2014.

Marx, Karl, and Frederick Engels. *Correspondence*. In MECW. Vols. 41–46. New York: International Publishers, 1985–1992.

McLellan, David. *Karl Marx: Interviews and Recollections*. New York: Barnes & Noble, 1981.

Most, Johann. *Kapital und Arbeit: Ein Populärer Auszug aus "Das Kapital" von Karl Marx*. Chemnitz: G. Rübner, n.d. [1873].

Musto, Marcello. "Introduction." In *Workers Unite! The International after 150 Years*, edited by Marcello Musto, 1–68. London: Bloomsbury, 2014.

Musto, Marcello. *Another Marx: Early Writings to the International*. London: Bloomsbury, 2018.

Nicolaevsky, Boris, and Otto Maenchen Helfen. *Karl Marx—Man and Fighter*. London: Methuen, 1936.

Rubel, Maximilien. *Bibliographie des œuvres de Karl Marx*. Paris: Rivière, 1956.

Steinberg, H.-J. *Sozialismus und Deutsche Sozialdemokratie*. Hannover: Verlag für Literatur und Zeitgeschehen, 1967.

Revolution and Radical Democracy: Marx Versus Post-Marxism

Kohei Saito

I. Introduction

The traditional Marxist project of "permanent revolution" that envisions a transition to socialism by taking over the state power through a proletarian revolution lost its appeal to the majority of the left after it was even more harshly criticized due to the collapse of the USSR. The "idea of communism" lost its plausibility, and it became an object of postmodern speculation.[1] Consequently, the opposition to capitalism remained largely absent in the last decades, as the "third way" suggested by social democrats was nothing but their adoption to the neoliberal policies. However, the experience of the last 30 years clearly shows that the global

---

This work was supported by JSPS Kakenhi Grant Number JP18K12188 as well as by the Ministry of Education of the Republic of Korea and the National Research Foundation of Korea (NRF-2018S1A3A2075204).

[1] Slavoj Žižek and Costas Douzinas, eds., *The Idea of Communism* (London: Verso, 2010).

K. Saito (✉)
Osaka City University, Osaka, Japan

© The Author(s) 2019   41
S. Gupta et al. (eds.), *Karl Marx's Life, Ideas, and Influences*, Marx, Engels, and Marxisms, https://doi.org/10.1007/978-3-030-24815-4_3

hegemony of neoliberal capitalism which claimed to bring about the "end of history," far from realizing free, democratic society, not only significantly enlarged economic inequality but also deepened structural crises such as financial instability, environmental destruction, and far-right xenophobia.

The world today direly needs a utopian imaginary, which social democracy cannot offer. In this situation, one of the last recourses to the left is the post-Marxian theory of "radical democracy."[2] Post-Marxists reinterpreted Marx's theoretical legacy through an attempt to deal with the "autonomy of the political," which enables envisioning the possibility of a radical social change in the twenty-first century. However, as the prefix "post" indicates, post-Marxists who advocate radical democracy, such as Ernesto Laclau, Chantal Mouffe, and Jacques Rancière, do not simply accept Marx's theory, but rather add—often critical—corrections. It is thus necessary to clarify what kinds of Marxist ideas remained and what was lost in this transition from Marxism to post-Marxism. As will be shown here, *socialism as democracy beyond capitalism* is the true legacy of Marx that the left needs to revitalize today in contrast to the uncritical celebration of the importance of *political* struggle and will as a way of changing the society.

To clarify this point, it is first necessary to understand Marx's unique conception of the modern separation of the economic and the political in the capitalist society. However, post-Marxists often miss Marx's point, and rather blame Marx's crude economic reductionism due to its negation of the autonomy of the political. In contrast, by highlighting the difference between the young and matured Marx, this paper explicates his vision of socialism beyond the modern dualism of the state and civil society. As a result, it will be clear that Marx's theory of revolution, which is tightly linked to his critique of political economy in *Capital*, does not negate the

---

[2] There are more liberal versions as a post-Marxist alternative to Marx's theory of revolution. See Axel Honneth, *The Idea of Socialism* (London: Polity, 2018), 53. Honneth's idea of socialism as "social freedom," however, has almost nothing to do with Marx's socialism by dismissing the dimension of economic equality, and it becomes quite unclear why it is still necessary to read Marx. The other, and more radical left alternative, is robust discussion on post-capitalism. Despite their strong emphasis on technological development such as automation and information technology, Nick Srnicek and Alex Williams's *Inventing the Future: Postcapitalism and a World without Work* (London: Verso, 2015) also clearly points to the need for the construction of the political subjectivity by drawing upon Laclau's theory of hegemony and radical democracy. This is why the current paper aims at examining whether radical democracy can be an effective socialist strategy.

autonomy of the political. In contrast to Laclau and Rancière, however, Marx did not believe that the autonomy of the political would lead to a radical social change and human emancipation. Rather, Marx's understanding of the political reveals the fetishism of post-Marxists in their uncritical celebration of the autonomy of the political.

II. The Modern Binary of the State and Society

"Society" as an independent sphere of communal and individual life distinguished from "the state" obviously existed before the rise of modernity. For example, it is possible to find various discussions on family and private property in ancient Greece and Rome.[3] However, it is also undeniable that after the seventeenth century, the relationship between the state and society attained a unique modern character. As a result of the loss of traditional communal ties in the modern society, the *bellum omnium contra omnes* among private individuals on the market came to threaten the public order, so that the reconstruction of the social and communal ties among the atomized individuals became a topic of theoretical reflection. For example, Thomas Hobbes and later Johann Gottlieb Fichte projected the modern subjectivity upon a "fiction" of the endless concurrence among atomized individuals in the "state of nature" and deduced how this endless conflict necessarily leads to the conscious reconstruction of the social bonds under the state through social contract and mutual recognition. In other words, the state as a universal communal realm must be consciously reconstructed in the face of fragmentation and atomization of individuals under the market economy. The fundamental ideology for the legitimation of the body politic here was "possessive individualism."[4]

Georg Wilhelm Friedrich Hegel criticized Fichte's solution of the authoritarian state and attempted to figure out the ways of mediating the universality of state governance and the particularity of individual desires without negating the modern subjectivity. However, his idea for the realization of social freedom in his *Philosophy of Right* also suffers from a certain ambivalence. On the one hand, the modern social division of labour realizes the relations of mutual material interdependence among

---

[3] Ellen Meiksins Wood, *Democracy against Capitalism: Renewing Historical Materialism* (Cambridge: Cambridge University Press, 1994), 239.

[4] C. B. Macpherson, *The Political Theory of Possessive Individualism: Hobbes to Locke* (Oxford: Oxford University Press, 2011).

free and equal persons, so the social tie in "civil society (*bürgerliche Gesellschaft*)" constitutes an essential component for the realization of "ethical life (*Sittlichkeit*)."[5] On the other hand, the immanent tendency of civil society to create economic inequality produces the rich and the poor called "rabble (*Pöbel*)," who cannot be integrated into the society but rather threaten to destroy the public social order. Neither the counter-measure of civil society such as "corporation (*Korporation*)" and "police (*Polizei*)" nor the state intervention can overcome this economic contradiction.[6]

Hegel's ambivalence is discernible here. While he recognized the need to mediate the state and civil society, he retained the old conception that emphasizes the uniquely modern "separation" of the public sphere and the private sphere. However, this distinction is destabilized by the reality, as the economic activity intrudes into the public sphere in the form of rabble. In other words, despite the separation of the economic and the political sphere, rabble reveals an intimate tie between the political and the economic. This is usually hidden, but the neutrality and the universality of the state are challenged with the deepening of the economic contradiction.

It was Marx who paid attention to this problem of the modern society. Modern capitalist society differs from pre-capitalist societies in that its primary aim of social production is not concrete goods for the sake of satisfying individual needs, but the valorization of capital as such. Furthermore, the relation of domination and obedience is emancipated from personal and political relationship, so that social relations come to be constituted under formally free and equal individuals. In the pre-capitalist societies, the appropriation of the surplus product of other people's labour is founded directly upon the relation of political domination. There was an original unity of the political and the economic. In contrast, exploitation of surplus in a capitalist society dissolves this tie and attains an appearance of being an act of exchange amongst equal individuals in the private sphere. Here exists the uniquely modern separation of the economic and

---

[5] When Hegel translated the term "civil society" which means "state" or "common wealth" to a German term *bürgerliche Gesellschaft*, he gave it a specific meaning. As a consequence, *bürgerliche Gesellschaft* cannot be simply reduced to the market, as it also includes *Korporation* and *Polizei*, so that it has a function to mediate the public ("the state") and the private ("the family").

[6] Frank Ruda, *Hegel's Rabble: An Investigation into Hegel's Philosophy of Right* (New York: Continuum, 2011).

the extra-economic, which leads to the separation of the public sphere from the private sphere, that is, the economic sphere is depoliticized as the sphere of private activities.

However, the separation does *not* mean that the state and civil society become fully independent of each other. Modern individuals who are liberated from tradition and customs attain a reflexive subjectivity with regard to value judgements and norms.[7] As seen earlier, this process also includes liberation from economic exploitation based on direct political and personal domination. However, modern atomized individuals are not entirely free. They are now subjected to a new type of domination and coercion which is impersonal—an anonymous domination by things acting independently of one's own will. This is what Marx called "reification." In other words, the reified power of things attains an enormous force in the production process and in the market, exerting the power of command in a *depoliticized form* over individual judgements and behaviours.

In this situation, however, the distinction between the private and the public inevitably becomes ambivalent and obscure. The sphere of civil society, though considered to be "private," actually comes to fulfil a "public role" of social integration and disciplining, contributing to the construction of the relations of domination. At the same time, the state, which is supposed to deal with universal matters and rights, follows the logic of capital, guaranteeing a system of private property as well as actively intervening into the market for economic growth. In this sense, the state fosters the "private" interests of a particular social group of capitalists. This is how the uniquely modern "unity in separation" of the state and the society or of the universality and the particularity emerges together with the appearance of their separation.[8]

Thus, according to Marx, the separation of the public and the private based on the separation of the state and civil society is an unstable one. Notably, this is not because the economic sphere fully covers and dominates the political sphere due to the expansion of the market activities and the corresponding formation of the sphere of the "social."[9] According to

[7] Jürgen Habermas, *Between Facts and Norms: Contributions to a Discourse Theory of Law and Democracy* (Cambridge, MA: MIT Press, 1998).

[8] John Holloway and Sol Picciotto, "Introduction: Towards a Materialist Theory of the State," in *State and Capital: A Marxist Debate*, ed. John Holloway and Sol Picciotto (London: Edward Arnold, 1978), 3.

[9] Hannah Arendt discussed this issue with the concept of "the social." Hannah Arendt, *The Human Condition* (Chicago: The University of Chicago Press, 1998). Wendy Brown's

Marx, there is no pure, ideal political realm which existed before the invasion of the social. Rather, he argues that the state as a political apparatus always already receives a uniquely capitalist "form determination (*Formbestimmung*)." The political form of state governance is inevitably tied to the economic relations of domination, as he points out in the *Grundrisse*:

> The specific economic form in which unpaid surplus labor is pumped out of the direct producers determines the relationship of domination and servitude, as this grows directly out of production itself and reacts back on it in turn as a determinant. On this is based the entire configuration of the economic community arising from the actual relations of production, and hence also its specific political form. It is in each case the direct relationship of the owners of the conditions of production to the immediate producers—a relationship whose particular form naturally corresponds always to a certain level of development of the type and manner of labor, and hence to its social productive power—in which we find the innermost secret, the hidden basis of the entire social edifice, and hence also the political form of the relationship of sovereignty and dependence, in short, the specific form of state in each case.[10]

Here one should not interpret this passage as a manifestation of Marx's crude economic reductionism. Marx's point is rather that the political sphere becomes a distinct sphere separated from the economic one under the capitalist mode of production, but it can never be fundamentally independent from the economic, insofar as it receives the uniquely capitalist political form. The political and economic problems are tightly interwoven in capitalism because the economic relations within the capitalist mode of production condition the relations of domination in the state.

As long as freedom and rights such as human rights are formal rights based on the relations of commodity exchange, they cannot fully overcome inequality and unfreedom under capitalism—this is why the political intervention of the welfare state in the market is fundamentally limited. Formal equality and freedom rather complement and legitimize the

Edgework (Princeton: Princeton University Press, 2005) also views the current challenge to democracy by neoliberalism in its economic domination over the political sphere. Both Arendt and Brown attempt to defend freedom proper in the political sphere, missing the fact that both the economic and the political are mutually constitutive social forms of capitalist relations.

[10] Karl Marx, *Capital*, vol. 3 (London: Penguin, 1993), 923. See also Soichiro Sumida, "Die Zusammenfassung der bürgerlichen Gesellschaft in der Staatsform," in *Marx-Engels-Jahrbuch 2017/2018* (Berlin: De Gruyter, 2018), 47.

exercise of private power that enables the command over and exploitation of the large number of workers by a few capitalists in the economic sphere, constituting more solid relations of domination and subordination than ever in favour of the ruling class. On the other hand, economic forces supported by the state enable the expanding and accelerating accumulation of capital. Conversely, the augmented power of reification coercively determines judgements, behaviours, and will in various spheres, facilitating the disciplining and domestication of the masses and increasing public order and social integrity.

Marx believed that in order to overcome the contradiction of the reified domination, it is necessary to abolish the dualism of the state and civil society. The problem is twofold. On the one hand, although the "public" meaning of the social activities of production significantly increases in our daily life due to the deepening of mutual dependence through the increasing social division of labour, the meaning of economic activities is largely limited to the "private" sphere, whose consequences are ascribed solely to individuals. On the other hand, although the state has a certain room for intervening in the market, the state and civil society are ultimately complementary to each other for the sake of maintaining capitalist relations. Therefore, formal rights within civil society cannot be expanded beyond a certain point, so that the state cannot be a tool to eradicate the truly negative aspects of civil society. This is why Marx argued for overcoming the uniquely modern unity in separation of the state and civil society for the sake of the "free development of individuals," demanding not only the "expropriation of the expropriators" but also the "annulment" of politics.[11]

III. MARX'S THEORY OF REVOLUTION

In order to comprehend what Marx envisioned with the transcendence of the capitalist mode of production, one needs to examine his theoretical development a little more carefully, especially because there are changes and continuities in his vision of revolution. Since his theory changed over time, its evaluation can significantly differ, depending on which text one focuses on. While post-Marxists often draw upon Marx's early texts such as *A Contribution to the Critique of Hegel's Philosophy of Right* and *The Communist Manifesto*, it is important to comprehend his political theory in relation to his later critique of political economy.

---

[11] István Mészáros, *Marx's Theory of Alienation* (London: Merlin Press, 2006), 160.

According to Alex Demirovic, there exists a "large consistency" in Marx's theory of revolution despite various theoretical changes.[12] And this continuity precisely lies in Marx's claim for the need to overcome the separation of politics and economy as well as the dualism of the state and civil society. As he argued in *On the Jewish Question*, modern representative democracy brings about political emancipation, so that occupations, births, and religious beliefs are regarded as non-political distinctions in civil society that belong to the private sphere. In contrast, the state serves as a public sphere which deals with universal issues free from private interests. However, Marx argues that under such a division of the state and civil society, the state as universal life of species-being is separated from the actual social life, so that individuals are "deprived of [their] real individual life and endowed with unreal universality." The life in the state becomes an unrealistic world of heaven because various inequality and unfreedom are preserved in reality in a depoliticized form in civil society. Even if people constitute the state according to the idea of democracy, they can participate in it merely as "the imaginary member of an illusory sovereignty." Marx calls this constitution of social communality based on such an unrealistic mediation "the perfect Christian state,"[13] claiming that such existence of the state expresses the alienated separation of the state and civil society.

The French Revolution is exemplary. This "Christian state" is a formally "democratic state." According to Marx, a revolution that aims only for "political emancipation" without challenging the modern dualism never brings about human emancipation in the end. Since the state attempts to establish "the real species-life of man devoid of contradictions," neglecting the atomized situation of divided private interests within the actual civil society, "it can achieve this only by coming into violent contradiction with its own conditions of life, only by declaring the revolution to be permanent."[14] The world in which formal equality and freedom dominate can exist only through the oppression of concrete inequalities and unfreedoms in civil society. Seeking only political emancipation without overcoming this contradiction in civil society, modern dualism would ultimately lead to a violent conformism—the coercive force that treats real inequalities as if they were equals. The realization of human emancipation requires overcoming the separation of civil society from the state and replacing the illusionary life with the real equality and freedom in social life.

---

[12] Alex Demirovic, "Rätedemokratie oder das Ende der Politik," *Prokla* 155 (2009): 186.
[13] Karl Marx, *On the Jewish Question*, MECW vol. 3, 154, 156.
[14] Ibid., 156.

It is thus necessary to go beyond the modern dualism of the private and the public, as well as the universal and the particular, through the radical transformation of civil society itself. This is the fundamental insight of the young Marx.

According to Demirovic, such a recognition is not limited to the young Marx. For example, Marx repeated the same claim in his analysis of the Paris Commune in *The Civil War in France*. As long as the separation between the state and civil society remains, there is no human emancipation. Marx argued that political emancipation brought about through the French Revolution only opposed the state as a "supernatural" power to civil society.

> It was, therefore, forced to develop, what absolute monarchy had commenced, the centralization and organization of state power, and to expand the circumference and the attributes of the state power, the number of its tools, its independence of, and its supernaturalist sway of real society which in fact took the place of the medieval supernaturalist heaven with its saints. Every minor solitary interest engendered by the relations of social groups was separated from society itself, fixed and made independent of it, and opposed to it in the form of state interest, administered by state priests with exactly determined hierarchical functions.[15]

Marx's argument in this passage is quite similar to his critique of the "perfect Christian state" in *On the Jewish Question*. The revolutionary character of the Paris Commune precisely lies in the "the reabsorption of the State power by society, as its own living forces instead of as forces controlling and subduing it, by the popular masses themselves, forming their own force instead of the organized force of their suppression."[16] The Commune aimed at establishing "truly democratic institutions" by realizing social production based on associated producers. With an expression that reminds of Lincoln, Marx characterized democracy in the Commune in the following way: "It was a Revolution against the State itself, this supernaturalist abortion of society, a resumption by the people for the people, of people's own social life. It was [...] a Revolution to break down this horrid machinery of class domination itself."[17] The Commune transformed the social production in order to overcome the alienated power of the state and regain the social communality.

[15] Karl Marx, *The Civil War in France*, MECW vol. 22, 484.
[16] Ibid., 487.
[17] Ibid., 486.

However, there are also theoretical changes in Marx's socialist strategy. His emphasis shifted from the permanent revolution based on the centralized state power to a reformist struggle based on trade unions and cooperatives. Marx in the *Communist Manifesto* emphasized the importance of taking the state power through political revolution led by a vanguard party. In other words, the plan was the nationalization of means of the production through the "dictatorship of the proletariat," and for the transition to socialism to be conducted through economic reforms from above. One could discern a certain instrumentalist understanding of the state here. In contrast, the late Marx found possibilities of the future in cooperatives—even if he did not abandon his critique of cooperativism in those years—and recognized the importance of social reforms such as the legislation of the ten-hour working day and the foundation of the public professional school. Instead of demanding the state-led reformations, he came to emphasize the need for the management of social production from the bottom-up association and trade union organization in a decentralized manner.[18]

Behind this transformation of Marx's view on socialism, there is his recognition that the existing capitalist state does not become an emancipatory tool for the socialist transition, even if the workers take the state power. Political reform alone cannot challenge the existing mode of production. In fact, Marx explicitly said in *Civil War in France* that the current form of the state is of no use for the sake of establishing socialism: "But the proletariat cannot [...] simply lay hold of the existent state body and wield this ready-made agency for their own purpose."[19] In the transition to socialism, the modern socialist state must be dissolved into the local-level system of governance based on the network of decentralized communes.

It is noteworthy that this change of Marx's view owes to the deepening of his critique of political economy. Although he never fully elaborated on his theory of the state in detail, he intended to comprehend the specifically modern relationship between the state and civil society in continuation with his critique of political economy. Marx pointed to the importance of comprehending the political form of the state in its relation to the economic forms of money and capital, although this relationship is hidden

---

[18] Ryusuke Ohashi, *Marx Shakaishugizo no Tenkan* [*The Transformation of Marx's View on Socialism*] (Tokyo: Ochanomizu Shobo, 1996), 22–3.
[19] Marx, *The Civil War in* France, MECW vol. 22, 533.

under the appearance of the separation of the economic and the extra-economic forces. In the reified world of formal democracy, the "private" power of civil society attains a "public" function to govern the masses through its economic power of disciplining and oppression, which supplements the enormous political power of the centralized state. This political form of the state cannot be emancipatory. Thus, it is necessary to transform the economic relations through association of workers in such a way that their reified power can be weakened, and the political form can be significantly transformed. This is why Marx claimed that without the transcendence of economic forms, it is not possible to realize "truly democratic institutions." Democracy must not be separated from the sphere of social production—"the reabsorption of the State power by society" through revolution. This is the fundamental condition for the establishment of socialism.

IV. Post-Marxist Critique of Marx's Historical Materialism

However, the Marxist theory of the state and permanent revolution has been denounced for its reductionistic attitude towards the multiplicity of the sphere of political struggles which reduces everything to the determination by the economic in the "last instance." According to the critics, Marx's theory of revolution is *apolitical* because politics is ultimately reduced to the law of history driven by economic forces. Dick Howard even argues that "revolution is an antithesis of the politics."[20] In a similar manner, various critics repeatedly pointed out that the socialist emancipation of humans would oppress the political dimension through the "administration of things." Hannah Arendt wrote:

> In Marx's ideal society these two different concepts are inextricably combined: the classless and stateless society somehow realizes the general ancient conditions of leisure from labor and, at the same time, leisure from politics. This is supposed to come about when the "administration of things" has taken the place of government and political action.[21]

---

[20] Dick Howard, *The Specter of Democracy* (New York: Columbia University Press, 2002), 20.
[21] Hannah Arendt, *Between Past and Future: Eight Exercises in Political Thought* (London: Penguin Books, 2006), 19–20.

Arendt's critique against the "administration of things" appears quite credible, especially because it transformed into "the administration of people" under Stalinism.

It was almost natural that Western Marxism and later post-Marxism aimed to overcome economic determinism of traditional Marxism, paying attention to the autonomy of non-economic spheres. Louis Althusser was particularly important in this context, as he problematized Marx's discussion of base/superstructure and attempted to replace it with the concept of "overdetermination," emphasizing the relative autonomy of the superstructure.[22] However, Althusser also suffered for a long time from Engels' notion of the determination in the "last instance" by the economic base. In contrast, post-Marxists, despite Althusser's strong influence on them, got rid of the notion of the "last instance" and developed its unique theory of the autonomy of the political.

For example, a major figure of post-Marxism, Jacques Rancière characterizes Marx's theory as "meta-politics." He argues that meta-politics treats "the political" as the false ideology and aims to dissolve it into "the social" as "truth."[23] As Slavoj Žižek succinctly puts it, Marxist politics from the standpoint of meta-politics is nothing but a "shadow-play" upon which the economic process as truth is projected.

> Marxist (or Utopian Socialist) *meta-politics*: political conflict is fully asserted, *but* as a shadow-theatre in which events whose proper place is on Another Scene (of economic processes) are played out; the ultimate goal of "true" politics is thus its self-cancellation, the transformation of the "administration of people" into the "administration of things" within a fully self-transparent rational order of collective Will.[24]

In meta-politics, there is thus no autonomy of the political, as politics is a mere reflection of the economic forces. If economy is organized according to "a fully rational order" beyond class antagonism, politics will be dissolved too because it is nothing but a tool to mitigate the economic conflict.

---

[22] Louis Althusser, *For Marx* (London: Verso, 2006).

[23] Jacques Rancière, *Disagreement: Politics and Philosophy* (Minneapolis: University of Minnesota Press, 1999), 82.

[24] Slavoj Žižek, *The Ticklish Subject: The Absent Centre of Political Ontology* (London: Verso, 1999), 190.

In this vein, Rancière criticizes the Marxist theory of ideology that reduces everything to the economic: "It is, in short, the concept in which all politics is canceled out, either through its proclaimed evanescence, or, on the contrary, through the assertion that everything is political, which comes down to saying that nothing is, that politics is only the parasitical mode of truth. Ideology is, finally, the term that allows the place of politics to shift endlessly, right to the dizzy limit: the declaration of its end."[25] Again, there is no space for politics in Marx's theory.

There is an inevitable impression that Marx neglected the importance of politics because he did not write much on this topic during his lifetime. Surely enough, Marx talked a lot about politics through his activities as a journalist and in the First International, but he did not elaborate on his own theory of politics. Consequently, critics can confidently argue that Marx's theory is class-centric, while politics is epiphenomenal. Economic equality is more important than political and social freedom. Thus, Axel Honneth writes: "The inevitable result is not only an inadequate understanding of politics, but also a failure to grasp the emancipatory potential of these same rights to freedom."[26] Western Marxists conclude that Marx's theory cannot deal with the manifestation of the political through the "new social movements" characterized with the non-economic differences and pluralities of identities.

In the middle of the collapse of the authority of traditional Marxism and the significant weakening of the left, post-Marxists explored the possibility of theorizing the political without falling into economic determinism. One of the most famous attempts can be found in the idea of "radical democracy" as a critique of liberal and deliberative democracy developed by Rancière, Laclau, and Mouffe. Despite theoretical differences,[27] they all agree on the need to reject historical materialism as determinism, emphasizing the incompleteness of the society. According to Laclau, for example, every identity must be fixed within a discursive space, but its articulation inevitably contains the exclusion of the other, so that it can never be complete. Therefore, identity is always fluid and modifiable. Class consciousness as the proletarian identity is no exception, as it also must be constructed through various discursive praxis. Laclau thus concludes that the "contradiction" of the economic sphere does not necessarily manifest as the political antagonism between capitalist and proletariat: "Antagonism does not necessarily mean contradiction."[28]

There is, so Laclau believes, no reason to be pessimistic about this. On the contrary, he argues that it is possible to utilize this fluidity of identities and to aim for the construction of the universal identity through the articulation of various interests, which he calls the construction of a "chain of equivalences" through hegemonic practice. When a certain particular identity occupies a hegemonic position, it loses its particularity and attains a kind of universality as an "empty signifier," under which all other particular identities are subsumed. This is the main condition for the emergence of a revolutionary mass movement. However, Laclau adds that even this universality cannot be truly universal, as long as the political constitution of such universal identity is characterized by antagonistic negation of the other and thus inevitably excludes this otherness. Therefore, radical democracy is incompatible with the "truth" of traditional Marxism that the proletarian class is a universal class: "This point is decisive: there is no radical and plural democracy without renouncing the discourse of the universal and its implicit assumption of a privileged point of access to 'the truth,' which can be reached only by a limited number of subjects."[29]

Rancière argues in a similar manner. Within the existing order of the state—what he calls "*police*"—goods and rights as well as social status and functions are justly allocated to its members in given relations of power. However, such universality of the state hides a certain exclusion in reality, for there is a group of people who do not possess their "part" due to this exclusion. The politics emerges at the moment, when these people utilize the universality of "equality" so as to disrupt the current allocation of shares within the state. According to Rancière, this occurs "by implementing a basically heterogenous assumption, that of a part of those who have no part."[30] In this moment, the particular interest of the excluded group intrudes into the universal and subverts the existing order of the police by showing the latter's particularity. There is a reversal of the universal and the particular. In contrast, within Marxism the proletariat is predetermined to incarnate the true universality, so that the perfect allocation of everything is determined in advance in socialism, and the administration of things excludes the possibility of the politics in Rancière's sense.

[28] Ernesto Laclau, *New Reflections on the Revolution of Our Time* (London: Verso, 1991), 8.

[29] Ernesto Laclau and Chantal Mouffe, *Hegemony and Socialist Strategy: Towards a Radical Democratic Politics* (London: Verso, 2001), 191–2.

[30] Rancière, *Disagreement*, 30.

Post-Marxism believes that since any universality inevitably contains a certain exclusion, any attempt to construct the true universality in the completeness of society—the proletarian socialist revolution—is bound to fail. However, this also means that the incompleteness of society contains the possibility of radically changing any existing order as well. In this sense, the possibility of a radical social transformation always exists. When the particularity which is marginalized and excluded from the current discursive constellation transforms itself into the universal, it subverts the existing order and realizes a new allocation of goods and rights. This is the true moment of politics as an "event."

V. Marx's Critique of Post-Marxism

Is the post-Marxist theorization of "event" worthy of the prefix "post" that takes over Marx's theory of revolution? As seen earlier, Laclau and Rancière believe that there is no total social emancipation under the absolute universality. According to them, the idea of communism is over because the economic contradiction can no longer occupy the position of "empty signifier" in an a priori way. Today, there are only incessant hegemonic struggles among various norms and interests seeking after the position of the incomplete universality. By extending the chain of equivalence over various groups, it is necessary to construct a new social movement, in which the marginalized and excluded groups come to occupy the position of the universality.

However, struggles in radical democracy inevitably cause more and more conflicts and dissensus, which must be accompanied by violence and abuse time to time, if they want to be truly radical. This poses a dilemma of how to protect radical democracy from disastrous consequences. Setting up a predetermined set of rules and norms to regulate forms of political struggles would also prevent political movements from attaining a radical consequence. On the other hand, since the political negotiations may not always be peaceful processes and could incur violent oppression by the state, there is no guarantee that they will lead to freedom and emancipation instead of war and conflicts. Post-Marxists criticized Marxist economic reductionism of the politics represented by "end of politics" and "die off (*absterben*)" of the state. However, the post-Marxist alternative of "declaring the revolution to be permanent" is also unfree.

Marx would agree with Laclau and Rancière that the moment when the singular comes to occupy the position of the universal is essential for the politics. However, as long as the circular process of the singular and the universal persists, Marx regards it as a proof that the social emancipation is not realized yet because new struggles must be always renewed and continued no matter what their costs might be. This makes a clear contrast to Laclau's and Rancière's positive view of the eternal construction of temporal universalities.[31] Marx rather seeks to put an end to this process of bad infinite and replace it with the social communality based on association.

However, let's assume for a moment that it were possible to avoid falling into a violent conflict without also ending up with mere deliberations and negotiations within a given normative framework. In that case, people would strive after the universalization of their own interests, and society would critically examine the validity of their claims and change "common sense." The distinction between the universality and the particularity would be constantly redrawn. As a result, formal equality and freedom would be expanded, so that new countermeasures would be set up against issues of gender and ethnicity, which abstract universalities cannot adequately deal with.

Of course, Marxism does not negate the importance of new achievements won through such a process. On the other hand, such a vision of society would be nothing but a deflated idea of communism, if it were regarded as the realization of human emancipation. If it is possible to achieve true freedom and universality by extending the formal rights within civil society, while the modern separation of the state and civil society can be taken for granted, the necessity to overcome capitalism is significantly obscured, and the establishment of socialism is no longer a necessary condition for realizing true democracy: "To treat this appearance as if it were the unmasked and ultimate reality is certainly no advance in the analysis of capitalism. It mistakes a problem for a solution, and an obstacle for an opportunity."[32] Thus, post-Marxism is not a socialist project. "No socialist strategy can be taken seriously that ignores or obscures the class barriers beyond which the extension of democracy becomes a challenge to capitalism."[33]

---

[31] Alex Demirovic, "Kritik der Politik," *Nach Marx: Philosophie, Kritik, Praxis*, eds. Rahel Jaeggi, and Daniel Loick (Berlin: Shurkamp, 2013), 478.

[32] Wood, *Democracy*, 282.

[33] Ellen Meiksins Wood, *The Retreat from Class: A New "True" Socialism* (London: Verso, 1986), 138.

What Marx wanted to highlight was not that politics is a "shadow-play," but that the state as the realm of social communality is fundamentally conditioned by the political form under the capitalist mode of production. Although there is the appearance of the separation of politics and economy, this separation also functions as a way of enabling capital's domination and coercion, so it is not possible to use this appearance of separation as a starting point of struggle for opening up the future society. This is why the transcendence of capitalism has a significant importance for human liberation in Marx's theory of socialist revolution.

However, this ultimate insight of Marx is significantly obscured by post-Marxists, when they got rid of the "privileged" status of economy and praised the autonomy of the political by juxtaposing various struggles. As Ellen Meiksins Wood points out, the uniquely modern separation of politics and economy de-economizes politics. Consequently, there are multiplicities of non-economic struggles, so that they attain the appearance of an autonomy that has nothing to do with economy. However, the idea of democracy that presupposes such a separation falls into "fetishism" by mystifying the relations of domination that exist underneath of the "separation" precisely because of the uniquely capitalist unity of the private and the public.[34] Consequently, the post-Marxist vision of new revolution of our time turns out to be insufficient and limited. Its fetishism may end up accepting capitalism and its inequality and unfreedom.

In contrast, the transcendence of the separation between the state and civil society begins with communally deciding the daily issues of production and distribution as a social matter. The democratization in the sphere of social production is the key for the democratization of politics.[35] Although Marx did not elaborate on this point, it is worth exploring the possibilities of such a new form of communal democracy that may look like something totally different from "politics" based on the current dualist separation—Demirovic calls this "the end of politics." In other words, there is the possibility of socialist democracy. Once liberated from reified economic forces and the relation of domination in capitalism, the new possibilities for social struggles in other non-economic spheres will deepen significantly. Furthermore, only when association takes back the social communality, and the state is freed from the political form prescribed by

[34] Ibid., 150.
[35] Michael Hardt and Antonio Negri, *Assembly* (Oxford: Oxford University Press, 2017), 147.

the capitalist economic relations, can the state get engaged with issues in a democratic manner that could not be conducted earlier because most of the social issues could not be dealt with politically in the capitalist mode of production. To overcome the anarchic competition in the market, socialism includes the "administration of the people" by the people for the sake of overcoming reification. Liberalism and socialism are incompatible.

Of course, since Marx did not talk much about revolution as such or about freedom and equality in socialist democracy, the current observation inevitably remains a fragmentary one. Yet, Marx's vision of the transcendence of the dualism of the state and civil society through revolution documents his original insight into the need for the true democracy, and this is exactly what is missing in post-Marxism due to its acceptance of capitalism.

BIBLIOGRAPHY

Althusser, Louis. *For Marx*. London: Verso, 2006.
Arendt, Hannah. *The Human Condition*. Chicago: The University of Chicago Press, 1998.
Arendt, Hannah. *Between Past and Future: Eight Exercises in Political Thought*. London: Penguin Books, 2006.
Brown, Wendy. *Edgework: Critical Essays on Knowledge and Politics*. Princeton: Princeton University Press, 2005.
Demirovic, Alex. "Rätedemokratie oder das Ende der Politik." *Proklra* 155 (2009): 181–206.
Demirovic, Alex. "Kritik der Politik." In *Nach Marx: Philosophie, Kritik, Praxis*, edited by Rahel Jaeggi and Daniel Loick, 463–85. Berlin: Shurkamp, 2013.
Hardt, Michael and Antonio Negri. *Assembly*. Oxford: Oxford University Press, 2017.
Holloway, John and Sol Picciotto. "Introduction: Towards a Materialist Theory of the State." In *State and Capital: A Marxist Debate*, edited by John Holloway and Sol Picciotto, 1–31. London: Edward Arnold, 1978.
Honneth, Axel. *The Idea of Socialism*. London: Polity 2018.
Howard, Dick. *The Specter of Democracy: What Marx and Marxists Haven't Understood and Why*. New York: Columbia University Press, 2002.
Laclau, Ernesto. *New Reflections on the Revolution of Our Time*. London: Verso, 1991.
Laclau, Ernesto. *On Populist Reason*. London: Verso, 2005.
Laclau, Ernesto and Chantal Mouffe. *Hegemony and Socialist Strategy: Towards a Radical Democratic Politics*. London: Verso, 2001.

Macpherson, C. B. *The Political Theory of Possessive Individualism: Hobbes to Locke.* Oxford: Oxford University Press, 2011.

Marx, Karl. *On the Jewish Question.* In MECW. Vol. 3. 146–74. New York: International Publishers, 1975.

Marx, Karl. *The Civil War in France.* In MECW. Vol. 22. 437–514. New York: International Publishers, 1986.

Marx, Karl. *Capital.* Vol. 3. London: Penguin, 1993.

Mészáros, István. *Marx's Theory of Alienation.* London: Merlin Press, 2006.

Ohashi, Ryusuke. *Marx Shakaishugizo no Tenkan.* Tokyo: Ochanomizu Shobo, 1996.

Rancière, Jacques. *Disagreement: Politics and Philosophy.* Minneapolis: University of Minnesota Press, 1999.

Ruda, Frank. *Hegel's Rabble: An Investigation Into Hegel's Philosophy of Right.* New York: Continuum, 2011.

Srnicek, Nick and Alex Williams. *Inventing the Future: Postcapitalism and a World without Work.* London: Verso, 2015.

Sumida, Soichiro. "Die Zusammenfassung der bürgerlichen Gesellschaft in der Staatsform." In *Marx-Engels-Jahrbuch 2017/2018*, 41–60. Berlin: De Gruyter, 2018.

Wood, Ellen Meiksins. *The Retreat from Class: A New "True" Socialism.* London: Verso, 1986.

Wood, Ellen Meiksins. *Democracy against Capitalism: Renewing Historical Materialism.* Cambridge: Cambridge University Press, 1994.

Žižek, Slavoj. *The Ticklish Subject: The Absent Centre of Political Ontology.* London: Verso, 1999.

Žižek, Slavoj and Costas Douzinas, eds. *The Idea of Communism.* London: Verso, 2010.

Marx' Research Project As a Future Science for Emancipatory Action: A Delineation

Michael Brie

I. Introduction

During every new crisis that proves the vulnerability of capitalism, *Capital* is quick to resurface in the media. Marx appears as a modern-day Cassandra, predicting the fall of the golden city, which re-announces itself in each of these crises. His works have this effect because in them the praise of capitalism's unique productiveness (in global historic perspective) and the analysis of the system's antagonistic dynamics and destructive force, alienation and loss of control are inextricably linked. As much as Marx's analysis of capitalism is acknowledged, however, too little reference is made to the conceptualization of communism that permeates his entire politico-economic oeuvre. Marx's question as to how precisely—*because* of the rule of capital valorization over labour—nature and society, and *within this framework* the conditions of a post-capitalist order, can develop, was mostly put *ad acta*. Obviously, the collapse of the Soviet Union contributed

Translated by Tim Jack

M. Brie (✉)
Institute for Critical Social Analysis of the Rosa Luxemburg Stiftung, Berlin, Germany

© The Author(s) 2019
S. Gupta et al. (eds.), *Karl Marx's Life, Ideas, and Influences*, Marx, Engels, and Marxisms, https://doi.org/10.1007/978-3-030-24815-4_4

61

to this state of affairs. In 1989/91, many believed that the ruins of the Soviet Union would likewise bury Marx's revolutionary oeuvre. The theory's hotbed, as it seemed, had gone cold. Only Marx's analysis of the actual state of a world dominated by capitalism seemed to survive. This assumption proved premature.

Marx, from the very beginning, struggled against the cleavage in the reception of *Capital* between pure analysis and the work's transformation-oriented aim. As it provides such a vivid and convincing analysis of the capitalist mode of production and forms of domination, many readers completely missed Marx's actual point. Referring to a letter by the textile entrepreneur Gustav Meyer, Marx wrote to his friend Ludwig Kugelmann in 1868: "Meyer's letter gave me great pleasure. However, he has partly misunderstood my exposition. Otherwise he would have seen that I depict *large-scale industry* not only as the mother of the antagonism, but also as the producer of material and intellectual conditions for resolving these antagonisms, though this cannot proceed *along pleasant lines*".[1] Marx's fundamental conviction of the inevitable demise of capitalism rested on a presumed *objective* process during which capitalism would produce the conditions for its transformation to communism—or otherwise the system's downfall into barbarism.

II. Three Introductory Methodological Remarks

Understanding *Capital* and Marx's conceptualization of the (capitalist) economy requires us to return to 1843/44. At this time, Marx set a course that would determine his further political and theoretical work. In particular against the backdrop of left-wing Hegelianism, a current of thought already in its terminal crisis at the time, his choice of course becomes comprehendible. Regarding this issue, it is important to point out three things: (1) Marx's values and basic assumptions, (2) his research questions, and (3) his methodology.

Turning from Kant to Hegel, Marx had written to his father in 1837: "There are moments in one's life which are like frontier posts marking the completion of a period but at the same time clearly indicating a new direction. [...] A curtain had fallen, my holy of holies was rent asunder, and new gods had to be installed. From the idealism which, by the way, I had

---

[1] Karl Marx, "Marx to Kugelmann, 11 July 1868," in MECW (London: Lawrence & Wishart, 1987), 42: 552.

compared and nourished with the idealism of Kant and Fichte, I arrived at the point of seeking the idea in reality itself. If previously the gods had dwelt above the earth, now they became its centre."[2] Five years later, after witnessing the reactionary backlash in Prussia, and being deeply involved in the intense debates and the left-wing Hegelians' bold search for new horizons and, as an editor of the *Rheinische Zeitung* newspaper, confronted with the social and political problems in Prussia's Rhine Province, Marx was ready to install other, new "gods". Max Weber describes such turning points as follows: "All research in the cultural sciences in an age of specialization, once it is oriented towards a given subject matter through particular settings of problems and has established its methodological principles, will consider the analysis of the data as an end in itself. It will discontinue assessing the value of the individual facts in terms of their relationships to ultimate value-ideas. Indeed, it will lose its awareness of its ultimate rootedness in the value-ideas in general. And it is well that [it] should be so. But there comes a moment when the atmosphere changes. The significance of the unreflectively utilized viewpoints becomes uncertain and the road is lost in the twilight. The light of the great cultural problems moves on. Then science too prepares to change its standpoint and its thinking apparatus and to view the streams of events from the heights of thought. It follows those stars which alone are able to give meaning and direction to its labors."[3] There are hardly better words to describe Marx's productive crisis in 1843, during which he rapidly wrote the texts compiled in the *German-French Annals* (1844), and which, through the direct influence of Engels' *Outline of a Critique of Political Economy*, then led Marx to focus his attention on political economy. Marx pinpointed new—communist—stars on the horizon, which he consequently followed thereafter.

An additional response to the importance of research questions is found in Immanuel Kant. In the preface to the second edition of *The Critique of Pure Reason*, Kant wrote about the founders of modern science Galileo Galilei and Isaac Newton: "They comprehended that reason has insight only into what it itself produces according to its own design; [...] for otherwise accidental observations, made according to no previously designed plan, can never connect up into a necessary law, which is yet what reason

---

[2] Karl Marx, "Marx to His Father, 10–11 November 1837," in MECW (London: Lawrence & Wishart, 1975), 1: 10, 18.
[3] Max Weber, *The Methodology of Social Sciences* (Glencoe: The Free Press, 1949), 112.

seeks and requires."[4] Understanding *Capital* requires particular consideration of the questions that the "appointed judge" Marx posed and reconstruction of his experimental arrangement. These questions, however, were formulated by Marx in the years following 1843. His experimental arrangement developed in a process that spanned two decades, during which he constantly revised his approaches. *Capital* is constructed as an "artistic whole",[5] and aims to condense the vast number of observations Marx had made into a "necessary law" which points towards communism.

Understanding thinkers like Marx, who develop new perspectives with such deep implications, requires a scientific-methodological approach that not only touches on Marx's values and the initial questions he strove to answer, but also reveals how he reached his conclusions and developed his categories and his methodology. The suggestive power of *Capital* lies in the stringent presentation that very impressively blends the logic of his line of thought with the wealth of empirical material. It is highly tempting to think that reality itself is speaking as a "craggy melody".[6] However, the "rational character of the thing"—there is no returning to the times before Kant—is a construction which itself does not immediately relate to the reality of things, but only to ideal objects, created within the theory itself. These objects are the theory's central categories. Based on the available empirical material, the chosen methodology defines the possible links between categories. As É. M. Čudinov writes, we need to remember the "activity of construction": "Not only is the essence non-observable. Usually it cannot even be derived from a set of phenomena. The constructive activity of thinking […] is the only possible form of perception. Based on a set of initial assumptions, researchers then need to establish a system of theoretical objects and formulas, through which then the essence of a particular phenomenon can reveal itself."[7] While the theoretical approach conditions the selection of empirical material, the theory also changes due to these choices. Inversely, this implies that the analysis of theories demands an accurate examination of the processes by which these theoretical objects were constructed, to which the theory then directly refers, and how they are subsequently *related* to each other. We are required to dissect how

---

[4] Immanuel Kant, *Critique of Pure Reason. Second Edition 1787* (Cambridge: Cambridge University Press, 1998), 109.

[5] Karl Marx, "Marx to Engels, 31 July 1865," in MECW (London: Lawrence & Wishart, 1987), 42: 173.

[6] Marx, "Marx to His Father, 10–11 November 1837," 18.

[7] É. M. Čudinov, *Priroda Naučnoi Istiny (Die Natur der wissenschaftlichen Wahrheit)* (Moskva: Izdatel'stvo političeskoj literatury, 1977), 222.

these constructs highlight essential contexts, or block us from seeing relevant processes, and how the empirical material was selected. These three reasons rule out any naïve direct approach to Marx's oeuvre.

III. Marx's "Value Ideas" and Critical Proletarian Communism

Marx formulated his research questions between 1843 and 1845 against the backdrop of the dissolution of left-wing Hegelianism. The contradiction between Hegel's system and the perceived reality of Prussia and Germany became unbearable. Arnold Ruge, who was closely tied to Marx until 1844, demanded a break from the "lazy contemplativeness of Hegelianism" and rekindling of "the Fichtean energy of the deed". He considered "the *concrete and meaningful 'ought'* of the self-knowing historical present" to be "the dialectic of history itself".[8] Against the backdrop of the crisis of left-wing Hegelianism, Marx, who worked as editor at the *Rheinische Zeitung* newspaper, witnessed social injustices, the dominance of the interests of major owners, and the ubiquitous limitations to essential liberal freedoms. In 1843, this led him to formulate in the *Critique of Hegel's Philosophy of Right* the central value idea that would guide his work over the coming decades. Marx transformed this into the demand to participate in the practical revolutionary overthrow of society until all forms of domination and exploitation were overcome: "The criticism of religion ends with the teaching that *man is the highest being for man*, hence with the *categorical imperative to overthrow all relations* in which man is a debased, enslaved, forsaken, despicable being."[9]

While therefore confronted in 1843 with the intellectual crisis of the movement of which he was a part, Marx, nonetheless, had begun to *search for practical approaches to universal emancipation by means of a universal revolution* of the real conditions of a real society. This was the guiding value idea that continuously drove him forward and provided the basis for his *critical proletarian communism*.[10] Organically, therefore, Marx attempted to

---

[8] Arnold Ruge, "Zur Kritik des gegenwärtigen Staats- und Völkerrechts (1840)," in *Die Hegelsche Linke. Dokumente zu Philosophie und Politik im deutschen Vormärz*, eds. Heinz Pepperle and Ingrid Pepperle (Leipzig: Reclam jun., 1985), 153.

[9] Karl Marx, "Contribution to the Critique of Hegel's Philosophy of Law. Introduction (1844)," in MECW (London: Lawrence & Wishart, 1975), 3: 182.

[10] Marx used the term "German, [...] critical communism" in 1851 with regard to the concepts developed by him and Engels to distinguish them from other forms of communism,

blend three approaches: a new notion of critique, a highly specific definition of communism, and a direct link to the proletarian movement of his time.

Let us begin with his notion of critique. Between 1843 and 1845, Marx gradually developed his new, five-tier approach to critical reflection: (1) critique of theoretical and practical awareness, as far as they apologetically relate to real conditions, or apply abstract moral standards from outside; (2) critique of actual forms of domination and exploitation as temporary forms of an antagonistic development; (3) critique as an effort to uncover those tendencies and elements that already transcend current society; (4) critical self-reflection by the truly emancipatory movements to clarify their goals, means, and strategies; and (5) the permanent criticism and self-criticism of the "enlighteners". Such criticism should become an organic part of these movements. This was a "Copernican revolution" of the notion of critique following upon both Kant and Hegel.[11] Marx saw critique as an organic element of *revolutionary practice*, as "the coincidence of the changing of circumstances and of human activity or self-change can be conceived and rationally understood only as *revolutionary practice*".[12] A critique, however, could only achieve this by being a conscious and self-disciplined reflection of the preconditions, conditions, strategies, and consequences of the practices aiming to transform society (Fig. 1).

While Marx's notion of critique therefore represents the first step on his new course, his conceptualization of communism is the second. From late 1843 onwards, Marx identified his emancipatory project with the terms socialism and communism. In early 1843, he still saw democracy as a "solved riddle of all constitutions",[13] and described democracy as the "genus Constitution".[14] One year later he wrote: "Communism is the riddle of history solved, and it knows itself to be this solution."[15] In October 1842, Marx had written that the *Rheinische Zeitung* newspaper "does not admit that communist ideas in their present form possess even

which they had criticized in the *Manifesto*. Karl Marx, "Revelations Concerning the Communist Trial in Cologne," in MECW (London: Lawrence & Wishart, 1979), 11: 455.

[11] See Kurt Röttgers, *Kritik und Praxis. Zur Geschichte des Kritikbegriffs von Kant bis Marx* (Berlin and New York: De Gruyter, 1975).

[12] Karl Marx, "Theses on Feuerbach," in MECW (London: Lawrence & Wishart, 1975), 5: 4.

[13] Karl Marx, "Contribution to the Critique of Hegel's Philosophy of Law," in MECW (London: Lawrence & Wishart, 1975), 3: 29.

[14] Ibid., 29.

[15] Karl Marx, "Economic and Philosophic Manuscripts of 1844," in MECW (London: Lawrence & Wishart, 1975), 3: 297.

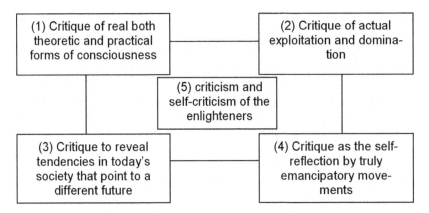

Fig. 1 Marx's concept of critique

theoretical reality, and therefore can still less desire their *practical realization*, or even consider it possible".[16] But, he had added: "We are firmly convinced that the real danger lies not in *practical attempts*, but in the *theoretical elaboration* of communist ideas, for *practical attempts, even mass attempts*, can be answered by *cannon* as soon as they become dangerous, whereas *ideas*, which have conquered our intellect and taken possession of our minds, ideas to which reason has fettered our conscience, are chains from which one cannot free oneself without a broken heart; they are demons which human beings can vanquish only by submitting to them".[17] One year later, he subscribed to exactly this idea of communism, held on to it for the rest of his life, and gave it a form that left a crucial mark on the twentieth century.

At this time, Marx aimed for radical solutions to the problems of his epoch. He therefore broke with Hegelian concepts that sought to mediate in some way the contradictions between bourgeois society (man as bourgeois) and the state (man as *citoyen*). Marx did not strive to develop new forms of mediating between these opposite poles; he aimed to dissolve the differences. Marx therefore redefined the term emancipation and in *On the Jewish Question* he wrote: "*All* emancipation is a *reduction* of the human world and relationships to *man himself.* [...] Only when the real,

[16] Karl Marx, "Communism and the Augsburg Allgemeine Zeitung," in MECW (London: Lawrence & Wishart, 1975), 1: 220.
[17] Ibid., 220f.

individual man [...] has become a *species-being* in his everyday life, in his particular work, and in his particular situation, only when man has recognized and organized his *'forces propres'* as *social* forces, and consequently no longer separates social power from himself in the shape of *political* power, only then will human emancipation have been accomplished."[18]

In these brief sentences, Marx gives his answer to the question posed by Rousseau in the "Social Contract" as to how a free association can be founded. He mentions two conditions: first, the forces of the individuals alienated from bourgeois society must be jointly appropriated and socially organized by them; second, these forces must be transformed into ways of free development of individuals. Through this double process of transformation every individual expression of life becomes directly social and every social activity follows its free self-development. A direct identity of social and individual development is established.

Third, from 1843 onwards, Marx combined his understanding of critique and communism with his orientation towards the new class of industrial proletarians. In particular, through his studies of the history of the great French Revolution, Marx had reached the conclusion that the more radically the question of emancipation is posed, the more its representatives will tend to be members of evermore disenfranchised groups of ever-lower social standing, who nonetheless decisively determine society. Both characteristics, according to Marx, applied to the proletariat. In bourgeois society, freedom was tied to private property, yet the class of those without property was rapidly expanding. While producing private property, the proletariat was excluded from it. Decisively, the new, exponentially increased capacity of capitalism to produce wealth was based precisely on this mechanism of exclusion. What then would happen if this class ever demanded emancipation? The political revolution would trigger a revolution of property ownership, a social revolution. An emancipation of this new class, Marx argued, was inconceivable without a communist transformation of the whole of society. However, from Marx' point of view, this class was the only power that could achieve it. This provided the cornerstone for his construct of critical proletarian communism: "Where, then, is the positive possibility of a German emancipation? Answer: In the formulation of a class with *radical chains.*"[19]

---

[18] Karl Marx, "*On the Jewish Question,*" in MECW (London: Lawrence & Wishart, 1975), 3: 168.

[19] Marx, "Contribution to the Critique of Hegel's Philosophy of Law. Introduction (1844)," 186.

Marx's critical communism as a structure, however, still lacked a foundation. His new method of critique had not yet been critically applied to any particular question, and therefore remained empty. The communist vision was nothing more than a promise of total emancipation and lifting of all alienation of social powers. It remained undefined. Betting on the proletariat as the agent of this universal emancipation was a bet on uncharted territory, and its guarantee of success was to lie in the presence of a bourgeois and industrializing society that gave rise to its own grave-diggers. As a theory, as well as politico-practically speaking, however, they still remained three separate elements. From there on, a spiralling, cyclical process took hold in Marx's work, which was guided by the materialist basis of his method of critique, the politico-economic foundation of his vision of communism, and his political commitment to ensuring the workers' movement became conscious of its historic role.[20] This triangle was the prism Marx used to focus his concept of universal emancipation and through which he aimed to enlighten his objects of analysis and of politics. Marx's oeuvre and his work after 1843/44 can be understood as such a "delving into" (Fig. 2).

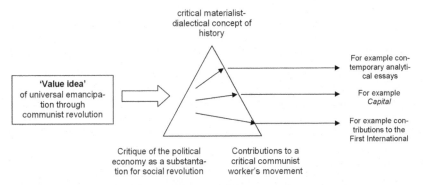

Fig. 2   Marx's prism of intervention

[20] Lutz Brangsch, "Das Kommunistische als Erzählung der Sozialdemokratie des 19. Jahrhunderts. Der 'Deutsche Kritische Kommunismus'," in *Das Kommunistische. Oder: Ein Gespenst kommt nicht zur Ruhe. Mit Beiträgen von Bini Adamczak, Friederike Habermann Und Massimo De Angelis*, ed. Michael Brie and Lutz Brangsch (Hamburg: VSA, 2016).

IV. CAPITAL AS A HISTORIC-MATERIALIST DRAMA

The most important outcome of Marx' lifelong research processes was of course the *Capital*. Too often it is read just as a mere analysis of the capitalist mode of production. But *Capital* is much more. It is definitely one of the greatest dramas in the European history of ideas, comparable to Plato's Republic, Hobbes' Leviathan, or Hegel's Phenomenology of the Mind. From the outset, Marx made his intentions very clear: "[T]hese petrified relations must be forced to dance by singing their own tune to them!"[21]

It is no coincidence that Marx, in the introduction to the first volume of what he planned in 1859 to become a series, but which was published under the title *A Contribution to the Critique of Political Economy*, provided some "brief remarks regarding the course of [his] study of political economy", in addition to a brief introduction of the "guiding principle" of his materialistic methodology. This introduction can also be seen as the *overture* to his opus magnum. The central themes are there: his opposition to domination and exploitation, the need for an informed economic analysis as the basis for any analysis of society, the history of humankind characterized by a historic sequel of antagonisms, and the perspective of their communist solution.

In *Capital*, a critical analysis of the capitalist mode of production was to reveal the emancipatory options to overcoming the system. A "correct approach" of social conditions, grounded ultimately in history, would, according to Marx, lead to "points which indicate the transcendence of the present form of production relations, the movement coming into being, thus FORESHADOWING the future".[22] Marx aimed to prove in *Capital* that the increasing maturity of "material conditions, and the combination on a social scale of the processes of production" also provided the basis for "contradictions and antagonisms of the capitalist form" to mature, and "thereby provide[d], along with the elements for the formation of a new society, the forces for exploding the old one".[23] This included revealing reactionary and barbaric counter-tendencies that were potentially capable of bringing down the entire emancipatory project. Marx in this regard stayed true to his five-tier approach to critique described earlier. Ernst Bloch condensed this approach

---

[21] Marx, "Contribution to the Critique of Hegel's Philosophy of Law. Introduction (1844)," 178.

[22] Karl Marx, "Outlines of the Critique of Political Economy (Rough Draft of 1857–58)," in MECW (London: Lawrence & Wishart, 1986), 28: 389.

[23] Karl Marx, *Capital*, Vol. I, in MECW (London: Lawrence & Wishart, 1996), 35: 504f.

applied by Marx in *Capital* into the following formula: "The dialectical-historical tendency science of Marxism is thus the mediated *future science of reality plus the objectively real possibility within it*, all this for the purpose of *action*."[24]

Marx closed the *Introduction* of 1859 with Dante's words: "At the entrance to science, as at the entrance to hell, the demand must be made: Qui si convien lasciare ogni sospetto. Ogni vilta convien che qui sia morta. [From Dante, Divina Commedia: Here all misgiving must thy mind reject. Here cowardice must die and be no more]."[25] In his book *Marx' Inferno: The Political Theory of Capital*, William Clare Roberts argues that "the structure of *Capital* lies in the structure of Dante's *Inferno*".[26] Clearly, *Capital* can be understood as a materialist drama of exploitation that closes with a perspective of liberation, of social revolution as its purifying purgatory. It subsequently aims to provide guidance to those who have got lost so that by going through *Inferno* they may find a path to liberation. The *Preface* is the road map.

If we interpret *Capital* as a drama in analogy to *Inferno* in Dante's *Divine Comedy* as William Clare Roberts supposes,[27] then the first act presents us with the transformation of a society of free and equal people who exchange commodities in a world in which the "the social character of men's labour appears to them as [...] a social relation, existing not between themselves, but between the products of their labour".[28] Hereafter, the *money fetish*, which they themselves have produced, rules them. This is the antechamber to Inferno. From here, we reach the second section of *Capital*, which at the same time constitutes the second act of the drama. It describes how the free and equal separate into a society where "the possessor of labour power" is forced into "bringing his own hide to market and has nothing to expect but—a hiding" to the benefit of "capitalists".[29] The very long third act develops this relation between both classes as a production of multiple forms of surplus value and wage, struggles over the mediation of the relation between both classes by

[24] Ernst Bloch, *The Principle of Hope* (Cambridge, MA: The MIT Press, 1995), 1: 285.

[25] Karl Marx, "A Contribution to the Critique of Political Economy," in MECW (London: Lawrence & Wishart, 1987), 29: 265.

[26] William Clare Roberts, *Marx's Inferno: The Political Theory of Capital* (Princeton: Princeton University Press, 2016).

[27] Dante's text consists of three parts: *Inferno*, *Purgatorio*, and *Paradiso*.

[28] Marx, *Capital*, Vol. 1, 83.

[29] Ibid., 186.

developing the real capitalist mode of production, as well as the struggle over legal interventions to regulate the relationship between capital and labour. These are sections three to six of *Capital*. In the fourth act, Marx develops the antagonism between capital and labour as the "General Law of Capitalist Accumulation" (section seven) of a reproductive relationship: "Accumulation of wealth at one pole is, therefore, at the same time accumulation of misery, agony of toil, slavery, ignorance, brutality, mental degradation, at the opposite pole, i.e., on the side of the class that produces its own product in the form of capital."[30] Part VIII of *Capital*, the so-called primitive accumulation, reconstructs the historic development of the classes of capitalists and workers and anticipates the expected negation of the capitalist mode of production through a social revolution as an exit from *Inferno*.

Marx takes the readers of *Capital* from a very general unit, commodities, through the intermediate stages of money and capital to surplus value and from there to the concrete general concept of capitalist accumulation.[31] He describes this accumulation as a process that turns everything into a commodity, antagonistically splits society into two, and subdues workers evermore completely. Marx's categories are theoretical objects that he enriches over the course of the text both in terms of categories and empirically. A spiral develops that underlies all four acts of the drama (Fig. 3). The relationships and the actors involved are thereby transformed and transform themselves.

V. Open Questions

The real drama of the development of the capitalist mode of production has unfolded in a way that Marx had not anticipated. The communist revolutions inspired by him did not take place in the centres of the capitalist world system but at the semi-periphery. The social systems that emerged from these revolutions have partly collapsed or have moved in a direction that includes the introduction of essential institutions of capital accumulation. At the same time, global capitalism is in the midst of

---

[30] Ibid., 640.

[31] Evald V. Ilyenkov, *The Dialectics of the Abstract and Concrete and Marx's Capital* (London: Progress Publishers, 1982); Viktor A. Vazjulin, *Die Logik des "Kapitals" von Karl Marx* (Norderstedt: Books on Demand, 2006); Helmut Reichelt, "Zum Problem der dialektischen Darstellung ökonomischer Kategorien im Rohentwurf des Kapitals," in *Geld—Kapital -Wert. Beiträge zur Marx-Engels-Forschung. Neue Folge 2007*, ed. Rolf Hecker, Richard Sperl, and Carl-Erich Vollgraf (Hamburg: Argument, 2007).

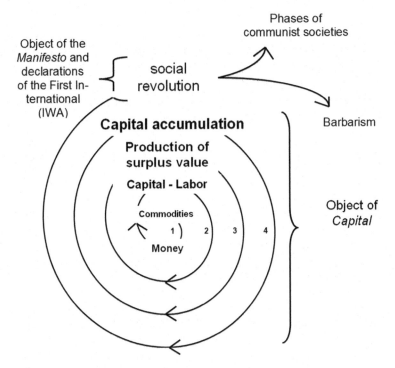

Fig. 3 Marx's *Capital* as a process in the form of a spiral

a multi-crisis that is resulting precisely from its global success. A renewed reading of *Capital* must face the real historical development of the last 150 years and this contradictory situation. This becomes clear when one talks about the starting point of *Capital*—the commodity as the elementary form of wealth in capitalist societies.

One of the fundamental difficulties of Marx's historic-materialist method is the unbelievable complexity of his object of critique. As sketched out in the introduction to his *Outlines of the Critique of Political Economy* (1857/58), Marx's path takes him from the abstract to the specific. Correspondingly, *Capital* begins with the following sentences: "The wealth of those societies in which the capitalist mode of production prevails, presents itself as 'an immense accumulation of commodities', its unit being a single commodity. Our investigation must therefore begin with the analysis of a commodity."[32]

---

[32] Marx, *Capital*, Vol. 1, 45.

These two sentences at the beginning of *Capital* rest on complex underlying assumptions. They assume the capitalist mode of production's rule over society and the terms *wealth*, *presents itself* and *commodity* are introduced. Then, Marx speaks of *unit*. A commodity here is as much a theoretically constructed object (category) as an object of direct contemplation under specific social conditions, staring anybody in the face who dares to enter a shopping mall. As practical experience immediately teaches, unlike in pre-capitalist societies, under the rule of the capitalist mode of production, merely securing one's existence is bound to the condition of commodity ownership. After the failed revolution of 1848, Heinrich Heine, whom Marx referred to as a friend in *Capital*, wrote in a poem in 1851: "But if thou hast nothing, friend, Go and hang thyself this minute; Only they who've aught on earth Have a claim for living in it." A larger part of the wealth on which mere survival depends, but not all of it, takes the commodity form. As Wolfgang Fritz Haug writes: "What kind of gaze then perceives the wealth of bourgeois society merely as a collection of commodities? It is the gaze of consumers. […] Only that part of wealth, which is up for sale is a commodity."[33]

While Marx in the introduction to the *Outlines* in 1857 still spoke very generally on the "division of labour, money, value, etc." as "abstract, general relations",[34] his confrontation with the Proudhonists led him to become more precise in two regards. First, Marx sought to debunk the idea that abolishing money would lead to a free exchange of goods based on the amount of working hours that goes into their production. Proudhonists, he was convinced, simply did not understand that the money form is a mere result of the commodity form. Marx's great efforts to derive money from commodities and his decision to begin his magnum opus with a complex presentation of value forms is only comprehensible against the backdrop of his specific politico-programmatic confrontation with Proudhonism. He therefore also warned Engels: "Should you write something, don't forget, 1. that it extirpates Proudhonism root and branch, 2. that the specifically social, by no means absolute, character of bourgeois production is analysed straight away in its simplest form, that of

[33] Wolfgang Fritz Haug, *Vorlesungen zur Einführung ins "Kapital"* (Köln: Pahl-Rugenstein, 1974), 42; see also Michael Heinrich, *Wie das Marxsche "Kapital" lesen. Teil 1: Leseanleitung und Kommentar zum Anfang des 'Kapital'* (Stuttgart: Schmetterling, 2016), 50ff.

[34] Karl Marx, "Outlines of the Critique of Political Economy (Rough Draft of 1857–58). Introduction," in MECW (London: Lawrence & Wishart, 1986), 28: 37.

the commodity."[35] In this regard, Marx's theory of money results from the internal conflict between socialist currents on the tangible options to overthrow capitalism. The political came before the scientific goal and both were inextricably linked. In 1859, *two* alternative socialist politico-economic approaches existed: Proudhon's elaborated theory and Marx's oeuvre, which had not yet matured to its full extent. The conflict within the socialist camp and the opposition to Proudhonism clearly made its mark on *Capital*. Without the documents of the deliberations of the International Workingmen's Association (IWMA), where they were controversial issues, the centrality of the struggle for shorter working days, salary increases, and union organization in *Capital* makes no sense.

Second, by emphasizing the dual nature of commodities (value and use value) Marx showed that—unlike previous socialist economists had assumed—capitalist exploitation (i.e. appropriation of unpaid work) does not contradict the law of value (the exchange of commodities based on the invested quantities of abstract labour), and actually becomes possible, in particular when the law is consistently applied. According to Marx, for their labour, workers receive a value commensurate to the cost of reproducing their labour power (if on a market). The law of value can by no means ensure that they receive the total value of the products their labour in capitalist businesses produces. The common assumption that fully applying the law of value is enough to overcome capitalism, according to Marx, remains blind to the fact that only after capitalism developed did this law of value become precisely the law regulating the dominant mode of production.

This argument too is owed to the divide in the socialist camp. The IWMA discussions focused on strategic questions: Can union struggles for higher wages be successful in the long term? What connection exists between the political emancipation of the working classes and their seizing of political power as the means to achieve this? Whether a reformist transformation of bourgeois capitalist societies is possible that, while retaining the economic institutions (private property, markets, competition, credit, banks, returns, etc.), can transform them into socialist, association-based forms was an open question. The Proudhonists defended this position. The aim was a new balance between the law of value, markets, competition, and state regulation. Out of free agreements between workers, and

[35] Karl Marx, "Marx to Engels, 22 July 1859," in MECW (London: Lawrence & Wishart, 1983), 40: 473.

within the existing system, a new system was to evolve from below. For the Proudhonists, the aim of socialist politics lay in ensuring the best possible favourable conditions for such a transformation.

Marx in contrast referred to revolution as the way to overcome capitalism. In his view, the establishment of a democratic dictatorship of the proletariat, by handing over the means of production to the working class, would initiate a complete overhaul of the modes of production and living and pave the way towards a communist society. In conscious reaction to the conditions for worker's reproduction, a total transformation of the modes of production and living could begin and in the long term provide opportunities for every individual's free development in solidarity with the development of all. Based on this position, in the IWMA, Marx promoted uniting the union and political struggles to conquer the state, the political independence of the workers' movement vis-à-vis bourgeois and petty bourgeois forces, a consistent orientation towards common property, and a dictatorship of the proletariat as the political expression of the rule of the working class.[36]

In view of this consideration, it should be noted that Marx's attempt to solve the socialist conflict over political economy led to a set of new problems that have remained unsolved until today. Two of them are worth considering briefly. They are closely related to the issues we have just discussed and are inspired by the work of Karl Polanyi. One initial problem with Marx's critique of the political economy is that *any* form of institutional mediation of social conditions now appears rooted in the capital relation. This is mainly the result of his concept of a communist society.[37] Communism was community-based for him.[38] He consciously and "logically" derived the relationship between capital and labour from that between the owners of commodities. Marx vehemently rejected the idea of Proudhonists that associative forms of production and free exchange were possible based on the value of labour.

---

[36] See Hannes Skambraks, *Das Kapital von Marx—Waffe im Klassenkampf. Aufnahme und Anwendung der Lehren des Hauptwerkes von Karl Marx durch die deutsche Arbeiterbewegung* (Berlin: Dietz, 1977); Marcello Musto, *Workers Unite! The International 150 Years Later* (New York and London: Bloomsbury Academic, 2014).

[37] On the relationship between work on *Capital* and Marx's understanding of a communist society, see W. S. Wygodski, *Das Werden der ökonomischen Theorie von Marx und der Wissenschaftliche Kommunismus.* (Berlin: Dietz, 1978).

[38] See Peter Ruben, "Die kommunistische Antwort auf die soziale Frage," *Berliner Debatte Initial* 9, no. 1 (1998).

From here, Marx evolved to a communist position. For him, communism constituted a society grounded on the indivisible common ownership of the means of production. As he wrote in *Capital*, the producers, as a "community of free individuals" would produce "with the means of production in common, in which the labour power of all the different individuals is consciously applied as the combined labour power of the community".[39] Marx added: "All the characteristics of Robinson's labour are here repeated, but with this difference, that they are social, instead of individual."[40] A communist society is imagined as a community and a monolithic subject. Individual property would exist only in the context of common ownership.[41] It would reveal itself as individual appropriation of social wealth through such a transformation of the mode of production, in which work for society contributes to the free development of each individual and becomes their primary life concern. For Marx, communism is a society in which the work of each and every individual becomes immediately social. Conversely, according to Marx, work for society would then appear directly as personal development. The interests of all members of society together and of each individual directly coincide in this model. It is therefore only consistent for Marx to assume that once on this course, all *bourgeois* forms of mediation of the commodity-money relation, laws, and the state would die off.

A society not characterized by the contradictions between individual, collective, and social developments, and in which the individual interests and collective interests of everybody coincide, is unachievable—a non-workable utopia. Marx in many instances suggests such a utopia. The expansion of freedom that communism promises inevitably creates new contradictions between individual, collective, and social forms of reproduction and development. According to the concept of socialism, the only difference would be that the form these struggles take would no longer exist within the framework of the primacy of capital accumulation. Not necessarily less severe, the contradictions would nonetheless lose their

---

[39] Marx, *Capital*, Vol. I, 89.

[40] Ibid.

[41] In *Capital*, where Marx delineates the perspective of a communist society, he writes: "But capitalist production begets, with the inexorability of a law of Nature, its own negation. It is the negation of negation. This does not re-establish private property for the producer, but gives him individual property based on the acquisitions of the capitalist era: i.e., on cooperation and the possession in common of the land and of the means of production." Marx, *Capital*, Vol. I, 751.

class character. One could also say that as these questions concern personal development, specific collective identities, and creative processes, such contradictions would hopefully no longer play out as a threat to personal subsistence. At the same time, they would gain a new dimension touching on people's innermost self-image.

Marx upheld a vision of a society in which the individual work and actions become immediately social as part of a single plan until his later writings as documented in his *Critique of the Gotha Programme*. The downside was that any reform that does not aim to abolish the institutions of bourgeois society, but instead strives to give them a new direction, could be considered a sham reform—at least for as long as the proletariat does not hold the political power. Such an approach considers breaking capital's dominance as essentially equal to systematically abolishing all market-based, legal, and political forms of mediation in modern societies. A form of socialism with room for markets becomes inconceivable. Furthermore, while a post-capitalist society faces considerable difficulties, the focus is merely on solving the contradictions of capitalism, with no regard for newly arising contradictions. This conceptualization of the capitalist economy was unable to anticipate the expansion of the social welfare state and social property,[42] the development of a mixed economy, and the society combining different logics.[43] It made the search for transformative strategies that go beyond capitalism and combine rupture, expansion of niches, and symbiotic development[44] all the more difficult. The ideologues of state party socialism firmly based themselves on these elements of Marx's approach. The concentration of all power at one centre appeared as consistently "Marxist". Its role as an indispensable representative of the mono-subject provided the legitimacy of the communist state party. Common property, the indivisible power of everybody, and the predominance of a single concept, communism, was the model. However, this socialism of the twentieth century failed. Based on a different perspective for a post-capitalist society, a contemporary critique of the capitalist economy will require a new take on the question of "[f]reedom in a complex society".[45]

---

[42] Horst Müller, *Das Konzept PRAXIS im 21. Jahrhundert: Karl Marx und die Praxisdenker, das Praxiskonzept in der Übergangsperiode und die latente Systemalternative* (Norderstedt: Books on Demand, 2015), 406ff.

[43] T. H. Marshall, *Citizenship and Social Class* (Cambridge: Cambridge University Press, 1950).

[44] Erik Olin Wright, *Envisioning Real Utopias* (London and New York: Verso, 2010), 273ff.

[45] Karl Polanyi, *The Great Transformation: The Political and Economic Origins of Our Time*, 2nd Beacon Paperback ed. (Boston, MA: Beacon Press, 2001), 257ff.

An up-to-date critique of the capitalist economy will among other concepts require revisiting Marx's starting point in *Capital*, his choice of the category of commodity. As Karl Polanyi showed, central goods for the reproduction of the capitalist mode of production are not produced as commodities. These are what he calls "fictitious commodity": "The crucial point is this: labor, land, and money are essential elements of industry; they also must be organized in markets; in fact, these markets form an absolutely vital part of the economic system. But labor, land, and money are obviously not commodities; the postulate that anything that is bought and sold must have been produced for sale [...] is emphatically untrue in regard to them."[46] If, however, the most essential goods—labour, natural resources, and money—are not commodities, but only to a limited and contested extent take on the form of commodities, this fundamentally changes the analysis of the capitalist mode of production. It is not the commodity as an elementary form of capitalist wealth that then forms the starting point of analysing capitalism, but rather the complex systems of earthly nature (the Gaia sphere), life worlds, social institutions, and culture under the primacy of capital accumulation (Fig. 4). If money is not

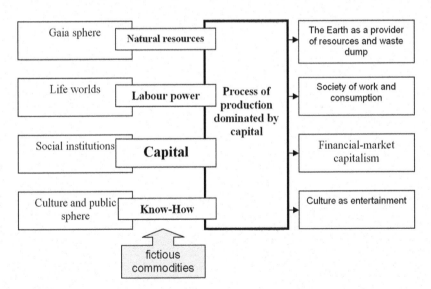

Fig. 4   The reproductive relationship of capitalist societies

[46] Polanyi, *The Great Transformation*, 75.

itself created through the movement of commodities, but created in the central bank-supported credit system, if labour force is not sold and the use of labour force instead only temporarily rented (and the willingness to do so is not fully ruled by the laws of the labour market), if natural resources and their reproduction do not essentially follow market laws, then this requires us to redefine the starting point of any, and in particular a historic-materialistic, analysis of the capitalist mode of production.

The specifically capitalist mode of production derives its "production factors" from the four mentioned systems. Under the primacy of capital accumulation, they are profoundly changed or destroyed. Capitalist wealth, expressed in the growth of the gross national product of goods on the market and of profit, is at odds with the wealth of natural diversity and a liveable environment, good work and good life, stable and legitimate social institutions, and the possibilities of a free cultural society.[47] The ancient concept of household or family management (*oikonomiké*) would have to be reformulated as Ecommony.[48] At the heart of such an economy would be the reproduction of those systems from which the *resources* stem and to which they return after careful use. Such a changed understanding of the capitalist mode of production also changes the perspective on strategies of fundamental reforms in capitalism and beyond. The old contrast between reform and revolution is receding in the face of a new Great Transformation that overcomes the capitalist market society. Both are needed at the same time—reforms that relativize the subordination of the commodities of a free life for all to capital accumulation and revolutionary ruptures that overcome the dominance of capital accumulation over the reproduction of nature, society, and culture.

With Beverly Silver, we could also say that the Marx-type struggles (capital vs. labour) are today being subdued by Polanyi-type struggles.[49] They are mainly struggles over the freedoms that ensure a good life[50] and

---

[47] Michael Brie, "Transformationen des Reichtums—Reichtum der Transformationen. Eine Vier-in-Einem-Perspektive," in *Futuring. Transformation Im Kapitalismus Über Ihn Hinaus*, ed. Michael Brie (Münster: Westfälisches Dampfboot, 2014).

[48] Friederike Habermann, *Ecommony: UmCARE zum Miteinander* (Sulzbach am Taunus: Ulrike Helmer Verlag, 2016).

[49] See Beverly J. Silver, *Forces of Labor. Workers' Movements and Globalization since 1870*, Cambridge Studies in Comparative Politics (Cambridge and New York: Cambridge University Press, 2003), 17ff.

[50] See Dieter Klein, ed., *Leben statt gelebt zu werden. Selbstbestimmung und soziale Sicherheit. Zukunftsbericht der Rosa-Luxemburg-Stiftung* (Berlin: Dietz, 2003); Alberto Acosta, "Das "Buen Vivir". Die Schaffung einer Utopie," *Juridikum*, no. 4 (2009); Eduardo Gudynas, "Buen Vivir. Das gute Leben jenseits von Entwicklung und Wachstum," in *Demokratie,*

against their subordination to capital accumulation and commodification. The strategic questions have shifted since the time of Marx. Four questions are now at its core: What are we permitted to create and use? How do we want to live? Which decisions do we want to take? And, to speak with Immanuel Kant: What is human? The focus of Adam Smith's classical work was the question of how to increase the production of commodities as the wealth of the nations. Now, 250 years later, it is about how to increase the production of real human wealth with less labour and fewer natural resources in a society based on solidarity, freedom, and equality.

This automatically brings us back to Marx. For him, wealth was nothing but

> the universality of the individual's needs, capacities, enjoyments, productive forces, etc., produced in universal exchange. [...] What is wealth if not the absolute unfolding of man's creative abilities, without any precondition other than the preceding historical development, which makes the totality of this development—i.e. the development of all human powers as such, not measured by any *previously given* yardstick—an end-in-itself, through which he does not reproduce himself in any specific character, but produces his totality, and does not seek to remain something he has already become, but is in the absolute movement of becoming?[51]

Such an approach would lead to a new concept for transformation.[52] We could also say that "value ideas" have moved on. New struggles are now the focus. The vision of a post-capitalist order that develops within these struggles has changed.

It is time to revisit *Capital*. We should take up the challenge, and again engage in the analysis of current capitalism as a "future science" for the purpose of action. The power of Marx's approach, as well as its limitations, can teach us to endeavour towards new breakthroughs and overcome the iron cage of the dominance of capital accumulation over nature, society, and life that fate casts us into. This requires a new concept for the critique of the capitalist economy and society.

Partizipation, Sozialismus. Lateinamerikanische Wege der Transformation, ed. Miriam Lang, vol. 96 (Berlin: Rosa-Luxemburg-Stiftung, 2012).

[51] Marx, "Outlines of the Critique of Political Economy (Rough Draft of 1857–58)," 411f.

[52] See Judith Dellheim et al., *Den Krisen entkommen. Sozialökologische Transformation* (Berlin: Karl Dietz, 2012); Dieter Klein, *Das Morgen tanzt im Heute. Transformation im Kapitalismus und über ihn hinaus* (Hamburg: VSA, 2013), http://www.rosalux.de/filead-min/rls_uploads/pdfs/sonst_publikationen/VSA_Klein_Das_Morgen.pdf.

BIBLIOGRAPHY

Acosta, Alberto. "Das 'Buen Vivir'. Die Schaffung einer Utopie." *Juridikum*, no. 4 (2009): 219–23.

Bloch, Ernst. *The Principle of Hope. Vol. 1.* Cambridge, MA: The MIT Press, 1995.

Brangsch, Lutz. "Das Kommunistische als Erzählung der Sozialdemokratie des 19. Jahrhunderts. Der 'Deutsche Kritische Kommunismus'." In *Das Kommunistische. Oder: Ein Gespenst kommt nicht zur Ruhe. Mit Beiträgen von Bini Adamczak, Friederike Habermann Und Massimo De Angelis*, edited by Michael Brie and Lutz Brangsch, 63–80. Hamburg: VSA, 2016.

Brie, Michael. "Transformationen des Reichtums—Reichtum der Transformationen. Eine Vier-in-Einem-Perspektive." In *Futuring. Transformation Im Kapitalismus Über Ihn Hinaus*, edited by Michael Brie, 194–241. Münster: Westfälisches Dampfboot, 2014.

Čudinov, É. M. *Priroda Naučnoi Istiny (Die Natur der wissenschaftlichen Wahrheit).* Moskva: Izdatel'stvo političeskoj literatury, 1977.

Dellheim, Judith, Lutz Brangsch, Frieder-Otto Wolf, and Joachim Spangenberg. *Den Krisen entkommen. Sozialökologische Transformation.* Berlin: Karl Dietz, 2012.

Gudynas, Eduardo. "Buen Vivir. Das gute Leben jenseits von Entwicklung und Wachstum." In *Demokratie, Partizipation, Sozialismus. Lateinamerikanische Wege der Transformation*, edited by Miriam Lang, 28–45. Berlin: Rosa-Luxemburg-Stiftung, 2012.

Habermann, Friederike. *Ecommony: UmCARE zum Miteinander.* Sulzbach am Taunus: Ulrike Helmer Verlag, 2016.

Haug, Wolfgang Fritz. *Vorlesungen zur Einführung ins "Kapital".* Köln: Pahl-Rugenstein, 1974.

Heinrich, Michael. *Wie das Marxsche "Kapital" lesen. Teil 1: Leseanleitung und Kommentar zum Anfang des 'Kapital'.* Stuttgart: Schmetterling, 2016.

Ilyenkov, Evald V. *The Dialectics of the Abstract and Concrete and Marx's Capital.* London: Progress Publishers, 1982.

Kant, Immanuel. *Critique of Pure Reason. Second Edition 1787.* Cambridge: Cambridge University Press, 1998.

Klein, Dieter, ed. *Leben statt gelebt zu werden. Selbstbestimmung und soziale Sicherheit. Zukunftsbericht der Rosa-Luxemburg-Stiftung.* Berlin: Dietz, 2003.

Klein, Dieter. *Das Morgen tanzt im Heute. Transformation im Kapitalismus und über ihn hinaus.* Hamburg: VSA, 2013. http://www.rosalux.de/fileadmin/rls_uploads/pdfs/sonst_publikationen/VSA_Klein_Das_Morgen.pdf

Marshall, T. H. *Citizenship and Social Class.* Cambridge: Cambridge University Press, 1950.

Marx, Karl. "Communism and the Augsburg Allgemeine Zeitung." In MECW. Vol. 1, 215–21. London: Lawrence & Wishart, 1975a.

Marx, Karl. "Contribution to the Critique of Hegel's Philosophy of Law." In MECW. Vol. 3, 3–129. London: Lawrence & Wishart, 1975b.

Marx, Karl. "Contribution to the Critique of Hegel's Philosophy of Law. Introduction (1844)." In MECW. Vol. 3, 175–87. London: Lawrence & Wishart, 1975c.

Marx, Karl. "Economic and Philosophic Manuscripts of 1844." In MECW. Vol. 3, 229–346. London: Lawrence & Wishart, 1975d.

Marx, Karl. "Letter to His Father, November 10–11, 1837." In MECW. Vol. 1, 10–21. London: Lawrence & Wishart, 1975e.

Marx, Karl. "*On the Jewish Question.*" In MECW. Vol. 3, 146–74. London: Lawrence & Wishart, 1975f.

Marx, Karl. "Theses on Feuerbach." In MECW. Vol. 5, 3–6. London: Lawrence & Wishart, 1975g.

Marx, Karl. "Revelations Concerning the Communist Trial in Cologne." In MECW. Vol. 11, 395–457. London: Lawrence & Wishart, 1979.

Marx, Karl. "Outlines of the Critique of Political Economy (Rough Draft of 1857–58)." In MECW. Vol. 28, 49–537. London: Lawrence & Wishart, 1986a.

Marx, Karl. "Outlines of the Critique of Political Economy (Rough Draft of 1857–58). Introduction." In MECW. Vol. 28, 17–48. London: Lawrence & Wishart, 1986b.

Marx, Karl. "A Contribution to the Critique of Political Economy." In MECW. Vol. 29, 257–417. London: Lawrence & Wishart, 1987.

Marx, Karl. *Capital.* Vol. I. In MECW. Vol. 35. London: Lawrence & Wishart, 1996.

Marx, Karl and Frederick Engels. Correspondence. In MECW. Vols. 40, 42. London: Lawrence & Wishart, 1983, 1987.

Müller, Horst. *Das Konzept PRAXIS im 21. Jahrhundert: Karl Marx und die Praxisdenker, das Praxiskonzept in der Übergangsperiode und die latente Systemalternative.* Norderstedt: Books on Demand, 2015.

Musto, Marcello. *Workers Unite! The International 150 Years Later.* New York and London: Bloomsbury Academic, 2014.

Polanyi, Karl. *The Great Transformation. The Political and Economic Origins of Our Time.* 2nd Beacon Paperback ed. Boston, MA: Beacon Press, 2001.

Reichelt, Helmut. "Zum Problem der dialektischen Darstellung ökonomischer Kategorien im Rohentwurf des Kapitals." In *Geld—Kapital -Wert. Beiträge zur Marx-Engels-Forschung. Neue Folge 2007*, edited by Rolf Hecker, Richard Sperl, and Carl-Erich Vollgraf, 87–104. Hamburg: Argument, 2007.

Roberts, William Clare. *Marx's Inferno: The Political Theory of Capital.* Princeton: Princeton University Press, 2016.

Röttgers, Kurt. *Kritik und Praxis. Zur Geschichte des Kritikbegriffs von Kant bis Marx.* Berlin and New York: De Gruyter, 1975.

Ruben, Peter. "Die Kommunistische Antwort Auf Die Soziale Frage." *Berliner Debatte Initial* 9, no. 1 (1998): 5–18.

Ruge, Arnold. "Zur Kritik des gegenwärtigen Staats- und Völkerrechts (1840)." In *Die Hegelsche Linke. Dokumente zu Philosophie und Politik im deutschen Vormärz*, edited by Heinz Pepperle and Ingrid Pepperle, 147–71. Leipzig: Reclam jun., 1985.

Silver, Beverly J. *Forces of Labor. Workers' Movements and Globalization since 1870*. Cambridge Studies in Comparative Politics. Cambridge and New York: Cambridge University Press, 2003.

Skambraks, Hannes. *Das Kapital von Marx—Waffe im Klassenkampf. Aufnahme und Anwendung der Lehren des Hauptwerkes von Karl Marx durch die deutsche Arbeiterbewegung*. Berlin: Dietz, 1977.

Vazjulin, Viktor A. *Die Logik des "Kapitals" von Karl Marx*. Norderstedt: Books on Demand, 2006.

Weber, Max. *The Methodology of Social Sciences*. Glencoe: The Free Press, 1949.

Wright, Erik Olin. *Envisioning Real Utopias*. London and New York: Verso, 2010.

Wygodski, W. S. *Das Werden der ökonomischen Theorie von Marx und der Wissenschaftliche Kommunismus*. Berlin: Dietz, 1978.

The Intimations of a Post-Capitalist Society in Marx's Critique of Political Economy

Peter Hudis

I. WHERE TO BEGIN ANEW IN DEVELOPING AN ALTERNATIVE TO CAPITALISM?

Two hundred years after Marx's birth, there is no problem more urgent to address, and difficult to resolve, than developing an *emancipatory* alternative to capitalism that can serve as a pole of attraction for masses of people. The need for this is becoming increasingly clear. Capitalism's insatiable drive to commodify the lifeworld is subjecting an array of human activities to monetary transactions while producing a level of environmental destruction that threatens the very basis of civilization. We have clearly reached the point, even putting the risk of imperialist wars aside, at which the question before us is whether humanity has a future if an alternative to capitalism fails to arise.

However, while growing numbers of people around the world today aspire for such an alternative, developing one is proving very difficult. There are at least two reasons for this. One is the very nature of capitalism, in which human relations take on the form of relations between things. Diverse products of labour can enter into quantitative relations with one

P. Hudis (✉)
Oakton Community College, Des Plaines, IL, USA

© The Author(s) 2019
S. Gupta et al. (eds.), *Karl Marx's Life, Ideas, and Influences*, Marx, Engels, and Marxisms, https://doi.org/10.1007/978-3-030-24815-4_5

another only if they share a common *quality*. That common quality is their *value*. However, as Marx noted, "[v]alue does not have its description branded on its forehead; it rather transforms every product of labor into a social hieroglyphic." Since value can only show itself in a relation between physical, material entities, it *appears* that what enables products to be exchanged is the natural property of the things themselves instead of a historically specific form of social labour. Capitalism is defined by a curious anomaly: it is a system that produces unprecedented levels of change and transformation at the same time as appearing to be an immutable fact of human existence. Capitalism *must* appear to the common imagination in this way, precisely because it is based on augmenting wealth computed in monetary terms as an end in itself.

The second reason that it has proven difficult to develop a viable alternative is the profound crises, and ultimate failures, of the numerous efforts to create "socialist" or "communist" regimes over the course of the last 100 years. Social democratic governments, both in the West and in parts of the developing world, have at times managed to promote valuable social reforms, but they ultimately failed to project an alternative to capitalism. Instead, they ended up capitulating to neoliberalism, which has itself provided an opening for resurgent xenophobic racism and narrow nationalism. The Marxist-Leninist regimes that came to power in much of the developing world succeeded, by and large, in asserting national sovereignty against imperialism, but they proved no less of a failure. Their substitution of "market anarchy" by statist command economies led to gross inefficiencies as well as some of the most repressive regimes on the planet. None succeeded in making a firm break from capitalism, as shown by the fact that virtually all of them ended up openly embracing actually existing capitalism.

So where do we begin developing an alternative? It cannot be devised by theoreticians irrespective of the actual struggles against existing society, by workers, peasants, women, racial and national minorities, and LGBTQ people. Masses of people, especially at critical turning points such as we face today, create forms of struggle and organization that seek to reverse the deleterious impact of capitalist social relations upon everyday life. These need to be listened to and built upon in developing an alternative— especially because so many of them express the need for non-hierarchical social relations that go beyond the horizon of both capitalism and statist "socialism." Yet, at the same time, today's nascent efforts to promote an alternative need a *theory* that can pinpoint the specific social relations that must be transformed in order to surmount the capitalist law of value. But what can serve as the *source* of such a theory if the approach of many socialists and communists failed to live up to the task? We cannot live by the truths of a different era. But neither can we turn our backs on history by ignoring important sources within the socialist and communist tradition that speak to our present-day concerns.

There is, of course, no more important source of socialist and communist thought than the work of Marx. While he is wildly credited (or condemned) for his exhaustive critique of the capitalist mode of production, it is often presumed that he had little or nothing to say about a post-capitalist society. So how could his critique of political economy—which has as its aim, as he famously stated, analyses of the law of motion of *capitalism*—have anything to tell us today about an alternative to it?

The answer first of all lies in the fact that Marx's work does not consist of a radical political economy; it instead represents a critique of the very foundations of political economy. Economics deals with *existing* formations while taking for granted the conditions that establish the possibility for their existence. The classical political economists—and even more so the neoclassical economists that succeeded them—viewed capitalism as a necessary expression and fulfilment of human nature. They therefore felt no need to highlight the transitory and historical nature of capitalism. They defined the future in terms of the temporal horizon of the present. Marx's theoretical project proceeds from a completely opposite standpoint. His greatest theoretical work, *Capital,* does not consist of a theory of capitalist *development.* It instead delineates capitalism's tendency towards crisis and *dissolution.* Marx could do so because he analysed capitalism from the conceptual standpoint of socialism. He grasps the reality of the present through the temporal horizon of the future. One of the few Marxists to understand this was Rosa Luxemburg. She wrote:

> The secret of Marx's theory of value, of his analysis of money, his theory of capital, his theory of the rate of profit, and consequently of the whole existing economic system is [...] the final goal, socialism. And precisely because, *a priori,* Marx looked at capitalism from the socialist's viewpoint, that is, from the historical viewpoint, he was enabled to decipher the hieroglyphics of capitalist economy.[1]

---

[1] Rosa Luxemburg, "Social Reform or Revolution," in *The Rosa Luxemburg Reader,* ed. Peter Hudis and Kevin B. Anderson (New York: Monthly Review Press, 2004), 150–1.

No one doubts that Marx criticized the utopian socialists for idle speculation about the future, just as it is widely known that he eschewed writing
blueprints about the new society. But that does not mean he lacked an
understanding of what is required for a socialist society to come into existence. His entire career consisted of a series of extended polemics against
other radical thinkers, from Proudhon to Lassalle, who in his view had a
defective understanding of the nature of socialism or communism. It was
on the basis of a distinctive understanding of "the final goal" that Marx
proceeded to analyse and delineate capitalism's tendency towards crisis
and dissolution.

Closer to our age, the Czech Marxist Humanist philosopher Karel
Kosik argued along similar lines concerning the radical divide between
Marx's project and traditional economics, in *Dialectics of the Concrete*:

> *Economics is the objective world of people and of their social products; it is not
> the objectual world of the social movement of things.* The social movement of
> things which masks social relations of people and their products is one par-
> ticular, historically transient form of economics. [...] This is where Marx's
> theory is a *critique* of economics in the proper sense of the word, it exhibits
> the *real movement of economic categories as a reified form of the social move-
> ment of people. This* critique discovered that the categories of the social
> movement of things are necessary and historically transient existential forms
> of the social movement of people.[2]

In sum, *Capital* is not an empirical critique of actually existing capitalist
societies. It is a *dialectical* critique of what is integral to them—the logic
of capital, grounded in the law of value. Dialectical analysis, as against
empiricist approaches, does not merely describe the nature of an existing
thing but explores its process of transition into what it is not. As much as
Marx tried to avoid speculating about the future, as a deeply *dialectical*
thinker he could not help but intimate its future transcendence. The transcendence that he had in mind, now that we have the full corpus of his
work available for study, turns out to be quite different from how most
post-Marx Marxists conceived of the new society. It is this dimension of
Marx's work, above all else, that speaks to the realities facing us today. I
will seek to demonstrate this by re-examining the intimations of a new
society found in Marx's critique of political economy.[3]

---

[2] Karel Kosik, *Dialectics of the Concrete: A Study on Problems of Man and the World*
(Dordrecht-Holland: D. Reidel), 115.

[3] For a fuller discussion of these issues, see Peter Hudis, *Marx's Concept of the Alternative
to Capitalism* (Chicago: Haymarket Books, 2013).

II. The Humanist Content of Marx's Value Theory of Labour

Capital cannot be understood if its central categories are viewed as eternal, quasi-natural factors that apply to all forms of society. Money, private property, and the market do not mean the same thing in capitalism as in pre-capitalist societies. Most importantly, Marx held that production for the sake of increasing value—or wealth in monetary terms—is unique to capitalism and capitalism alone. It does not exist before it or after it. Value is not the same as material wealth, which does exist in all societies. *This distinction is the pivot upon which the entirety of Marx's critique of capital turns.*

The distinguishing mark of capitalism is that labour assumes a value *form*. Value, or wealth measured in monetary terms, is the expression of a specific form of social labour. Hence, labour "as such" is *not* the source of value. According to Marx, only a particular *kind* of labour is the source of value. A commodity's value is determined not by the *actual* amount of time taken to produce it but by the *socially necessary labour time* established on a global level. If value were determined by actual labour time, workers would be made to work as slowly as possible, since the greater the labour time, the greater is the amount of accumulated value. That never happens, of course, because the value of commodities is determined not by actual labour time but by *socially necessary labour* time over which workers have no control. This average varies continuously, due to technological innovations that increase the productivity of labour. It is communicated to the agents of production behind their backs, through the laws of competition. As capitalism progresses, concrete labour—the varied kinds of labour employed in making use-values—becomes increasingly dominated by labour that conforms to an abstract average, termed by Marx as "abstract labour." Abstract labour—*and abstract labour alone*—is the substance of value, which takes the phenomenal form of exchange value in the market.

Value is a rather *abstract* category, which makes it all the easier to overlook the fact that it expresses a peculiar kind of human activity: *labour that is constrained by a time determination that is outside the workers' control.* Once labour assumes a *dual* form in which abstract labour dominates concrete labour, productive activity ceases to be the expression of the workers' creativity, but instead becomes a monotonous, thing-like form that suppresses it. This *reification* of the workers' concrete, sensuous activity in the drive to generate greater wealth in abstract, monetary form is the essence of capitalism.

Hence, Marx's theory of value marks a radical break from classical political economists like Ricardo. The assumption among many followers as well as critics of Marx is that both have the same labour theory of value but draw different conclusions from it, since Marx singles out the existence of surplus value—the difference between the value of labour power and the value of the product—whereas Ricardo does not. In other words, it is assumed that both have a quantitative theory of value—that is, so many hours of labour determine the value of the product. It logically follows from this assumption that "Marxism" is a more radical version of Ricardianism, in that it seeks to effect a "fair" redistribution of value by providing workers with a greater share of the surplus product.

In fact, nothing could be further from the truth. Unlike Ricardo, Marx does not have a quantitative labour theory of value. He does not hold that actual labour time, or concrete labour, is the source of value. Concrete labour is only the source of *use-values*. He emphasizes again and again that the substance of value is *abstract* labour—a *qualitative* determination that Ricardo, like all classical political economists, simply ignored. Ironically, most established Marxists have also ignored it, as seen in their failure to grasp that value production applies only to capitalism, *precisely because it is a product of the peculiar form of social labour that is specific to capitalism—abstract or alienated labour.*

These distinctions are not a matter of scholastic hair-splitting, since they directly determine the understanding of the alternative to capitalism. All societies devote a certain amount of time to labour; if actual labour time is the source of value, it follows that all societies—including socialist ones—are defined by value production. *The social form of labour that is peculiar to capitalism becomes treated as an immutable, transhistorical fact of human existence.* The whole point and purpose of *Capital*—to take issue with those who transform "into eternal laws of nature and reason the social forms springing from the present mode of production"[4]—is turned on its head. Once value production is assumed to be a permanent feature of the human landscape, it follows that "socialism" is defined as little more than a "fair" redistribution of value. The real problem—*the reduction of human relations to relations between things*—is rendered invisible.

This standpoint has largely defined both Social-Democratic and Stalinist approaches. The discrepancy between the amount of value produced by workers and the amount they receive in wages would be solved, they

[4] Karl Marx and Friedrich Engels, *Manifesto of the Communist Party*, in MECW (New York: International Publishers, 1976), 6: 501.

claimed, through state management of the economy. Yet this approach ignores the real problem—the fact that labour (and other human relations) takes on a value form. The ultimate expression of value is *money*. Money is a non-sensuous abstraction, but human beings are sensuous, concrete beings. It is hardly "natural" to measure a person by how much money they are "worth." But it seems completely natural from a capitalist viewpoint, since people count in its eyes only to the extent that they augment value and profit. Those who focus on the redistribution of value, without targeting the existence of value production, therefore naturalize and render invisible the very thing that makes capitalism a dehumanizing system.

Moreover, attempts to "abolish" surplus value by redistributing value— fine as that may be for temporarily redressing some of the inequities of capitalism—ultimately prove quixotic, since they leave untouched the social relations that give rise to these inequities. *Surplus value follows from value production—not the other way around.* The value of a commodity is produced by *labour power*, which is *not* the same as living labour. This distinction between living labour and labour power is the pivot of Marx's theory of surplus value and profit. Labour power is the only commodity that is capable of producing a greater value than itself. To try to eliminate surplus value and profit while leaving intact the abstract or alienated labour that defines the expenditure of human labour power is akin to cutting off the head of hydra while leaving its body intact. It is only a matter of time before the head grows back—nay, before many more heads grow back! Such has been the fate of statist "socialism" in the twentieth century.

The *categories* employed by Marx in *Capital* anticipate these later developments, since they disclose that the law of value rests upon a specific set of *alienated* human relations. An exit from capitalism is not possible without uprooting them. *There is no other solution.* As Marx wrote in 1844, "All emancipation is a reduction of the human world and relationships to humanity itself."[5] *This perspective never left him.*

The radical depth of Marx's humanist critique of capital is often unrecognized, even by insightful commentators. For example, David Harvey has recently argued that Marx did not really have a labour theory of value; he says many have confused Marx with Ricardo's labour theory of value. He rests this on the claim that the value created in production is illusory so long as it is not realized through market transactions. He writes: "I take

---

[5] Karl Marx, "*On the Jewish Question,*" in MECW (New York: International Publishers, 1975), 3: 168.

the value created in production to be only a potential value until it is realized. An alternative way would be to say that the value is produced but then the value is lost if there is no demand for it in the market."[6] But if abstract labour, as Marx insists, is the substance of value, how can the value of which it is the substance be "lost"? Does this not imply that abstract labour's existence also depends on the market? Marx clearly says the opposite, however, in *Capital*: "The value of a commodity is expressed in its price *before* it enters into circulation, and it is therefore a precondition of circulation, not its result."[7]

To be sure, realization is a major component of expanded reproduction. However, what is "realized" in market exchange is not value but *capital*. The value is already there, "*before* it enters into circulation." If capital cannot be exchanged for money, then the value embodied in it is *destroyed*. The destruction of capital is of course integral to capitalism; it especially occurs during recessions and depressions, when less profitable units of capital are allowed to go under in favour of more profitable ones. But what drives this process is not the inability to sell the product due to a lack of effective demand on the market, but rather a *decline in the rate of profit* due to the growth of the organic composition of capital relative to the employment of living labour.

This has crucial ramifications. If the value of a commodity does not truly exist until it is realized in exchange, it follows that the elimination of value production—and the transcendence of capitalism—hinges on the management of exchange relations. Organizing the arrangement of *things*, such as prices, commodities, and markets, becomes viewed as the pivot of creating a non-capitalist society. Harvey himself suggests that a revival of Keynesian welfare-state policies that more equitably redistribute surplus value is the path that can best promote an exit from capitalism. Aside from the fact that there is little evidence that Keynesian measures, even at their best, ever seriously challenged capitalism, such market-based "solutions" leave untouched the social form of labour that grounds capitalist social existence. The emphasis on the management of *things*, via organizing exchange, leaves aside the need to transform *human* relations.

[6] See "Marx's Law of Law of Value: A Debate Between David Harvey and Michael Robert," *Michael Roberts blog*, April 2, 2018: https://thenextrecession.wordpress.com/2018/04/02/marxs-law-of-value-a-debate-between-david-harvey-and-michael-roberts.

[7] Karl Marx, *Capital*, Vol. I, trans. Ben Fowkes (New York: Penguin, 1976), 260.

Here is where it becomes essential not to treat categories like "money," "value," and "exchange value" as abstract, quasi-natural categories without reference to the specific social (that is, human) relations of which they are the expression. Money, for instance, does not mean the same thing in pre-capitalist societies (defined by the exchange of use-values) as in capitalism (in which use-values are produced for the sake of exchange). In capitalism, money is the universal equivalent, and a universal equivalent becomes possible only insofar as labour assumes a value form. Since abstract labour is the substance of value, "value requires above all an independent form by means of which its identity with itself may be asserted."[8] This independent form is money. The more abstract labour dominates concrete labour, the more all-pervasive becomes the drive to augment value; and the more this continues, the more value must posit an abstract "self-identity with itself." This means that the logic of capital compels money to assume a form independent of the concrete, material properties that makes its existence possible.

The increasingly abstract nature of money makes modern capitalism more unstable and turbulent. Bubbles abound, and monetary crises increase in frequency and severity. But here is where it gets tricky. Many critics tend to see such financial crises as the decisive issue, which leads them to argue that greater governmental control and regulation of financial (and capital) markets can produce an exit from capitalism. However, this overlooks the fact that financial or monetary crises are made possible (and necessary) by the evermore abstractive character of human social activity. As a result, the need to transform the specific human relations that necessitate that money take the form of an abstract universal is not addressed. We are left with a critique of capitalism that fails to keep its finger on the pulse of human relations.

Hence, grasping *Capital*'s intimation of a post-capitalist society requires being attentive to Marx's *distinctive* theory of value. As the U.S. Marxist-Humanist philosopher Raya Dunayevskaya wrote:

> Marx's primary theory is a theory of what he first called "alienated labor" and then "abstract" or "value-producing" labor. He analyzed commodities and showed that the exchange of commodities in general had been exchanged more or less sporadically for centuries before capitalism.

---

[8] Ibid., 255.

Capitalism begins when the capacity to labor [be]comes a commodity. ... Hence, it is more correct to call the Marxist theory of capital not a labor theory of value, but a value theory of labor.[9]

In essence what [Marx] said to Smith and Ricardo was: You thought your task was done with the discovery of labor as the source of value. In reality, it has just begun. If that theory means anything at all, it means that you must deal with man, the laborer, directly. ... Marx's analysis of labor—and this is what distinguishes him from all other Socialists and Communists [of] his day *and* of ours—goes much further than the economic structure of society. His analysis goes to the actual *human* relations.[10]

III. The Expansive Vision of Freedom in *Capital*

We are now in a position to directly turn to the intimations of a post-capitalist society in *Capital*. Remarkably, the fullest discussion appears in the section that delineates capitalism's ultimate *inhumanity*—commodity fetishism. This fetishism is very difficult to dispel, since, "the social relations between private labours appears as what they are, i.e. they do not appear as direct social relations between persons in their work, but as material relations between persons and social relations between things."[11] Since fetishism is an adequate expression of real social relations, it is not self-evident that even the best minds can avoid succumbing to it. The mystery of commodities only "vanishes," Marx writes, once we encounter "other forms of production."[12]

He first turns to the past by briefly surveying pre-capitalist economic forms in which common ownership of the means of production prevail. Relations of personal dependence predominate, in which "there is no need for labour and its products to assume a fantastic form different from their reality." No abstract medium, such as exchange value, mediates human relations; direct social labour prevails, not indirect social labour. Marx would continue this line of investigation until the end of his life, as seen in his voluminous writings of the 1870s and 1880s on communal forms in India, China, Russia, Indonesia, North Africa, and among the Native Americans of North and South America.[13]

[9] Raya Dunayevskaya, *Marxism and Freedom, from 1776 Until Today* (Lanham, NJ: Humanities Books, 2000), 138.

[10] Ibid., 55, 60.

[11] Marx, *Capital*, Vol. 1, 165–6.

[12] Ibid., 169.

[13] See Kevin B. Anderson, *Marx at the Margins: On Nationalism, Ethnicity, and Non-Western Societies* (Chicago: University of Chicago Press), 2010.

He then turns to the *future*, writing: "Let us finally imagine, for a change, an association of free men, working with the means of production held in common." It may be helpful to pause here and ask what it means for the means of production to be held in common. It does not refer to a merely formal transfer of private ownership to public or state entities. Transferring the property deed from private to collective is a mere *juridical* relation, which does not necessarily free the working class from class domination. Marx explicitly refers to "free men" owning the means of production, which means they exert effective and not just nominal control over the labour process. *And of course, that is not possible unless the workers democratically control the labour process.*

He then states that in a post-capitalist society, products become "directly objects of utility" and do not assume a value form. Exchange value and universalized commodity production come to an end. Producers decide how to make, distribute, and consume the total social product.[14] He invokes neither the market nor the state as the medium by which this is achieved. He instead envisions a planned distribution of labour time by producers who are no longer subjected to socially necessary labour time. Abstract labour is abolished, since *actual* labour time becomes the measure of social relations instead of an average that we do not control.

Marx goes on to state that "[w]e shall assume, but only for the sake of a parallel with the production of commodities, that the share of each individual producer in the means of subsistence is determined by his labor time."[15] What is the "parallel"? Is he suggesting that socially necessary labour time and value production continue under socialism? No, he is not. He is saying that a "parallel" exists with the old society insofar as there is an equal exchange—producers labour for so many actual hours and receive goods produced in an equivalent amount of actual hours. But the *content* of this exchange is radically different from what prevails in capitalism, since it is defined by a freely associated exchange of *activities* instead of an exchange of *commodities* based on an abstract average over which workers have no control. Distribution of the elements of production on the basis of actual labour time represents a radical break from capitalism, since this signals that the peculiar social form of labour—the split between abstract and concrete labour—has been abolished.

[14] Marx, *Capital*, Vol. I, 171–2.
[15] Ibid., 172.

The distinction between actual labour time and socially necessary labour time is critical, since conflating them leads to the erroneous view that value production continues to operate in a socialist society. Georg Lukács erred in this direction in his *Ontology of Social Being* and *The Process of Democratization*. He writes:

> For Marx, labor exploitation can exist under socialism if labor time is expropriated from the laborer, since the share of every producer to the means of production is determined by his labor time. ... For Marx, the law of value is not dependent upon commodity production ... according to Marx these classical categories are applicable to any mode of production.[16]

Lukács misreads Marx's phrase about a *parallel* with the production of commodities as suggesting an *identity* between commodity production and the forms that prevail in socialism. The logical conclusion—which is shared by both market and statist socialists—is that socially necessary labour time is an inevitable part of human existence that will always be with us. But if that is so, it follows that abstract labour, with all its alienated and dehumanizing characteristics, will also be with us always. This amounts to nothing less than defining the new society by the principles that govern capitalism.

In contrast, Marx repeatedly stresses that in socialism or communism—the two mean the same thing in his work and do not note distinct historical stages—socially necessary labour time is *abolished*. Time no longer confronts the worker as a person apart; instead, time becomes the space for human development. He writes in *Capital* Volume II:

> With collective production, money capital is completely dispensed with. The society distributes labor power and means of production between the various branches of industry. There is no reason why the producers should not receive paper tokens permitting them to withdraw an amount corresponding to their labor time from the social consumption fund. But these tokens are not money; they do not circulate.[17]

And in an earlier draft of *Capital*, he wrote that in socialism or communism

---

[16] Georg Lukacs, *The Process of Democratization*, trans. Norman Levine (Albany: SUNY Press, 1991), 120–1.

[17] Karl Marx, *Capital*, Vol. II, trans. D. Fernbach (New York: Penguin, 1978).

[t]he general character of labor would not be given to it only by exchange; its communal character would determine participation in the products. The communal character of production would from the outset make the product into a communal, general one. The exchange initially occurring in production, which would not be an exchange of exchange values but of activities determined by communal needs and communal purposes, would include from the beginning the individual's participation in the communal world of products ... labor would be *posited* as general labor prior to exchange, i.e., the exchange of products would not in any way be the *medium* mediating the participation of the individual in general production. Mediation of course has to take place.[18]

These and other passages show that it is not true that Marx never discussed a future post-capitalist society; references to it are found throughout his work. This does not mean that Marx forgot his critique of utopianism. Nor does it suggest (as John Holloway put it) that "to locate [communism] in the future is in effect to leave us in the grip of the [vanguard] party, a form of struggle that has failed and miserably so."[19] The idea of a vanguard party that "brings" communist consciousness to the masses "from without" was alien to Marx and only entered "Marxism" through one of his bitterest political enemies—Ferdinand Lassalle.[20] Lassalle first propagated the idea that "vehicles of science" such as himself were needed to bring socialist consciousness to the workers, who presumably can attain only trade union consciousness through their own activity—a notion that he directly passed on to Karl Kautsky, who in turn passed it on to Lenin. There is not a hint of such a conception in Marx, who proclaimed from start to finish that "the emancipation of the working class is the task of the working class itself." As the text of the *Grundrisse* and *Capital* shows, nothing stops one from "imagining" the future while steering clear of the notion that communist consciousness is brought to the masses irrespective of their spontaneous struggles. *And this is possible because the future is immanent in the struggles of workers against capital.*

[18] Karl Marx, *Economic Manuscripts of 1857–58*, in MECW (New York: International Publishers, 1986), 28: 108.
[19] John Holloway, "Read *Capital*: The First Sentence," *Historical Materialism* 23, no. 3 (2015): 8.
[20] See Peter Hudis, "Political Organization," in *The Marx Revival*, ed. Marcelo Musto (Cambridge: Cambridge University Press, forthcoming 2019).

The fullest expression of Marx's views on post-capitalist society is found in his 1875 *Critique of the Gotha Programme*. In this critique of his own followers, he distinguishes between two phases of socialism or communism: the first, as it emerges from the womb of the old society; the second, as it stands on its own foundations. He states that with the initial, lower phase, the producers "do not exchange their products; just as little does the labor employed on the product appear here *as the value* of these products, as a material quality possessed by them, since now, in contrast to capitalist society, individual labor no longer exists in an *indirect* fashion but *directly* as a component part of the total labor."[21] Generalized commodity exchange comes to an end in the first, initial phase of socialism, since abstract labour, the substance of value that enables products of labour to be universally exchanged, no longer exists. With democratic, freely associated control of the means of production, the producers themselves, and not some external force like socially necessary labour time, govern their interactions. And since labour loses its dual character, value production comes to an end—not only in the higher but also in the "lower," *initial* phase of socialism or communism.

Labour itself, however, does not come to an end in the new society. Instead, in the lower phase, it serves as a measure for distributing the social product. "The individual producer receives back from society—after the deductions have been made—exactly what he gives to it. What he has given to it is his individual *quantum* of labour." Individuals receive from society a voucher or token that they have "furnished such and such an amount of labour" and from it obtain "the social stock of means of consumption as much as the amount of labour costs."[22] As in *Capital*, Marx is *not* suggesting that the worker's labour is computed on the basis of a social *average* of labour time, but rather by the actual amount of hours performed in a given cooperative or enterprise.

Of course, this is only the lower phase of socialism or communism—it is still defective. The new society that emerges from the womb of the old one is incomplete, since "bourgeois right" remains. *But what does this mean*, since with the lower phase the workers control the means of production and the bourgeois class is already eliminated? He is simply repeating the same point made in *Capital* that there is a "parallel" with commodity production

---

[21] Karl Marx, *Critique of the Gotha Program*, in MECW (New York: International Publishers, 1989), 24: 85.

[22] Ibid., 86.

in the very restricted sense that an exchange of equivalents persists. As with capitalist "bourgeois right," what you get from society depends on what you give to it. But this *quid pro quo* is a world removed from the exchange of *abstract* equivalents. *What is exchanged are human activities, not products bearing a value form.* People now learn how to master themselves and their environment on the basis of a time determination that does not confront them as a person apart. Only when they have achieved this mastery will it become possible to reach "[f]rom each according to their ability, to each according to their need" in a higher phase. At that point, the *quid pro quo* is left behind. With the end of the division between mental and manual labour and the achievement of the "all-round development of the individual," a higher phase is reached in which actual labour time no longer serves as a measure of social relations.

Marx's discussion of the lower phase is not a normative view of how a socialist society emerging from the womb of capitalism *ought* to be organized. He is not writing a blueprint for the future. As he states in the *Critique*, once production relations have been thoroughly transformed on a systematic, societal level, a new form of "distribution of the means of consumption results *automatically*."[23] Marx is thinking out what society will be like once it has freed itself from the dual character of labour and value production, but the specific details depend on factors that cannot be known in advance.

Perhaps the biggest misconception of all is to confuse Marx's discussion of the first phase of socialism or communism with "the dictatorship of the proletariat." The latter is instead a *political* transitional stage *between* capitalism and the new society. The *Critique* clearly states: "Between capitalist and communist society lies the period ... in which the state can be nothing but *the revolutionary dictatorship of the proletariat*."[24] It is a transitional stage in which the vast majority—*not a minority party*—seizes control of the means of production by divesting the old classes of their property right. It utilizes democratic means, as suggested by the Paris Commune of 1871, to eliminate class domination by revolutionizing the social relations of production. Once socialism is arrived at, the dictatorship of the proletariat becomes superfluous, since by then the proletariat ceases to exist, because classes as a whole cease to exist.

[23] Ibid., 95.
[24] Ibid.

By confusing the "dictatorship of the proletariat" with the initial phase of socialism, far too many have assumed that the state—which in some form prevails in the political transition period—also continues in a post-capitalist society. In contrast, Marx held that the state is an "excrescence" of class society that is superseded in socialism.[25]

IV. Post-Marx Marxism Versus *Marx's* Marxism

Tragically, the intimations of a new society found in *Capital* did not inform the perspectives of post-Marx Marxism. Most dismissed any discussion of a future socialist society as a reversion to utopianism. And the few who delved into the social forms of the future tended to define socialism by the elimination of "market anarchy" in favour of a state plan. Yet the state plans that defined the USSR and Mao's China did not lead to a viable, *emancipatory* alternative to capital.

To be sure, a number of valiant attempts were made to transcend capitalism—and none was more valiant than the 1917 Bolshevik Revolution. Yet Lenin himself made no secret of the fact that as of 1917 the Bolsheviks had given very little thought as to how to create a socialist society. Their decision to "storm the heavens" and take power in 1917 was a remarkable achievement, but they were woefully unprepared for what happens after. By the late 1920s, under the weight of growing isolation, a counter-revolution led by Stalin consumed the revolution from within, leading to outright state capitalism.

Of course, Stalin declared in 1936 that by eliminating the free market and private property, the USSR had established "socialism." This was followed, in 1944, by his announcement that the law of value continues to operate in the USSR. Stalin admitted (through one of his ideologues, Wassili Leontief) that the existence in the USSR of universalized commodity production, wage labour, exchange value, and an average rate of profit meant that the USSR operated according to the law of value—which everyone until then viewed as integral to capitalism. But no need to worry, Stalin declared, the state plan will ensure that that the surplus product is "fairly" distributed to the masses. This was no scholastic debate. It defined the terms under which the communist (and much of the socialist) movement

[25] Karl Marx, *The Ethnological Notebooks*, ed. Lawrence Krader (Assen: Van Gorcum, 1972), 329.

viewed a post-capitalist society for decades afterwards.[26] Value production, abstract or alienated labour, and universalized commodity production became widely accepted as compatible with "socialism." Mao Tse-Tung (to give one striking example), who learned his "Marxism" not from Marx but from Stalin, took it for granted that commodity production and value production exists under socialism. He took this revisionism even further by adding the preposterous claim that class struggle also exists under "socialism"—which will presumably be around for hundreds of years until "full communism" arrives. As a result, the communist movement lost sight of the need to target the alienated human relations that make value production possible.

Today we live in a different era, in which it has become clear that a completely different approach is needed. Here is where Marxist-Humanism's emphasis on creating a philosophically grounded alternative to capitalism comes in. If the problem of capitalism is unequal distribution, there is no need to transform human relations; a mere change in tax policy will suffice. If the problem is the existence of private property, there is also no need to transform human relations; a mere change in the deed of ownership will suffice. But if the problem is value production—central to which is the domination of actual labour time by socially necessary labour time—then the only way to overcome capitalism is to create new human relations in which time becomes "the space for human development."

In sum, if the critique of capitalism is limited to the surface, phenomenal level, the understanding of the alternative to capitalism will be limited to the surface, phenomenal level. Marx did not have a superficial or phenomenal understanding of the logic of capital; and this is why his critique of political economy—despite his objections to utopianism—provides important insights into what constitutes an alternative to both "free market" capitalism and the state capitalism that called itself communism.

As I argue in *Marx's Concept of the Alternative to Capitalism*, this does not mean that "the answer" to the alternative to capitalism is found in Marx. What matters most of all is not what Marx said in 1843 or 1883, but what Marxism means today, after a century of aborted revolutions, as well as the emergence of new forces of liberation—such as national minorities, women, LGBTQ people and others who were not prioritized by earlier generations of Marxists. Re-examining Marx's work with new eyes

---

[26] See Raya Dunayevskaya, "A New Revision of Marxian Economics," *American Economic Review* 34, no. 3 (September 1944), 533–7.

is where our work begins, not where it ends. But without a proper beginning, it is not possible to find our way to an end. Philosophy, it is often said, is a perpetual search for a proper beginning, and that is just as true when it comes to envisioning alternatives to capitalism.

BIBLIOGRAPHY

Anderson, Kevin B. *Marx at the Margins: On Nationalism, Ethnicity, and Non-Western Societies*. Chicago: University of Chicago Press, 2010.

Dunayevskaya, Raya. "A New Revision of Marxian Economics." *American Economic Review* 34, no. 3 (September 1944): 533–7.

Dunayevskaya, Raya. *Marxism and Freedom, from 1776 Until Today*. Lanham, NJ: Humanities Books, 2000.

Holloway, John. "Read *Capital*: The First Sentence." *Historical Materialism* 23, no. 3 (2015): 3–26.

Hudis, Peter. *Marx's Concept of the Alternative to Capitalism*. Chicago: Haymarket Books, 2013.

Hudis, Peter. "Political Organization." In *The Marx Revival*, edited by Marcelo Musto. Cambridge: Cambridge University Press, 2019 [forthcoming].

Kosik, Karel. *Dialectics of the Concrete: A Study on Problems of Man and the World*. Dordrecht-Holland: D. Reidel, 1977.

Lukacs, Georg. *The Process of Democratization*. Translated by Norman Levine. Albany: SUNY Press, 1991.

Luxemburg, Rosa. "Social Reform or Revolution." In *The Rosa Luxemburg Reader*, edited by Peter Hudis and Kevin B. Anderson. New York: Monthly Review Press, 2004.

Marx, Karl. *The Ethnological Notebooks*. Edited by Lawrence Krader. Assen: Van Gorcum, 1972.

Marx, Karl. "On the Jewish Question." In MECW. Vol. 3, 175–87. New York: International Publishers, 1975.

Marx, Karl. *Capital*. Vol. I. Translated by B. Fowkes. New York: Penguin, 1976.

Marx, Karl. *Capital*. Vol. II. Translated by D. Fernbach. New York: Penguin, 1978.

Marx, Karl. *Economic Manuscripts of 1857–58*. In MECW. Vol. 28, 5–540. New York: International Publishers, 1986.

Marx, Karl. *Critique of t Gotha Programme*. In MECW. Vol. 24, 81–99. New York: International Publishers, 1989.

Marx, Karl and Frederick Engels. *Manifesto of the Communist Party*. In MECW. Vol. 6, 477–519. New York: International Publishers, 1976.

Roberts, Michael. "Marx's Law of Law of Value: A Debate Between David Harvey and Michael Robert." *Michael Roberts blog*, April 2, 2018. Accessed at https://thenextrecession.wordpress.com/2018/04/02/marxs-law-of-value-a-debate-between-david-harvey-and-michael-roberts

Recovering Marx: Steps Towards a Breakdance

Peter Beilharz

I. Recovering Marx: Stedman Jones

We are all, these days, in recovery. The times are out of joint, and nothing much seems to hold, certainly not any imaginary centre. Some of us are recovering Marx, and there is a great deal of activity in these quarters. What did Marx come to say? And, how does this wisdom travel across all the spaces and time zones that we now inhabit? These are two major questions that animate our curiosity, and while they are related, they are clearly not the same. They invite distinct responses, the first philological, the second applied or adaptive.

This essay invites a breakdance, a sequence in six steps around these issues and themes, punctuated in between by a segue which leads on. The first three steps take in major new works on Marx by Gareth Stedman Jones, Jason Barker and Marcello Musto. Three distinct steps follow. They inquire into the history of recent Marx reception in Australia, one each for three successive journals: *Arena* into the 1960s, *Intervention* into the

P. Beilharz (✉)
Sichuan University, Chengdu, China

Curtin University, Bentley, WA, Australia

© The Author(s) 2019   103
S. Gupta et al. (eds.), *Karl Marx's Life, Ideas, and Influences*, Marx,
Engels, and Marxisms, https://doi.org/10.1007/978-3-030-24815-4_6

1970s and *Thesis Eleven* into the 1980s and since. There also appears to be a dissonance here between the global Marx revival and an enthusiasm for Marx in the antipodes which is past tense or at the very least different.

The biography of Marx, especially that which is theoretically interesting, has until recently been thin on the ground. A generation ago, the most substantial work would have been that which came from the pen of David McLellan, which was innovative not least because he understood the importance of the *Grundrisse*. Gareth Stedman Jones has also been dancing with Marx, and before then Engels, for a long time. Recently we had his introduction to the Penguin edition *Communist Manifesto*, where the editorial is longer than the text. Now we have his even longer biography, *Karl Marx—Greatness and Illusion*, in the same league as the girth of *Capital* itself.[1]

Who was Karl Marx? How do we remember him? How do others remember him?

Easy, in the realm of vox pop. He was the guy who caused the Russian Revolution, right? Big guy, grumpy, beard.

No, sorry, that was Lenin, different time and place. Bald guy, professional revolutionary. Marx died in England in 1883. Lenin then was still in short pants, and in a rather different part of the world. And 1917 was a world away. And perhaps there were some other, more material than ideological issues involved in the Russian Revolution as well. This was not just a matter of ideas, or ideology. Ideas matter, but they do not change the world in themselves.

The irony of history is that Marx would come to be identified with Soviet Communism. This identification proved to be fatal, in more ways than one. As the liberal, or sceptical, father of sociology, Max Weber wrote to his friend, the young Hungarian hothead Georg Lukács, that the Russian Revolution would set the cause of socialism back by a hundred years.

Time's up, after 2017, though there remains no shortage of anticapitalist activity on the streets. As for socialism, understood as the construction of a new social order, the process looks like it is taking even longer. How, in the meantime, to unhook these moments, times and places? Who was Marx, disinterred out from under the dead weight of the Russian Revolution?

---

[1] Gareth Stedman Jones, *Karl Marx—Greatness and Illusion* (Cambridge: Belknap at Harvard, 2016).

Gareth Stedman Jones has been working on this very big book for a long time. The result, as George Steiner put it in the *Times Literary Supplement*, is no friend to elegance. But it is an astonishing achievement, even if the result is overwhelming. This book is so big that it is hard to read; you get sore wrists.

Stedman Jones seeks to develop an approach which makes his book freestanding, so that at any given point you do not need to head to the shelf or to Wiki to keep up with the narrative of the nineteenth century. The devil of the book is in its detail. This is not a book that can be criticized for omission. Stedman Jones sets out to relocate Marx, if not to replace him. The nuance of his life and times is dealt with in detail and in finesse. Attention is duly paid to both text and context.

Texts matter, as the Bolsheviks did not know many of them, and made Marx up in their own image. As Stedman Jones observes, for example, Marx refers twice in passing to the idea of the dictatorship of the proletariat; Lenin turns it into a core principle of Marxism. Marx uses the word party to refer to his handful of followers; Lenin turns this into the combat, or vanguard party of disciplined revolutionaries. Context matters, as the story of Marx is also, in Stedman Jones' telling, well distant, long gone. Marx's world is different to Lenin's, which is different to ours. Moreover, Marx became stuck in the vision of his own youth. He was also, as Zygmunt Bauman used to say, a youthful hothead from the Rhine.

The core thesis of the book here is that Marx takes on an apocalyptic worldview in the 1840s, and fails to revise it as the world of capitalism and liberal reform change in the second half of the century. Whatever this world is, it is before Bolshevism, before 1917. The young Marx is a romantic, a poet; maybe, in this way of thinking, he should have stayed there. Later he is a journalist, and as Stedman Jones observes, it is his columns in the *New York Daily Tribune* which are the most influential of his work in his own time; maybe he should have stuck with journalism. In between times, he was a philosopher, but this was the least of his impacts. During most of his lifetime, his followers could be counted on fingers and toes, though his enemies were apparently more numerous.

Stedman Jones covers all this beautifully. Family, religion, philosophy, money, poverty, friends, enemies, Engels, health, Hegel, exile, housing, character, Paris, London, Manchester, Shakespeare, tippling—it is all there. Most of all, there are Marx's ghosts, Bourgeoisie and Proletariat, the class actors who become locked into Marx's choreography.

Stedman Jones has written famously in the past about the language of class. His argument is not that class does not matter, but that Marx conjured up his own class actors from the revolutionary period of his youth. By the time of *Capital*, however, the working class was busy doing other things, organizing for reform, picking up the consumption side of the Industrial Revolution, looking to its gains and not only its losses.

In this telling of the story, Marx is put back in his box—the one marked German Philosopher, Nineteenth Century. This is an approach pioneered by Leszek Kołakowski, whose own views on Marx began with the observation that "Karl Marx was a German philosopher." It is a useful corrective to the Bolshevik appropriation, which turns Marx into Lenin, or else engages in the lazy play of Russian dolls.

This telling of the story sidesteps the 1960s, and the rediscovery of Marx as the advocate of freedom and emancipation. It is silent on the contemporary rediscovery of Marx by Thomas Piketty and the Occupy Movement. In this, it keeps Marx too far away. Marx's critical legacy still matters.

It does, however, unhook Marx from the cartoon Marxism of popular culture. It insists on the distance between Marx and the authors of Soviet Communism.

Marx and Lenin never met. Neither did Marx and Weber, the stoical voice of classical sociology. Weber is the better additive to Marx, sober and sceptical rather than redemptive in temper. After all, as thinkers such as Lukács and Loewith anticipated, Marx and Weber together would become the rational basis of the Frankfurt School and the tradition of Critical Theory, the critique of commodification and rationalization combined. Even Weber, however, was too optimistic in his prediction. Who these days speaks of Socialism in Our Time?

Ours is not the world Marx diagnosed in the 1840s, or misread in the 1860s. The imperative that we might do better, however, remains. As those who follow Marx, we still face both challenges—text and context, philology and extension, thinking and application.

II. Marx Returns: Barker

Jason Barker takes a different tack to Stedman Jones, at once more irreverent and more cutting-edge. This is a new genre, a new spin, avant-garde, as far as Marx scholarship is concerned. For Barker, *Marx Returns* neither as comedy nor farce but as something new.[2]

---

[2] Jason Barker, *Marx Returns* (Washington, DC: Zero, 2017).

How did it all begin in this telling? First, there was Marx, in Trier, Roman city, grapevines. Then there was Engels, in Manchester. Hell on earth, for some; fox hunting for some others. Then there was industry. Engels and Ermen, cotton at Manchester, Salford and Eccles. Then there was steel; Sheffield, Ford and Detroit, Stalin, Man of Steel, Magnitogorsk. Then there were two Chinese Revolutions, one in 1949 and another more recently. Industry everywhere.

Now there is the Marx Industry. Today there is a flood of books. Spurred on by Marx's 200th birthday, the Marx Industry is primed. The good news is that its products are better than ever, perhaps because of the distance that we might now take from Marx, perhaps because Marx has been unhooked from the Soviet experiment, allowed to breathe again after *The Death of Stalin*. These days even the *Economist* has given Marx a place at the table.

As befits the times, there are some fresh genres here—the play, the film, the graphic novel. There are ambient books, such as *Love and Capital*, or *Mrs Engels*, for which there were other precedents. Eisenstein planned to film *Capital*. Goytisolo's postmodern farce chased the *Marx Family Saga*; and there is the Canadian cartoon pastiche with Disney, *The Communist Manifesto*, as funny as it is disturbing. There are truly exceptional new scholarly works, such as Sven Erik Liedman's *Marx—A World to Win*[3] and Marcello Musto's *Another Marx*.[4] There is even a book called *Circling Marx*.[5] Or, is he circling us? There are witty and well-executed artworks, at an arm's length such as Christopher Crouch's *Lenin in Perth*. And there are new fictions, such as Jason Barker's *Marx Returns*. He's back! There is something about repetition here, or eternal return.

Jason Barker is Professor of English in South Korea. How does he bark? Jason goes for the gothic. This is Marx's story, with jokes and new dialogue added in to Marx's fury with his carbuncles and interest in chess and differential calculus. Marx suffered a great deal from pain in the ass; likely, he became a pain in the ass to those around him. The family always short; Engels pleading for him to finish, please finish that big book. So there is comedy here, as well as tragedy. Trotsky caricatured Hilferding as the bent-back professor lurching turtle-like with his big book, *Das Finanzkapital*, on his back. Marx's favoured image was Prometheus, but when it came to his book, the better image may rather be Sisyphus.

---

[3] Sven-Eric Liedman, *Marx—A World to Win* (London: Verso, 2018).
[4] Marcello Musto, *Another Marx: Early Manuscripts to the International* (London: Bloomsbury, 2018).
[5] Peter Beilharz, *Circling Marx. Essays 1980–2020* (Leiden: Brill, forthcoming-b).

Marx's life was dominated by numbers, large and small, from mathematicians to bailiffs, from zero to infinity. His mother, among others, teased him about the chronic absence of capital. But there is much more here. The story has a strong sense of atmosphere. There is effluvium, and poetry, intrigue and poverty. This is a book that relies not least on smell, and smells, Dante's Inferno. *Pfui, Teufel!* Barker evokes, and pokes. He makes his subjects all too human. This indeed is one of his main axes. Why was Marx so obsessed with the writing of one book, *Capital*?

Thus his wife, Jenny: "Did you ever stop to consider that your writing might be making you ill, Karl?" Or as his father put it, you can choose Jenny or the Book. The result of his life's labour and his family's tragedy was a work that remains incomplete. It is as though Marx needed not to finish. Look only at the last two chapters: chapter 32 is socialist revolution arriving unannounced, like a final curtain in the dance hall; chapter 33 is Mr. Peel on the Swan River, Perth again. The story of *Capital* begins with the commodity form and ends up somewhere near where the British first planted that Chenin blanc on the land of the local indigenous people, the *Wadjuk Noongar*. No joke!

There is pathos here, as well as humour. Karl is connected to his son Edgar and his symbolic toy locomotive; the loss of a later son, Guido, and the dedicated travails of his brilliant and tragic daughters follow. For the new world is also a world of motion, and locomotion, as well as anguish and inertia.

The story that Barker tells is incredibly witty, clever and creative. It is amusing and entertaining as well as instructive. Perhaps it is directed to those who already know, which might explain the need for explanatory notes in a book ostensibly heading in the direction of fiction. But *Marx Returns* suggests both a combination of rare talents and a will to create, both themselves attributes of Karl Marx. The book is in a strange way mimetic, just as mimesis is also innovative, a world away.

So is the joke on us? Maybe. Bernard Shaw wanted to insist that all revolutionary ideas begin as massive jokes. This is a stimulating book, which manages to wear the immensity of its learning lightly.

Jason Barker is among other things director of the movie *Marx Reloaded* (2011). In the Age of the Screen, Marxism must also need perchance to be visual. Better than *The Matrix*, this is less neomarxism than Marx Neo. Perhaps Marx did not need to write the Big Book after all. These days you can watch the results of the longer story on your phone. Or look out the window. Marxism remains, as Kenneth Burke put it a long time ago, a way of seeing. You don't necessarily need to know it in order to see it; but it probably helps.

III. Another Marx: Musto

As Marcello Musto announces in his new biography, we are in the midst of a Marx Revival. Only now does it become possible seriously to unhook Marx from those who claimed to make a revolution in his name. I am unsure as to how complete this historic uncoupling process is; but there is certainly a Marx Revival going on. Some very good new works on Marx have appeared over the last few years; there is clearly an ongoing process of recovery, discovery, and reappropriation or reconstruction. *Another Marx—Early Manuscripts to the International* is one of its finest achievements. It is presented as a kind of biography, though it is segmented rather than complete or historically exhaustive. It is, I think, primarily a work of philosophical and sociological insight, presented in biographical and historical form.

Musto's dance makes three moves, following three parts of the book or vital moments in Marx's path. These steps are as follows. We begin with the early work, from youth to Paris. The second step involves the development of the critique of political economy. The third covers political militancy from the First International to Bakunin. All of which is, as you might say, well known. But his book suggests a starting over. And, as I shall suggest, there is something special in the combination of skills and insights that Musto brings to his task which serves to set this book apart.

To begin, it is as though we hardly know Marx at all, or at least that we only know the iceberg peaks. As Musto reminds, earlier Marxists had very little of the corpus actually available to them. In the English language, readers only had the most important manuscripts available to them into the 1960s and 1970s. This situation is continually improving. We have 50 volumes of the *Collected Works* in English. In German, we are still only up to volume 65 of the planned 114 volumes of *Marx-Engels-Gesamtausgabe* (*MEGA*²). We discover that there are not only economic and philosophical manuscripts or ethnological or mathematical notebooks, but also ecological notebooks. *Und so weiter* ... And this is indeed one important image that emerges from Musto's book. Marx's work consists of a partial list of actually published works, and a mountain, an immense accumulation of notebooks. For this is how Marx actually worked, how he combined reading, research, and critique and writing. The notebooks were Marx's laboratory.

How might we read Marx, now, and why? The situation resembles the state of play in Gramsci Studies, where there are clear distinctions between philologists and reconstructionists, or between those who want first to get clearly what Gramsci had to say and those who view his writing as a tool-box whose purpose is to explain and address the present. For the philologists, the first task is to read and understand the *Prison Notebooks* in all their rich complexity. For the reconstructionists, the task is to seek intellectual orientation from these texts and especially their key themes, hegemony *usw.*, and then turn to the pressing tasks of the day, in a world that sometimes seems light years away from the interwar period of Gramsci.[6]

Musto's task here is to begin by rereading Marx, text and context, with full attention to both. The result is in a sense uncanny, as it both places Marx at that distance and makes him our peer or contemporary, as we struggle with those ongoing tasks of reading, writing, researching and thinking the contemporary for ourselves. Musto does not address the problems of the present directly, but he leaves the door open to this possibility. This is, to my way of thinking, a serious advance on works like Jonathon Sperber's *Karl Marx*, which seek to recover Marx by putting him in a nineteenth-century box, past tense, all context, history of the past rather than of our present.[7]

In the longer conversation that might follow, we will need again, also it seems to me, to reassess the paths not followed by the bullyboys of Bolshevism. This will include rethinking so-called Western Marxism, the traditions of the Frankfurt School, council communism, *Socialisme ou Barbarie*, the legacies of East European critical theory and so on. For, as Musto reminds, the most powerful ethical legacy of Karl Marx was the enthusiasm for emancipation or autonomy of self-development based on the cultivation of dependence or community.

So how does this book work? Musto has a fine combination of skills and attributes. He demonstrates sensitive and sophisticated linguistic and philological skills, acute historical sensibilities and the capacity to hear wide-ranging philosophical and political economic resonances. He has voice, but he also has a good ear. Marcello Musto understands the deep complexity of his subject, including his appalling medical history and desperate poverty. He combines a fine sense of detail, for example concerning Trier, with a clear sense of the philosophical substance of Marx's project as it moves from Paris to London via Ireland and the Paris Commune, pointing later to the Russian Road. There are fine reminders of the importance

---

[6] Peter Beilharz, "From Marx to Gramsci to Us—From Laboratory to Prison and Back," *Thesis Eleven* 132 (2016).

[7] Jonathon Sperber, *Karl Marx—A Nineteenth Century Life* (New York: Liverwright, 2013).

of sarcasm and style in Marx, as in the famous burrowing mole, but also the representation of Herr Vogt as a perfectly detailed skunk. Musto pulls all this together; but he also knows full well that Marx's brilliance was the result or product of his cultures, and it is plain that he too knows these cultures, as best as one could coming so much later.

A last word: this book is beautifully written and rendered by Patrick Camiller, and a pleasure to read. It is the best book written on Marx since Karl Korsch published *Karl Marx* in 1938. Eighty years is a long time to wait, but perhaps, like capital itself, the Marx scholarship itself is now also accelerating. Moreover, this is a Marx whose compass is pointed to today, with all the complexity and depth of implication which that involves. This is a great achievement, suggestive of more to come. For understanding, like Marx's lifework, is bound to remain unfinished.

Segue ... Interval

Clearly, the global Marx revival proceeds apace. As mentioned earlier, there are other major works too. Two major works focus on the early Marx. Stathis Kouvelakis has delivered a major volume on *Philosophy and Revolution from Kant to Marx*.[8] Michael Heinrich is in the process of publishing a major and massive multivolume project working intensively out of the German materials. These are vitally important works of Marx scholarship, for as Musto observes, in order really to enter this labyrinth it would be necessary not only to reread Marx hermeneutically but also to reread what he read. How many of us read Proudhon, or Bauer or Hess, rather than summaries of Marx's renditions of them and all the other formative thinkers that went into this mix?

This would, of course, be the work of a lifetime. Other new works follow different paths or lines of curiosity. Terrell Carver, unsung hero of careful Marx analysis since his *Karl Marx—Texts on Method*, 1975, has now published his postmodern primer *Marx*, a clever volume pitched frontally at the young reader who might imagine Marx alongside their own visage in those endless selfies.[9] In *Marx and Russia* James White offers a different approach to Liedman's biography.[10] Where Liedman paints the big picture, he also seeks to do justice to the connection, which

[8] Stathis Kouvelakis, *Philosophy and Revolution, From Kant to Marx* (London: Verso, 2018).
[9] Terrell Carver, *Marx* (Oxford: Polity, 2018).
[10] James D White, *Marx and Russia* (London: Bloomsbury, 2018).

is indeed serious, to Liebig and Schorlemmer, to agriculture and chemistry. If we want to know more about how Marx thought, this may be a more useful line of association than the endless later fuss concerning Darwin. White, for his part, follows the Russian Road more seriously than anyone in writing on Marx in English since Teodor Shanin. White takes as his point of departure the fine, and marginalized if perhaps bloodless, trilogy of Leszek Kołakowski. *Main Currents of Marxism* remains a monumental work, one that has likely been sidelined because of the left's difficulty in placing Kołakowski as an apostate, one who knows the field extremely well but is also past it. White looks to connecting up the Russian lineage in detail, its continuities and deep ruptures, from Sieber and Kovalelsky as well as Danielson and Zasulich to Bogdanov and finally, fatally, Stalin, diverging along the way with Plekhanov to the Darwinist orthodoxy that came to be known as diamat and histomat and with Lenin to vanguardism, beyond the earlier consensus of the First International that the emancipation of the workers could only take place by their own effort. White's strong claim is that Marx's work shifts significantly from early to later views of the history of capitalist development, from universal to specific. White argues that the Russian Road was symptomatic not of a weakness for Russian exceptionalism, so much as an opening to non-classical paths of industrial development, all those that diverged from the British model of capitalism and the feudalism-capitalism-socialism procession implied by the *1859 Preface*.

As I have suggested in *Circling Marx*, there is even such a possible interpretation of the famous double ending in chapters 32 and 33 of the first volume of *Capital*, and here we begin to arc gently towards our final three dance steps, in the direction of the antipodes.[11] Chapter 32 of *Capital* is often taken to be the proper culmination of the text and its choreography. The structure of the argument is in fact dissonant. The logic of *Capital* seems to demonstrate its capacity for self-reproduction, give or take claims about the tendency of profit rate to fall, crisis tendencies and so on. The arrival of proletarian revolution as announced in chapter 32 is without structural support in the argument that goes before. The proletariat is largely absent from major parts of the book, except as the carrier of suffering and endless toil until death. Capital is its subject, more than labour, even though we know from the early work that capital is nothing but stored-up labour, or labour power. The content of chapter 33

---

[11] Beilharz, *Circling Marx*, Introduction.

turns rather to the possibility of further capitalist development through the settlement of lands such as Australia.

Much earlier, in the *Neue Rheinische Zeitung* for 1850, Marx had suggested again another possible projection for capitalist development, different to systematic colonization or to any possibilities suggested by the Russian or kindred Roads:

> Thanks to Californian gold and the tireless energy of the Yankees, both coasts of the Pacific Ocean will soon be as populous, as open to trade and as industrialised as the coast from Boston to New Orleans is now. And then the Pacific Ocean will have the same role as the Atlantic has now and the Mediterranean had in antiquity and in the Middle Ages—that of the great water highway of world commerce; and the Atlantic will decline to the status of an inland sea, like the Mediterranean.[12]

Capitalist hyper-development would be urged even further on by the results of the Chinese Revolution. Social and socialist alternatives would become even more remote and difficult to imagine. Clearly global Marxists would have their work cut out, in this new scenario where even interpreting the world would become a major renewed challenge. This is one other impulse which calls out the Marx revival.

IV. In Australia: *Arena*

There is less evidence of any such revival in Australia, though there remains serious innovation in application, for example in the work of Bryan and Rafferty on *Capitalism with Derivatives*,[13] which echoes out through the recent work of Negri and Hardt. The political economists are still at work. As to Marx scholarship, the picture is different. Perhaps the global international division of intellectual labour has changed; perhaps post-Marxism rules down under. For we are all, in some sense or other, after Marx. The intellectual scene in Australia is still comparatively small, and its mainstream culture is one of relative prosperity and well-fed complacency. The activity of the prominent social movements of former times has become constricted. There has been a structural transformation in the university

---

[12] Quoted in Rolf Hosfeld, *Karl Marx, an Intellectual Biography* (New York: Berghahn, 2013), 85.

[13] Dick Bryan and Michael Rafferty, *Capitalism and Derivatives* (London: Palgrave Macmillan, 2006).

system, which for better and for worse was a privileged space for Marxist inquiry in the previous generation. Marxism has lost its place in the foundational teaching of the universities; no, rather it is foundational teaching itself which has been elided. Who teaches Marx these days? Or Weber, Durkheim, Simmel, Freud? PowerPoint rules; knowledge is masticated into bite-size pieces. Texts are deemed too difficult for students, even in the most established of universities, where the new buzzword is apparently something called *relatability*, whose premise is that students can only learn about matters that are already within their cultural universes. Why go to university at all? (Oh, wrong question!)

This was not always so. Even a generation back, Marx was a staple in liberal arts teaching in Australia. And Marxism was in a state of revival on the left. Consider *Arena*, founded in 1963 in the wake of Hungary and Khruschev and the global emergence of Marxist humanism and revisionism. The first editorial, in its first issue, called for a renewal of Marxism; and it was to become known for its interest in the new strata of the intellectually trained and the recombination of manual and mental labour. The work of Eugene Kamenka was one early textual point of reference, though the *Arena* thesis perhaps anticipated the ideas of Gorz and Mallet and later Sohn Rethel. In the late 1960s, students, more than workers, were on the march, though both came together in the Moratoria against the war in Vietnam. These were the days of the dreams of worker-student alliance, and of Western Maoist fantasies about something to be figured as a cultural revolution in the metropoles.

Arena in its prime was a remarkable achievement. Here our sample is issue number 19:1969. The student movement was a leading motif and enthusiasm attracting wide discussion. Another pioneering paper here was the Maoist Humphrey McQueen's early critique of labour movement racism, anticipating the publication of his decisive work *A New Britannia* in 1970. But there is more, and it is closer to the pulse of Marx and Marxist theory. Zawar Hanfi translates and introduces Feuerbach's *Preliminary Theses*. Alastair Davidson contributes a major and comprehensive survey of and engagement with Althusser. Bruce McFarlane engages with the political economy of Wolfsohn, Horvath and Mandel. All this in one issue, and more.

Arena was not a promoter of Althusser so much as of its own homespun rural romanticism. It did not sponsor William Morris, but some of its ambitions were reminiscent of that kind of Marxism. Having been flagged by Davidson, Althusser caught on elsewhere.

This is not the place for an assessment of the reception of Althusser in Australia. It was widespread, even though the emergent Marxist cultures of Melbourne and Sydney were to be German and French, in caricature. Even the humanist pages of *Arena* were open to its discussion. While Foucault, structuralism and poststructuralism were to become more influential in Sydney, there were also strong impulses to German thinking into the later 1970s from George Markus, The Sydney-Konstanz Capital analysis group and Wal Suchting, all working out of Sydney University's Department of General Philosophy. The Althusser Effect here was like the earlier Beatles Effect. Some local rock bands copied the Beatles; others picked up on their own emergent strategy, which was to write songs for themselves. In Australia, one important aspect of the Althusser Effect was that we began to read not only *Reading Capital*, but also Marx's *Capital*. Capital Reading Classes sprung up. The group we ran as students at Monash, where Davidson and Hanfi were among our teachers, had up to 30 participants meeting weekly. In its early days the Political Economy Movement did indeed look something like a movement, with annual conferences bringing together a thousand or so. Davidson and Hanfi taught us Marx and Gramsci and much else besides, verse and line. Others, such as art historian Bernard Smith, were thinking through the texts for themselves as they wrote their own leading studies of imperialism and cultural traffic.[14]

Perry Anderson's recent *New Left Review* memoir of a period meeting with Althusser touches on some of these issues in the antipodes. Anderson recalls with mutual amusement Althusser's encounter with a visiting Australian, very likely Alastair Davidson, who had become acquainted with Althusser, Poulantzas, Buci-Glucksmann, Laclau and Mouffe, Godelier, Lefebvre and other major drivers of French Marxism in the cusp of the 1980s. Although famously hostile to historicism, Althusser begins with the observation that we did not, even then, really have a clear sense of the reception, or global invention of Western Marxism in recent times, the hegemony of Anderson's own mapping notwithstanding:

Althusser to Anderson: Who had really taken his ideas up, and what had they done with them? An anecdote symbolized for him their fate. An Australian had visited him one day to say that the universities in Australia were in an

---

[14] See Peter Beilharz, *Imagining the Antipodes: Culture, Theory and the Visual in the Work of Bernard Smith* (Melbourne: Cambridge University Press, 1997).

uproar between the supporters of Althusser and the foes of Althusser. Life had been made impossible by their quarrels—above all by the bellicosity of the Althusserians. ... My ideas in Australia—Althusser spoke as if with a comic despair, about an *ultima thule* of the workers movement.[15]

The antipodes may otherwise have figured as the great unknown southern land in the northern imagination, rather than as a small mythical island to the north of Britain. But Ben Brewster had translated Althusser, complete with Glossary, so that we might in the south also follow the compass of the *New Left Review*. So, we all read Althusser, even in the antipodes. And, indeed, Althusser became the leading light of the next major moment in the life of Marxist journals in Australia.

V. In Australia: *Intervention*

It arrived in 1972, and it was called, appropriately, *Intervention*. Perhaps the best parallel elsewhere would have been *Theoretical Practice*, which first appeared in London in 1970. We also read *Theoretical Practice*, and we read Hindess and Hirst. (Later we all read E. P. Thompson's *Poverty of Theory*, and many of us ran to the other side of the boat. But this was already the last gasp of Althusserian Marxism, after 1978.) *Intervention*, however, in 1972 was home-grown, originally combining perhaps two key impulses: a dedication to the immense theoretical revolution announced by Louis Althusser; and the recognition that Australian Marxists must know their own history, after the example of Lenin in *The Development of Capitalism in Russia*. So here there was a familiar tension, that between Marx's theory and its application.

There were many key actors on *Intervention*, but two signal influences were those of Grant Evans and Kelvin Rowley. They were associated with the Left Tendency of the Communist Party of Australia, whose local politics were rather inflected by a kind of Maoist culturalism in Sydney and those of emergent Eurocommunism in Melbourne. The Althusserians had predictably little effect on the daily business of the Communist Party. They could just as well have been speaking Japanese, as far as the Central Committee was concerned.

---

[15] Perry Anderson, "An Afternoon with Althusser," *New Left Review* 113 (September 2018): 66.

The first issue of *Intervention* included papers on pastoral capitalism, sociology and Marxism, Lefebvre and Althusser. The second issue included analysis of Japan, radical history and Gramsci; the third focused on technocratic labourism, Korsch, Luxemburg and Marcuse. In the fourth, among other things, Keith Tribe worried the status of the *Grundrisse*, always bound to be a troubling text for those who believed in *Capital* as a work of the science of history. Into its later years, *Intervention* shifted from Melbourne to Sydney, and the French influence became more apparent. Editorials now were privileging Nietzsche. "Our motto: No more reformations!" Marx was looking more like the problem. So that by 1983 there appeared *Beyond Marxism. Interventions after Marx*. French philosophy was in the air; New Philosophy was also in the air. The best and brightest of the Sydney radicals turned their minds to French theory; and their contribution to the broader field is considerable. Barry Hindess arrived in Canberra, and in Sydney others such as Paul Patton did a great deal to promote work such as that of Deleuze. There was a flourishing of theory in Sydney, and it was French.

Intervention thus now reads like a capsule of the intellectual history of its times. The journal continued to engage closely with white Australian history and political economy, the latter now supplemented by the work of *The Journal of Australian Political Economy* (JAPE, b 1977). Its cultural interests went into projects such as *Local Consumption* and concerns with media, leading on to enthusiasms for Baudrillard and the Foucault Effect. The moment of Althusser could not be sustained. In retrospect, it seems less than entirely clear how Althusser came to dominate discussion so radically. Althusser's arguments were too heavily hermetic and scholastic to be long maintained. The undercurrent of feminism in *Intervention* played out through brilliant work in the wake of French feminism, from Liz Grosz to Rosi Braidotti and Meaghan Morris to Moira Gatens. The energies expressed in Sydney split the Philosophy Department, famously, into Traditional and Modern, and General, the split brought on first over whether Marxism belonged in the curriculum, and then over the legitimacy of feminism. Other things were happening in Melbourne.

VI. In Australia: *Thesis Eleven*

The first issue of *Thesis Eleven* appeared late in 1980 in Melbourne. It also looks now like something from the past: Western Marxism and critical theory, with an inflection more German than French, and combining enthusiasm for the Lukács of *History and Class Consciousness* with the power of insight in Gramsci's *Prison Notebooks*. The students of Lukács, Fehér and Heller had arrived 18 months earlier in Melbourne, Szelenyi in Adelaide, the Markuses in Sydney. Alastair Davidson had translated Gramsci already in 1968.[16] So the power trio of Western Marxism was there: Gramsci, Lukács, Korsch, Rosa Luxemburg on piano, these mediated for us in our twenties by local presences such as Davidson, Heller and Markus. We were influenced by the first generation of the Frankfurt School, and the early Habermas, *Socialisme ou Barbarie*, and even by council communism. Bauman had passed through Canberra in 1970, declining the offer of a chair there, heading on to his new home in Leeds. Castoriadis was to become a significant influence and a major contributor to the journal. Johann Arnason and David Roberts were further to mediate all this learning. For editing a Marxist journal, and what comes after, is also clearly a learning process.

The first issue of *Thesis Eleven* was entitled "Whither Marxism?" as much of all discussion in this period coalesced around the issue of the crisis of Marxism. It carried the views of Davidson, on Marx; Heller, on radical philosophy; Arnason, on this very crisis of Marxism; Markus, on the forms of Marx's critical economy; and Backhaus, in his pioneering text, on the value form in Marx. Three other papers were more strictly historical. There was a piece on labour history, by N. W. Saffin; a document from Gramsci, on the transition; and an arcane but brilliant piece by Steve Wright on J. A. Dawson and the Southern Advocate for Workers Control. It did not miss Wright's attention that Dawson published the first edition of Pannekoek's *Workers Councils* in Melbourne in 1950. We, in the southlands, were part of a long tradition of intellectual *emarginati*. Wright's own contribution came to include the landmark study *Storming Heaven— Class Composition and Struggle in Autonomist Marxism*.[17] His work belongs to a fine filament of Italian Marxism in the antipodes which includes that of his teacher, Davidson, and the later brilliant Gramsci scholar Peter Thomas.

What did *Thesis Eleven* come to be? For our 100th issue in 2010, we commissioned George Steinmetz to read the backfile and discern some

---

[16] Peter Beilharz, *Alastair Davidson—Gramsci in Australia* (Leiden: Brill, forthcoming-a).

[17] Steve Wright, *Storming Heaven—Class Composition and Struggle in Italian Autonomist Marxism* (London: Pluto, 2002).

trends.[18] The result? It was no surprise: as the journal proceeds through time, there is less and less work on Marx, much more on after Marx, or seeking to apply and extend the critical tradition. But there is also a blip in reference to Marx in these pages, after 1995. The critical horizon of the journal shifted from capitalism to modernity, a shift consistent with the leading trends in East European critical theory from Heller and Fehér to Bauman. In the case of Markus, the interest expanded from capital to culture.

As it approaches its fourth decade, the achievement and character of *Thesis Eleven* remain difficult to discern. The journal became more pluralized and given to puzzling over problems of the world, such as, in these days, populism, nationalism, watersheds, empires, technologies, indigenous and other modernities and so on. There have been recent issues on Gramsci, on the work of the Markuses, and Lukács, and further work on Castoriadis and Bauman.[19] Forty years on, the moment of Western Marxism has also passed, while the practice of critical theory has become a massive and open canopy. The interests of the editors have expanded dramatically, to take in more of popular culture and rock music, the creativity of the quotidian, matters of place, time and division as well as high art and culture as traditionally conceived. And whatever the depth of its distance from a project such as *Intervention*, there was a constant need for *Thesis Eleven* also to deal with issues of place, in the antipodes as elsewhere. So there is both extension and application work here, and work given to revaluing our own traditions and thinkers.

Where is Marx, in all this? Subsumed, transformed, repeated via creative mimesis; periodically reconsidered. Certainly, there are other impulses at work, such as that shown by the local followers of *Historical Materialism*. As for me, personally, *Capital* remains my desert island book, the one to which I most constantly return and imbibe from, the *Grundrisse* fast on its tail. Those of us who follow Marx celebrate the revival, and hope still to

---

[18] George Steinmetz, "Thirty Years of Thesis Eleven: A Survey of the Record and Questions for the Future." *Thesis Eleven* 100 (2010); and see thesiseleven.com for recent activities of the journal http://thesiseleven.com

[19] See James Dorahy, *The Budapest School: Beyond Marxism* (Leiden: Brill, 2019); Jonathon Pickle and John Rundell, eds., *Critical Theories and the Budapest School* (London: Routledge, 2018); Peter Beilharz, *Zygmunt Bauman—Dialectic of Modernity* (London: Sage, 2000); Peter Beilharz, ed., *The Bauman Reader* (Oxford: Blackwell, 2000); Peter Beilharz, *Working With Zygmunt Bauman: Sociology and Friendship* (Manchester: Manchester University Press, forthcoming-c).

pass on this legacy. There is still so much to learn, and to change, even for us on the margins. Marx returns; we return. The repetition is additive, and qualitative; over all these years since Marx, it represents an immense accumulation of radical culture. So do we go on, dancing our lives away, hoping for better, hoping ever for more. Here is the rose; dance away!

BIBLIOGRAPHY

Anderson, Perry. "An Afternoon with Althusser." *New Left Review* 113 (September 2018): 59–68.

Barker, Jason. *Marx Returns*. Washington, DC: Zero, 2017.

Beilharz, Peter. *Imagining the Antipodes: Culture, Theory and the Visual in the Work of Bernard Smith*. Melbourne: Cambridge University Press, 1997.

Beilharz, Peter, ed. *The Bauman Reader*. Oxford: Blackwell, 2000a.

Beilharz, Peter. *Zygmunt Bauman—Dialectic of Modernity*. London: Sage, 2000b.

Beilharz, Peter. "From Marx to Gramsci to Us—From Laboratory to Prison and Back." *Thesis Eleven* 132 (2016): 77–86.

Beilharz, Peter. *Alastair Davidson—Gramsci in Australia*. Leiden: Brill, forthcoming-a.

Beilharz, Peter. *Circling Marx. Essays 1980–2020*. Leiden: Brill, forthcoming-b.

Beilharz, Peter. *Working With Zygmunt Bauman: Sociology and Friendship*. Manchester: Manchester University Press, forthcoming-c.

Bryan, Dick and Michael Rafferty. *Capitalism and Derivatives*. London: Palgrave Macmillan, 2006.

Carver, Terrell. *Marx*. Oxford: Polity, 2018.

Dorahy, James. *The Budapest School: Beyond Marxism*. Leiden: Brill, 2019.

Hosfeld, Rolf. *Karl Marx, an Intellectual Biography*. New York: Berghahn, 2013.

Kouvelakis, Stathis. *Philosophy and Revolution, From Kant to Marx*. London: Verso, 2018.

Liedman, Sven-Eric. *Marx—A World to Win*. London: Verso, 2018.

Musto, Marcello. *Another Marx: Early Manuscripts to the International*. London: Bloomsbury, 2018.

Pickle, Jonathon, and John Rundell, eds. *Critical Theories and the Budapest School*. London: Routledge, 2018.

Sperber, Jonathon. *Karl Marx—A Nineteenth Century Life*. New York: Liverwright, 2013.

Stedman Jones, Gareth. *Karl Marx—Greatness and Illusion*. Cambridge: Belknap at Harvard, 2016.

Steinmetz, George. "Thirty Years of Thesis Eleven: A Survey of the Record and Questions for the Future." *Thesis Eleven* 100 (2010): 67–80.

White, James D. *Marx and Russia*. London: Bloomsbury, 2018.

Wright, Steve. *Storming Heaven—Class Composition and Struggle in Italian Autonomist Marxism*. London: Pluto, 2002.

On the Notion of "Workers' Control" in Marx and Marxists (1871–1917): A Survey

Babak Amini

I. On the Idea of "Workers' Control"

The notion of "workers' control" has been used to cover a wide range of phenomena, from limited workers' supervision of working conditions to full workers' management of the social relation of production. It has also been deployed within a broad ideological spectrum including Marxism, anarcho-syndicalism, guild socialism, and Social Democracy.[1] Therefore, it is by no means limited to Marxism. In fact, Marxism has always had an

---

[1] For diversity on the notion among the various schools of thoughts, see Immanuel Ness and Dario Azzellini, eds., *Ours to Master and to Own: Workers' Control from the Commune to the Present* (Chicago: Haymarket, 2011); Dario Azzellini and Michael Kraft, eds., *The Class Strikes Back: Self-Organised Workers' Struggles in the Twenty-First Century* (Leiden: Brill, 2018); Maximilien Rubel and John Crump, eds., *Non-Market Socialism in the Nineteenth and Twentieth Centuries* (New York: Palgrave Macmillan, 1984); Catherine Mulder, *Transcending Capitalism through Cooperative Practices* (Basingstoke: Palgrave Macmillan, 2015); Bernard Shaw, ed., *Fabian Essays* (London: Allen & Unwin, 1948); Gregory K. Dow, *Governing the Firm: Workers' Control in Theory and Practice* (Cambridge and New York: Cambridge University Press, 2003).

B. Amini (✉)
London School of Economics, London, UK

© The Author(s) 2019
S. Gupta et al. (eds.), *Karl Marx's Life, Ideas, and Influences*, Marx, Engels, and Marxisms, https://doi.org/10.1007/978-3-030-24815-4_7

uneasy relationship with this notion either for its ideological flexibilities that could facilitate as much an anti-political radical left stance as a class-collaborationist liberal position, or for its conceptual antagonism with much of the actual twentieth-century socialist systems.

It is in the latter sense, in opposition to the most hegemonic forms of Marxism in the twentieth century, that the notion is utilized in this chapter to trace the conceptual genesis of a vision of communist society based on Marx's notion of a "society of free and associated producers".[2] Some might take an issue with such a radical interpretation of the idea of "workers' control" whose common use in theory and practice has set far less revolutionary criteria. One can argue in response that for workers to have an *actual* control over the relations of production, which goes beyond the limits of the sphere of production, they must break from not only capital towards socialization of the means of production but also the state towards the associated administration of society.[3] Workers remain under the spur of capital and its market imperatives even if they are given supervisory or participatory rights. They remain subject to the will of bureaucratic organs of the centralized state even if they are formally in control of the means of production. In emphasizing the "*workers'* control", it seeks to make a distinction with the visions of the future society based on the state or the party control. Therefore, this chapter surveys the *theoretical* manifestations of a concept defined *a priori* rather than the evolution of the notion employed *a posteriori* through concrete experiences.

The temporal boundary adapted in this essay is from 1871, when Marx published his reflections on the Paris Commune in *Civil War in France* to just before the February Revolution of 1917. There are more reasons behind this deliberation beyond space considerations. Although the genesis of the concept can certainly be found in earlier writings of Marx such as the *Grundrisse* and *Capital*, Volume I, the experience of the Paris Commune (1871) invoked new ideas in Marx about the organization of the post-capitalist society. Conversely, the experience of the February Revolution had profound effects on Marxist theorists on the political form of the revolutionary transition and the nature of socialist society. It is precisely the exclusion of the effects of this momentous event from the inquiry that helps to highlight its transformative effects on Marxist thoughts on classical Marxism and beyond.

---

[2] Karl Marx, *Theories of Surplus Value (Part 3)* (Moscow: Progress Publishers, 1971), 157.
[3] For example, see Paul Mattick, "Workers' Control," in *Anti-Bolshevik Communism* (Monmouth: Merlin Press Ltd., 2007), 211–31.

The chapter illustrates the extent to which the idea of "workers' control" finds different expression in Marx and some of the Marxist theorists between 1871 and the February Revolution. Needless to say, not all Marxist thinkers of this period and not all of their writings could be analysed within the confines of this chapter. Therefore, it is not a comprehensive survey even within the chosen period; its hope, nevertheless, is to at least provide a ground for further investigation. However, certain peculiarities surface from the selection, suggesting that the most "prominent" Marxist theorists of this period did not in fact have as much to say about the notion of "workers' control" as compared to more "marginal" figures. Reasons behind this and the need to re-examine Marx's writings on this notion are discussed in the concluding section.

The major themes that emerged from the survey resolve around the centrality of self-emancipation of the working-class to democratically control the socialized means of production through federations of associated producers. This implies that the question of the state and its role in such revolutionary transformation looms large in these accounts. Some theorists, especially Marx and Engels, were also keenly aware of the fact that such a realm of freedom is unattainable as long as capitalist market imperatives are left in place.

II. Brief Remarks on the Historical Context

The different takes and emphasis on the notion of "workers' control" that we will see should be proximally understood in terms of the varieties of political contexts that demanded different theoretical struggles. Two underlying historical trends, one general to the period and the other particular to the national context, can be recognized.

In was in this period that socialist parties emerged and, especially in continental Europe, gained traction towards becoming mass parties.[4] Although they faced serious hurdles in translating their mass support into political power due to electoral disenfranchisement and state repression, the rapid expansion of the working class provided the social force behind these parties. In the meanwhile, this period saw the growth of the union

---

[4] See Dick Geary, ed., *Labour and Socialist Movements in Europe before 1914* (Oxford: Berg, 1989); Geoff Eley, *Forging Democracy the History of the Left in Europe, 1850–2000* (Oxford: Oxford University Press, 2002).

movement, which was not always in sync with the socialist movement in either ideological orientation or organizational domination.[5]

Marxism had its own trajectory in this period which, albeit rapidly becoming one of the most dominant theoretical orientations among the radicals, had by no means remained unchallenged. The gulf that erupted within the International Workingmen's Association (IWMA) between the anarchists and Marxists continued to widen for the next four decades.[6] Anarchist thought continued to play a major influence on radical thinkers, especially in Russia, France, and the Southern European countries.[7] Therefore, Marxist theoreticians felt obliged to clearly distinguish themselves, sometimes even at the cost of rejecting some positive aspects of anarchist thoughts. Another development that concerned Marxists particularly until the end of the 1900s was the significant shift within the labour movement towards syndicalism.[8]

There were specific trends within each country that strongly influenced the native theoretical development. It was only in Germany that Marxism became the official doctrine of the Social Democratic Party of Germany (SPD)—a party that enjoyed an exceptional hegemony within the Left and unparalleled organizational capacity which soon translated into parliamentary strength. The party was also responsible for the establishment of the union and, therefore, had a close relationship with it, albeit not without tensions, especially later in the 1900s. In France, there was a strong presence of Proudhonism and Blanquism until the end of the 1890s and then the continued influence of anarchism and syndicalism within the socialist and labour movement into the twentieth century. Therefore, the French Marxists had to carve a space within these ideologies which often involved

[5] See Donald Sassoon, *One Hundred Years of Socialism: The West European Left in the Twentieth Century* (London: Tauris, 2014), 1–30; Stefano Bartolini, *The Political Mobilization of the European Left, 1860–1980: The Class Cleavage* (Cambridge: Cambridge University Press, 2000); Ira Katznelson and Aristide R. Zolberg, eds., *Working-Class Formation: Nineteenth-Century Patterns in Western Europe and the United States* (Princeton: Princeton University Press, 1986).

[6] See Marcello Musto, "Introduction," in *Workers Unite! The International 150 Years Later*, ed. Marcello Musto (New York: Bloomsbury, 2014), 51–63.

[7] See David Berry and Constance Bantman, eds., *New Perspectives on Anarchism, Labour and Syndicalism: The Individual, the National and the Transnational* (Newcastle: Cambridge Scholars, 2010); Peter H. Marshall, *Demanding the Impossible: A History of Anarchism* (London: HarperCollins, 1992), esp. part V.

[8] See Marcel van der Linden and Wayne Thorpe, eds., *Revolutionary Syndicalism: An International Perspective* (Aldershot: Scolar, 1990).

leveraging on the deep-seated anarcho-syndicalist sensibilities of the French working class. In the United Kingdom, the hegemony of reformism within the labour movement which gave rise to the Labour Party left little room for radical socialist tendencies. The Irish situation, although under the influence of British socialism, had more room for radicalism insofar as it could be linked to the project of independence. It should not come as a surprise that the Marxist intellectuals in the United Kingdom, the United States, and Ireland gravitated towards the breathing space that was created after the emergence of the Industrial Workers of the World (IWW). Russia was a profoundly different case. Given the weakness of the social base due to the level of industrialization and the autocratic absolutist state, the most pressing challenge of the Russian socialists appeared to be the democratization of the state to create political space for reforms. However, the Tsar Regime proved itself incapable of undergoing any democratic reform.

The process of proletarization of the population intensified exponentially after the outbreak of World War I,[9] but the state clampdown on political agitation and socialist parties' capitulation to the imperialist project in the hope of finding a stronger foothold in the sphere of formal politics substantially interrupted the radical project within the socialist camp. Furthermore, the imperial rivalry in the lead-up to and the disastrous consequences of the war presented Marxist intellectuals with new questions to grapple with. This is why there is no text in the survey that was published during the war.

III. "Workers' Control" in Marx and the Early Marxists

Karl Marx (1818–1883)

There is much in Marx's works prior to 1871 that speaks to the idea of "workers' control". However, the developments within the IWMA and the Paris Commune had profound effects on his conception of the form of future society. In the General Rules of the IWMA, originally written in 1864 but updated in 1871, Marx and Engels restate the fundamental motto of the International "that the emancipation of the working classes

---

[9] See Antoine Prost, "Workers," in *The Cambridge History of the First World War*, ed. Jay Winter (Cambridge: Cambridge University Press, 2014).

must be conquered by the working classes themselves ... [and] that the economical emancipation of the working classes is, therefore, the great end to which every political movement ought to be subordinated as a means".[10] As he (and Engels) said repeatedly on numerous occasions, what mattered was that

> the emancipation of the working class must be achieved by working class itself. Hence we [in the workers' party] cannot cooperate with men who say openly that the workers are too uneducated to emancipate themselves, and must first be emancipated from above by philanthropic members of the upper and lower middle class.[11]

They also cautioned strongly against allowing the leadership of the working-class party to fall into the hands of such an element.[12] They held on uncompromisingly to this principle.

Albeit the subordination of the political movement to the economic emancipation, they put utmost emphasis on the importance of "the conquest of political power" as the "great duty of the working class".[13] They also underscored the fact that the working class cannot collectively engage in such political actions "except by constituting itself into a political party, distinct from, and opposed to all old parties formed by the propertied classes".[14] Therefore, Marx's idea of "workers' control" is far from an anarcho-syndicalist understanding. It sees the constitution of political parties as "indispensable" to "the triumph of social revolution",[15] even though political movement remains instrumentally subordinate to the ultimate end of the economic emancipation of the working class by the working class itself. They further believed that the working class must use its forces in economic struggles "as a lever for its struggle against the political power of landlords and capitalists".[16] In other words, "in the

[10] Karl Marx and Friedrich Engels, "General Rules of the International Working Men's Association," in *Workers Unite*, 265.

[11] Karl Marx, and Frederick Engels, "Circular Letter to August Bebel, Wilhelm Liebknecht, Wilhelm Brucke and Others," in MECW (London: Lawrence & Wishart, 1989), 24: 269.

[12] Ibid.

[13] Marx and Engels, "General Rules of the International Working Men's Association," 268.

[14] Ibid.

[15] Ibid.

[16] Karl Marx and Friedrich Engels, "[On the Political Action of the Working Class and Other Matters]," in *Workers Unite*, 285.

militant state of the working class, its economical movement and its political action are indissolubly united".[17]

In his *Civil War in France* (1871), Marx analysed the emergence and the development of the Paris Commune and assessed its theoretical implications. He argued that the Paris Commune showed that "the working class cannot simply lay hold of the ready-made State machinery, and wield it for its own purposes".[18] This is because the structure of the modern state has been formed through its historical evolution, due to both political struggle of classes (and class fractions) and economic changes in society, in ways that the state power and its organs reflect the capitalist social relation.[19] The Commune was "the direct anthesis of the [Second] Empire" that sought to supersede not only the form of a particular class character of that state but "class rule itself",[20] which required a fundamental transformation of the state and its key organs such as the army, the policy, the government, the educational institutions, and the judiciary. At the core of such transformation lay one fundamental principle to create the "the basis of really democratic institutions"[21]: "While the merely repressive organs of the old governmental power were to be amputated, its legitimate functions were to be wrested from an authority usurping preeminence over society itself, and restored to the responsible agents of society."[22] The "expansive political form" of government that the Commune sought to establish was "local municipal liberty".[23]

But this transformation could not be limited to the political sphere. Marx believed that the Commune as "essentially a working-class government [is] the produce of the struggle of the producing against the appropriating class".[24] Hence, the political form that the Commune sought to establish could "serve as a lever for uprooting the economical foundations upon which rests the existence of classes, and therefore of class rule".[25] This implied the transformation of private property into "mere instruments

[17] Ibid.
[18] Karl Marx, "The Civil War in France," in MECW (London: Lawrence & Wishart, 1986), 22: 328.
[19] Ibid., 328–9.
[20] Ibid., 330–1.
[21] Ibid., 334.
[22] Ibid., 332–3.
[23] Ibid.
[24] Ibid.
[25] Ibid.

of free and associated labour".[26] Such a cooperative society of free and associated producers whose vision had to be "emphatically international",[27] what Marx simply identified as "communism", was to "regulate national production upon a common plan, thus taking it under their own control".[28]

Further elaboration of Marx's radical understanding of "workers' control" appears in *Critique of the Gotha Programme* (1875) in which Marx offered a sharp critique of the draft of the programme of the Socialist Workers' Party of Germany. In response to the demand for state-assisted cooperatives under the democratic control of workers, Marx argued that "instead of arising from the revolutionary process of the transformation of society, the 'socialist organisation of the total labour' 'arises' from the 'state aid' that the state gives to the producers' co-operative societies which the state, not the worker, 'calls into being'".[29] He believed such a scheme could not lead to a revolutionary transformation of the capitalist social relation. He further questioned the seemingly democratic appeal of the demand: "[W]hat does 'control of the working people by the rule of the people' mean? And particularly in the case of working people who, through these demands that they put to the state, express their full consciousness that they neither rule nor are ripe for rule."[30] Therefore, creation of the conditions for a cooperative society to transcend the capitalist social relation of production was only valuable, Marx argued, "only insofar as they are the independent creations of the workers and not protégés either of the governments or of the bourgeois".[31] Through such a critique, Marx emphasized the need for achieving an actual rather than formal control by the workers.

Regarding the question of the transformation of the state in a communist society, Marx wrote here that in the period of political transition from capitalism to communism, the state undergoes a phase that "can be nothing but the revolutionary dictatorship of the proletariat".[32] We must note that this was a critique of Lassallean socialism that "treat[ed] the state

---

[26] Ibid., 335.

[27] Ibid., 338.

[28] Ibid., 335.

[29] Karl Marx, "Marginal Notes on the Programme of The German Workers' Party," in MECW (London: Lawrence & Wishart, 1989), 24: 93.

[30] Ibid.

[31] Ibid., 94.

[32] Ibid., 95. This phrase has been notoriously abused by later Marxists even though Marx himself rarely used it throughout his corpus.

rather as an independent entity that possesses its own 'intellectual, ethical and libertarian bases'".[33] Marx qualified the notion of the "dictatorship of the proletariat" in his *Notes on Bakunin's Statehood and Anarchy* (1874–1875) where he responded to the charges that Mikhail Bakunin made against him. The notion

> implies that as long as the other classes, above all the capitalist class, still exist, and as long as the proletariat is still fighting against it (for when the proletariat obtains control of the government its enemies and the old organisation of society will not yet have disappeared), it must use forcible means, that is to say, governmental means.[34]

Therefore, the proletariat must use the power of the state to accelerate the process of transforming the economic condition that constitutes it as a class, so as to abolish "its own character as wage labourer and hence as a class".[35] In response to Bakunin's rhetorical question as to whether the whole of the proletariat can stand at the head of the government, Marx said "CERTAINLY! For the system starts with the self-government of the communities."[36]

In *Capital*, Volume III, Marx began a discussion about the supervisory and managerial role by a general acknowledgement that it "arises where the direct production process takes the form of a socially combined process, and does not appear simply as the isolated labour of separated produces".[37] Therefore, it emerges in two forms: as an organizational necessity of "any combined mode of production" in general but also in all modes of production where there is an opposition between the director producers and the owners of the means of production".[38] What is specific about work of supervision and management under capitalism is that it is "directly and inseparably fused [ ] with the productive functions that all combined social labour assigns to particular individuals as their special work".[39] The infusion implies that the work of supervision does not necessarily have to be performed by the capitalists, just as the capitalist can become "superfluous

---

[33] Ibid., 94.
[34] Karl Marx, "Notes on Bakunin's *Statehood and Anarchy*," in MECW (London: Lawrence & Wishart, 1989), 24: 517.
[35] Ibid., 519.
[36] Ibid.
[37] Karl Marx, *Capital*, Vol. III (London: Penguin Classic, 1991), 507.
[38] Ibid.
[39] Ibid., 510.

as a functionary in production".[40] Marx referred to the cooperative factories as a proof of this superfluidity whose conditions of possibility emerge
at a certain stage of the development of capitalism. A crucial difference is
that "in the case of a cooperative factory, the antithetical character of the
supervisory work disappears, since the manager is paid by the workers
instead of representing capital in opposition to them".[41] Nevertheless, "the
cooperative factories run by workers themselves are, within the old form,
the first example of the emergence of a new form, even though they naturally reproduce in all cases, in their present organization, all the defects of
the existing system, and must reproduce them".[42] For Marx, freedom in
the realm of natural necessity

> can consist only in this, that socialized man, the associated producers, gov-
> ern the human metabolism with nature in a rational way, bringing it under
> their collective control instead of being dominated by it as a blind power;
> accomplishing it with the least expenditure of energy and in conditions most
> worthy and appropriate for their human nature. But this always remains a
> realm of necessity. The true realm of freedom, the development of human
> powers as an end in itself, begins beyond it, though it can only flourish with
> this realm of necessity as its basis.[43]

The true realm of freedom cannot be achieved unless the realm of necessity falls under the actual control of associated producers, beyond mechanisms of economic or political domination. This cannot be accomplished
within the wage system[44] or through market economy,[45] or on the basis of
centralized state control. This captures the essence of what Marx called a
"society of free and associated producers".[46]

Friedrich Engels (1820–1895)

Engels published a series of articles entitled *The Housing Question*
(1872–1873) as a critical intervention in the debate about the housing
shortage in the major industrial cities. The text criticized the schemes

[40] Ibid., 511.
[41] Ibid., 512.
[42] Ibid., 571.
[43] Ibid., 959.
[44] Marx, "Marginal Notes on the Programme of The German Workers' Party," 92.
[45] Karl Marx, *Capital*, Vol. II (London: Penguin Classics, 1992), 390, 434.
[46] Karl Marx, *Theories of Surplus Value (Part 3)* (Moscow: Progress Publishers, 1971), 157.

proposed by Proudhonian and Lassallean socialists regarding the solution to the housing crisis as insufficient to transform the capitalist social relation and, therefore, to address the root cause of the problem. In the last part, he countered the Proudhonist "redemption" scheme,[47] as characterized in Arthur Mülberger's writings, with respect to the seizure of the means of production. He argued that

> the "actual seizure" of all the instrument of labour, the taking possession of the industry as a whole by the working people, is the exact opposite of the Proudhonist "redemption". In the latter case, the individual worker becomes the owner of dwelling, the personal farm, the instrument of labour, in the former case, the "working people" remain the collective owner of the houses, factories and instruments of labour, and will hardly permit their use, at least during a transitional period, by individuals or associations without compensation for the cost. In the same way, the abolition of property in land is not the abolition of ground rent but its transfer, if in a modified form, to society. The actual seizure of all the instruments of labour by the working people, therefore, does not at all preclude the retention of rent relations.[48]

Some of the most substantive discussions relevant to the idea of "workers' control" in Engels in this period are found in Part III of *Anti-Dühring: Herr Eugen Dühring's Revolution in Science* (1878).[49] Like Marx, Engels was adamant in his critique of Lassallean state socialism in using the existing state machinery to fundamentally transform the capitalist social relation.[50] He argued that

---

[47] Engels defined the Proudhonian notion of "redemption" as follows: "the abolition of rented dwellings is proclaimed a necessity, and couched in the form of a demand that every tenant be turned into the owner of his dwelling". They proposed that this would be done by fully compensating the previous house owner and the occupants (i.e. the previous tenant) would continue to pay the equivalent amount of the previous rent annually to the society in return for the possession of the house. According to Mülberger (as quoted by Engels), this entailed that "society ... transforms itself in this way into a totality of free and independent owners of dwelling". Frederick Engels, "The Housing Question," in MECW (London: Lawrence & Wishart, 1988), 23: 327.

[48] Ibid., 386.

[49] Part of the book, which includes much of the discussion presented here, was published separately in 1880 under the title *Socialism: Utopian and Scientific.*

[50] Echoing Marx, Engels said in his preface to the 1888 English edition of *Communist Manifesto* that the political programme of the Manifesto "has in some details become antiquated". This was because the experience of the Paris Commune has proven that "the working class cannot simply lay hold of the ready-made state machinery, and wield it for its own

the transformation, either into joint-stock companies, or into state owner-ship, does not do away with the capitalistic nature of the productive forces. [...] The modern state, no matter what its form, is essentially a capitalist machine, the state of the capitalists, the ideal personification of the total national capital. The more it proceeds to the taking over of productive forces, the more does it actually become the national capitalist, the more citizens does it exploit. The workers remain wage-workers—proletarians. The capitalist relation is not done away with. It is rather brought to a head. But, brought to a head, it topples over.[51]

This essentially rejects nationalization as a revolutionary strategy. However, the state ownership of productive forces does not offer a solution, "con-cealed within it are the technical conditions that form the elements of that solution".[52] As for the solution, he wrote that it

can only consist in the practical recognition of the social nature of the mod-ern forces of production, and therefore in the harmonising of the modes of production, appropriation, and exchange with the socialised character of the means of production. And this can only come about by society openly and directly taking possession of the productive forces which have outgrown all control except that of society as a whole.[53]

Therefore, the solution lies only through socialization of means of pro-duction, in the sense of the society (not the "state") having open and direct (not conditional or indirect) control. It is within such an arrange-ment that "at last, [ ] the real nature of the productive forces of today, the social anarchy of production gives place to a social regulation of produc-tion upon a definite plan, according to the needs of the community and of each individual".[54] Note that Engels did not foresee a substitution of the social anarchy of production by a state-planned economy but a socially regulated one that is for the benefit not just of the community as a whole but also of each individual.

purpose". Frederick Engels, "Preface to the 1888 English Edition of the *Manifesto of the Communist Party*," in MECW (London: Lawrence & Wishart, 1988), 26: 518.
[51] Frederick Engels, "*Anti-Dühring*," in MECW (London: Lawrence & Wishart, 1988), 25: 265–6.
[52] Ibid., 266.
[53] Ibid.
[54] Ibid., 267.

Regarding the revolutionary process of such transformation, he wrote that "the proletariat seizes political power and turns the means of production in the first instance into state property. But in doing this, it abolishes itself as proletariat, abolishes all class distinctions and class antagonisms, abolishes also the state as state".[55] However, contrary to those who interpreted this as validating a (long) transitional period in which the workers' state in its capacity as the possessor of the means of production remains until it "naturally" withers away, it is crucial to note that he also stated that "[t]he first act by virtue of which the state really constitutes itself [as] the representative of the whole of society—the taking possession of the means of production in the name of society—this is, at the same time, its last independent act as a state".[56] It is, hence, its first and last act as a state after which its interference in the social relation becomes progressively superfluous until "the government of persons is replaced by the administrative of things".[57]Afterwards, "now under the dominion and control of man", "[t]he laws of his own social action, hitherto standing face to face with man as laws of nature foreign to, and dominating him, will then be used with full understanding, and so [be] mastered by him".[58] Such a control over social forces that govern human existence would at last usher the realm of freedom.

Social domination is not limited to the state. Engels saw the capitalist market competition as another subjugating force. In the same text, Engels criticized Dühring's idea of a federation of economic communes in which market competition between them, conditioned upon the freedom of movement of people between different communes, was preserved. Dühring distinguished this from the cooperative ownership of the workers' association which he believed "would not exclude material competition and even the exploitation of wage-labour".[59] In a discussion that resembles a critique of market socialism, Engels argued that Dühring's scheme preserved effective competition between different communes so that "things are removed from the sphere of competition, but men remain subject to it".[60]

---

[55] Ibid.
[56] Ibid.
[57] Ibid., 268.
[58] Ibid., 270.
[59] As quoted in Ibid., 274.
[60] Ibid., 275.

In his introduction to Marx's *The Civil War in France* (1891), Engels interpreted the shortcomings and confusions of the Commune in terms of its political and economic characters respectively based on the dominance of Proudhonians and Blanquists among the French working class.[61] He stated, for example, that, with the exception of associations in large industries, Proudhonians saw associations as "sterile, even harmful, because it was a fetter on the freedom of the worker".[62] But since, by the time of the Commune, there was a massive shift towards large-scale industries in France,

> by far the most important decree of the Commune instituted an organisation of large-scale industry and even of manufacture which was not only to be based on the association of the workers in each factory, but also to combine all these associations in one great union; in short, an organisation which, as Marx quite rightly says in *The Civil War*, must necessarily have led in the end to communism, that is to say, the direct opposite of the Proudhon doctrine.[63]

He rejects the Blanquist revolutionary strategy based on small, highly disciplined groups of men, organized in strictly centralized groups, "not only to seize the helm of state, but also by a display of great, ruthless energy, to maintain power until they succeeded in sweeping the mass of the people into the revolution and ranging them round the small band of leaders". He argued that this profoundly contradicts the political form of society envisioned by the Commune.

> In all its proclamations to the French in the provinces, it appealed to them to form a free federation of all French Communes with Paris, a national organisation which for the first time was really to be created by the nation itself. It was precisely the oppressing power of the former centralised government, army, political police, bureaucracy, which Napoleon had created in 1798 and which since then had been taken over by every new government as a welcome instrument and used against its opponents—it was precisely this power which was to fall everywhere, just as it had already fallen in Paris.[64]

---

[61] Frederick Engels, "Introduction to Karl Marx's *The Civil War in France*," in MECW (London: Lawrence & Wishart, 1988), 27: 185.

[62] Ibid., 188.

[63] Ibid.

[64] Ibid., 188–9.

Hence, by drawing attention to the contradictions between the actual requirements of the movement and the formal orientations of these two ideologies, Engels highlighted the natural tendency of an emancipatory movement such as the Commune towards coordinated associations at all productive levels to freely manage the society.

Engels went on to make sense of the radical measures that the Commune took such as recallability as a way "not to lose against its only just conquered supremacy"[65] by subverting the measures that were used to undermine their power. The Commune took the recallability and capping wages in order to disrupt the historical transformation of the state and its organs "from servants of society into masters of society".[66] In opposition to the "superstitious belief" common among Germans regarding the state as the "'realisation of the idea', or the Kingdom of God on Earth",[67] Engels argued that

> the state is nothing but a machine for the oppression of one class by another, and indeed in the democratic republic no less than in the monarchy; at best an evil inherited by the proletariat after its victorious struggle for class supremacy, whose worst sides the victorious proletariat, just like the Commune, cannot avoid having to lop off at once as much as possible until such time as a generation reared in new, free social conditions is able to throw the entire lumber of the state on the scrap heap.[68]

In this sense, Engels saw the notion of the dictatorship of the proletariat exemplified in the Paris Commune.

Engels distinguished such self-government from various co-determination schemes. He wrote a critique on the draft of the Erfurt Programme, which was to replace the Gotha Programme as the core programme of the SPD. While raising caution in presenting details regarding the exact form of the self-governing structure in a short document such as the Erfurt Programme, Engels recommended adding the following point: "Complete self-government in the provinces, districts and communes through officials elected by universal suffrage. The abolition of all local and provincial authorities appointed by the state."[69] Regarding the question of regulation of industries, he said against co-determination-type models that

[65] Ibid., 189.
[66] Ibid., 190.
[67] Ibid.
[68] Ibid.
[69] Frederick Engels, "A Critique of the Draft Social-Democratic Programme of 1891," in MECW (London: Lawrence & Wishart, 1988), 27: 229.

we would be taken in good and proper by labour chambers made up half of workers and half of entrepreneurs. For years to come, the entrepreneurs would always have a majority, for only a single black sheep among the workers would be needed to achieve this. If it is not agreed upon that in cases of conflict both halves express separate opinions, it would be much better to have a chamber of entrepreneurs and in addition an independent chamber of workers.[70]

Engels shared the key elements of Marx's understanding of "workers' control" and pushed them forward in his writings during and after Marx's death. His thoughts were surely affected but not hampered by the significant developments in the socialist movement in Germany and internationally, especially after the relaxation of the anti-socialist laws in Germany and the founding of the Second International. Nevertheless, Engels remained committed to the idea of "workers' control" as the key pillar of an emancipatory socialist vision.

William Morris (1834–1896)

Morris was one of the earliest British Marxists who, with the support of Engels, co-founded the Socialist League in 1885 after his break from the Social Democratic Federation (SDF).[71] Before the clashes with the founder of the Social Democratic Federation, Henry Hyndman, Morris co-authored a piece with him called *A Summary of the Principle Socialism* (1884). Perhaps under the influence of Hyndman, the state played a more central role in this piece than in the later writings of Morris. Seemingly equating the state with the people as a whole, they called for

the immediate management and ownership of the railways by the state, so that in land communications of the country, [it] may be under the control of the people at large, and carried on for their benefit, regard

[70] Ibid., 230.

[71] The question as to whether William Morris should be considered as a "Marxist" is rather contentious (cf. E. P. Thompson, *William Morris: From Romantic to Revolutionary* (New York: Pantheon Books, 1976); G. D. H. Cole, *Socialist Thought. Marxism and Anarchism, 1850–1890* (London: Macmillan, 1954), 419; Florence Boos and William Boos, "The Utopian Communism of William Morris," *History of Political Thought 7*, no. 3 (1986)). Given the broad scope of Marxism adapted in this chapter that includes libertarian interpretations, we can safely categorize Morris under this banner.

being had to the full remuneration of the labour of all who are engaged in the work of transport.[72]

This, however, remains uncritical of the limits of nationalization and the actual content of the purported "control" by "the people".

In the *Manifesto of the Socialist League* (1885), he and his co-author E. Belfort Bax wrote that "the workers, although they produce all the wealth of society, have no control over its production or distribution".[73] The programme condemned both nationalization and state socialism "whose aim it would be to make concessions to the working class while leaving the present system of capital and wages still in operation".[74] In the second edition of the *Manifesto*, he weighed on the need for the socialists to gain political power, not in the sense of "exercise of the franchise, or even the fullest development of representative system", but a "direct control by the people of the whole administration of the community, whatever the ultimate destiny of that administration is to be".[75] He believed that the practical steps towards communism would create the opportunity to establish "the decentralized voluntary organization of production".[76]

In *Socialism from the Root Up* (1888), Morris envisioned the future social organization whose political aspect comprises "an organized body of communities, each carrying on its own affairs, but unified by a delegated federal body, whose function would be the guardianship of the acknowledged principles of society".[77]

One of the most intriguing expressions of the idea of "workers' control" in Morris is found in his critique of Edward Bellamy's extremely popular book *Looking Backward*, published in 1888. Morris criticized

---

[72] William Morris and H. M. Hyndman, *A Summary of Principles of Socialism* (London: The Modern Press, 1884), 58; reproduced in David Reisman, ed., *Democratic Socialism in Britain: Classic Texts in Economic and Political Thought 1825–1952* (London: Pickering & Chatto, 1996), 3.

[73] William Morris and E. Belfort Bax, *The Manifesto of The Socialist League* (London: Socialist League Office, 1885), 5; reproduced in Reisman, *Democratic Socialism in Britain*.

[74] Ibid., 7.

[75] William Morris and E. Belfort Bax, "The Manifesto of The Socialist League—Second Edition," William Morris Internet Archive. www.marxists.org/archive/morris/works/1885/manifst2.htm.

[76] Ibid.

[77] William Morris, "Socialism from the Root Up," in *Political Writings: Contributions to Justice and Commonwealth 1883–1890*, ed. Nicholas Salmon (Bristol: Thoemmes Press, 1994), 612.

Bellamy's vision of a socialist society that was "satisfied with modern civilization" and under centralized state control. This is why Bellamy had to "put forward his scheme of the organization of life; which is organized with a vengeance. His scheme may be described as State Communism, worked by the very extreme of national centralization".[78] Morris believed that such an overarching state is alienating for the individual. Instead,

> it will be necessary for the unit of administration to be small enough for every citizen to feel himself responsible for its details, and be interested in them [or in] that individual; that man cannot shuffle off the business of life on to the shoulders of an abstraction called the State, but must deal with it in conscious association with each other.[79]

For Morris, the aim of communism is as much to nurture "variety of life" as to facilitate the equality of conditions in order to bring about the realm of freedom.[80]

Paul Lafargue (1842–1911)

Lafargue, the co-founder of the Federated Socialist Workers' party of France in 1880, was one of the earliest Marxist theoreticians in France (and Spain) who played a key role in reshaping the French workers' movement after the Commune. In *Socialism and Nationalization* (1882), he called nationalization of certain industries "socialism for the capitalists", marking "the last form of capitalist exploration".[81] He gave the example of nationalization of some industries such as electric telegraph or the press as a way to keep the sector profitable for the speculators while maintaining control of the industries in the hands of the capitalists. He remarked that "in capitalist society a private industry only becomes a State service in order to better serve the interest of the bourgeoisie. [...] The state, by centralising administration, lessens the general charges; it runs the service at a smaller cost".[82] He believed that nationalization would open up the state to corruption. As for whether such measures would simplify the

---

[78] William Morris, "Looking Backward," in *Political Writings of William Morris*, ed. A. L. Morton (London: Lawrence and Wishart, 1984), 250.

[79] Ibid., 253.

[80] Ibid.

[81] Paul Lafargue, "Socialism and Nationalisation," *Socialist Standard* (February 1912): 43.

[82] Ibid.

process of expropriation for the workers' party, he argued that the danger would by far outweigh the advantages.

Although the first revolutionary act, according to Lafargue, must be to cease the central power as the precondition for the workers' party to begin the process of economic expropriation, "those who busy themselves with State-Socialism, that is to say, those who demand the nationalisation or municipalisation of certain services, do not trouble at all about the lot of the workers engaged in them. [...] The workshops of the State and municipality are prisons quite as bad as private workshops, if not worse [...] they are bent beneath an authority that is more powerfully hierarchic; they can neither combine nor strike". After a period of revolutionary transition during which the workers' government would increase its administrative and economic capacity, "with the needs of consumption and the powers of production scientifically calculated, consumption as well as production will be free".

In *Our Goal* (1889), Lafargue conceived of the solution to the "situation created by capitalist centralization" in the socialists' demand that

> all the centralized labor instruments, such as the railroads, factories, textile works, mines, large farming properties, banks, etc. become national property and be given over to the associated workers, who will operate them with a contract laying out conditions, not for the profit of a few capitalists, donothings and thieves, but for the profit of the entire nation.[83]

The emphasis on the transfer of the means of production to the associated producers is the key difference between this demand and that of state socialism. In other words, "if the industries already taken over by the state [...] don't fulfill the socialist ideal, it's because they aren't run by the associated workers in the interests of the nation, but by functionaries in a budgetary interest".[84]

Jules Guesde (1845–1922)

Guesde, a key figure in the early propagation of Marxism in France, met with Marx in London in 1880 and drafted the programme of the French Workers' Party. The Preamble, which according to Engels was dictated to

[83] Paul Lafargue, "Our Goal," Paul Lafargue Internet Archive. www.marxists.org/archive/lafargue/1899/04/our-goal.htm.

[84] Ibid.

Guesde,[85] distinguished between private and collective properties and argued that the former was increasingly eliminated by industrial progress as the latter was further constituted by the very development of capitalism. However, the collective appropriation could only come about by the revolution action of the proletariat "organized in a distinct political party".[86] The Preamble further recognized that the movement for the emancipation of the working class must aim at "the political and economic expropriation of the capitalist class and the return to community of all the means of production".[87] In the political section, the Programme demanded "the Commune to be master of its administration and its policing".[88] In the economic section, it demanded "prohibition of all interference by employers in the administration of workers' friendly societies, provident societies, etc., which are returned to the exclusive control of the workers".[89]

Guesde wrote in *The Social Problem and Its Solution* (1905) that

> it is only collectively that the workers, comprising the entire nation, can and ought to possess the means of wealth (mines, railways, canals, factories, etc.) socially operated. Capitalist evolution itself supplies the necessary elements, material and intellectual, of this appropriation and of this production by and for society now become a vast co-operative commonwealth.[90]

He emphasized the role of the state in this process, albeit not in its repressive form, arguing that

> [t]his economic expropriation—which would allow [] the expropriated full participation in the benefits accruing from social appropriation—must be preceded by a political expropriation, the establishment of the Socialist

---

[85] Fredrich Engels, "Engels to Eduard Bernstein," in MECW (London: Lawrence & Wishart, 1988), 46: 147.

According to a letter from Engels to Eduard Bernstein (25 October 1881), the theme to the programme was dictated to Guesde in the presence of Engels and Paul Lafargue.

[86] Jules Guesde and Karl Marx, "The Programme of the Parti Ouvrier," Jules Guesde Internet Archive. www.marxists.org/archive/marx/works/1880/05/parti-ouvrier.htm. This is the full translation of the programme and, in important ways, it is different from the translation of the Preamble that is provided in MECW, Vol. 24, 340.

[87] Ibid.

[88] Ibid.

[89] Ibid.

[90] Jules Guesde, "The Social Problem and Its Solution," Jules Guesde Internet Archive. www.marxists.org/archive/guesde/1905/jan/x01.htm

Republic being only realisable by a proletariat master of the State and acting in conformity with the law, since it itself will be and make the law.[91]

However, the question as to whether this "proletariat master of the State" indicates the class origin of the state administrators or the fundamental character of the administrative structure is unclear.

Daniel De Leon (1852–1914)

De Leon was already a Marxist before joining the Socialist Labor Party of America (SLP) in 1890. Writing soon after the SLP's break from the Knight of Labour and the formation of The Socialist Trade and Labor Alliance in 1895, De Leon defined socialism, in *Reform or Revolution* (1896), on the basis of the common ownership of the means of production, abolition of wage system, and the end of class society in which the state in its repressive form has withered away. However, he emphasized the importance of the coordinating role of the state without which no harmony can be achieved. Without going into its organizational structure, he argued that "[the society] needs this central directing authority" so the "cooperative commonwealth" with all its divisions of labour can work harmoniously.[92] He clearly distanced himself from the anti-political left by emphasizing that the economic and political issues and struggles cannot be separated and must be simultaneously tackled.

His position began to shift towards Industrial Unionism from 1904 onwards. In *The Burning Question of Trade Unionism* (1904), he saw some truths in both pro- and anti-union positions but criticized both for failing to understand the transformative potential of unions because they limit their vision to the present form of unions. He instead advocated for industrial unionism. He extended his criticism to the socialist strategy towards unions by arguing that "unless the political aspect of the labour movement is grasped, Socialism will never triumph; and that unless its trade union aspect is grasped, the day of its triumph will be the day of its defeat".[93] For him, it was in the political aspect of unionism that the spell of revolution lay.

---

[91] Ibid.

[92] Daniel De Leon, "Reform or Revolution," in *Daniel De Leon: Speeches and Editorials* (New York: New York Labor News, 1940), 7–8.

[93] Daniel De Leon, *The Burning Question of Trade Unionism* (New York City: National Executive Committee Socialist Labour Party, 1904), 27.

His involvement with the founding of the Industrial Workers of the World (IWW), albeit tenuous, radicalized his political view on the role of the industrial union. His anti-state stance became more pronounced in *Socialist Reconstruction of Society* (1905):

> Capitalist society requires the political State: accordingly, its economics translate themselves into political tenets; Socialist society, on the contrary, knows nothing of the political State: in Socialist society the political State is a thing of the past, either withered out of existence by disuse or amputated according to as circumstances may dictate.[94]

He linked that with the emergence of the industrial organization of the working class both as the economic foundation of the future society and the political movement to hollow out the state. Therefore, he identified the goal of the method of political struggle at the ballot as a "purely destructive" weapon.[95]

In *Industrialism* (1906), he argued that socialism is not the simple overthrow of private ownership and its replacement with public or state ownership. "Socialism is that social system under which the necessaries of production are owned, controlled, and administered by the people, for the people, and under which, accordingly, the cause of political and economic despotism having been abolished, class rule is at the end."[96] Accordingly, industrialism is an economic organization of the whole of the working class under one big union.[97]

The idea of "workers' control" in the trajectory of De Leon's thought was quite akin to the syndicalist notions. However, he insisted on distinguishing the position of Industrial Unionism from the syndicalist inclination towards direct action and frontal attack against the state, which he thought was very particular to the European context.[98] The goal of Industrial Unionism was "the substitution of the political state with the industrial government", aiming at "a democratically centralized govern-

[94] Daniel De Leon, *Socialist Reconstruction of Society: The Industrial Vote* (New York: Socialist Labor Party, 1925), 31.

[95] Ibid., 36. De Leon ran unsuccessfully for public office several times in the 1890s and the 1900s.

[96] Daniel De Leon, "Industrialism," in *Industrial Unionism: Selected Editorial* (New York: National Executive Committee Socialist Labor Party, 1920), 35.

[97] Ibid.

[98] Daniel De Leon, "'Syndicalism'", *Industrial Unionism: Selected Editorial* (New York: National Executive Committee Socialist Labor Party, 1920), 46–7.

ment, accompanied by the democratically requisite 'local self-rule'".[99]
Therefore, Industrial Unionism grasps the chief principle of the government to be "the central and local administrative authorities of the productive capabilities of the people".[100]

Karl Kautsky (1854–1938)

Kautsky was the leading Marxist theorist of the SPD. In *State Socialism* (1881) and *The Abolition of the State* (1881), he argued that, even though it might seem that the precondition for the emancipation of the proletariat is the abolition of the state, the proletariat needed the power of the state to preserve its class rule by disintegrating the other classes. He concluded by saying that "the abolition of the government and the state are not the first act of the proletariat revolution but the last consequence of this".[101] Therefore, the task of the proletariat was "not to destroy, but to conquer the state. The next goal of the proletariat consists of becoming the ruling class. Everything else must be subordinated to this purpose".[102]

In *The Free Society* (1882), his vision had a pronouncedly nationalistic angle. He noted that "not the prosperity of the individual, not the prosperity of the commune, the prosperity of the nation will be the highest goal of the free society to which everything else has to submit itself".[103] Regarding the structure of such free society, he said that it "will be a federation of nations and not of groups or communes; whose production will be left neither to free choice no[r] to the spontaneous formation of groups, no[r] even to sheer force of social attraction; instead, production will be placed under the direction of a well-organized administration".[104]

Kautsky was one of the leading architects of the Erfurt Programme (along with Eduard Bernstein and August Bebel). In a book entitled *Class Struggle* (1892), Kautsky elaborated on the Erfurt Programme. He recognized the state as having the requisite dimensions for the establishment of the "socialist

[99] Daniel De Leon, "Industrial Unionism," *Industrial Unionism: Selected Editorial* (New York: National Executive Committee Socialist Labor Party, 1920), 64.
[100] Ibid.
[101] Karl Kautsky, "Die Abschaffung des Staates," *Der Sozialdemokrat*, no. 51 (1881); translation by Noa Rodman available at https://libcom.org/library/abolition-state-karl-kautsky.
[102] Ibid.
[103] Karl Kautsky, "The Free Society," Karl Kautsky Internet Archive. www.marxists.org/archive/kautsky/1881/state/3-freesoc.htm.
[104] Ibid.

or co-operative commonwealth", which coexisted with the nation.[105] He envisioned a society in which the means of production in large industries, which are generally compatible with cooperative production, are owned by the state while leaving the small-scale production in the realm of private ownership. His vision of a socialist society in this writing shows profound incompatibilities with the idea of "workers' control". He stated that

> [i]t is true that socialist production is irreconcilable with the full freedom of labor, that is, with the freedom of the labor to work when, where, and how he wills. But this freedom of labor is irreconcilable with any systematic, co-operative form of labor, whether the form be capitalist or socialist.[106]

Finally, in such a socialist society, "where all the means of production are in a single hand, there is but one employer, [and] to change [jobs] is impossible".[107]

In *On the Day after the Social Revolution* (1902), he delved into some of the issues that might arise shortly after the outbreak of the revolution. Regarding the process of expropriation, he did not rule out the possibility of capitalists selling their enterprises directly to the workers who worked there so that they could operate them cooperatively. But he also suggested that "capital would find its most extensive and generous purchaser in the State and municipalities and for this very reason the majority of the industries could pass into the possession of the states and municipalities".[108] Furthermore, regarding the question of how to keep the workers in "labour" after the revolution, he relied on a "democratic discipline" of the kind that a union uses during a strike. He preserved a level of variation with respect to the organization of labour in different industries. In industries such as the railways,

> the democratic organization can be so formed that laborers choose delegates, who will constitute a sort of parliament, which will fix the conditions of labor and control for government of the bureaucratic machinery. Other industries can be given over to the direction of the unions, and others again can be operated co-operatively.[109]

Furthermore, he emphasized the impossibility of the abolition of money and wages.

---

[105] Karl Kautsky, *Class Struggle (Erfurt Program)*, trans. William E. Bohn (Chicago: Charles H. Kerr & Company, 1910).

[106] Ibid., 149.

[107] Ibid., 150.

[108] Karl Kautsky, *The Social Revolution*, trans. A. M. and May Wood Simon (Chicago: Charles H. Kerr & Company, 1916), 113.

[109] Ibid., 127.

James Connolly (1868–1916)

Connolly, one of the founding members of the Irish Socialist Republican Party (ISRP), was keenly aware of the importance of "workers' control" within socialism. In a remarkable passage, he argued in *State Monopoly Versus Socialism* (1899) that "Socialism properly implies above all things the co-operative control by the workers of the machinery of production; without this co-operative control the public ownership by the State is not Socialism—it is only State capitalism".[110] He separated ownership from control and argued that "the ownership by the State of all the land and materials for labour, combined with the co-operative control by the workers of such land and materials, would be Socialism".[111]

In *Parliamentary Democracy* (1900), he contrasted the parliamentary democracy under capitalism that merely gives workers the right to choose their masters with the socialist society in which

> the freedom of the revolutionist will change the choice of rulers which we have today into the choice of administrators of laws voted upon directly by the people; and will also substitute for the choice of masters (capitalists) the appointment of reliable public servants under direct public control. That will mean true democracy—the industrial democracy of the Socialist Republic.[112]

After his clashes with E. W. Stewart over trade union and electoral strategies of the ISRP and emigration to the United States in 1904, Connolly founded the Irish Socialist Federation (ISF) in New York in 1907. By this time, Connolly's thoughts were deeply influenced by his involvement with the IWW. He declared the neutrality of the ISF towards existing political parties while continuing the revolutionary fight at the economic level through the economic organizations of the IWW. He advocated for the formation of a new political party of the workers by the IWW to unify the revolutionary socialist forces.[113]

Similar to De Leon, Connolly argued that the "political institutions are not adapted to the administration of industry. Only industrial organisations are adapted to the administration of a co-operative commonwealth

---

[110] James Connolly, "State Monopoly versus Socialism," *The Workers' Republic* 2, no. 3 (10 June 1899): 5.

[111] Ibid.

[112] James Connolly, "Parliamentary Democracy," *The Workers' Republic* 4, no. 5 (22 September 1900): 6.

[113] James Connolly, "A Political Party of the Workers," *The Harp* 1, no. 1 (1908): 9–10.

that we are working for".[114] Instead of the territorially based political institutions that compose the coercive forces of capital,

> the workers in the shops and factories will organize themselves into unions, each union comprising all the workers at a given industry; that said [the] union will democratically control the workshop life of its own industry, electing all foremen etc., and regulating the routine of labour in that industry in subordination to the needs of society in general.[115]

Hence, for Connolly, the structure of the new society necessarily begins in the workshops and upwardly cascades to the rest of the industrial organization until "it reaches the culminating point of national executive power and direction".[116] The top level would be "administrated" by "a committee of experts elected from the industries and professions of the lands".[117] This conception of socialism

> destroys at one blow all the fears of a bureaucratic State, ruling and ordering the lives of every individual from above, and thus gives assurance that the social order of the future will be an extension of the freedom of the individual, and not the suppression of it. In short, it blends the fullest democratic control with the most absolute expert supervision.[118]

Although his ideas, like those of De Leon, came close to syndicalism, he insisted, in *Political Action* (1908), that industrial organizations should coexist with a pluralist socialist party that embraced "all shades and conceptions of socialist political thought".[119] He further clarified his conception of socialist political parties, where he defined two types of socialist parties: one made up of purely revolutionary individuals with clear ideological orientation and understanding of the economics of capital, and another, whose primary role is to educate and direct the class consciousness towards the revolutionary line. He believed that even though the second type ran the risk of confusion, the first had a tendency towards "dictation and despotism" that sought to "purify its ranks by expulsion".[120]

---

[114] James Connolly, *Socialism Made Easy* (Glasgow: Socialist Labour Press, 1917), 15.
[115] Ibid.
[116] Ibid.
[117] Ibid.
[118] Ibid.
[119] James Connolly, "Political Action," *The Harp* 1, no. 7 (July 1908): 7.
[120] Ibid., 6.

Vladimir Lenin (1870–1924)

It is difficult to talk positively about the ideas of Lenin in this period regarding the notion of "workers' control". Even though in *Draft and Explanation of a Programme of Social-Democratic Party* (1895–1896), he echoed Marx in that "the emancipation of the workers must be the act of the working class itself",[121] most of his writings in this period carried a rather patronizing view of the working class.

In one of his most famous writings, *What Is to Be Done?* (1902), Lenin expressed some of his most troubling statements about the revolutionary potential of the working class. He wrote that

> there could not have been Social-Democratic consciousness among the workers. It would have to be brought to them from without. The history of all countries shows that the working class, exclusively by its own effort, is able to develop only trade union consciousness. ... The theory of socialism, however, grew out of the philosophical, historical, and economic theories elaborated by educated representatives of the propertied classes, by intellectuals.[122]

Against the spontaneous actions of the masses, he argued that such a movement "leads to its subordination to bourgeois ideology ... for the spontaneous working-class movement is trade-unionism ... and trade-unionism means the ideological enslavement of the workers by the bourgeoisie".[123] His intention was not to undermine mass movement as such but to define the immediate task in the presence of such movement not in terms of "bowing to the spontaneity of this movement; i.e. reducing the role of the Social-Democracy to mere subservience to the working class movement as such".[124] Instead, he considered such mass movements at any given time to present the party with new theoretical, political, and organizational tasks to grapple with. Only through the activities of Social Democracy, whose task was to enter among the masses as "theoreticians,

---

[121] Vladimir Lenin, "Draft and Explanation of a Programme for the Social-Democratic Party," in Lenin Collected Works (London: Lawrence & Wishart, 1962), 2: 97.

[122] Vladimir Lenin, "What Is to Be Done?", in Lenin Collected Works (London: Lawrence & Wishart, 1961), 5: 375. Later in the same document, he elaborated on this idea with regard to class political consciousness, saying it "can be brought to the workers only from without, that is, only from outside the economic struggle, from outside the sphere of relations between workers and employers"; ibid., 422.

[123] Ibid., 384.

[124] Ibid., 390.

as propagandist, as agitators, and as organizers"[125] and whose relation to the economic struggle of the working class was one of "executive groups",[126] that we could ensure "the stability of the movement as a whole and carry out the aims both of Social-Democracy and of trade unions proper".[127] On the other hand, if we "begin with a broad workers' organization, which is supposedly most 'accessible' to the masses ... we shall achieve neither the one aim nor the other".[128]

In an article published in February 1905 entitled "Two Tactics", Lenin maintained his criticism of the position that assumed a subordinate and pliable position of the party to the movement. He held that "[i]t was in the name of independent activity of the proletariat that the 'organization-as-process' theory was invented, a theory that justified disorganization and glorified the anarchism of the intellectuals".[129] He distinguished between two types of independent activity of the proletariat: one that "possessed of revolutionary initiative" and another "that is undeveloped and is held in Leading-strings".[130] In June of that year, he published *A New Revolutionary Workers' Association* (1905) in which he analysed the impact of the Russian Liberation Union. The group sought to organize militia to overthrow the autocracy and establish a constitutional assembly whose structure would consist only of "groups of workers (mainly from one and the same workshop); (2) factory councils; (3) district meetings; and (4) committees of the Workers' Union".[131] Lenin believed that "by fighting for freedom without close connection with the proletarian struggle for socialism" such independent non-party organizations could "play a role that objectively amounts to promoting the interests of bourgeoisie".[132]

Similarly, in *Two Tactics of Social-Democracy in the Democratic Revolution* (1905), he called the Social Revolutionary Party's (SR) use of the term "Revolutionary Communes" revolutionary phrase-mongering since it disguises the errors and shortcomings of an experience (possibly the Paris Commune) in the distant past. His issue with the use of the term as by the

---

[125] Ibid., 425.

[126] Ibid., 457.

[127] Ibid., 460.

[128] Ibid.

[129] Vladimir Lenin, "Two Tactics," in *Lenin Collected Works* (London: Lawrence & Wishart, 1962), 8: 149.

[130] Ibid., 155.

[131] Vladimir Lenin, "A New Revolutionary Workers' Association," in *Lenin Collected Works* (London: Lawrence & Wishart, 1962), 8: 499.

[132] Ibid., 502.

SR was that it restricted its role to spreading the insurrection. However, Lenin insisted that such a revolutionary government would have other concrete administrative works to conduct, including a series of reforms.

Perhaps some of the most positive accounts by Lenin regarding "workers' control" can be found in his writings in the immediate aftermath of the 1905 Revolution. As he contemplated on the events of the 1905 Revolution in Russia, Lenin began to express more favourable statements about the political role of the Soviets and showed new directions in his thinking about the revolutionary potential of the working class. In *Our Tasks and the Soviet of Workers' Deputies* (1905), Lenin addressed the question of "how to divide, and how to combine the tasks of the Soviet and those of the Russian Social-Democratic Labour Party".[133] He argued that since the Soviet emerged as a result of the General Strike, which itself had both economic and political dimensions, the economic struggles could still be carried forward under a broad umbrella of political parties. With regard to the political dimension of the Soviet, he believed that it "should be regarded as the embryo of a provisional revolutionary government" and that it "should proclaim itself the provisional revolutionary government of the whole of Russia as early as possible, or should set up a provisional revolutionary government".[134] More than marking a fundamental change in Lenin's view on the revolutionary capacities of the working-class self-organization, it was meant to serve as a strategic appeal to meet the dire need for the formation of a political centre of gravity, sufficiently deep-rooted within the masses including the soldiers, the peasants, and the intelligentsia.

In the *Lessons of the Commune* (1908), Lenin reassessed the legacy of the Commune "as a splendid example of the unanimity with which the proletariat was able to accomplish the democratic tasks which the bourgeoisie could only proclaim".[135] He praised the Commune's actions saying that "without any particularly complex legislation, in a simple, straightforward manner, the proletariat, which had seized power, carried out the democratisation of the social system, abolished the bureaucracy, and made all official posts elective".[136] Its mistakes, according to Lenin, were that it did not seize the money capital from the banks and wage frontal assault on Versailles.

---

[133] Vladimir Lenin, "Our Tasks and the Soviet of Workers' Deputies," in *Lenin Collected Works* (London: Lawrence & Wishart, 1962), 10: 19.

[134] Ibid., 21.

[135] Vladimir Lenin, "Lessons of the Commune," in *Lenin Collected Works* (London: Lawrence & Wishart, 1962), 13, 476.

[136] Ibid.

Rosa Luxemburg (1871–1919)

Much of Luxemburg's political writings in this period is dedicated to a perceptive dissection of revolutionary actions. Furthermore, her characterization of capitalism as fundamentally anarchic limited her vision of radical possibilities of economic organization under socialism. Nevertheless, she always remained perceptively critical of various hurdles in the way of creative expression of the masses. Therefore, what we can get from Luxemburg's thought in this period is not so much the specificities of the idea of "workers' control" but a political philosophy of revolutionary praxis, firmly anchored on the spontaneous and creative potential of the masses, and fiercely against any structure that would come in the way of such actions.

In *Social Reform or Revolution* (1898), she acknowledged the significance of trade unions and parliamentary struggles to raise awareness and consciousness of the proletariat and organize them into a class. However, she cautioned that "if they are considered as instruments for the direct socialization of the capitalist economy, they lose not only their supposed effectiveness, but also cease to be a means of preparing the working class for the proletarian conquest of power".[137] She believed that achieving socialism through "an unbroken chair of continually growing reforms"[138] is a fantasy. Rather than automatically emerging out of the daily struggles of the working class, socialism is "the consequence of only the ever growing contradictions of capitalist economy and the comprehension by the working class of the unavoidability of the suppression of these contradictions through a social transformation".[139] The essence of the revolutionary praxis is "to recognize the direction of this development and then, in the political struggle to push its consequences to the extreme".[140]

However, her dedication to the SPD's mass party politics also limited her vision in some respects. In an important piece on the organizational question of the Russian Social Democracy, Luxemburg renounced the model of political organization based on "splintering, complete autonomy,

---

[137] Rosa Luxemburg, "Social Reform or Revolution," in *Rosa Luxemburg Reader*, ed. P. Hudis and K. B. Anderson (New York: Monthly Review Press, 2004), 141.
[138] Ibid.
[139] Ibid., 142.
[140] Ibid., 143.

and self-government for local organizations" as "the distinguishing feature of the burdensome and politically outmoded old organizational forms".[141] Instead, she called for a centralized mass party whose distinguishing character from Blanquist centralism is that it carries the "authoritative expression of the will of the conscious and militant vanguard of the workers; vis-à-vis the separated groups and individuals among them".[142] But particularly after the militant wave of strikes in 1905 and the Russian Revolution in that year, Luxemburg paid a lot of attention to the creative potential of spontaneous movements. In *Mass Action* (1911), she repeated her criticism of a party structure whose centralized form rested on a small party executive. Instead, she argued that "every step forward in the struggle for emancipation of the working class must at the same time mean a growing intellectual independence of its mass, its growing self-activity, self-determination, and initiative".[143] She saw the historical essence of the proletarian struggle in "the proletarian masses not needing 'leaders' in a bourgeois sense, that they are themselves leaders".[144]

In *The Mass Strike, Political Party and Trade Union* (1906), she argued that Social Democracy and syndicalism both assumed that the spontaneous will of the masses can be decided upon at will. On the contrary, she believed that this was a "historical phenomenon, which, at a given moment, could result from social conditions with historical inevitability".[145] Regarding the unforeseeable consequences of such spontaneous actions, she said that "even the relations of the worker to the employer are turned around since the January General Strike and the strikes of 1905 which followed upon it, the principle of the capitalist 'mastery of the house' is de facto abolished".[146] In fact, it is through apparently chaotic actions that "a feverish working organization" emerges.[147]

---

[141] Rosa Luxemburg, "Organizational Questions of Russian Social Democracy," in *Rosa Luxemburg Reader*, ed. P. Hudis and K. B. Anderson (New York: Monthly Review Press, 2004), 249–50.

[142] Ibid., 253.

[143] Rosa Luxemburg, "Mass Action," Rosa Luxemburg Internet Archive. www.marxists.org/archive/luxemburg/1911/08/29.htm.

[144] Ibid.

[145] Rosa Luxemburg, "The Mass Strike, Political Party and Trade Union," in *Rosa Luxemburg Reader*, ed. P. Hudis and K. B. Anderson (New York: Monthly Review Press, 2004), 170.

[146] Ibid., 186.

[147] Ibid.

Anton Pannekoek (1873–1960)

Although Pannekoek is known as one of the most prominent theorists of council communism, his writings prior to 1917 have a significantly different tone, very much revolving around the left wing of the SPD, albeit with his characteristic creativities. In his *Two Sorts of Reforms* (1908), he tried to carve out a third way between reformism and revolution by arguing for radical reformism as a revolutionary process. While empowering and radicalizing the workers, such radical reforms would prove unachievable within capitalism, making the need for a revolutionary transcendence evident. After achieving power, the working class must rapidly engage with the suppression of the cause of poverty through a socialization process by making the state machinery work in its interest. He continued this line of argument in his *Hope in the Future* (1912) where he maintained that those radical reforms resisted by the bourgeoisie and those measures that they fail to implement would radicalize the working class into a "peaceful and imperceptible passing of society to socialism".[148] In response to Kautsky's criticism of his *Two Sorts of Reforms*, Pannekoek clarified his position about the revolution further in *Marxist Theory and Revolutionary Tactics* (1912) by defining it as a *process*.[149]

In *Socialism and Anarchism* (1913), he presented the layout of the revolutionary transformation from capitalism to socialism. None of the chief characteristics of different phases of this transformation clearly speaks to the idea of "workers' control". Regarding the question of the state, the society would still require "an effective economic and carefully planned system of production and the avoidance of all useless waste of material and labour-power, in one word, organization".[150] In other words, the state "becomes a corporate body with purely economic function". Therefore, the political system after the victory of the proletariat "will be governed by the same principles which the workers now employed in their fighting organizations: equality of rights for all members, expression of the will of the whole in legal provisions and resolutions which each must obey, execution of the will of the majority by an executive".[151]

---

[148] Anton Pannekoek, "Hope in the Future," Anton Pannekoek Internet Archive. www.marxists.org/archive/pannekoe/1912/hope-in-future.htm.

[149] Such a process-oriented approach to revolution continued to play a central role in his thinking after his turn to council communism after 1917.

[150] Ibid., 127.

[151] Anton Pannekoek, "Socialism and Anarchism," *The New Review* 1, no. 5 (1913): 147.

He contrasted his view with both parliamentary socialism and syndical-ism in *Socialism and Labour Unionism* (1913), the former considering the work of other labour organizations such as unions unnecessary, and the latter believing that the working class is always already revolutionary and dismissing the crucial role of the party. Contrary to Industrial Unionists, Pannekoek argued that the labour union movement was revolutionary precisely insofar as it did not pursue revolutionary aims but focused on improving the working conditions and gathering the masses in great organizations.

IV. Concluding Remarks

The survey highlights a pattern in which the most prominent Marxist the-orists of this period did not in fact have as much to say about the notion of "workers' control" as the more "marginal" figures. A reason behind this is that much of the energy of the Marxist theorists in this period went into efforts to build lasting institutions to assert working-class power and to fight the most egregious aspects of capitalism and the state through day-to-day struggles. In the background of these preoccupations was the general tendency among Marxists to push the discussion of the forms of future society into the "day after the revolution". Therefore, contempla-tion on the notion of "workers' control" seemed insignificant. This was in sharp contrast with the general tendency among anarchists and syndicalists to engage in prefigurative politics that sought to reflect the foundations of the future society in its transformative practices here and now. This is an important reason why some of the lesser-known Marxist figures, especially those who had closer affinity to anarchist and syndicalist thoughts, are accentuated in the survey.

The unique contribution of Marx (and Engels, though not without tensions with respect to some of his writings and his interpretations of Marx) to this debate lies precisely in his staunch defence of those working-class movements that sought to increase the political capacities of the working class to carry out transformative processes and in his fierce cri-tique of their shortcomings in seeing those reforms as ends, while main-taining prefiguration as an essential part of the revolutionary process itself. This synthesis became clear to him after he encountered the experience of the Paris Commune and its prefigurative politics. The spirit behind his critique of the Gotha Programme regarding the tendency to postpone the abolition of the wage system, the capitalist market relations, and the capitalist form of the state to the day after the revolution rather than as part of the revolutionary programme of the party is such understanding of the importance of prefigurative politics. Such synthesis overcomes the tendency in socialist movements, which all-too-often become a reality, to sacrifice self-emancipation for creating the institutions of working-class power.

The events following the Russian and German Revolutions had profound effects on the theoretical understanding of "workers' control" within Marxist thoughts. They showed clearly the revolution's demand for a radical understanding of "workers' control" as the transformative basis of the future society. The thrust of these movements soon forced a major shift among the Marxist theoreticians. Profoundly different writings emerged from those experiences within the main canon of Marxism, at least for some time. Numerous articles, pamphlets, and books by Lenin, Kautsky, Luxemburg, Pannekoek, as well as Antonio Gramsci, Karl Korsch, Otto Rühle, Ernst Däumig, Max Adler, Otto Bauer, and Herman Gorter, directly engaged with the question of Soviets and councils in the process of revolutionary transformation. As the Russian Revolution began to lose some of its most emancipatory potential in the face of harsh post-war realities, certain political decisions by the Bolshevik leadership, as well as the failure of revolutionary attempts in Central and Western Europe, a new trend of Marxist thinkers formed what came to be known as "left-communism". It was within this tradition that much of the later writings on "workers' control" took place. This notion resurfaced during different phases, most notably during the "long 1960s" and again in the twenty-first century. After the collapse of the Soviet Union, there is once again room for rethinking and recovering such traditions which lay the ground for an emancipatory form of communism in which socialism and democracy are seen as an inseparable unity.

BIBLIOGRAPHY

Azzellini, Dario and Michael Kraft, eds. *The Class Strikes Back: Self-Organised Workers' Struggles in the Twenty-First Century*. Leiden: Brill, 2018.

Bartolini, Stefano. *The Political Mobilization of the European Left, 1860–1980: The Class Cleavage*. Cambridge: Cambridge University Press, 2000.

Berry, David and Constance Bantman, eds. *New Perspectives on Anarchism, Labour and Syndicalism: The Individual, the National and the Transnational*. Newcastle: Cambridge Scholars, 2010.

Boos, Florence and William Boos. "The Utopian Communism of William Morris." *History of Political Thought 7*, no. 3 (1986): 489–510.

Cole, G. D. H. *Socialist Thought: Marxism and Anarchism, 1850–1890.* London: Macmillan, 1954.

Connolly, James. "State Monopoly versus Socialism." *The Workers' Republic* 2, no. 3 (10 June, 1899): 5–7.

Connolly, James. "Parliamentary Democracy." *The Workers' Republic* 4, no. 5 (22 September, 1900): 5–6.

Connolly, James. "A Political Party of the Workers." *The Harp* 1, no. 1 (January, 1908a): 9–10.

Connolly, James. "Political Action." *The Harp* 1, no. 7 (July, 1908b): 6–7.

Connolly, James. *Socialism Made Easy.* Glasgow: Socialist Labour Press, 1917.

De Leon, Daniel. "Reform or Revolution." In *Daniel De Leon: Speeches and Editorials.* New York: New York Labor News, 1940.

De Leon, Daniel. *The Burning Question of Trade Unionism.* New York City: National Executive Committee Socialist Labour Party, 1904.

De Leon, Daniel. "Industrial Unionism." In *Industrial Unionism: Selected Editorial,* 62–5. New York: National Executive Committee Socialist Labor Party, 1920a.

De Leon, Daniel. "Industrialism." In *Industrial Unionism: Selected Editorial,* 34–6. New York: National Executive Committee Socialist Labor Party, 1920b.

De Leon, Daniel. "'Syndicalism'." In *Industrial Unionism: Selected Editorial,* 43–7. New York: National Executive Committee Socialist Labor Party, 1920c.

De Leon, Daniel. *Socialist Reconstruction of Society: The Industrial Vote.* New York: Socialist Labor Party, 1925.

Dow, Gregory K. *Governing the Firm: Workers' Control in Theory and Practice.* Cambridge and New York: Cambridge University Press, 2003.

Eley, Geoff. *Forging Democracy the History of the Left in Europe, 1850–2000.* Oxford: Oxford University Press, 2002.

Engels, Frederick. "*Anti-Dühring.*" In MECW. Vol. 25, 5–312. London: Lawrence & Wishart, 1988a.

Engels, Frederick. "A Critique of the Draft Social-Democratic Programme of 1891." In MECW. Vol. 27, 217–32. London: Lawrence & Wishart, 1988b.

Engels, Frederick. "The Housing Question." In MECW. Vol. 23, 317–91. London: Lawrence & Wishart, 1988c.

Engels, Frederick. "Introduction to Karl Marx's *The Civil War in France.*" In MECW. Vol. 27, 179–91. London: Lawrence & Wishart, 1988d.

Engels, Frederick. "Preface to the 1888 English Edition of the *Manifesto of the Communist Party.*" In MECW. Vol. 26, 512–18. London: Lawrence & Wishart, 1988e.

Engels, Fredrich. "Engels to Eduard Bernstein." In MECW. Vol. 46, 144–50. London: Lawrence & Wishart, 1988.

Geary, Dick, ed. *Labour and Socialist Movements in Europe before 1914.* Oxford: Berg, 1989.

Guesde, Jules. "The Social Problem and Its Solution." Jules Guesde Internet Archive. www.marxists.org/archive/guesde/1905/jan/x01.htm.

Guesde, Jules, and Karl Marx. "The Programme of the Parti Ouvrier." Jules Guesde Internet Archive. www.marxists.org/archive/marx/works/1880/05/parti-ouvrier.htm.

Katznelson, Ira and Aristide R. Zolberg, eds. *Working-Class Formation: Nineteenth-Century Patterns in Western Europe and the United States*. Princeton: Princeton University Press, 1986.

Kautsky, Karl. "Die Abschaffung des Staates." *Der Sozialdemokrat*, no. 51 (1881). Translation by Noa Rodman; available at https://libcom.org/library/abolition-state-karl-kautsky.

Kautsky, Karl. "The Free Society." Karl Kautsky Internet Archive. www.marxists.org/archive/kautsky/1881/state/3-freesoc.htm.

Kautsky, Karl. *Class Struggle (Erfurt Program)*. Translated by William E. Bohn. Chicago: Charles H. Kerr and Company, 1910.

Kautsky, Karl. *The Social Revolution*. Translated by A. M. and May Wood Simon. Chicago: Charles H. Kerr and Company, 1916.

Lafargue, Paul. "Our Goal." Paul Lafargue Internet Archive. www.marxists.org/archive/lafargue/1899/04/our-goal.htm.

Lafargue, Paul. "Socialism and Nationalisation." *Socialist Standard* (February, 1912): 43.

Lenin, Vladimir. "What is to be Done?" In *Lenin Collected Works*, Vol. 5, 347–530. London: Lawrence & Wishart, 1961.

Lenin, Vladimir. "Draft and Explanation of a Programme for the Social-Democratic Party." In *Lenin Collected Works*. Vol. 2, 93–121. London: Lawrence & Wishart, 1962a.

Lenin, Vladimir. "Lessons of the Commune." In *Lenin Collected Works*, Vol. 13, 475–8. London: Lawrence & Wishart, 1962b.

Lenin, Vladimir. "A New Revolutionary Workers' Association." In *Lenin Collected Works*, Vol. 8, 499–510. London: Lawrence & Wishart, 1962c.

Lenin, Vladimir. "Our Tasks and the Soviet of Workers' Deputies." In *Lenin Collected Works*, Vol. 10, 17–28. London: Lawrence & Wishart, 1962d.

Lenin, Vladimir. "Two Tactics." In *Lenin Collected Works*, Vol. 8, 148–57. London: Lawrence & Wishart, 1962e.

Luxemburg, Rosa. "Mass Action." Rosa Luxemburg Internet Archive. www.marxists.org/archive/luxemburg/1911/08/29.htm.

Luxemburg, Rosa. "The Mass Strike, Political Party and Trade Union." In *Rosa Luxemburg Reader*, edited by P. Hudis and K. B. Anderson, 168–99. New York: Monthly Review Press, 2004a.

Luxemburg, Rosa. "Organizational Questions of Russian Social Democracy." In *Rosa Luxemburg Reader*, edited by P. Hudis and K. B. Anderson, 248–65. New York: Monthly Review Press, 2004b.

Luxemburg, Rosa. "Social Reform or Revolution." In *Rosa Luxemburg Reader*, edited by P. Hudis and K. B. Anderson, 128–67. New York: Monthly Review Press, 2004c.

Marshall, Peter H. *Demanding the Impossible: A History of Anarchism.* London: HarperCollins, 1992.

Marx, Karl. *Theories of Surplus Value (Part 3).* Moscow: Progress Publishers, 1971.

Marx, Karl. "The Civil War in France." In MECW. Vol. 22, 307–59. London: Lawrence & Wishart, 1986.

Marx, Karl. "Marginal Notes on the Programme of The German Workers' Party." In MECW. Vol. 24, 81–99. London: Lawrence & Wishart, 1989a.

Marx, Karl. "Notes on Bakunin's *Statehood and Anarchy.*" In MECW. Vol. 24, 485–526. London: Lawrence & Wishart, 1989b.

Marx, Karl. *Capital.* Vol. III. London: Penguin Classic, 1991.

Marx, Karl. *Capital.* Vol. II. London: Penguin Classics, 1992.

Marx, Karl and Frederick Engels. "Circular Letter to August Bebel, Wilhelm Liebknecht, Wilhelm Brucke and Others." In MECW. Vol. 24, 253–69. London: Lawrence & Wishart, 1989.

Marx, Karl and Friedrich Engels, "General Rules of the International Working Men's Association." In *Workers Unite: The International 150 Years Later*, edited by M. Musto, 265–8. New York and London: Bloomsbury, 2014a.

Marx, Karl and Friedrich Engels. "On the Political Action of the Working Class and Other Matters." In *Workers Unite: The International 150 Years Later*, edited by M. Musto, 283–6. New York and London: Bloomsbury, 2014b.

Mattick, Paul. *Anti-Bolshevik Communism.* Monmouth: Merlin Press Ltd., 2007.

Morris, William. "The Manifesto of The Socialist League—Second Edition." William Morris Internet Archive. www.marxists.org/archive/morris/works/1885/manifst2.htm.

Morris, William. "Looking Backward." In *Political Writings of William Morris*, edited by A. L. Morton, 247–53. London: Lawrence and Wishart, 1984.

Morris, William. "Socialism from the Root Up." In *Political Writings: Contributions to Justice and Commonweal 1883–1890*, edited by Nicholas Salmon, 495–622. Bristol: Thoemmes Press, 1994.

Morris, William and E. Belfort Bax. *The Manifesto of The Socialist League.* London: Socialist League Office, 1885.

Morris, William and H. M. Hyndman. *A Summary of Principles of Socialism.* London: The Modern Press, 1884.

Mulder, Catherine. *Transcending Capitalism through Cooperative Practices.* Basingstoke: Palgrave Macmillan, 2015.

Musto, Marcello. "Introduction." In *Workers Unite! The International 150 Years Later*, edited by Marcello Musto, 1–68. New York: Bloomsbury, 2014.

Ness, Immanuel and Dario Azzellini, eds. *Ours to Master and to Own: Workers' Control from the Commune to the Present.* Chicago: Haymarket, 2011.

Pannekoek, Anton. "Hope in the Future." Anton Pannekoek Internet Archive. www.marxists.org/archive/pannekoe/1912/hope-in-future.htm.

Pannekoek, Anton. "Socialism and Anarchism." *The New Review* 1, no. 4 (1913a): 122–7.

Pannekoek, Anton. "Socialism and Anarchism." *The New Review* 1, no. 5 (1913b): 147–52.

Prost, Antoine. "Workers." In *The Cambridge History of the First World War*, edited by Jay Winter, 325–57. Cambridge: Cambridge University Press, 2014.

Reisman, David, ed. *Democratic Socialism in Britain: Classic Texts in Economic and Political Thought 1825–1952*. Vol. 3. London: Pickering & Chatto, 1996.

Rubel, Maximilien and John Crump, eds. *Non-Market Socialism in the Nineteenth and Twentieth Centuries*. New York: Palgrave Macmillan, 1984.

Sassoon, Donald. *One Hundred Years of Socialism: The West European Left in the Twentieth Century*. London: Tauris, 2014.

Shaw, Bernard, ed. *Fabian Essays*. London: Allen & Unwin, 1948.

Thompson, E. P. *William Morris: From Romantic to Revolutionary*. New York: Pantheon Books, 1976.

van der Linden, Marcel and Wayne Thorpe, eds. *Revolutionary Syndicalism: An International Perspective*. Aldershot: Scolar, 1990.

King, Marx, and the Revolution of Worldwide Value

Andrew J. Douglas

> *A society that performs miracles with machinery has the capacity to make some miracles for men if it values men as highly as it values machines. … [We] built a cotton economy for three hundred years as slaves on which the nation grew powerful. … We, too, realize that when human values are subordinated to blind economic forces, human beings can become human scrap.*[1]

> *Something is wrong with capitalism. … We are not interested in being integrated into* this *value structure.*[2]

[1] Martin Luther King, Jr., Speech to the United Automobile Workers, Detroit, 17 April 1961.
[2] Martin Luther King, Jr., Speech to the SCLC National Advisory Committee, 27 November 1967.

A. J. Douglas (✉)
Morehouse College, Atlanta, GA, USA

I. INTRODUCTION

"I am convinced," Martin Luther King, Jr., said in 1967, "that if we are to get on the right side of the world revolution, we as a nation must undergo a radical revolution of values."[3] This is one of the more resounding lines from King's corpus, and one of the most frequently cited. It is often taken to capture the essence of King's later radicalism, a sense of the political commitment and moral urgency that he ascribed to a "second" and more "substantive" phase of his life's work. That second phase sought to organize a more penetrating and comprehensive assault on what he called the "evil triplets" of racism, violence, and poverty. It is no secret that King became increasingly outspoken in his dissatisfaction with capitalism and the ways in which racism and violence had been interwoven into the structural workings of the economy and polity of the United States. But readers of King still need a better understanding of the nature, and legacy, of his critique of capitalism, both within and beyond the context of the United States. How, we might ask, is King's call for a "revolution of values" affected by the production and circulation of value in capitalist society?

Though King's analysis moved beyond, often against, key assumptions and conceptual tools of Marxist thought, Marx's way of thinking about capital as "value in motion" provides a generative starting point for addressing this question.[4] Consider Marx's account of the "commodity-form" under capitalism and how the market actor's singular and largely compulsory focus on the exchange of money can be said to "conceal a social relation."[5] Marx argued that the coordination of human labour and activity, the human interdependencies that King catalogued under the rubric of an "inescapable network of mutuality," had become sustained in the modern period by a logic of capital accumulation, or a distinctive pressure put upon capitalists—and into the neoliberal era, essentially *all* market actors—to pursue not only profit, but also sustained growth through the creation of viable outlets for reinvestment.[6] What we are compelled to

---

[3] Martin Luther King, Jr., "Beyond Vietnam: A Time to Break Silence" [1967], in *The Radical King*, ed. Cornel West (Boston: Beacon, 2016), 214.

[4] See Karl Marx, *Capital: A Critique of Political Economy, Vol. 1*, trans. Ben Fowkes (New York: Penguin, 1992), 255–6. See also Karl Marx, *Capital: A Critique of Political Economy, Vol. 2*, trans. David Fernbach (New York: Penguin, 1993), 211.

[5] See Marx, *Capital, Vol. 1*, 149.

[6] See Martin Luther King, Jr., "Letter from Birmingham Jail," in *Gospel of Freedom: Martin Luther King, Jr.'s Letter from Birmingham Jail and the Struggle That Changed a Nation*, ed. Jonathan Rieder (New York: Bloomsbury, 2014).

value and devalue in capitalist society is largely dependent upon its movement through cycles of accumulation and reinvestment. This movement,
this "value in motion," is itself dependent upon the reproduction of social
inequalities, which have significant temporal and spatial dimensions, as
well as discernible racial dimensions.

In order to grasp capitalism's racial character, it is necessary to stretch a
Marxist analysis, as Frantz Fanon put it, or to strike out onto the terrain of
what contemporary scholars refer to, following Cedric Robinson, as the
theory of racial capitalism.[7] If "capital can only be capital when it is accumulating," if capital "can only accumulate by producing and moving
through relations of severe inequality among human groups," if "accumulation requires loss, disposability, and the unequal differentiation of human
value," then, as Jodi Melamed has argued, we ought to explore how "racism enshrines the inequalities that capitalism requires."[8] We ought to
explore how racism has become, in Michael Dawson's words, a necessary
"background condition" that enables capitalist society by shaping and
normalizing its inequalities.[9] The theory of racial capitalism, which I
unpack in various ways throughout the essay, is meant not merely to call
attention to the "capitalist 'origins' of race and racism." The driving point,
as Nikhil Pal Singh says, is that "racial differentiation is intrinsic to processes of capitalist value-creation and speculation." And into the twentieth
and twenty-first centuries especially, such processes have turned an "ideal-
ized game of merit and chance into a stacked deck."[10] These ways of thinking about valuation, the circulation of capital, and the racial dimensions of
the capitalist value-form prove immensely helpful to the task of recon-
structing King's critique of political economy.

King, for his part, claimed to have read *Capital* by himself over the
Christmas holiday in 1949.[11] Well known is King's avowal of a dialectical

---

[7] See Frantz Fanon, *The Wretched of the Earth*, trans. Richard Philcox (New York: Grove, 2005), 5. See also Cedric J. Robinson, *Black Marxism: The Making of the Black Radical Tradition* (Chapel Hill: University of North Carolina Press, 2000).

[8] Jodi Melamed, "Racial Capitalism," *Critical Ethnic Studies* 1, no. 1 (Spring 2015): 77. See also Jodi Melamed, *Represent and Destroy: Rationalizing Violence in the New Racial Capitalism* (Minneapolis: University of Minnesota Press, 2011).

[9] Michael C. Dawson, "Hidden in Plain Sight: A Note on Legitimation Crises and the Racial Order," *Critical Historical Studies* (Spring 2016): 143–61.

[10] Nikhil Pal Singh, "On Race, Violence, and So-Called Primitive Accumulation," *Social Text 128* 34, no. 3 (September 2016): 30–1.

[11] See Martin Luther King, Jr., *Stride Toward Freedom: The Montgomery Story* (Boston: Beacon, 2010), 78.

methodology, which in its emphasis on processes and interconnections and the movement of parts within social totalities helps to demystify the social relations sustained by the circulation of capital. But in the context of a discussion of King, it makes sense to explore parallels with the revisionist approach spawned by Robinson's work in part because Robinson situated the critique of racial capitalism within an account of an indigenous Black radical tradition, one born of the lived struggles of Black people and that, by its nature, exceeds the terms of European discourse. There is no doubt that the theory of racial capitalism is meant partly to expose the limitations of European radicalism, and especially the ways in which Marxist materialism has been made to rationalize or even dismiss both racialism and the spiritual distinctiveness of indigenous Black struggle. Robinson did not highlight King's critique of political economy. He opted instead to survey the contributions of an earlier generation of Black scholar-activists, including W. E. B. Du Bois and C. L. R. James. But King can and should be aligned with this tradition, as a figure who factored the history of Black liberation struggle into a creolized appropriation of European intellectual legacies and who came to regard institutionalized practices of capital accumulation as organically interwoven with racial partition, dispossession, disinheritance, exploitation, and underdevelopment—in short, racial violence.

The imperative, King said, is to get on the right side of world revolution and to embrace a radical revolution of values. "We must rapidly begin the shift from a thing-oriented society to a person-oriented society," for "when machines and computers, profit motives and property rights, are considered more important than people, the giant triplets of racism, extreme materialism, and militarism are incapable of being conquered."[12] King saw in capitalist modernity an unprecedented, world-historical expansion of human productive and social capacity. But he also saw a "glaring contradiction" in the irrational and immoral persistence of material poverty and racial segregation, the unacceptable persistence of what he called "the other America." It is precisely in his attentiveness to the substance of this signal contradiction that the contours of a theory of racial capitalism emerge in his work. The following discussion begins with a brief commentary on how King's spiritual commitments and deference to the distinctiveness of indigenous Black protest complicated his reception of Marxism. It then considers King's analysis of the concentration of Black poverty in American cities before turning to explore the anti-imperialist

---

[12] King, "Beyond Vietnam: A Time to Break Silence," 214.

and internationalist dimensions of his critical theory. Ultimately, the essay speaks to how capitalism reproduces the unequal differentiation of human value, how it does so in racial terms, and how this process complicates the call, King's call, for a revolution of values.

II. "Approaching Spiritual Death"

The philosopher Nikolai Berdyaev, with whom King was familiar, wrote in a 1935 essay on Marxism that without the "spiritual element" there "cannot be talk about the attainment of the totality of life." The spiritual element, which found expression in King's own Christian theological commitments, adds an initial layer of complexity to King's critique of racial capitalism. Throughout his life, King had to reckon with anti-communist hysteria, including American attitudes towards Marxism, and the spirituality question was central to his manoeuvring. But King's public disavowal of Marxism underscores not only the difficulties he faced in wresting his thinking from the political-economic conservatism of a rights-based liberalism. It also vivifies the ways in which his mature critique of racial capitalism exceeded the terms of European radicalism and exhibited distinctive features of the Black radical tradition.

In that 1935 essay, Berdyaev would go on to claim that the "materialist" tradition of Marxist or Communist thought "wants to return to the proletariat the means of production alienated from him, but it does not at all want to return the spiritual element of human nature alienated from him, spiritual life." Berdyaev argued that "man belongs not only to the kingdom of Caesar, but also to the Kingdom of God," and that "man possesses a higher dignity and totality, *a value of life*, if he is a person."[13] While King "'believed that Marx had analyzed the economic side of capitalism right'" (and more on this later), he, like Berdyaev, worried that, as he said in 1966, "Marx didn't see the spiritual undergirdings of reality."[14] There is a temptation to read King's emphasis on the spiritual, along with his concern that "materialism" had mushroomed into one of modern society's great evils, as an expression of an overriding idealism of sorts, a sign that his conceptual and methodological moorings discourage any sustained critique of political economy. It is not clear that King ever really

---

[13] N. A. Berdyaev, "Marxism and the Conception of Personality," *Christendom*, no. 2 (December 1935), http://www.berdyaev.com/berdiaev/berd_lib/1935_400.html.
[14] King, "Speech at SCLC Staff Retreat," 20.

understood materialism in a strict Marxian sense of the term. As his former college professor Melvin Watson pointed out to him in a 1953 letter, in an effort to correct King's reading of Marx, "Marx's position was that the culture, thoughts, in fact, the whole life of man is conditioned ... *by the means of production.*" This "variety of materialism is very difficult to refute," Watson said, and it is, especially for a Baptist preacher steeped in Christian idealism, "a very disturbing phenomenon."[15] But King's point, like Berdyaev's, was just that a strict methodological materialism does not capture the spiritual dimensions of anti-capitalist protest; nor does it honour the ways in which a more satisfactory or sustainable social order would make room for the cultivation of spiritual or other meaning-making human activities. And as King put his theological commitments into working relation with the Black freedom struggle, his philosophy began to take on characteristic features of the Black radical tradition.

Part of what makes the Black radical tradition, Robinson said, is "the renunciation of actual being for historical being," or the preservation of "the integral totality of the people themselves," a people whose values and principles and ideals exceed the terms of Western modernity. What emerged from indigenous Black struggle in the modern period was a "revolutionary consciousness that proceeded from the whole historical experience of Black people and not merely from the social formations of capitalist slavery or the relations of production of colonialism."[16] The spiritual occupies a central place here, not as an opiate, not as evidence of a reactionary ideological consciousness, but as part of the psychology of active and sustained resistance. This is evident in various stages of King's activism. He went to Albany, Georgia, to join a people "straightening its back," a people working through the *spiritual renewal* that it needed to initiate and sustain collective resistance. He went to Chicago to foment something similar, a "*spiritual transformation* of the ghetto." He went to Memphis to express his "*spiritual connection* with labour," and he found there an audience moved by how his exemplary determination to fight on, his indefatigable courage, was itself reflective of "a *good spirit.*"[17] The spiritual dimension

---

[15] Melvin Watson, "Letter to King," in *The Papers of Martin Luther King, Jr., Vol. II: Rediscovering Precious Values, July 1951–November 1955*, ed. Clayborne Carson, Ralph E. Luker, Penny A. Russell, and Pete Holloran (Berkeley: University of California Press, 1994), 156–7.

[16] Robinson, *Black Marxism*, 168–9.

[17] See Jason Sokol, *There Goes My Everything: White Southerners in the Age of Civil Rights, 1945–1975* (New York: Vintage, 2007), 93–4; Thomas F. Jackson, *From Civil Rights to*

emerges organically from a people in movement and has a sort of autopoi-etic function, working to persuade the foot soldiers, King included, to stay the course, to keep on the right side of the world revolution, despite the seductiveness of what Robinson called "actual being," what we might call the inertial allure of White capitalist modernity and its "materialist" prom-ises of wealth, status, and "all of the other shallow things."[18]

King's worry about an approaching "spiritual death" was none other than a concern about the prospective annihilation of a people and its resis-tance struggles. And it is important to emphasize that this concern is cen-tral to the critique of racial capitalism, which trains focus not only on the exploitation of labour and resources, but also on the ways in which logics of capital accumulation render Black people vulnerable to premature death, both corporeally and spiritually. "Accumulation under capitalism is necessarily exploitation of labor, land, and resources," Melamed says, but it is also "a system of expropriating violence on collective life itself."[19] At issue is a "technology of antirelationality," the "production of social sep-arateness—the disjoining or deactivating of relations between human beings (and humans and nature)—needed for capitalist exploitation to work."[20] Melamed goes on to cite Ruth Wilson Gilmore's seminal defini-tion of racism as "the state-sanctioned and/or extra-legal production and exploitation of group-differentiated vulnerabilities to premature death, *in distinct yet densely interconnected political geographies.*"[21] It is remarkable how well this theoretical framework applies to King's life and work. King was concerned with how Black people had been partitioned and rendered vulnerable, within what he referred to repeatedly as the "inescapable net-work of mutuality," and in ways that could both feed capital accumulation and foreclose the development of alternative modes of human relation and

Human Rights: Martin Luther King, Jr., and the Struggle for Economic Justice (Philadelphia: University of Pennsylvania Press, 2009), 279; Michael K. Honey, "To The Mountaintop: 'Let Us Develop a Kind of Dangerous Unselfishness,'" in *All Labor Has Dignity*, ed. Michael K. Honey (Boston: Beacon, 2011), 181.

[18] See Martin Luther King, Jr., "The Drum Major Instinct," in *The Radical King*, ed. Cornel West (Boston: Beacon, 2016), 264.

[19] Melamed, "Racial Capitalism," 78. See Dawson, "Hidden in Plain Sight" and Nancy Fraser, "Expropriation and Exploitation in Racialized Capitalism: A Reply to Michael Dawson," *Critical Historical Studies* (Spring 2016): 163–78.

[20] Melamed, "Racial Capitalism," 78.

[21] Ruth Wilson Gilmore, "Race and Globalization," in *Geographies of Global Change: Remapping the World*, ed. R. J. Johnson, Peter J. Taylor, and Michael J. Watts (New York: Wiley-Blackwell, 2002), 261; emphasis added.

valuation. King argued in 1966 that "racism is based on the affirmation that the very being of a people is inferior," and that "the ultimate logic of racism is genocide."[22] This conception of racism, this concern with the systematic annihilation of a people, undergirds King's mature critique of how capitalism works as a system of expropriating violence on collective life itself, as I argue in the next two sections.

III. "The Glaring Contrast of Poverty and Wealth"

King moved beyond the terms of European radicalism, but he "believed that Marx had analyzed the economic side of capitalism right." Part of what this means is that King, ever the dialectician, was generally sympathetic with the grand development narrative, the idea that human history can be understood in terms of an ongoing struggle to expand social and productive capacity and that capitalist modernity reflects both historically unprecedented capaciousness and, contradictorily, the persistence of internal obstacles, what Marx referred to as the "fetters," to further development.[23] "Capitalism carries the seeds of its own destruction," King wrote in 1951. "I am convinced that capitalism has seen its best days in America, and not only in America, but in the entire world. It is a well-known fact that no social institution can survive when it has outlived its usefulness. This, capitalism has done. It has failed to meet the needs of the masses."[24] And King was always fond of the maxim "from each according to his ability, to each according to his needs," which he seems to have regarded as a speculative ideal of sorts, a fugitive vision of a more publicly oriented political economy, one in which human needs are prioritized, in which labour is rendered socially valuable—or "socially necessary," in Marxist terms—only insofar as it is made to serve human needs. The insinuation is that King was worried about how the ideological superstructure of capitalist modernity—established laws and political ideas, shared principles, indeed shared *values*—prevents further development of productive and

[22] King, "Speech at SCLC Staff Retreat," 7, 8.
[23] See Karl Marx's "Preface" to *A Contribution to the Critique of Political Economy* (1859), https://www.marxists.org/archive/marx/works/1859/critique-pol-economy/preface.htm.
[24] Martin Luther King, Jr., "Will Capitalism Survive," in *The Papers of Martin Luther King, Jr., Volume VI: Advocate of the Social Gospel, September 1948–March 1963*, ed. Clayborne Carson, Susan Carson, Susan Englander, Troy Jackson, and Gerald L. Smith (Berkeley: University of California Press, 2000), 104.

social capacity, further development of our very ability to relate to one another in ways that serve human needs, both material and spiritual.

And yet, King went beyond the critique of ideology as that operation is conventionally understood. Beyond the demystification of epistemic commitments, King sought to expose a mode of domination built into the material reproduction of capitalism's social form. This aspect of his critique is put on more vivid display as his thinking developed into the mid- to late 1960s, and as he sought to work through the "glaring contrast of poverty and wealth." The historian Thomas Jackson has shown that by about 1966 King began to argue against not only "lonely islands of poverty in a vast sea of prosperity," but also against the ways in which White privilege and prosperity were themselves conditioned by racial partitioning and Black underdevelopment, how increased capaciousness for some was bought necessarily at the expense of others. Of course, King sought to vivify the irrationality of economic inequality and distributive injustice. "Our nation is now so rich, so productive," he said, "that the continuation of persistent poverty is incendiary because the poor cannot rationalize their deprivation."[25] But more to the point, King argued that "depressed living conditions for Negroes are a *structural part of the economy*," that "certain industries are based upon the supply of low-wage, under-skilled and immobile non-white labor."[26]

This line of thinking came alive for King during his time in Chicago, during a period that, as David Garrow has shown, "would hasten the expansion of his own critical perspective on American society."[27] In Chicago, King began to speak more openly about the racial dimensions of systemic economic exploitation. A "total pattern of exploitation" is "crystallized in the slum," he said, and this situation exists simply "because someone profits by its existence." Following James Bevel and others, King spoke of "a system of internal colonialism," a "situation [that] is true only for Negroes."[28] Here, we can begin to garner clues about the spatial or geographical dimensions of King's critique of racial capitalism. At issue is the way in which White wealth and privilege are maintained through, to quote Gilmore again, "the state-sanctioned and/or extra-legal production

[25] Martin Luther King, Jr., "Freedom's Crisis," *The Nation* (1966).

[26] Ibid.; emphasis added. See also Jackson, *From Civil Rights to Human Rights*, 250–1.

[27] Garrow, *Bearing the Cross*, 430.

[28] For a brief history of the use of the term "internal colonialism" in the United States, see Ramón A. Gutiérrez, "Internal Colonialism: An American Theory of Race," *Du Bois Review*, 1, no. 2 (2004): 281–95.

and exploitation of group-differentiated vulnerabilities to premature death, in distinct yet densely interconnected political geographies." For King, the spatial concentration of Black poverty engendered vulnerability to premature death, both for individuals and for the group, for what Robinson referred to as "the integral totality of the people." And the urban slum, what King referred to in this moment as "the Chicago problem," was evidence of what Melamed has described as a "technology for reducing collective life to the relations that sustain neoliberal democratic capitalism," a "dialectic in which forms of humanity are separated (made 'distinct') so that they may be 'interconnected' in terms that feed capital."[29] It is worth quoting Melamed at length on this point:

> Although at first glance, dense interconnections seem antithetical to amputated social relations, it is capitalism's particular feat to accomplish differentiation as dense networks and nodes of social separateness. Processes of differentiation and dominant comparative logics create 'certainties' of discreteness, distinctness, and discontinuity—of discrete identities, distinct territorializations and sovereignties, and discontinuities between the political and the economic, the internal and the external, and the valued and the devalued. In the drawing of the line that constitutes discrete entities and distinguishes between the valued and the devalued, people and situations are made incommensurable to one another as a disavowed condition of possibility for world-systems of profit and governance.[30]

In his effort to come to grips with the "Chicago problem," King emerged as a critic who was deftly attuned to the ways in which Black "antirelationality" was densely interwoven with and made to serve circuits of capital accumulation, often through the production of Black vulnerability. He underscored the point that Black people had been partitioned, isolated, immobilized, stigmatized, in essence *devalued*, and that this was a "structural part of the economy."

Consider Marx's definition of devaluation, which is simple in itself, but is quite useful for thinking about how the value of Black lives is affected by the social movement of capitalist production and exchange. If we think of capital as "value in motion," we can think of devaluation as what happens whenever and wherever its motion is disrupted. Whenever and wherever the "process of reproduction is checked," Marx said, both "use-value

---

[29] Melamed, "Racial Capitalism," 78.
[30] Ibid., 78–9.

and exchange-value go to the devil."[31] Devaluation must also be seen as "the underside to overaccumulation."[32] Whenever and wherever accumulated surplus is at pains to find viable outlets for reinvestment or absorption, what ensues is the non-production of value, or what we might describe more fittingly, highlighting the artificial or manufactured character of the system itself, as the production of non-value. As the rate of profit tends to slow system-wide, we are confronted with, as Marx put it, "overproduction, speculation crises and surplus capital alongside surplus population."[33] The result is always devaluation. This simple revelation is profoundly significant for how we might understand King's call for a "revolution of values."

Deindustrialization, offshoring, and other forms of capital flight have decimated Black communities in the United States, most proximately in the urban north and the so-called Rust Belt. And though such decimation came into more widespread public consciousness in the decades after King's death, in the wake of the accumulation crises of the 1970s and during the subsequent neoliberal reforms of the 1980s, King appeared to have seen the writing on the wall, as his reflections on the "Chicago problem" and his anti-war arguments indicate. In various ways, King found himself pushing back against efforts to resolve the internal contradictions of capital accumulation, efforts by capitalist actors, working in concert with the state, to invest in various ways overseas, to resume circulatory processes that had slowed on the domestic front by creating overseas markets for the absorption of surplus. Throughout the post-war period, such efforts introduced new modes of racial exploitation. It was a "new jungle," King said to a group of packinghouse workers in 1962, made possible by "the shining glittering face of science," by "automation and the runaway shop."[34] The point is that what King referred to as a deadening sense of "nobodyness," a sense of neglect and societal worthlessness that he began to read into the material and psychic life of the Black ghetto of the 1960s, was wrought by devaluation—of labour, of education, of

---

[31] Karl Marx, "Theories of Surplus Value," https://www.marxists.org/archive/marx/works/1863/theories-surplus-value/ch17.htm.

[32] David Harvey, *The Limits to Capital* (New York: Verso, 2006), 192.

[33] Karl Marx, *Capital: A Critique of Political Economy*. Vol. 3, trans. David Fernbach (New York: Penguin, 1993), 351.

[34] Martin Luther King, Jr., "Thirteenth Convention, United Packinghouse Workers of America, Minneapolis, Minnesota, May 21, 1962," in *All Labor Has Dignity*, ed. Michael K. Honey (Boston: Beacon, 2011), 51.

infrastructure, indeed of Black lives as such. This kind of racially marked devaluation must be seen as an effect of the spatial flight of the circulation of capital.[35]

Michael Denning has pointed out that "under capitalism, the only thing worse than being exploited is not being exploited."[36] Today we might well refer to "wageless life," to a new manifestation of "surplus population" that, in the words of the *Endnotes* collective, "need not find itself completely 'outside' capitalist social relations. Capital may not need these workers, but they still need to work. They are thus forced to offer themselves up for the most abject forms of wage slavery in the form of petty production and services—identified with informal and often illegal markets of direct exchange arising alongside failures of capitalist production."[37] Wagelessness presents itself, of course, as a major problem for the reproduction of an economy built on the continuous circulation of consumption dollars. And though King knew that "no matter how dynamically the [capitalist] economy develops and expands it does not eliminate poverty," he argued, in 1967, that "we have come to a point where we must make the nonproducer a consumer or we will find ourselves drowning in a sea of consumer goods." He argued that "we must create full employment or we must create incomes. People must be made consumers by one method or the other."[38] It is tempting to read this emphasis on the expansion of consumption power as a sort of temporal fix to systemic accumulation crises, an approach that might buy a little time for the continued circulation of capital and does nothing to challenge underlying structural contradictions, or indeed racial capitalism's social relations. King was ambivalent on this matter, to be sure. But I wager that in his effort to foment a "revolution of values," in his effort to rethink "this value system," King sought to imagine an economy for which consumption would be driven not by the reproduction of capitalism, not by the reproduction of the unequal and obscured social relations that make accumulation possible, but by the service of human needs. His emphasis on propping up consumption power must be understood in the context of this broader critique.

---

[35] See, for example, King, "Letter from Birmingham Jail."
[36] Michael Denning, "Wageless Life," *New Left Review* 66 (November–December 2010).
[37] See "Misery and Debt," *Endnotes* 2 (2010): 30f15.
[38] King, *Where Do We Go from Here*, 172.

And indeed this broader critique of the reproduction of capitalism, of an economic structure marked by "value in motion," is evident in King's articulation of a strategy of urban "dislocation," which began to emerge in earnest in the summer of 1967. King knew that capital accumulates by "producing and moving through relations of severe inequality among human groups—capitalists with the means of production/workers without the means of subsistence, creditors/debtors, conquerors of land made property/the dispossessed and removed."[39] And he sought to galvanize an active countermovement that could challenge the reproduction of racial capitalism on the people's terms. He began to call on Black citizen-activists and their allies "to dislocate the functioning of a city," to, as it were, throw sand into the gears of the circulation of capital.[40] Beyond Chicago, King sought to take a poor people's campaign to Washington, to foment a sort of occupy movement that could, in effect, shut it down. If folks could "just camp ... and stay," he said, "the city will not function." Such a movement, he imagined, could be "as dramatic, as dislocative, as disruptive, as attention-getting as the riots without destroying life or property."[41] The crucial point is just that King's call for "dislocation," a call born of an evolving attentiveness to the racially marked relations and processes that feed capital accumulation, can be understood as part of a movement to reconstruct how human beings relate to and value one another, a strategy that, we are now beginning to see more clearly, is deeply resonant with the Black radical tradition.

III. "Social Stability for Our Investments"

Land concerns were also a consistent pillar of King's global vision, as evidenced by, for example, his early interest in the Indian Bhoodan Movement and, of course, his mature defence of the Northern Vietnamese struggles for land reform.[42] By 1967, and to the consternation of so many in and outside of the Movement, King offered an apology of sorts for a Northern Vietnamese "revolutionary government seeking self-determination," a "government that had been established not by China—for whom the

[39] Melamed, "Racial Capitalism," 77.
[40] Martin Luther King, Jr., cited in Garrow, *Bearing the Cross*, 574.
[41] Ibid., 579, 582.
[42] On the Indian Bhoodan or Land Gift Movement of the 1950s, see Martin Luther King, Jr., "My Trip to the Land of Gandhi," in *A Single Garment of Destiny: A Global Vision of Justice*, ed. Lewis V. Baldwin (Boston: Beacon, 2012), 107.

Vietnamese have no great love—but by clearly indigenous forces that included some communists." For the peasants of the Vietnamese country-side, King said, "this new government meant real land reform, one of the most important needs in their lives."[43]

Too often appreciation of King's internationalism is hemmed in by a narrow reading of his opposition to the Vietnam War. Such a reading, supported to be sure by King's own insistence that "our government is more concerned about winning an unjust war in Vietnam than winning the war against poverty here at home," reduces the economic dimension of King's antimilitarism to a matter of opportunity costs, as if the only relevant question had to do with domestic budgetary priority, how best to allocate federal expenditure.[44] But King was clear that "the need to *maintain social stability for our investments* accounts for the counterrevolutionary action of American forces in Guatemala" and explains why "American helicopters are being used against guerrillas in Cambodia and why American napalm and Green Beret forces have already been active against rebels in Peru." The systemic need for the continuous circulation of capital and the ongoing expansion of its spatial boundaries, the dynamic structural imperative of the global market economy, accounts for "our alliance with the landed gentry of South America" and explains why we see "individual capitalists of the West investing huge sums of money in Asia, Africa, and South America, only to take the profits out with no concern for the social betterment of the countries." King described post-war U.S. imperialism in terms of a stubborn global class politics, an elite refusal "to give up the privileges and the pleasures that come from the immense profits of overseas investments."[45] The implication, on a deeper theoretical plane, is that warfare had become a crucial resource in the capitalist struggle to resolve escalating accumulation crises. What King sought to confront, in essence, was a proactive government movement seeking to establish and maintain overseas markets for the absorption of economic surplus. King's anti-war arguments ought to be seen as part of a long tradition of left criticism of military surplus spending, which he might have described as "military Keynesianism."[46]

[43] King, "Beyond Vietnam: A Time to Break Silence," 206–7.

[44] King, "Local 1199," 165.

[45] King, "Beyond Vietnam: A Time to Break Silence," 213–14.

[46] Forged initially by the early-century contributions of Rosa Luxemburg, the critical theorization of military stimulus spending experienced a watershed moment in the late 1960s, with the publication of Paul A. Baran and Paul Sweezy's *Monopoly Capital: An Essay on the American Economic and Social Order* (New York: Monthly Review, 1966). See also Rosa

The key forebear of that longer tradition of left criticism once said that "an industrial army of workmen, under the command of a capitalist, requires, *like a real army*, officers [managers], and sergeants [foremen overlookers], who, while the work is being done, command in the name of the capitalist."[47] For so long, within the left tradition, it was presumed that the "silent compulsion" of market relations would come to supplant more violent dispossession and expropriation of land and labour, that the naked violence that Marx read into capitalism's "prehistory" would over time take on a more covert *modus operandi*. It was presumed that market rationalization would obscure the ways in which "free" living labour would continue to be thrust into impoverishment and expendability, that the work of critique of ideology would thus become an increasingly salient weapon in the ongoing class struggle. Fair enough. Critique of ideology is crucial work. But here again, it is important to invoke the theory of racial capitalism, as the privileged vantage of European radicalism has not always registered the real violence, racial and otherwise, that King and other twentieth-century Black radicals have borne prophetic witness to. From the vantage of Black labour and wageless life worldwide, there is and has been nothing *analogous* about the role of military discipline and management in the production and circulation of value. Capital accumulation requires *real armies*, commanding and supervising market relations on a global scale. And in this, racial domination plays an essential role.

Recent historical work has documented the ways in which early capitalism specialized in, as Nikhil Pal Singh puts it, a "form of commercial privateering backed but unimpeded by sovereign power and most fully realized in slavery, settler colonialism, and imperialism."[48] Certainly the "conscription, criminalization, and disposability of poor, idle, or surplus labour—the historical process of forcibly 'divorcing the producers from the means of production' that for Marx is capitalism's precondition"—has always relied upon "racial differentiation as a directly violent yet also flexible and fungible mode of ascription." But, as Singh goes on to point out, "there has been no period in which racial domination has not been woven into the management of capitalist society."[49] The "state-sanctioned force and violence originally required to create wage labour" has not disappeared into the era of mature,

Luxemburg, *The Accumulation of Capital,* trans. Agnes Schwarzschild (New York: Routledge, 2003).

[47] Marx, *Capital,* Vol. I, 172; emphasis added.

[48] Nikhil Pal Singh, *Race and America's Long War* (Oakland: University of California Press, 2017), 79.

[49] Ibid.

consolidated global capitalism. Indeed in our own time, force and violence is "retained in the forms of hierarchy and competition between workers, in the social requirements of policing unwaged labor that has migrated to poverty and the informal economy, and in imperial and nationalist interpellations of the urban and metropolitan working classes."[50] King spoke of expanded social and productive capacity under capitalism, population increase and improved living conditions, as we have seen, but he also underscored as the precondition of these their dialectical underside, the production of human scrap, the disposability of living labour, the omnipresent threat of systematic annihilation of a people. Here we would do well to recall, quoting Singh again, that the "constant, violent dislocation of these two processes requires constant management in the form of police and military solutions—that is, directly coercive interventions." We would do well to keep in mind that capital accumulation "spurs forms of moral, temporal, and spatial sequestration that become part of the framework of crisis management, through which the simultaneous production of growth and death can be viewed less as a contradiction than as a necessary dimension of historical progress."[51] It cannot be denied that in this, and to say it again, racial ascription and domination play an essential role.

These sobering considerations can be read back into King's suspicions of global capitalism in richly generative ways. The imperial expansion of the capitalist value-form has put more and more human beings in relation to one another in ways that feed the production and circulation of capital. And as Samir Amin reminds us, "far from progressively 'homogenizing' economic conditions on a planetary scale," this historical process has produced racial inequality and uneven geographical development, a "permanent asymmetry" in which is "affirmed, with violence still greater than that contemplated by Marx, the law of pauperization that is indissolubly linked to the logic of capital accumulation."[52] This is precisely what has become of the "inescapable network of mutuality," what will remain of it, King feared, unless enough conscientious objectors step up to confront—actively and politically, and not merely through the cultivation of moral conscience or right perception—the war-making and imperial offensives that reproduce the conditions for the production and circulation of value worldwide.

It is important to note that King's anti-war arguments were carved against a burgeoning mid-century Black internationalism, at a time when

---

[50] Ibid., 96–7.
[51] Ibid.
[52] Samir Amin, *The Law of Worldwide Value* (New York: Monthly Review, 2010), 84.

he found himself immersed in what Brandon Terry has called the "problem-space of black power."[53] This was a context in which a "resurgence of Marxist thought in black political life helped enable a shift away from the discourse of *inclusion* and *citizenship rights*, toward emphases on *oppression* and *domination*," but also a context in which pan-African commitments augured a renewed sense of global anti-capitalist solidarity.[54] King's "second phase" marked his reorientation towards criticism of structures of oppression and domination, and it could be argued that this context also enabled his pan-Africanism in compelling ways. As Terry goes on to point out, "King often invoked African Americans' connection to Africa, and suggested modes of transnational solidarity," though "his formulations placed less emphasis on the idiom of 'racial' ancestry than resonant and shared features of racial oppression between colonialism and Jim Crow."[55] And in this way, King's internationalism hewed closer to the spirit of Bandung, the spirit of an anti-capitalist nonaligned movement born of a global Southern alliance, a resonant and shared experience of racial and colonial oppression. It is telling that for King, the 1955 gathering in Bandung, spearheaded by 29 Asian and African delegations caught in the throes of anti-imperialist struggle, was better understood as a popular movement than as a national or bourgeois one. "More than one billion three hundred million of the colored peoples of the world have broken aloose from colonialism and imperialism," King said to a crowd in St. Louis in 1957. "*They* have broken aloose from the Egypt of colonialism. … *They* assembled in Bandung some months ago."[56]

IV. "THESE ARE REVOLUTIONARY TIMES"

Nearly a decade later, King spoke again of politics and of where the future might go. He urged solidarity with grass-roots struggles of various kinds. "All over the globe men are revolting against old systems of exploitation

---

[53] Brandon M. Terry, "Requiem for a Dream: The Problem-Space of Black Power," in *To Shape a New World: Essays on the Political Philosophy of Martin Luther King, Jr.*, ed. Tommie Shelby and Brandon M. Terry (Cambridge, MA: Harvard University Press, 2018).

[54] Ibid., 313.

[55] Ibid, 315.

[56] Martin Luther King, Jr., "'A Realistic Look at the Question of Progress in the Area of Race Relations,' Address Delivered at St. Louis Freedom Rally," in *The Papers of Martin Luther King, Jr., Volume VI: Advocate of the Social Gospel, September 1948–March 1963*, ed. Clayborne Carson, Susan Carson, Susan Englander, Troy Jackson, and Gerald L. Smith (Berkeley: University of California Press, 2007), 175–6; emphasis added.

and oppression," he said, "and out of the wounds of a frail world, new systems of justice and equality are being born. The shirtless and barefoot people of the land are rising up as never before. The people who sat in darkness have seen a great light." It is incumbent upon all of us, he said, to "support these revolutions."[57] In the United States, King was drawn to a burgeoning Black youth movement that had begun its own revolution of values through indigenous confrontation with "actual being." It was "precisely when young Negroes threw off their middle-class values that they made an historic social contribution," he said.[58] And it is perhaps worth noting that, in the last year of his life especially, King was tempted to move out of his non-violent comfort zone in an effort to grapple with modes of indigenous protest against the coming of the new phase of the capitalist economy, often riotous protest against what critics refer to today as the neoliberal world order.[59]

It is remarkable how well King's mature reflections on political economy transcend their historical genesis. As the historian Thomas Holt has documented, into the 1970s and 1980s, into the accumulation crises of the early neoliberal era, "blacks found themselves the late-arriving guests as the feast for an expanding middle class was ending." In the throes of deindustrialization, as the "post-production" domestic economy came to resemble "a zero-sum game rather than an expanding pie, policies of racial preference became the scapegoat for a tightening labor market and concentration of educational opportunities."[60] Today scholars argue that the rapid economic growth of the mid-twentieth century is beginning to look more and more like the great historical exception and that the zero-sum tendencies of the neoliberal era indicate a likelihood that no type or degree of government intervention can do much to build out prosperity or even sustain an existing middle class. If the new economy is fraught with accumulation crises and is moving towards a zero-sum relation between winners and losers, then we ought to expect a new era of politicization, a future resistance that sets out to work both within and beyond conventional channels of liberal democracy, as King envisioned half a century ago. The mature King knew all too well that "some Americans would need to

[57] King, "Beyond Vietnam: A Time to Break Silence," 215.
[58] King, "A New Sense of Direction."
[59] See Martin Luther King, Jr., *The Trumpet of Conscience* (Boston: Beacon, 2011).
[60] Thomas C. Holt, *Children of Fire: A History of African Americans* (New York: Hill and Wang, 2010), 354, 357.

give up privileges and resources for others to live in decency." And he knew all too well that "that took politics."[61]

In 1967, King said that "there is nothing except a tragic death wish to prevent us from reordering our priorities so that the pursuit of peace will take precedence over the pursuit of war … nothing to keep us from molding a recalcitrant status quo with bruised hands until we have fashioned it into a brotherhood."[62] But surely the obstacles, from ideological and fetishistic obfuscation to the emboldened interests of counterrevolution, were far more formidable, far more complex, than King led on. This, of course, King knew all too well. In the last years of his life especially, King battled through fits of depression, a recurring sense that he was chasing a fool's errand. Many in his inner circle, including veteran anti-capitalist soldiers such as Bayard Rustin and Stanley Levinson, sought to persuade King that the United States was just not yet ready for radical political-economic restructuring. And yet King soldiered on. Part of what he gave us, in his last years especially, was a compelling critical theory, a diagnostic account of racial capitalism. And this was no fool's errand. Perhaps now more than ever, King's critique, especially when read in complementary relation to the resurgence of interest in Marxism, can help to motivate incisive thinking about the obstacles that foreclose realization of a more just world as well as the enduring activist legacy of the Black radical tradition.

BIBLIOGRAPHY

Amin, Samir. *The Law of Worldwide Value.* New York: Monthly Review, 2010.

Baran, Paul A. and Paul Sweezy. *Monopoly Capital: An Essay on the American Economic and Social Order.* New York: Monthly Review, 1966.

Berdyaev, N. A. "Marxism and the Conception of Personality." *Christendom*, no. 2 (December 1935). http://www.berdyaev.com/berdiaev/berd_lib/1935_400.html.

Dawson, Michael C. "Hidden in Plain Sight: A Note on Legitimation Crises and the Racial Order." *Critical Historical Studies* (Spring 2016): 143–61.

Denning, Michael. "Wageless Life." *New Left Review* 66 (November–December 2010): 70–97.

Endnotes Collective. "Misery and Debt." *Endnotes 2* (2010).

Fanon, Frantz. *The Wretched of the Earth.* New York: Grove, 2005.

---

[61] Jackson, *From Civil Rights to Human Rights*, 251.
[62] King, "Beyond Vietnam: A Time to Break Silence," 215.

Fraser, Nancy. "Expropriation and Exploitation in Racialized Capitalism: A Reply to Michael Dawson." *Critical Historical Studies* (Spring 2016): 163–78.

Garrow, David J. *Bearing the Cross: Martin Luther King, Jr., and the Southern Christian Leadership Conference.* New York: HarperCollins, 2004.

Gilmore, Ruth Wilson. "Race and Globalization." In *Geographies of Global Change: Remapping the World,* edited by R. J. Johnson, Peter J. Taylor, and Michael J. Watts. New York: Wiley-Blackwell, 2002.

Gutiérrez, Ramón A. "Internal Colonialism: An American Theory of Race." *Du Bois Review* 1, no. 2 (2004): 281–95.

Harvey, David. *The Limits to Capital.* New York: Verso, 2006.

Holt, Thomas C. *Children of Fire: A History of African Americans.* New York: Hill and Wang, 2010.

Jackson, Thomas F. *From Civil Rights to Human Rights: Martin Luther King, Jr., and the Struggle for Economic Justice.* Philadelphia: University of Pennsylvania Press, 2009.

King, Jr., Martin Luther. "A New Sense of Direction." *Worldview* (April 1972): 5–12.

King, Jr., Martin Luther. "Minutes of the National Advisory Committee." In David J. Garrow, *Bearing the Cross: Martin Luther King, Jr., and the Southern Christian Leadership Conference,* 581. New York: HarperCollins, 2004.

King, Jr., Martin Luther. "'A Realistic Look at the Question of Progress in the Area of Race Relations,' Address Delivered at St. Louis Freedom Rally." In *The Papers of Martin Luther King, Jr., Volume VI: Advocate of the Social Gospel, September 1948–March 1963,* edited by Clayborne Carson, Susan Carson, Susan Englander, Troy Jackson, and Gerald L. Smith, 175–6. Berkeley: University of California Press, 2007a.

King, Jr., Martin Luther. "Will Capitalism Survive?" In *The Papers of Martin Luther King, Jr., Volume VI: Advocate of the Social Gospel, September 1948–March 1963,* edited by Clayborne Carson, Susan Carson, Susan Englander, Troy Jackson, and Gerald L. Smith, 104–7. Berkeley: University of California Press, 2007b.

King, Jr., Martin Luther. *Stride Toward Freedom: The Montgomery Story.* Boston: Beacon, 2010a.

King, Jr., Martin Luther. *Where Do We Go From Here: Chaos or Community?* Boston: Beacon, 2010b.

King, Jr., Martin Luther. "Local 1199, New York City, March 10, 1968." In *All Labor Has Dignity,* edited by Michael K. Honey, 153–66. Boston: Beacon, 2011a.

King, Jr., Martin Luther. *The Trumpet of Conscience.* Boston: Beacon, 2011b.

King, Jr., Martin Luther. "United Automobile Workers Union, Detroit, Michigan, April 17, 1961." In *All Labor Has Dignity,* edited by Michael K. Honey, 23–30. Boston: Beacon, 2011c.

King, Jr., Martin Luther. "My Trip to the Land of Gandhi." In *A Single Garment of Destiny: A Global Vision of Justice*, edited by Lewis V. Baldwin, 100–9. Boston: Beacon, 2012.

King, Jr., Martin Luther. "Letter from Birmingham Jail." In *Gospel of Freedom: Martin Luther King, Jr.'s Letter from Birmingham Jail and the Struggle That Changed a Nation*, edited by Jonathan Rieder, 169–86. New York: Bloomsbury, 2014.

King, Jr., Martin Luther. "Beyond Vietnam: A Time to Break Silence." In *The Radical King*, edited by Cornel West, 201–20. Boston: Beacon, 2016a.

King, Jr., Martin Luther. "The Drum Major Instinct." In *The Radical King*, edited by Cornel West, 253–64. Boston: Beacon, 2016b.

King, Jr., Martin Luther. "Speech at SCLC Staff Retreat." The Archives of the King Center for Nonviolent Social Change, Atlanta, GA, n.d.

Luxemburg, Rosa. *The Accumulation of Capital*. New York: Routledge, 2003.

Marx, Karl. *A Contribution to the Critique of Political Economy*, 1859; reprint, https://www.marxists.org/archive/marx/works/1859/critique-pol-economy/preface.htm.

Marx, Karl. "Theories of Surplus Value." https://www.marxists.org/archive/marx/works/1863/theories-surplus-value/ch17.htm.

Marx, Karl. *Capital*. Vol. 1. New York: Penguin, 1992.

Marx, Karl. *Capital*. Vol. 2. New York: Penguin, 1993a.

Marx, Karl. *Capital*. Vol. 3. New York: Penguin, 1993b.

Melamed, Jodi. *Represent and Destroy: Rationalizing Violence in the New Racial Capitalism*. Minneapolis: University of Minnesota Press, 2011.

Melamed, Jodi. "Racial Capitalism." *Critical Ethnic Studies* 1, no. 1 (Spring 2015): 76–85.

Robinson, Cedric J. *Black Marxism: The Making of the Black Radical Tradition*. Chapel Hill: University of North Carolina Press, 2000.

Singh, Nikhil Pal. "On Race, Violence, and So-Called Primitive Accumulation." *Social Text 128* 34, no. 3 (September 2016): 27–50.

Singh, Nikhil Pal. *Race and America's Long War*. Oakland: University of California Press, 2017.

Sokol, Jason. *There Goes My Everything: White Southerners in the Age of Civil Rights, 1945–1975*. New York: Vintage, 2007.

Terry, Brandon M. "Requiem for a Dream: The Problem-Space of Black Power" In *To Shape a New World: Essays on the Political Philosophy of Martin Luther King, Jr.*, edited by Tommie Shelby and Brandon M. Terry, 290–324. Cambridge, MA: Harvard University Press, 2018.

Watson, Melvin. "Letter to King." August 14, 1952. In *The Papers of Martin Luther King, Jr., Vol. II: Rediscovering Precious Values, July 1951–November 1955*, edited by Clayborne Carson, Ralph E. Luker, Penny A. Russell, and Pete Holloran, 156–7. Berkeley: University of California Press, 1994.

Fetishism and Exploitation Marx - 150 and Marx 200: What Has Changed?

Paula Rauhala

I. Introduction

"Marx's critical theory of fetishism has become a central point of reference for a 'modern' understanding of Marxism which is represented by, among others, intellectuals who wish to distance themselves from the antiquated dogmas of 'traditional Marxism,'" Jan Hoff, a proponent of the contemporary German New Reading of Marx (*Neue Marx-Lektüre*), probably the most popular Marxist approach in Germany today, wrote in 2009.[1] This position raises an interesting question: Why does the emphasis on fetishism differentiate between a "modern" and an "antiquated" reading of *Capital*?

The modern reading to which Hoff refers dates back to around 1968 and is especially connected to the Frankfurt school. A glance at the literature that appeared in Germany at the time of the centennial anniversary of *Capital* (1967) and on the 150th anniversary of Marx's birth (1968) indicates that readers of *Capital* who followed the critical theory of the

---

[1] Jan Hoff, *Marx Worldwide: On the Development of the International Discourse on Marx since 1965*, trans. Nicholas Gray (Leiden: Brill, 2017), 138.

P. Rauhala (✉)
Tampere University, Tampere, Finland

© The Author(s) 2019
S. Gupta et al. (eds.), *Karl Marx's Life, Ideas, and Influences*, Marx,
Engels, and Marxisms, https://doi.org/10.1007/978-3-030-24815-4_9

Frankfurt school typically perceived the concept of fetishism as key to the book. In East Germany, the fetishism theme was not as central in the most important readings of *Capital* at the time. Later, the leading East German expert on Marx's use of this concept, Thomas Marxhausen, even once made the pun that some West German authors fetishize the concept of fetishism.[2]

Many valid reasons justified the increased interest in reading *Capital* through the lens of fetishism in the Federal Republic of Germany (FRG) in the 1960s. This chapter presents the argument that these reasons were not pertinent in the East at the time and were no longer relevant at Marx's bicentennial in 2018.

In this chapter, discussions on the centennial anniversary of *Capital* and the 150th anniversary of Marx's birth in 1967–68 are considered, as are discussions that took place 50 years later, in 2017–18, prompting the question—what has changed? It will be argued that an interpretation of *Capital* that emphasized the concept of fetishism answered the problems encountered by its West German readers in the late 1960s much better than a more traditional reading, in which Marx's theory of surplus value plays a more prominent role. The interpretation of the 1968 generation of the Frankfurt school is, however, still popular today, 50 years later. The argument presented in this chapter is that some of the key ideas of this approach to *Capital* are becoming more and more anachronistic, as the world has changed from what it was in 1968.

There are a number of possible explanations for why a reading of *Capital* that focuses on Marx's theory of fetishism made more sense than a more traditional reading in Frankfurt during the 1960s. The first and most obvious is that it follows in the tradition of Western Marxist discussions on alienation and reification. Unlike the first generation of the Frankfurt school, this generation of their students, inspired by the publication of *Grundrisse* in 1953 in the German Democratic Republic (GDR), embraced *Capital* as Marx's main philosophical work, rather than viewing it primarily as a study in economics. Instead, they thought *Capital* contains a much broader social theory. This is probably partly because most readers of *Capital* in the West were philosophers or sociologists, whereas in the East, mostly economists were considered competent commentators

---

[2] Thomas Marxhausen, "Fetischismusfetischismus 'linker' Marxologie. Bemerkungen zur Marxverfälschung durch Ulrich Erckenbrecht, 'das Geheimnis des Fetischismus' Grundmotive der Marxschen Erkenntniskritik," *Hallesche Arbeitsblätter zur Marx-Engels-Forschung* 6 (1979).

on *Capital*. This fact may seem trivial, but the reasons for this state of affairs are connected to the fundamental differences between West and East German societies.

Another reason why the focus on the concept of fetishism in *Capital* made sense in Frankfurt in the 1960s is that Marx's theory of fetishism was applied in the West German context to both forms of modern, industrial societies, that is, capitalism and state socialism—at least implicitly. Thirdly, the fetishism theory offers an explanation for the ongoing question of Western Marxists: Are workers still interested in overthrowing capitalism? This question was especially urgent in West Germany during the years of the *Wirtschaftswunder* (economic miracle), an exceptionally long period of economic growth after World War II that benefitted not only owners but also workers. The theory of fetishism brings to the forefront the structural effects of the capitalist market economy. The real relations appear in inverted forms. The system of class exploitation appears as an egalitarian market system in which individuals pursue success in the sphere of equality and freedom. In 1968 FRG, it seemed that workers, who were relatively well off, had taken this appearance more or less for granted. The rebelling students' theoretical role model, Herbert Marcuse, even announced on the podium of the Free University in West Berlin, at the height of the student revolts in 1967, that workers were no longer able to see the destructive nature of the system, which offered comfortable unfreedom. Only outcasts and intellectuals were able to see the real relations.[3]

During the past 50 years, which separate the Marx jubilee of 1967–68 from that of 2017–18, the world has changed. After decades during which a challenger to the capitalist system still existed, global capitalism is now returning to business as usual. The shortening of the work day in the West has stagnated since the 1970s.[4] Income inequality has increased.[5] Also, the link between productivity growth and the growth of real wages has been broken. Even in Germany, the link between the increase in labour productivity and the growth of real wages has been severed since the 1990s, and

[3] Herbert Marcuse, "Ziele, Formen und Aussichten der Studentenopposition," *Das Argument* 45 (1967): 399–400.

[4] Christoph Hermann, *Capitalism and the Political Economy of Work Time* (London and New York: Routledge, 2015), 1.

[5] Anwar Shaikh, *Capitalism, Competition, Conflict, Crisis* (Oxford: Oxford University Press, 2016), 755.

the level of inequality between the rich and the poor has increased.[6] For these reasons, the main argument of Marx's *Capital* that capitalism is a system of private profit making by exploiting wage labour, rather downplayed in the *Neue Marx Lektüre*, is today much more relevant than it was in 1960s West Germany. Therefore, in contrast to much of the Frankfurtian reading of Capital, today, a more topical reading of the book appreciates fetishism as a crucial concept of Marx's critique, and yet, according to this reading the concept of fetishism can only be understood correctly in connection to the theory of surplus value.

II. The 150th Anniversary of *Capital* and the Bicentennial of Marx's Birth, 2017–18

The reading of *Capital*, formulated by the students of the first generation of the Frankfurt school around 1968, was still popular in Germany on the 150th anniversary of its publication and on the bicentennial of Marx's birth in 2017–18, and it has gained popularity elsewhere in the world. This reading does not consider the imperative of profit making at the expense of wage labour as the most important aspect of Marx's analysis of capitalism. Rather, it finds the key insights of *Capital* within the first chapter of the first volume, in the analysis of the commodity, in which Marx does not yet comment on wage labour and capital. Indeed, this reading connects Marx's theory of fetishism primarily to the topics of the first three chapters—that is, commodities and money.

Unlike in the reading defended here, in the *Neue Marx Lektüre*, the essence of capitalism is not found in bourgeois class relations, but in commodity production and in the fact that labour produces value in the first place. In the words of Michael Heinrich, probably the most notable follower of the Frankfurtian tradition of reading *Capital* in Germany today, the problem of capitalism is "the rule of value over humans."[7] Politically, it follows that the goal is not primarily overcoming class exploitation and capital as an objectified form of bourgeois class relations, but overcoming the various forms of "impersonal domination,"

---

[6] Oliver Nachtwey, *Germany's Hidden Crisis: Social Decline in the Heart of Europe*, trans. David Fernbach and Loren Balhorn (London and New York: Verso, 2018), 112–3, 116.

[7] Heinrich, Michael, *An Introduction to the Three Volumes of Karl Marx's Capital*, trans. Alexander Locascio (New York: Monthly Review Press, 2012), 77. See also Rakowitz, Nadja, *Einfache Warenproduktion. Ideal und Ideologie* (Freiburg: ça ira, 2000), 86.

that is, commodities, money, capital, and the state.[8] Heinrich motivates his reading with a critique of traditional Marxism.

> The simple ideas of traditional 'Marxist political economy,' centered around labor and exploitation and heavily relying on the false falling rate of profit, cannot help very much to understand contemporary capitalism. But a 'critique of political economy,' centered around 'form analysis,' fetishism and a monetary theory of value and capital can help very well.[9]

Another influential reader of *Capital*, who contrasts his own reading to traditional Marxism, is Moishe Postone. Being a student of Iring Fetscher, the political science professor at the Goethe University of Frankfurt from the early 1960s until the late 1980s, Postone is probably the most eminent proponent of the Frankfurtian reading of *Capital* in the Anglophone world.

In Postone's reading of *Capital*, the target of Marx's critique is not class domination, that is, the private ownership of the means of production and the exploitation of wage labour. Rather, the problem of capitalism is the form of social labour itself, the fact that labour produces value as abstract social labour. According to Postone, "The system constituted by abstract labor embodies a new form of social domination. It exerts a form of social compulsion whose impersonal, abstract, and objective character is historically new."[10]

Consequently, the working class should not seek the abolition of the appropriation of unpaid surplus labour by the owning classes. Instead, it should aim to overcome the "value creating labour" itself.[11] This is because, according to Postone's reading of Marx, "social domination in capitalism does not, on its most fundamental level, consist of the domination of people by other people, but in the domination of people by abstract social structures that people themselves constitute."[12] Fetishism instead of exploitation is the key concept of Marx's book, because capitalism is characterized by "self-generated structural domination," which

[8] Heinrich, Michael, *An Introduction to the Three Volumes*, 222.

[9] Heinrich, Michael, "Relevance and Irrelevance of Marxian Economics," *New School Economic Review* 1, no. 1 (2004): 57.

[10] Moishe Postone, *Time, Labor and Social Domination. A Reinterpretation of Marx'* (Cambridge: Cambridge University Press, 2003), 158–9.

[11] Ibid., 63.

[12] Ibid., 30.

"cannot be fully grasped in terms of class exploitation and domination," but rather, as "a historical dynamic beyond the control of the individuals constituting it."[13]

In the more traditional reading of *Capital* defended in this writing, the specificity of a society in which the capitalist mode of production is dominant, compared to other class societies, is that the appropriation of surplus labour is mediated by the market, and therefore, is not observable and not personal. Like in all other forms of class societies, the work day of a worker is divided into necessary and surplus labour. In capitalism, however, the distribution of the product of both parts of the work day among the working class and the owning classes (industrial capital, money-dealing capital, commercial capital, and landed property) is mediated through market mechanisms. The value added appears in the fetishized forms of wage, profit, commercial profit, interest, and land rent. Therefore, fetishism is a crucial concept, and it is present in all three books of *Capital*. The fetishisms of commodities and money are just the beginning of the story, and after the fourth chapter of the first volume, the concept of fetishism is always related to surplus value and to the mechanisms of its production, circulation, and distribution.

Unlike this reading, in which the essence of capitalism is explained by the concepts of capital and wage labour, for Postone, "Marx seeks to grasp the core of capitalism with the categories of commodity and value."[14] Hence, if we follow Postone's reading, it follows that Marx would present his critique of capitalism already before presenting the transformation of money into capital, and before demonstrating how the division of the work day into necessary and surplus labour is under bourgeois relations of production, reflected in the monetary categories of wage, profit, interest, commercial profit, and land rent. The political implication of Postone's reading is that the primary goal should not be overcoming the system of class exploitation based on the appropriation of surplus labour, but overcoming "value" altogether.[15] In a more traditional reading, as defended herein, the essence of capitalism cannot be found in the first chapter of *Capital*, and the political conclusions drawn from the book are related to the bourgeois class relations and not to the existence of value, commodities, and money, as such.

[13] Ibid., 31.
[14] Ibid., 131.
[15] Ibid., 26.

The Frankfurtian reading of *Capital* has also influenced contemporary readers of the text in the Anglophone world. Among them is Peter Hudis, who writes that Marx's

> primary concern is with the way social relations in modern society take on the *form* of value. His main object of critique is the *inverted* character of social relations in capitalism, where *human* relations take on the form of relations between *things*. There is little doubt that Marx's critique of capitalism centres upon a critique of value-production.[16]

As noted, this interpretation of *Capital*, which identifies commodities and money, and fetishism escorting these forms, as the main target of Marxian critique of capitalism, has its roots in West Germany around the year 1968. In the coming sections, it will be argued that 50 years ago in West Germany, there were good reasons to emphasize Marx's theory of commodity fetishism instead of the theory of surplus value and to emphasize impersonal domination in Marx's theory, instead of class rule. These reasons are embedded in the specific context of reading *Capital* in divided Germany around 1967–68. The next section will provide an overview of this peculiar historical situation.

III. Centennial Anniversary of *Capital* and 150th Anniversary of Marx's Birth in East and West Germany, 1967–68

In 1968, Germany was divided into the GDR and the FRG. The settings for Marx and Marxist research in both states were very different. The year 1968 marked a historical break in both German states, and also for the research on Marx and Marxism. What is common in both states is that Marx's works became more readily available during the jubilee. The years preceding 1968 had been also politically interesting in both states. With regard to the argument presented in this chapter, the most important factor in West German society at the time was the rise of the student movement, while in the East, the most important events were de-Stalinization and economic reforms.

---

[16] Peter Hudis, *Marx's Concept of the Alternative to Capitalism* (Leiden and Boston: Brill, 2012), 8.

In GDR, Marx belonged to the official canon of the socialist state, which professed a Marxist-Leninist ideology. This meant not only that Marxist research had plenty of resources, but also that the Socialist Unity Party (*Sozialistische Einheitspartei Deutschlands*, SED) interfered with the research, which made genuine research difficult.

East Germany is, however, especially interesting for research on Marx, and increasingly so from 1967 on, when editorial work on the historical-critical edition of Marx's and Engels' works, *Marx-Engels-Gesamtausgabe* (MEGA), started in East Berlin. The project, which Stalin had suppressed, was continued on the centennial of Marx's *chef d'oeuvre*. On that day, September 14, 1967, the organ of the Communist Party of the Soviet Union (*Pravda*) and the organ of the SED (*Neues Deutschland*) announced that the Institute of Marxism Leninism in Moscow and the Institute of Marxism Leninism in East Berlin would continue to work on MEGA.[17] The darkest years of Stalinism were over. New volumes would not appear before 1975, but during the 1950s and 1960s, serious research on Marx's work, Marxian economics, and Marxism were revived. Also, the 41 volumes of *Marx-Engels-Werke* (MEW), which first appeared during the "Karl Marx year" in 1953, were completed on the sesquicentennial of Marx's birth—May 5, 1968.[18]

Another factor enforcing the revival of credible scientific research and relatively free and critical discussion on the Marxian political economy was the New Economic System (*Neues ökonomisches System*, NES), a promising reform programme of the socialist economy during the early 1960s.[19] The NES spurred not only practical but also theoretical debates on fundamental problems of Marxian economics, Marx's method, and interpretations of *Capital*.

---

[17] "Gesamtausgabe der Werke von Marx und Engels," *Neues Deutschland*, September 14, 1967, 1–2.

[18] "Marx-Engels-Werkausgabe vollständig erschienen," *Neues Deutschland*, May 5, 1968, 2. Both publication projects trained a considerable number of experts on Marx's and Engels' thought: Beiträge zur Marx-Engels-Forschung. Neue Folge (2006) presents 160 short biographies of the editors of MEW, MEGA, and the Soviet collected works of Marx and Engels, Sočinenija. "Kurzbiografien," in *Beiträge zur Marx-Engels-Forschung. Neue Folge. Sonderband 5. Die Marx-Engels-Werkausgaben in der UdSSR und DDR* (1945–1968), ed. Carl-Erich Vollgraf, Richard Sperl, and Rolf Hecker (Hamburg: Argument Verlag, 2006).

[19] See, for example, Klaus Steinitz and Dieter Walter, *Plan–Markt–Demokratie. Prognose und langfristige Planung in der DDR–Schlussfolgerungen für morgen* (Hamburg: VSA-Verlag, 2014); Günter Krause, *Wirtschaftstheorie in der DDR* (Marburg: Metropolis-Verlag, 1998).

In West Germany, the Cold War atmosphere—not in the form of communism as in the East but in the form of anti-communism—presented challenges for Marxist research and for dealing with Marx's ideas in an academic context. During the 1950s, the country had only a few Marxian academics, and until 1968, few of Marx's works had been published in the West. This situation changed during the 1960s. What was important for the Marx research in Frankfurt was that during the 1960s, Iring Fetscher published a student edition of Marx's and Engels' texts. Fetscher, known for his critiques of Soviet Marxism, was a professor of political science at the Goethe University of Frankfurt, and Moishe Postone's teacher.

One of the volumes of Fetscher's student edition contained the first section "commodities and money" from the first edition of *Capital*. This text became important for new readings of *Capital* among the younger generation of the Frankfurt school, given that Marx's presentation of the value form and commodity fetishism differ in this first edition from the subsequent, commonly used editions.[20] Michael Heinrich reports that this text was seen as "the 'missing link' between the 'Grundrisse' and later editions of 'Capital'."[21]

The Marx jubilee of 1967–68 made Marx's works more available not only in the East, but also in the West. In 1967, on the 100th anniversary of *Capital*, an edition of the three volumes appeared, as *Europäische Verlagsanstalt* (EVA) published a licensed edition of *Capital* by East German Dietz Verlag. At the same time, the *Grundrisse* appeared for the first time in the West, and later, *Theories of Surplus Value*. The jubilee was the formal reason for the publication of Marx's original texts, but another reason was the increased demand for those texts among radicalized youth.

Frankfurt was not only the stronghold of the Marxist critical theory, but also, from the mid-1960s, the hub of the "anti-authoritarian wing" of the student movement. The reading of *Capital*, emphasizing fetishism and impersonal domination in Marx's critique, came into being in close proximity to this group of students and young researchers.

[20] See Hans-Georg Backhaus, "Zur Dialektik der Wertform," in *Beiträge zur Marxistischen Erkenntnistheorie*, ed. Alfred Schmidt (Frankfurt am Main: Suhrkamp, 1969), 129.

[21] Michael Heinrich, "Reconstruction or Deconstruction?," in *Re-reading Marx: New Perspectives after the Critical Edition*, ed. Riccardo Bellofiore and Roberto Fineschi (London: Palgrave Macmillan, 2009), 73.

In 1968, university students changed the whole of West German society, but especially shook its highly elitist university culture. The appearance of what is nowadays called the *Neue Marx Lektüre* is tightly connected to these events. Hans-Jürgen Krahl, who was a student of Adorno, was politically and theoretically the leading figure of the movement in Frankfurt, as Rudi Dutschke was in Berlin. Krahl was not only a political figure, but also one of the most important representatives of the new philosophical readings of *Capital.*

The background for the rise of the student movement was, as Georg Fülberth explains, the short supply of fresh labour power in the FRG after the building of the Berlin Wall in 1961.[22] After World War II and until 1961, the miraculously growing economy of the FRG benefitted from educated labour streaming from the East to the West. After erection of the wall, the sudden increased need for highly qualified labour opened the doors of the academy to the children of non-academic parents. These students encountered a conservative university culture and the rigid, undemocratic structures of the university institution. This generation of students relaxed the academic culture, and they revolted outside universities by opposing the emergency laws (*Notstandsgesetzgebung*), the Vietnam War, and the bourgeois media embodied by the *Springer* house, which was central in stirring up negative attitudes towards the protesting students.

At the same time, the meaning of being academically educated changed. Before World War II, university students in the most educated countries (Germany, France, and Britain) accounted for no more than "one tenth of one per cent of their joint populations."[23] By the late 1980s, "in educationally ambitious countries, students formed upwards of 2.5 per cent of the *total* population."[24] FRG was among the countries where the number of university students multiplied by four to five from 1960 until 1980.[25] This meant that the children of the middle class or even of working-class families gained access to the West German academy.[26] This partly explains the shift among academic students from conservative attitudes to leftist attitudes.

---

[22] Georg Fülberth, "Linke Hoffnungen, linke Chancen, linkes Versagen?" in *Pankover Vorträge* 152. *1968—Bilanz und ungelöste Probleme* (Berlin: Helle Panke, 2010), 48.

[23] Eric Hobsbawm, *Age of Extremes: The Short Twentieth Century 1914–1991* (London: Abacus, 1995), 295.

[24] Ibid.

[25] Ibid., 296.

[26] Wolfgang Abendroth, "Der Weg der Studenten zum Marxismus," *Z. Zeitschrift für Marxistische Erneuerung* 113 (March 2018): 104.

Even if the anti-authoritarian wing of the West German student movement had assumed the typical West German anti-communist attitude, as Wolfgang Abendroth puts it, the lasting result of the happenings of the year 1968 in West Germany was the end of official anti-communism and anti-Marxism.[27] The Communist Party of Germany (*Kommunistische Partei Deutschlands*, KPD) was legally banned from 1956 onwards. In 1968, the state cancelled the ban on the KPD. Dealing with Marxism was no longer "a cardinal sin," as Adorno had described it in 1962, in his lecture on Marx's critique of political economy.[28] This is the context from which the new reading of *Capital* emerged.

IV. The Concept of Fetishism in the Reading of *Capital* Around 1968

Although he taught many students, Adorno himself did not write much about *Capital*, but he made good use of the concepts of Marx's critique of political economy, such as commodity fetishism, ideology, and the idea of real abstraction. Many of Adorno's students came to emphasize these themes as well. Ernst Theodor Mohl explains:

> In an exclusive tutorial at the beginning of the 1960s, he [Adorno] explained to me the section on fetish and the subject-object inversion which follows from it in such a way that I was subsequently able to avoid taking an economistically foreshortened perspective on Marx's critique of capitalism.[29]

Similarly, Jan Hoff explains that,

> according to [Hans-Jürgen] Krahl, Adorno's legacy was the transmission of the consciousness of emancipation characteristic of the Western Marxism of the interwar period through his specific reference to the categories of reification, fetishisation, mystification and second nature.[30]

---

[27] Ibid., 107–8.

[28] Theodor W. Adorno, "Theodor W. Adorno on 'Marx and the Basic Concepts of Sociological Theory': From a Seminar Transcript in the Summer Semester of 1962," *Historical Materialism* 26, no.1 (2018): 164.

[29] Ernst Theodor Mohl, "Ein Reisebericht," in *In Memoriam Wolfgang Jahn: Der ganze Marx—Alles Verfasste veröffentlichen, erforschen und den 'ungeschriebenen' Marx rekonstruieren* (Hamburg: Argument Verlag, 2002), 18–19. Quoted after: Hoff, *Marx Worldwide*, 77.

[30] Hoff, *Marx Worldwide*, 28–29.

Another student of Adorno, Hans Georg Backhaus, later noted that "essentially, all of my writings deal with one and the same theme: the problem of fetishism."[31]

Why was the concept of fetishism so central for the young generation of readers of Marx from the Frankfurt school? Why is this concept supposed to make a difference between "a traditional" and a "modern," or a "non-dogmatic," reading of Marx's mature work?

In one important event in the context of the student revolts, in the fully packed Auditorium Maximum of the *Freie Universität* in West Berlin in 1967, Herbert Marcuse explained that the one-dimensional society had managed to integrate the working class. According to Marcuse, the only opposition left consisted of intellectuals, hippies, and outcasts.[32] Only these groups were able to see behind the thoroughly bureaucratized order, which was repressing the majority of the people by satisfying their needs and creating more and more false needs.

Similarly, a key question for Marcuse, in his talk at the Summer school in Korčula in 1964, had been:

[W]hy should the overthrow of the existing order be a vital necessity for people who own, or can hope to own, good clothes, a well-stocked larder, a TV set, a car, a house and so on, all within the existing order?[33]

Also, in *One-Dimensional Man* (1964), which appeared in a German translation by Alfred Schmidt in 1967, Marcuse traces the reasons for the diminishing revolutionary potential of the Western working class. As Marcuse puts it, people seemed to "find their soul in their automobile, hi-fi set, split-level home, [and] kitchen equipment."[34] Marcuse and those following him suggested that workers were not able to see the true nature of the system.

What "system" does Marcuse actually address in his critique? It is interesting that Marcuse, more or less explicitly, targets his critique at both systems—capitalism and state socialism. An indication of this is that he

---

[31] Hans-Georg Backhaus, *Dialektik der Wertform: Untersuchungen zur Marxschen Ökonomiekritik*, 2nd ed. (Freiburg: Ça ira, 2011), 34; translation mine.

[32] Marcuse, "Ziele, Formen und Aussichten," 399.

[33] Herbert Marcuse, "Socialism in the Developed Countries," in *Marxism, Revolution and Utopia: Collected Papers of Herbert Marcuse*, ed. Douglas Kellner and Clayton Pierce (London and New York: Routledge, 2014), 6: 179.

[34] Herbert Marcuse, *One Dimensional Man: Studies in the Ideology of Advanced Industrial Society*, 2nd ed. (London and New York: Routledge, 2002), 11.

also applies the general terms "industrial civilization" and "industrial society" more often than the word "capitalism." Marcuse claims that "[t]echnology serves to institute new, more effective, and more pleasant forms of social control and social cohesion." Then, the "totalitarian tendency of these controls" is "creating similarities in the development of capitalism and communism."[35] This is a "comfortable, smooth, reasonable, democratic unfreedom" which "prevails in advanced industrial civilization."[36] Instead of the satisfaction of true needs, industrial society offers "repressive satisfaction."[37] Hence, one possible interpretation of Marcuse's assertions is that the real social relations remain hidden in both forms of industrialized and consumerist societies. As Douglas Kellner explains in the preface to the second edition, the book was "taken up by the emergent New Left as a damning indictment of contemporary Western societies, capitalist and communist."[38]

Claiming that the workers were alienated in their comfortable everyday existence can, of course, also be criticized as patronizing, as if the radical students or university professors who came from middle-class families knew better what the workers should aspire to. From today's perspective, it seems likely that the continually rising standard of living, shortened weekly work hours, and relatively good working conditions in both German states did, after all, satisfy many true and vital needs of wage workers.

Even if Marcuse traces some real developments, not all of the working class was satisfied. Especially in France and Italy, revolting students joined forces with striking workers. In West Germany, common struggles of students and workers were not so common, despite the economic recession, which had set in by 1966. One reason might have been, along with the relative weakness of the West German worker's institutions, as Wolfgang Abendroth explains, the students' "Adornian" language.[39] It is not easy to draw practical conclusions from Adorno's Marxism, and Adorno himself warned against doing so. As Alex Demirovic puts it, some of those who wanted to turn theory into practice reasoned that practice equals

---

[35] Ibid., xlvi.
[36] Ibid., 3.
[37] Ibid., 9.
[38] Douglas Kellner, "Introduction to the Second Edition," in *One Dimensional Man: Studies in the Ideology of Advanced Industrial Society*, 2nd ed. (London and New York: Routledge, 2002), xi.
[39] Abendroth, "Der Weg der Studenten zum Marxismus."

confrontation with the police.[40] As Adorno predicted, those who drew such an extreme conclusion often got disappointed, and therefore, became turncoats later.[41] The distance between the Frankfurtian students, the forms of their practice, and the workers might explain, in part, why Marx's description of how things are not as they immediately appear appealed to the followers of the Frankfurt school much more than a reading in which class conflict is seen as apparent.

Adorno was an influential teacher of the students. In the transcript made by Adorno's student Hans-Georg Backhaus of Adorno's lecture on 1962, the ideas of fetishism, real abstraction, character mask, and second nature play a prominent role. In Adorno's reading of *Capital*, the main problem Marx deals with is the constitution of economic facts. Whereas neoclassical economics aims at a mathematically precise description of established facts, Marx's critique, instead, reveals the mechanisms that constitute these facts in the first place.[42]

For Adorno, exchange is a process of abstraction, which does not take place in thought, but in social reality. The parties of exchange, whether they are conscious of it or not, reduce use values into their labour values during the process of exchange. Thus, they conduct a real abstraction, a conceptual operation in reality.[43] This abstraction is a result of people's own actions in the market, and yet, they encounter it as a coercive external reality, which becomes more violent, the less people are conscious of its operation. This abstraction also makes the relations behind the things appear as properties of these things themselves.[44] This is not just an appearance; it is not a question of a false consciousness. The structure of social reality is such that consciousness really is determined by being.[45] Individuals are at the mercy of the market forces.

---

[40] Alex Demirovic, "Die 'Ideen von 1968' und die inszenierte Geschichtslosigkeit," in *Emanzipation als Versöhnung. Zu Adornos Kritik der »Warentausch«-Gesellschaft und Perspektiven der Transformation*, ed. Iring Fetscher and Alfred Schmidt (Frankfurt am Main: Verlag Neue Kritik, 2002), 39.

[41] Ibid.

[42] Adorno, "Theodor W. Adorno on 'Marx and the Basic Concepts of Sociological Theory'," 163. See also Backhaus, "Zur Dialektik der Wertform," 139.

[43] Adorno, "Theodor W. Adorno on 'Marx and the Basic Concepts of Sociological Theory'," 156.

[44] Ibid., 159–60.

[45] Ibid., 160.

Adorno does not present, however, a circulationist model of the "commodity economy." He emphasizes that not only products are commodified, but labour power also is sold as a commodity. Workers are free to change from one employer to the other, but are, in any case, forced to sell their labour power and to give away unpaid labour to the capitalist class. A contract without the compulsion to perform unpaid surplus labour is not an option. Capitalists, for their part, are also at the mercy of external forces. They do not have personal reasons to strive for profit. They do it because they carry the character mask of capital.[46] Fetishism and the impersonal form of domination are at the centre of Adorno's reading of *Capital*.

What about the East German readers of *Capital*? Did they represent "the traditional reading," in which the concept of fetishism was neglected? At the least, it is safe to say that East German readers of *Capital* did not neglect this concept.[47] For example, Walter Tuchscheerer, in his book *Bevor das Kapital entstand* (1968), claims that the concepts of commodity and money fetishism offer the key to understanding Marx's theory of value.[48] However, Fred Oelßner, an important politician and the head of the Institute for Social Sciences at the Academy for Social Sciences of the central committee of SED (*Akademie für Gesellschaftswissenschaften beim ZK der SED*), writes in his preface to the book that the author, in places, overemphasizes the importance of commodity and money fetishisms in *Capital*.[49] Oelßner also refers to the examiners of Tuchscheerer's doctoral thesis, who criticized the same point.

[46] Ibid., 161–2.

[47] As also Jan Hoff emphasizes, especially the research carried on a few years later by an East German researcher of the MEGA project, Thomas Marxhausen, is still worthwhile for anyone interested in the development of the concept of fetishism in Marx's thought. See Thomas Marxhausen, "Die Theorie des Fetischismus im dritten Band des 'Kapitals'," in *Beiträge zur Marx-Engels Forschung* 25 (1988): 209–43; Thomas Marxhausen, "Fetischcharakter der Ware," in *Historisch-Kritisches Wörterbuch des Marxismus*, ed. Wolfgang Fritz Haug (Hamburg: Argument Verlag, 1999), 4: 343–54.

[48] Walter Tuchscheerer, *Bevor das Kapital entstand. Die Herausbildung und Entwicklung der ökonomischen Theorie von Karl Marx in der Zeit von 1843 bis 1858*, ed. Gerda Tuchscheerer (Berlin: Akademie-Verlag, 1968), 373.

[49] Fred Oelßner, "Vorwort," in *Bevor das Kapital entstand: Die Herausbildung und Entwicklung der ökonomischen Theorie von Karl Marx in der Zeit von 1843 bis 1858*, ed. Gerda Tuchscheerer (Berlin: Akademie-Verlag, 1968), 15.

Tuchscheerer's book is certainly one of the most important East German books on how *Capital* came about. Later, one of the most important figures of the Frankfurtian student movement and of the new readings of *Capital*, Ernst Theodor Mohl, calls the chapter of Tuchscheerer's book that traces the development of Marx's theory of fetishism "admirable." [50] This is because it "avoids the economistic foreshortening characteristic of previous discussion in the East," and instead, highlights "the qualitative, socially critical aspects of Marx's doctrine of value."[51]

Tuchscheerer's book appeared in the GDR during the Karl Marx jubilee in 1968 and was published simultaneously in FRG. The book probably influenced the new readings of *Capital* in the West as well,[52] as did probably another important book, *The Story of a Great Discovery* (*Istorii a odnogo velikogo otkrytii a K Marksa: k sozdanii u "Kapitala"*, 1965) by Vitaly Vygodsky, translated from Russian into German in the GDR to honour the centennial anniversary of *Capital* in 1967. The book deals with Marx's different manuscripts during the course of his research from 1850 until 1863. In the beginning of his book, Vygodsky notes that Marx overcame the fetishism (in addition to the empiricism and ahistoricism) typical of the bourgeois political economy very early, by explaining that the objective appearances of human labour are essentially forms of the appearance of the relations between human beings.[53] In *Poverty of Philosophy* (1847), Marx "formulated the most important theses of his economic doctrine: The relations of production are not, as in the opinion of bourgeois economists, relations between things but relations between people with reference to things," Vygodsky reminds readers.[54] Thus, Vygodsky by no means ignores the centrality of fetishism in Marx's critique of political economy. However, even if the concept of fetishism gained some attention in the East German discussions, the Frankfurtian way of elaborating on it was a distinctively Western phenomenon.

[50] Ernst Theodor Mohl, "Germany, Austria and Switzerland," in *Karl Marx's Grundrisse: Foundations of the Critique of Political Economy 150 Years Later*, ed. Marcello Musto (London and New York: Routledge, 2008), 194.

[51] Ibid.

[52] Rolf Hecker, "Hans-Georg Backhaus: Die Dialektik der Wertform," *Utopie kreativ* 94 (August 1998): 90.

[53] Vitaly Vygodsky, *The Story of a Great Discovery*, trans. S.V. Salt (Tunbridge Wells: Abacus Press, 1974), 20.

[54] Ibid. See also, Karl Marx, *The Poverty of Philosophy*, in MECW (London: Lawrence & Wishart, 1976), 6: 165.

V. AN ENCOUNTER BETWEEN EAST AND WEST

In a talk at the conference organized for the centennial of *Capital*, *100 Jahre das Kapital* in Frankfurt am Main, the translator of Marcuse's *One-Dimensional Man* and Adorno's assistant, Alfred Schmidt, presented an influential interpretation of Marx's method in *Capital*. According to Jan Hoff, "Schmidt's paper represents a kind of 'birth document' for what was a new phenomenon in postwar West Germany: the intensive and sophisticated engagement with the critique of political economy."[55]

Given that the *Neue Marx Lektüre* is known as a distinctively Western way of reading Marx, it is noteworthy that in the context of Schmidt's presentation, an interesting discussion between Schmidt and an East German delegate took place. This discussion helps to examine why the concept of fetishism was so central in the West, and at the same time, perhaps caused some unease in the East. This conference was an exceptional event in the sense that the organizer, the Institute of Political Science of the Goethe University of Frankfurt, headed by Iring Fetscher, had invited a very heterogeneous group of Marxist and non-Marxist researchers—among them, an official delegation consisting of the top political economists of GDR.

Schmidt's reading of *Capital* differed fundamentally from the East German reading of the work. For Schmidt, a sense of all of Marx's categories is critical. The laws of the political economy are an expression of such a society in which people do not yet control their own societal forces. Schmidt explained that the objectified appearances of human labour are products of our activity, forming a coercive, objective second nature. Different from capitalism, in communism, there would not be any forces or conditions existing independently of us, Schmidt announced.[56]

In other words, this philosopher claimed that all of the categories researched by Marx—commodities, money, capital, and wage—emerge from our own separate and non-reflected actions and belong exclusively to capitalism. Then, under socialism, *Capital* would be a useless book. From Schmidt's perspective, dialectical materialism was by no means an ontological hypothesis of the structure of reality, but instead, a description of the state of affairs in a capitalist society, in which thought is determined by

---

[55] Hoff, *Marx Worldwide*, 81.

[56] Alfred Schmidt, "Zum Erkenntnisbegriff der Kritik der politischen Ökonomie," in *Kritik der politischen Ökonomie heute: 100 Jahre 'Kapital'*, ed. Walter Euchner and Alfred Schmidt (Frankfurt am Main and Wien: Europäische Verlagsanstalt and Europa Verlag, 1968), 57.

being. People face the objectified appearances of their own labour as independent forces, and their own actions result in the laws of the economy, reminiscent of natural laws.

Schmidt also expressed the same idea in a collection of essays titled *Folgen einer Theorie*, which appeared on the centennial of *Capital*: economic determinism applies as long as humans do not control their own societal forces.[57] Ingo Elbe sums up Schmidt's conclusion: Marx's message was not an automatism of liberation, but liberation from the automatism of an irrational mode of socialization.[58]

Karl Bichtler, the head of the Department of Political Economy of Socialism in the East German Academy of Sciences, criticized Schmidt's basic premise, saying that as an aggregate result of the intersecting actions of individual economic actors, certain economic laws emerge. This is why we need to sit in this conference, Bichtler quipped.[59] In other words, for him, it was clear that laws and forces that are independent of economic actors still existed not only in capitalism, but also in state socialism.

Why did Alfred Schmidt's reading of *Capital* seem so problematic to Bichtler? In the Eastern bloc, every student of political economy had to read *Capital*, even if the book was not read as a manual for a planned economy. Most of Marx's categories and laws were considered specific to capitalism, but some very general laws were thought to operate in socialism as well. In the official celebrations of *Capital*, organized two weeks earlier in East Berlin, the Head of State Walter Ulbricht ascertained that the laws included the law of value, the law of the economy of time, and the so-called law of the congruence of the forces and relations of production.[60]

The law of value was considered to apply because some means of production, most of the raw materials, intermediate goods, and consumption

[57] Alfred Schmidt, "Über Geschichte und Geschichtsschreibung in der materialistischen Dialektik," in *Folgen einer Theorie: Essays über ›das Kapital‹ von Karl Marx*, ed. Ernst Theodor Mohl (Frankfurt am Main: Suhrkamp, 1967), 111.

[58] Ingo Elbe, *Marx im Westen. Die neue Marx-Lektüre in der Bundesrepublik seit 1965*, 2nd rev. ed. (Berlin: Akademie Verlag, 2010), 68.

[59] See *Kritik der politischen Okonomie heute. 100 Jahre 'Kapital'*, ed. Walter Euchner and Alfred Schmidt (Frankfurt am Main and Wien: Europäische Verlagsanstalt and Europa Verlag, 1968), 56.

[60] Walter Ulbricht, *Die Bedeutung des Werkes "Das Kapital" von Karl Marx für die Schaffung des entwickelten gesellschaftlichen Systems des Sozialismus in der DDR und den Kampf gegen das staatsmonopolistische Herrschaftssystem in Westdeutschland* (Berlin: Dietz Verlag, 1967).

goods were produced as commodities for exchange.[61] Unlike in capitalism, even if the products of labour appeared as commodities and money, the utilization of the commodities and money as capital was to be prevented.[62] Still, the law of value, it was believed, had not lost its validity.

However, commodity–money relations were considered subordinate to the socialist relations of production.[63] Whereas the determining characteristic of commodity production is the anarchistic regulation of the social production *ex post*, via the functioning of the law of value, in the state socialism, it was considered the task of the central planners. By the 1960s, however, it had become evident that the economy was not under the control of the central planners, partly because they had to base their decisions on incomplete information.[64] Companies did not always give correct information to the central planners, because it was not in their own best interests.[65] This is because the directors of the companies wanted to secure as many resources and encumber as few obligations for their companies as possible. The interests of the companies, and of individuals, did not coincide with the interests of the rest of the society—"yet," as was often added. Hence, the relations between producers were not transparent, so to say, which was one of the challenges of centralized planning.

The problems related to the diverging interests and incomplete information given to planners were among the most important reasons reform was needed, which GDR realized in the form of the New Economic System, launched in 1963. New Economic System aimed to improve the productivity of labour, the utilization of material resources, and the system of planning by introducing market elements in the form of enforcing monetary categories, increasing the independence of companies, and providing economic incentives.

Against this backdrop, it is easy to understand why Bichtler criticized Schmidt's presentation. From Bichtler's perspective, in a complex modern society, certain economic laws emerge from the actions of individual

[61] N. A. Zagalow et al., *Lehrbuch politische Ökonomie: Sozialismus*, trans. Hermann Mertens, Ingrid Stolte, and Günter Wermusch (Frankfurt/Main: Verlag Marxistische Blätter, 1972), 252ff.

[62] Ibid., 62.

[63] Ibid., 256.

[64] See, for example, Elmar Altvater, "Rationalisierung und Demokratisierung. Zu einigen Problemen der neuen ökonomischen Systeme im Sozialismus," *Das Argument* 39 (1966), 286.

[65] Jiří Kosta, Jan Meyer and Sibylle Weber, *Warenproduktion im Sozialismus; Überlegungen zur Theorie von Marx und zur Praxis in Osteuropa* (Frankfurt am Main: Fischer Taschenbuch Verlag, 1973), 159.

producers and consumers. The task of economics was to understand and make use of these laws for the purpose of achieving political goals. Getting these laws under control was not a simple task, nor was the abolishment of such laws in a complex modern system of production and exchange.

Schmidt's answer to Bichtler's critique was that Bichtler wrongly considers the objectivity of the laws of political economy as a positive aspect of *Capital*; the objectivity of these laws was the object of Marx's critique. One should not fetishize in theory what is already fetishized in reality.[66] Schmidt also got support from Oskar Negt, another important Frankfurtian theorist, who insisted that the scientific (*Naturwissenschaftlichen*) concepts—meaning the objective laws of the economy—in Marx's work have to be understood with their disappearance in communism in mind.[67]

Hence, one aspect of the disagreement could be that Marx's concept of fetishism—not so much fetishism of capital, but fetishism of commodities and money—enables a critique of the Eastern reading of Marx, and of some aspects of the state socialist society. Ernest Mandel also explicated such a critique in the conference. Mandel inquired of Bichtler whether fetishism, alienation, and ideology necessarily escort the state socialist variant of commodity production.[68]

The abolition of commodities and money was surely far from the realities of the GDR at the time. The country was struggling with much more concrete and acute problems. However, the critique presented by Western Marxists is interesting from the perspective of both theory and practice. With regards to social reality, state socialism seemed to be far from how Marx had envisioned post-capitalist society. A top-down order and lack of democracy and freedom of speech characterized the state socialism of the twentieth century. In addition, the state socialism seemed to share some core values with the Western capitalist societies of the time. In both systems, productionism and consumerism reigned. The workers did not have control over production and were offered a subordinate role in the workplace. Consent for the top-down order was bought with the promise of a rising standard of living and increasing possibilities to consume. In this

---

[66] See *Kritik der politischen Ökonomie heute*, 57.

[67] Ibid., 56.

[68] Ibid., 343–4.

respect, Marcuse's pairing of the two systems traces something interesting, even if his poetic critique does not offer a precise analysis of either one.[69] From the perspective of Frankfurtian readers of *Capital*, East Germans seemed to fetishize the socially specific economic forms (such as commodities, money, profit, interest, and wage) and laws (such as the law of value) presented by Marx in *Capital*. In the opinion of the Frankfurtians, Marx used these categories exclusively in a critical sense, including the categories of commodities and money. In the postscript from the editors of the conference publication *100 Jahre Kapital*, Walter Euchner and Alfred Schmidt write that economists from East Germany formulate Marx's critique of political economy as a positive theory of economics, and therefore, the critical sense of Marx's project tends to get lost.[70] In the same spirit, the "father" of the *Neue Marx Lektüre* Hans Georg Backhaus claims later that as Marxism-Leninism understood Marx's political economy affirmatively as a positive political economy, it functioned as a legitimation of the new system of domination.[71] Different from this, critical theory understands Marx's critique negatively, as a critique of fetishized forms. In other words, for the East German economists, it was clear that state socialism was essentially a commodity-producing society; for the Frankfurtians, instead, the term "socialist commodity production" did not make any sense.[72]

As readers of *Capital*, Bichtler and Schmidt operated in very different social realities. The questions they sought to answer with the help of the book were different. In the East, economists were mainly considered competent commentators of *Capital*, whereas in the West, Marxian theory was

---

[69] See Wolfgang Fritz Haug, "Das Ganze und das ganz Andere," in *Antworten auf Herbert Marcuse*, ed. Jürgen Habermas (Frankfurt am Main: Suhrkamp, 1968), 50–72.

[70] Walter Euchner and Alfred Schmidt, "Nachwort der Herausgeber," in *Kritik der politischen Ökonomie heute: 100 Jahre ›Kapital‹*, ed. Walter Euchner and Alfred Schmidt (Frankfurt am Main and Wien: Europäische Verlagsanstalt and Europa Verlag, 1968), 359.

[71] Hans-Georg Backhaus, *"Über den Doppelsinn der Begriffe "Politische Ökonomie" und "Kritik" bei Marx und in der Frankfurter Schule,"* in *Wolfgang Harich zum Gedächtnis: eine Gedenkschrift in zwei Bänden*, ed. Stefan Dornuf und Reinhard Pitsch (München: Müller & Nerding Verlag, 2000), 2: 19. Similar views are expressed by Heinrich, "Relevance and Irrelevance," 54, and Postone, *Time, Labor and Social Domination*, 170–1.

[72] See Backhaus, Hans-Georg, "Materialien zur Rekonstruktion der Marxschen Werttheorie," in *Gesellschaft. Beiträge zur Marxschen Theorie*, eds. H. G. Backhaus, G. Brandt, and G. Dill et al. (Frankfurt am Main: Suhrkamp Verlag, 1978), 11: 59.

rarely studied in economic departments. While Bichtler was interested in finding solutions to the practical problems of the state socialist planned economy, Schmidt was not at all concerned with such issues. Moreover, the Cold War drove the perspectives of each side ever farther away from each other.

The mainstream of the East German reading of *Capital* was grounded on very specific historical circumstances and on the practical problems of a centralized planned economy. Similarly, reading *Capital* in the context of the 1968 generation of the Frankfurt school and the anti-authoritarian wing of the student movement was peculiar. For the radicalized students, reading *Capital* through the concept of fetishism made much more sense than a more traditional reading. The historically specific societal conditions of the divided Germany during the years of the Cold War are, however, no longer current. Therefore, it is time to reconsider both readings, including the now dominant Western interpretation.

VI. Conclusion

There were many good reasons for the emphasis on fetishism, second nature, and real abstraction in West Germany around 1968. First, in the FRG, the readers of *Capital* were not economists, but philosophers acquainted with the "Western Marxist" discourse of alienation and reification. Even if Marxist theory entered the West German academy during the 1960s, mainly the social sciences and humanities departments tolerated it. Second, Marx's theory of fetishism—not related to capital and wage labour, but to commodities and money—offered tools for the critique of both forms of the "industrial society," capitalism and state socialism.[73] Third, and most important for emphasis on fetishism might be that around 1968, students arose as an independent force in society. Their revolutionary mood clashed with the objective conditions of the working class. Until the late 1960s, there had been a long period of growth, and not only capital but also labour had benefitted. The globally "regulating capitals," that is, the most competitive capitals, were—in many cases—located in West Germany. These companies could pay much higher wages than the companies in other countries were able to pay.[74]

[73] See Postone, *Time, Labor, and Social Domination*, 7.
[74] See Shaikh, *Capitalism, Competition, Conflict, Crisis*, 265ff. I thank Miika Kabata for this comment.

In such exceptional historical conditions, focusing on the problem of fetishism was, for many radicals, more interesting than focusing on the theory of surplus value. These reasons are less weighty today, because the move to shortening of the work day has stagnated, the connection between the growth of productivity and of wages has been broken, and the welfare state is under attack. A more traditional reading of *Capital*, focusing on the theory of surplus value, provides better justification than the reading of the 1968 generation to explain why the length of the work day is a question of life and death for the representatives of capital today.

Moreover, what remains to be done elsewhere is to demonstrate that a more "traditional" reading of *Capital*, focusing on the theory of surplus value, not only makes more sense in present times, but also is more accurate. The main targets of Marx's critique are bourgeois relations of production and how these relations are portrayed in the bourgeois political economy, and not the fetishism of commodities or money as such. Fetishisms of commodities and money are, to a lesser or greater degree, present wherever a market exists. Therefore, it might make sense to apply the concept of fetishism of commodities and money to the state socialism of the twentieth century as well.

Fetishism of capital is, however, another story. Fetishism of capital is related to the specifically capitalist relations of production—the relationship between capital and wage labour. Only in the beginning of the first volume of *Capital* does Marx talk about fetishism of commodities and money. From the fourth chapter of volume I onwards, Marx discusses the bourgeois relations of production, and from this chapter on, he links the concept of fetishism to the capital relation—that is, to the theory of surplus value—and the theme of fetishism runs through all three volumes. The problem of fetishism of capital is related to the constant and variable, fixed and circulating capital, to the production of relative surplus value, to the wage form, to the yearly rate of surplus value, to the rate of profit, and finally, to the commercial profit, interest, and land rent. Thus, what remains to be done elsewhere is to demonstrate the meaning of the concept of fetishism in all three volumes of the book, and how, even if eminently central, the concept of fetishism gains its proper meaning only in connection to the theory of surplus value. In capitalism, fetishism serves to hide the fact that the source of all value is labour, and thus, covers exploitation of wage labour, even if the social relations immediately appear as free and equal market exchanges.

There are, however, positions in the structure of production and exchange, where the social relations are much less covered by the objective appearances of these relations, by the commodity form, money form, wage form, or by the forms of profit, rent, and interest. These positions are the positions of the employer and the employee, in the "fierce struggle over the limits of the working day."[75] As Marx goes through the early legislation restricting the length of the work day, he quotes factory inspectors who talk about "'small thefts' of capital from the labourer's meal and recreation time."[76] Marx comments on this by saying that, "it is evident that in this atmosphere the formation of surplus value by surplus labour, is no secret."[77] In the struggle over the length of the work day, the real relations are laid bare.

Today, the struggle over the length of the work day is once again apparent, even in Germany. Marx's theory of surplus value makes much more sense today than it did 50 years ago in the globally privileged FRG. In the changed circumstances, the "traditional" reading does not seem quite so antiquated anymore, but instead, seems plausible, even common sense. Therefore, Jan Hoff and other followers of Alfred Schmidt should reconsider "the antiquated dogmas of traditional Marxism." The only reason for this is that the antiquated form of society was restored in the decades following 1968.

Bibliography

Abendroth, Wolfgang. "Der Weg der Studenten zum Marxismus." *Z. Zeitschrift für Marxistische Erneuerung* 113 (March 2018): 101–8.

Adorno, Theodor W. "Theodor W. Adorno on 'Marx and the Basic Concepts of Sociological Theory': From a Seminar Transcript in the Summer Semester of 1962." *Historical Materialism* 26, no. 1 (2018): 154–64.

Altvater, Elmar. "Rationalisierung und Demokratisierung. Zu einigen Problemen der neuen ökonomischen Systeme im Sozialismus." *Das Argument* 39 (1966): 265–89.

Backhaus, Hans-Georg. "Zur Dialektik der Wertform." In *Beiträge zur Marxistischen Erkenntnistheorie*, edited by Alfred Schmidt, 128–52. Frankfurt am Main: Suhrkamp, 1969.

---

[75] Karl Marx, *Marx's Economic Manuscript of 1864–1865*, ed. Fred Moseley (Leiden and Boston: Brill, 2015), 894.

[76] Karl Marx, *Capital Volume I*, in MECW (London: Lawrence & Wishart, 1996), 35: 250.

[77] Ibid.

Backhaus, Hans-Georg. "Über den Doppelsinn der Begriffe 'Politische Ökonomie' und 'Kritik' bei Marx und in der Frankfurter Schule." In *Wolfgang Harich zum Gedächtnis: eine Gedenkschrift in zwei Bänden*. Vol. 2, edited by Stefan Dornuf und Reinhard Pitsch, 12–213. München: Müller & Nerding Verlag, 2000.

Backhaus, Hans-Georg. *Dialektik der Wertform. Untersuchungen zur Marxschen Ökonomiekritik*, 2nd ed. Freiburg: Ça ira, 2011.

Backhaus, Hans-Georg. "Materialien zur Rekonstruktion der Marxschen Werttheorie 3." In *Gesellschaft. Beiträge zur Marxschen Theorie*. Vol. 11, edited by Hans Georg Backhaus, 16–117. Frankfurt am Main: Suhrkamp Verlag, 1978.

Demirovic, Alex. "Die 'Ideen von 1968' und die inszenierte Geschichtslosigkeit." In *Emanzipation als Versöhnung. Zu Adornos Kritik der »Warentausch«-Gesellschaft und Perspektiven der Transformation*, edited by Iring Fetscher and Alfred Schmidt, 30–49. Frankfurt am Main: Verlag Neue Kritik, 2002.

Elbe, Ingo. *Marx im Westen: Die neue Marx-Lektüre in der Bundesrepublik seit 1965*, 2nd rev. ed. Berlin: Akademie Verlag, 2010.

Euchner, Walter and Alfred Schmidt. "Nachwort der Herausgeber." In *Kritik der politischen Ökonomie heute. 100 Jahre ›Kapital‹*, edited by Walter Euchner and Alfred Schmidt, 359. Frankfurt and Wien: Europäische Verlagsanstalt and Europa Verlag, 1968.

Fülberth, Georg. "Linke Hoffnungen, linke Chancen, linkes Versagen?" In *1968— Bilanz und ungelöste Probleme. Pankower Vorträge* 152, edited by Helle Panke, 47–56. Berlin: Helle Panke, 2010.

Haug, Wolfgang Fritz. "Das Ganze und das ganz Andere." In *Antworten auf Herbert Marcuse*, 2nd ed., edited by Jürgen Habermas, 50–72. Frankfurt am Main: Suhrkamp Verlag, 1968.

Hecker, Rolf. "Hans-Georg Backhaus: Die Dialektik der Wertform." *Utopie kreativ* 94 (August 1998): 89–92.

Heinrich, Michael. "Relevance and Irrelevance of Marxian Economics." *New School Economic Review* 1, no. 1 (2004): 54–8.

Heinrich, Michael. "Reconstruction or Deconstruction? Methodological Controversies about Value and Capital, and New Insights from the Critical Edition." In *Re-reading Marx: New Perspectives after the Critical Edition*, edited by Riccardo Bellofiore and Roberto Fineschi, 71–98. London: Palgrave Macmillan, 2009.

Heinrich, Michael. *An Introduction to the Three Volumes of Karl Marx's Capital*. Translated by Alexander Locascio. New York: Monthly Review Press, 2012.

Hermann, Christoph. *Capitalism and the Political Economy of Work Time*. London and New York: Routledge, 2015.

Hobsbawm, Eric. *Age of Extremes: The Short Twentieth Century 1914–1991*. London: Abacus, 1995.

Hoff, Jan. *Marx Worldwide: On the Development of the International Discourse on Marx since 1965*. Translated by Nicholas Gray. Leiden: Brill, 2017.

Hudis, Peter. *Marx's Concept of the Alternative to Capitalism.* Leiden and Boston: Brill, 2012.

Kellner, Douglas. "Introduction to the Second Edition." In *One Dimensional Man: Studies in the Ideology of Advanced Industrial Society,* 2nd ed., IX–XXXVIII. New York and London: Routledge, 2002.

Kosta, Jiří, Jan Meyer, and Sibylle Weber, *Warenproduktion im Sozialismus: Überlegungen zur Theorie von Marx und zur Praxis in Osteuropa.* Frankfurt am Main: Fischer Taschenbuch Verlag, 1973.

Krause, Günter. *Wirtschaftstheorie in der DDR.* Marburg: Metropolis-Verlag, 1998.

"Kurzbiografien." In *Beiträge zur Marx-Engels-Forschung. Neue Folge. Sonderband 5. Die Marx-Engels-Werkausgaben in der UdSSR und DDR (1945–1968),* edited by Carl-Erich Vollgraf, Richard Sperl, and Rolf Hecker, 471–524. Hamburg: Argument Verlag, 2006.

Marcuse, Herbert. "Ziele, Formen und Aussichten der Studentenopposition." *Das Argument* 45 (1967): 398–407.

Marcuse, Herbert. *One Dimensional Man: Studies in the Ideology of Advanced Industrial Society,* 2nd ed., London and New York: Routledge, 2002.

Marcuse, Herbert. "Socialism in the Developed Countries." In *Marxism, Revolution and Utopia: Collected Papers of Herbert Marcuse.* Vol. 6, edited by Douglas Kellner and Clayton Pierce, 169–80. London and New York: Routledge, 2014.

Marx, Karl. *The Poverty of Philosophy.* In MECW. Vol. 6, 105–212. London: Lawrence & Wishart, 1976.

Marx, Karl. *Capital,* Volume I. In MECW. Vol. 35. London: Lawrence & Wishart, 1996.

Marx, Karl. *Marx's Economic Manuscript of 1864–1865.* Edited by Fred Moseley. Leiden and Boston: Brill, 2015.

Marxhausen, Thomas. "Fetischismusfetischismus 'linker' Marxologie. Bemerkungen zur Marxverfälschung durch Ulrich Erckenbrecht, 'das Geheimnis des Fetischismus' Grundmotive der Marxschen Erkenntniskritik." *Hallesche Arbeitsblätter zur Marx-Engels-Forschung* 6 (1979): 91–6.

Marxhausen, Thomas. "Die Theorie des Fetischismus im dritten Band des 'Kapitals'." *Beiträge zur Marx-Engels Forschung* 25 (1988): 209–43.

Marxhausen, Thomas. "Fetischcharacter der Ware." In *Historisch-Kritisches Wörterbuch des Marxismus.* Vol. 4, edited by Wolfgang Fritz Haug, 343–54. Hamburg: Argument Verlag, 1999.

Mohl, Ernst Theodor. "Ein Reisebericht." In *In Memoriam Wolfgang Jahn: Der ganze Marx—Alles Verfasste veröffentlichen, erforschen und den 'ungeschriebenen' Marx rekonstruieren,* 13–32. Hamburg: Argument Verlag, 2002.

Mohl, Ernst Theodor. "Germany, Austria and Switzerland." In *Karl Marx's Grundrisse: Foundations of the Critique of Political Economy 150 Years Later,* edited by Marcello Musto, 189–201. London and New York: Routledge, 2008.

Nachtwey, Oliver. *Germany's Hidden Crisis: Social Decline in the Heart of Europe*. Translated by David Fernbach and Loren Balhorn. London and New York: Verso, 2018.

Oelßner, Fred. "Vorwort." In *Bevor das Kapital entstand: Die Herausbildung und Entwicklung der ökonomischen Theorie von Karl Marx in der Zeit von 1843 bis 1858*, edited by Gerda Tuchscheerer, 7–16. Berlin: Akademie-Verlag, 1968.

Postone, Moishe. *Time, Labor and Social Domination: A Reinterpretation of Marx's Critical Theory*. Cambridge: Cambridge University Press, 2003.

Rakowitz, Nadja. *Einfache Warenproduktion: Ideal und Ideologie*. Freiburg: Ça ira, 2000.

Schmidt, Alfred. "Über Geschichte und Geschichtsschreibung in der materialistischen Dialektik." In *Folgen einer Theorie: Essays über ›das Kapital‹ von Karl Marx*, edited by Ernst Theodor Mohl, 103–29. Frankfurt am Main: Suhrkamp, 1967.

Schmidt, Alfred. "Zum Erkenntnisbegriff der Kritik der politischen Ökonomie." In *Kritik der politischen Ökonomie heute: 100 Jahre 'Kapital'*, edited by Walter Euchner and Alfred Schmidt, 30–43. Frankfurt am Main and Wien: Europäische Verlagsanstalt and Europa Verlag, 1968.

Shaikh, Anwar. *Capitalism: Competition, Conflict, Crisis*. Oxford: Oxford University Press, 2016.

Steinitz, Klaus and Dieter Walter. *Plan–Markt–Demokratie: Prognose und langfristige Planung in der DDR–Schlussfolgerungen für morgen*. Hamburg: VSA-Verlag, 2014.

Tuchscheerer, Walter. *Bevor das Kapital entstand: Die Herausbildung und Entwicklung der ökonomischen Theorie von Karl Marx in der Zeit von 1843 bis 1858*. Edited by Gerda Tuchscheerer. Berlin: Akademie-Verlag, 1968.

Ulbricht, Walter. *Die Bedeutung des Werkes "Das Kapital" von Karl Marx für die Schaffung des entwickelten gesellschaftlichen Systems des Sozialismus in der DDR und den Kampf gegen das staatsmonopolistische Herrschaftssystem in Westdeutschland*. Berlin: Dietz Verlag, 1967.

Vygodsky, Vitaly. *The Story of a Great Discovery: How Marx Wrote "Capital"*. Translated by S.V. Salt. Tunbridge Wells: Abacus Press, 1974.

Zagalow, N. A. et al. *Lehrbuch politische Ökonomie: Sozialismus*. Translated by Hermann Mertens, Ingrid Stolte, and Günter Wermusch. Frankfurt/Main: Verlag Marxistische Blätter, 1972.

PART II

On the Critique of Political Economy

Marx's Observations on the Classical Theory of Interest

Jan Toporowski

I. Introduction

Despite its incompleteness, Marx's discussion of interest represents one of the first serious responses to the Ricardian theory of interest. It contains insights of great value for understanding how his vision of capitalism and finance was evolving and the direction in which it was evolving.

Section "Ricardo's Theory of Interest" examines Ricardo's theory of interest, enunciating what may be referred more broadly as the classical theory of interest. Section "Marx on Interest" describes Marx's critical reassessment of that theory. Despite his departure from the classical theory of interest, Marx's theory remained located in the "classical" capitalism of his time, when finance was external to the capitalist system of reproduction, in the sense that capitalist finance was acquired through primitive accumulation, or borrowed from banks less involved in intermediation

---

This chapter arises out of discussions with Anwar Shaikh and Riccardo Bellofiore, neither of whom is responsible for the remaining errors in it.

J. Toporowski (✉)
SOAS University of London, London, UK

© The Author(s) 2019
S. Gupta et al. (eds.), *Karl Marx's Life, Ideas, and Influences*, Marx, Engels, and Marxisms, https://doi.org/10.1007/978-3-030-24815-4_10

211

between capitalists. In Section "Interest in a "Pure Capitalist" Economy: A "Transfer" Theory of Interest", the theory is extended beyond Hilferding to modern finance capital and the changed function of the rate of interest when capitalist financing is internal to the capitalist system of reproduction.

II. RICARDO'S THEORY OF INTEREST

The rate of interest plays a subsidiary part in David Ricardo's political economy. In his *Principles of Political Economy*, the discussion of interest is placed towards the end of the book, well after his exposition of the principles of production and distribution. His key doctrine—that the rate of interest is ultimately determined by the rate of profit—even more sharply distinguishes his monetary theory from the modern monetary theory descended from Wicksell. It is in the light of Wicksell's theory that Ricardo's is too often interpreted.

Ricardo had first put forward the doctrine that that rate of interest is determined by the rate of profit in 1810 in his observations on "The High Price of Bullion," where he denied what came to be the later Keynesian or neoclassical notion that the rate of interest depends on the demand for money, relative to its supply, or, in Ricardo's words, on "the abundance of paper money; that if it were too abundant, interest would fall, and if not sufficiently so, interest would rise." He went on: "It can, I think, be made manifest, that the rate of interest is not regulated by the abundance or scarcity of money, but by the abundance or scarcity of that part of capital, not consisting of money." As evidence to support this, Ricardo quoted a passage from Chapter 2, Book II of Adam Smith's *The Wealth of Nations* in which Smith argued that money is not an input into production and serves only to circulate the inputs of production. Elsewhere, in chapter 4 of that book, Smith had argued that the extraction of gold from newly discovered mines in North America had greatly increased the quantity of money, but did not lower the rate of interest. Ricardo concluded that "the rate of interest... [is] regulated by the profits on the employment of capital, and not by the number or quality of the pieces of metal, which are used to circulate its produce."[1]

---

[1] David Ricardo, *The High Price of Bullion: A Proof of the Depreciation of Bank Notes*, in *The Works and Correspondence of David Ricardo, Volume III, Pamphlets and Papers, 1809–1811*, ed. Piero Sraffa (Cambridge: Cambridge University Press, 1951), 88–9.

In the same year, 1810, in his letter to the editor of the *Morning Chronicle* concerning Sir John Sinclair's pamphlet criticizing the Bullion Report, Ricardo took issue with Sinclair's notion that an increase in the circulation of bank notes would reduce the rate of interest. Sinclair had written that if the note issue and coinage circulating in Britain of £40 million were reduced, the rate of interest would rise: "how much would not the rate of interest be cramped? Whereas if ... [the note issue and coinage were raised] bearing an interest of 4 per cent and the whole of it actively employed in various industrious pursuits, it cannot be doubted, that the prosperity of the country would increase with a celerity, and be carried to a height, which would not otherwise have been attainable." Ricardo commented, "If this reasoning be just, how incalculable would the prosperity of the country become, if the Bank would increase their notes to 100 millions and lend them at 3 per cent."

Ricardo went on:

> If Sir John will take the trouble to consult the 4th chap. 2d book, of Dr A. Smith's celebrated work, he will there see it undeniably demonstrated, that the rate of interest for money is totally independent of the nominal amount of the circulating medium. It is regulated solely by the competition of capital, not consisting of money. The real amount of the circulating medium, with the same amount of commerce and confidence, must always be the same; it may, indeed, be called 100 million, or 20 millions, but the real value of the one or the other sum must be the same.[2]

In his chapter in the *Principles* on currency and banks, Ricardo reinforced this view:

> The whole business, which the whole community can carry on, depends on the quantity of its capital, that is, of its raw material, machinery, food, vessels, etc. employed in production. After a well-regulated paper money is established, these can neither be increased nor diminished by the operations of banking. If then, the State were to issue the paper money of the country, although it should never discount a bill, or lend one shilling to the public, there would be no alteration in the amount of trade; for we should have the same quantity of raw materials, of machinery, food and ships; and it is probable, too, that the same amount of money might be lent, not always at 5 per cent. Indeed, a rate fixed by law, when that might be under the market rate,

<hr>

[2] Ibid., 143.

but at 6, 7, or 8 per cent., the result of the fair competition in the market between the lenders and the borrowers.[3]

Ricardo expanded on this in a chapter on "The Effects of Accumulation on Profits and Interest," confusingly placed earlier in the *Principles*, where it is chapter XXI and separated from chapter XXVII, "On Currency and Banks," by chapters on "Bounties on Exportation ...," "On Bounties on Production," and Adam Smith's doctrine on Rent, "On Colonial Trade, and On Gross and Net Revenue." In that earlier chapter, Ricardo conceded that the rate of interest may deviate temporarily from the rate of profit: "The rate of interest, though ultimately and permanently governed by the rate of profit, is however subject to temporary variations from other causes."[4] Those causes could be a shortage of sales revenue in the case of a manufacturer, or even credit inflation: "If by the discovery of a new mine, by the abuses of banking, or by any other cause, the quantity of money be greatly increased, its ultimate effect is to raise the price of commodities in proportion to the increased quantity of money; but there is always an interval, during which some effect is produced on the rate of interest."[5]

Ricardo had little time for the Keynesian notion that emerged a century later that the long-term rate of interest, rather than the short-term rate in the money markets, is the one relevant to capital accumulation: "The price of funded property [i.e., the yield on bonds] is not a steady criterion by which to judge of the rate of interest."[6] This is because in wartime, the stock market is "loaded" by the funding operations of the government, and in peacetime, is so boosted by the operations of sinking funds (to pay off the national debt) and the demand of risk-averse investors, depressing "the rate of interest on these securities below the general market rate."[7] Different rates of interest are payable according to the term of the bond. At the same time, the quarterly interest payments on the national debt regularly squeeze the money market, causing sharp increases in the rate of interest in that market.

---

[3] David Ricardo, *On the Principles of Political Economy and Taxation*, in *The Works and Correspondence of David Ricardo Volume I*, ed. Piero Sraffa and Maurice Dobb (Cambridge: Cambridge University Press, 1951), 365. The Usury Laws at the time when Ricardo was writing restricted the rate of interest to a maximum of 5 per cent.

[4] Ibid., 297.

[5] Ibid., 298. See also G. L. S. Shackle, "Foreword," in *Value Capital and Rent*, by Knut Wicksell (London: George Allen and Unwin, 1954).

[6] Ibid.

[7] Ricardo, *On the Principles of Political Economy and Taxation*, 298.

In an intriguing footnote, Ricardo took issue with Jean-Baptiste Say over a question that had bothered French political economy since the days of the Physiocrats. Like François Quesnay and Adam Smith, Say had deplored the offering of public loans at rates of interest in excess of the 5 per cent that agriculture, manufacturing, and commerce could afford, drawing capital away from productive employment in those activities. Ricardo dismissed such worries:

To the question 'who would lend money to farmers, manufacturers and merchants, at 5 per cent per annum, when another borrower, having little credit, would give 7 or 8 per cent?' I reply, that every prudent and reasonable man would. Because the rate of interest is 7 or 8 per cent there, where lender runs extraordinary risks, is this any reason that it should be equally high in those places where they are secured from such risks? M. Say allows, that the rate of interest depends on the rate of profits; but it does not, therefore, follow, that the rate of profits depends on the rate of interest. One is the cause, the other the effect, and it is impossible for any circumstances to make them change places.[8]

III. Marx on Interest

Marx's first reflections on the rate of interest appear in the notes that were subsequently published as Part III of *Theories of Surplus Value*. In an Addenda entitled "Revenue and It's Sources. Vulgar Political Economy," Marx argued that with capitalist production, a new type of financing emerges, which he called "interest-bearing capital." This acquires the character of a fetish, an existence apparently independent of capitalist production. Marx wanted to challenge this by arguing that in industrial capitalism, the interest is paid from surplus value. On this basis, the polemics against interest of contemporary critics such as Proudhon, attributing the evils of capitalism to excessive interest or usury, were "fetishistic." Usury, Marx argued, was a feature of mercantile capitalism, rather than industrial capitalism.[9] In industrial capitalism, interest circulates between capitalists in the sense that an individual capitalist can decide whether to lend his (money) capital out at interest or employ it himself in the process of production.[10]

---

[8] Ibid., 297–300. See also Jan Toporowski, *Theories of Financial Disturbance: An Examination of Critical Theories of Finance from Adam Smith to the Present Day* (Cheltenham: Edward Elgar, 2005), 17–25.

[9] Karl Marx, *Theories of Surplus Value Part III* (Moscow: Progress Publishers, 1971), 487.

[10] Ibid., 477–8.

In his notes, therefore, Marx's main point was to emphasize that, under capitalism, interest acquires a new social and economic significance because it is now paid out of surplus value, which requires the circulation of money through industrial production. However, his notes are inconclusive and leave at least two ambiguities. First of all, there is the ambiguity over whether interest is paid out of hoards of accumulated profits—in which case, the current flow of profits forms less of a constraint on interest payments. Indeed, if the hoard is large enough, then current profitability may be unnecessary, and the requirement that the rate of profit should be at least equal to, if not greater than the rate of interest, proves unnecessary. The second ambiguity arises in the accounting for interest payments. If interest is paid between capitalists, then an individual capitalist's income no longer just depends on the "profit of enterprise" that is left over after payment of interest on the money capital borrowed. The individual capitalist's income must also include the interest received on money capital lent out earlier to other capitalists. Marx' admission that the capitalist may decide to be a money capitalist or a functioning capitalist already concedes that individual capitalists are not irrevocably committed to one or the other means of earning money from their money capital. It, therefore, suggests that more recent Marxist attempts to revive the critique of usury, by separating out a rentier capitalist class from a productive capitalist class oppressed by high interest, may be vulnerable to this kind of fetishistic thinking. But to break out of these ambiguities, it is necessary to break too with the classical theory of interest.

Marx attempted to deal with these ambiguities in Vol. III of *Capital*. Here, he was evidently influenced by the dissent of Thomas Tooke, and to a lesser extent, John Stuart Mill from the real interest rate theory of David Ricardo and Adam Smith. Ricardo had argued that the rate of interest is "ultimately and permanently governed by the rate of profit."[11] Tooke and Mill had argued that the rate of interest was disturbed by too many monetary factors to make this a reliable relationship. Tooke put forward the idea that it was the average rate of interest that was under the influence of the rate of profit and "... the dissenting positions of Tooke and J.S. Mill on the interest-profit relationship in the 1820s heavily influenced Marx in developing a conception of the rate of interest as an autonomous variable in the sense of being determined by forces independent of the rate of

---

[11] Ricardo, *On the Principles of Political Economy and Taxation*, 297.

profit."[12] Amid the "disorderly mass of notes, comments and extracts," Marx's editor Friedrich Engels found the key chapters on the rate of interest "in the main, complete."[13] In the draft that became Volume III of *Capital*, and which he then intended to revise, Marx concluded that it was the *average* rate of interest over a span of years that was determined by the *average* rate of profit. But this does not mean that all firms earn an average rate of profit—something worth bearing in mind at a time when many Marxist economists attach crucial importance to aggregate, or average, rates of profit. In fact, there is a spread of profit rates at any one time and a spread of interest rates.[14] In that sense, there was no "natural rate of interest" or marginal profit on capital, as enunciated by Joseph Massie and later by Knut Wicksell. "In any event the average rate of profit is to be regarded as the ultimate determinant of the maximum limit of interest."[15] Moreover, in times of speculation, interest can be paid out not out of profit, but out of borrowed capital, and such Ponzi financing, as Minsky would later call it, may be sustained for a while. However, such borrowing to pay interest is usually the prelude to crisis. This borrowing raises the rate of interest and, as Marx put it, transforms "bankrupt swindlers" into "respectable and solvent capitalists."[16]

With these exceptions, however, Marx was adamant that the rate of interest is paid out of current profits. He quoted the *Economist* magazine of January 22, 1853 "The relation between the sum paid for the use of capital and the capital expresses the rate of interest as measured in money." And "The rate of interest depends 1) on the rate of profit; 2) on the proportion in which the entire profit is divided between the lender and the borrower." Then, quoting from Joseph Massie's *An Essay on the Governing Causes of the Natural Rate of Interest*, "If that which men pay as interest for the use of what they borrow, be a part of the profits it is capable of producing, this interest must always be governed by those profits... The natural rate of interest is governed by the profits of trade to particulars."[17] Marx went further along Ricardian lines, although it is not clear whether he was here citing the classical view of interest that he proposed to criticize,

---

[12] Matthew Smith, *Thomas Tooke and the Monetary Thought of Classical Economics* (Abingdon, UK: Routledge, 2011), 212.

[13] Fredrick Engels, "Preface," in MECW (London: Lawrence & Wishart, 1998), 37: 6.

[14] Karl Marx, *Capital*, Vol. III, in MECW (London: Lawrence & Wishart, 1998), 37: 365–6, 512.

[15] Ibid., 360.

[16] Ibid., 513–15.

[17] Ibid., 358–9.

or giving his own view: "we shall find that a low rate of interest generally corresponds to periods of prosperity or extra profit, a rise in interest rates separates prosperity and its reverse, and a maximum of interest up to a point of extreme usury corresponds to the period of crisis."[18] Nevertheless, Marx went on, "the rate of interest also has a tendency to fall quite independently of the fluctuations in the rate of profit" due to the expansion of the class of rentiers with surplus money savings. Moreover, "the development of the credit system and the attendant ever-growing control of industrialists and merchants over the money savings of all classes that is effected through the bankers, and the progressive concentration of these savings in amounts which can serve as money capital, must also depress the rate of interest."[19]

Marx's own view was stated in the next passage about the average rate of interest, which he linked with the long-term rate of interest. "To determine the average rate of interest we must (1) calculate the average rate of interest during its variations in the major industrial cycles; and (2) find the rate of interest for investments that require long-term loans of capital." This long-term rate, Marx thought, was more or less stable.[20] This led Marx to conclude that there is

> no such thing as a natural rate of interest in the sense in which economists speak of a natural rate of profit and a natural rate of wages… unlike the general rate of profit, there is, on the one hand, no general law to determine the limits of the average rate of interest as distinct from the continually fluctuating market rates of interest, because it is merely a question of dividing the gross profit between two owners of capital under different title; on the other hand, the rate of interest—be it the average or market rate prevalent in each particular case—appears as a uniform, definite and tangible magnitude in a quite different way from the general rate of profit.[21]

In addition to identifying (in passing) the importance of the long-term rate of interest, which was put forward 70 years later by Keynes as the key financial instrument for business investment, Marx also anticipated Keynes's "euthanasia of the rentier"—the notion that a permanently low rate of interest would finally induce business to invest. In Marx's version, a reduction of the rate of interest to zero would turn the money capitalists

---

[18] Ibid., 360.

[19] Ibid., 361–2.

[20] Ibid., 362, 366. In the twentieth century, Keynes and Kalecki argued that it was this long-term rate of interest that is relevant to business investment.

[21] Ibid., 362, 364–5, also 366–8.

into functioning capitalists in order to earn a positive return on their money.[22] But that, in turn, implies that money and functioning capitalists are more or less the same individuals or institutions. Marx's repeated equation of equivalence between the *average* rate of interest and the *average* rate of profit reinforces the idea that capitalist interest is paid from surplus value in general, but not necessarily from the surplus value produced at the time of the interest payment.

Here, it is worth recalling Joseph Schumpeter's criticism of the doctrine that lay at the origins of the Ricardian theory of interest, Nicholas Barbon's notion, enunciated in 1690, that interest is the "Rent of the Wrought or Artificial Stock"—namely, the capital stock.[23] For Schumpeter, this led to the nineteenth-century classical view that economic activity is determined by "real" factors, resources, and commodities, over which money is a mere veil. He observed: "Thus we easily slip into a position that may be characterized by the equivalent propositions that the business firm earns interest or that the lender receives profit—not as would seem more natural to the unprejudiced mind, an income *sui generis* of which profit is merely the most important course."[24]

There remains the second ambiguity referred to at the start of this section, the accounting for the interest paid and its receipt by other capitalists. In a sense, this clarified itself with the evolution of interest-bearing capital in the final years of Marx's life, the emergence of finance capital, and the development of Marx's financial theory in Hilferding's *Finance Capital*. With finance capital, the money-capitalist and the functioning capitalist are merged into the modern corporation or the holding company, operating symbiotically with the banking system (or investment banking in capital market economies). It is only after Hilferding and the discussion of "pure credit" in Wicksell and Schumpeter that we can understand fully how capitalist interest involves the circulation of surplus value in the form of accumulated money profits, but that interest is disconnected from the rate of profit. With the concentration and development of the money markets, the rate of interest represents the rate of exchange between different types of financing.[25] The following section examines the functioning of the rate of interest in such a "pure" capitalist economy.

[22] Ibid., 378.

[23] Nicholas Barbon, *A Discourse of Trade* (London: Milbourn, 1690).

[24] Joseph A. Schumpeter, *History of Economic Analysis* (New York: Oxford University Press, 1954), 330.

[25] Rudolf Hilferding, *Finance Capital A Study of the Latest Phase of Capitalist Development* (London: Routledge and Kegan Paul, 1981): 268–9.

IV. Interest in a "Pure Capitalist" Economy: A "Transfer" Theory of Interest

To understand properly Marx's theory of interest, it needs to be put into the context of the capitalism of his time, and the evolution of that capitalism. Marx's observations on interest came during the transition in the relationship of capitalists with finance from one in which finance is external to industrial capitalists, controlled by banks and wealthy pre-industrial (merchant) capitalists, and subject to religiously sanctioned legal restrictions, to a relationship in which finance is internal to industrial capitalists, who can "fund" their long-term plant and equipment with long-term obligations, in the form of bonds or shares, and short-term rates of interest are no longer restricted. To some degree, this shift is reflected in the change in the yield curve (the relationship between the long-term rate of interest to the short-term rate) that occurred at the time when Marx was writing. When Ricardo was enunciating his "classical" theory of interest, the long-term rate of interest (his "price of funded property") was the rate on bonds issued by the government and the great trading companies. That rate was more unstable than the short-term rate of interest that was constrained by the Usury Laws. With the abolition of those laws, in 1844, and even later in the same century, with the development of markets for long-term company finance, the situation was reversed: The short-term rate of interest became more unstable than the long-term rate.[26]

Marx's ambiguities are complicated by his choice of labour value as numéraire. In pursuit of this, the notion of interest as Massie's "rent on stock" is associated in Volume II of *Capital* with the use of gold as money. Marx placed the production of gold in the sector producing means of production, and therefore using labour and having a rate of profit that corresponds to Ricardo's and the rate of profit in manufacturing.[27] But capitalist banking and finance were always more like a "credit club" of capitalists. The origins of capitalist credit lie in the discounting of bills by "merchant" or "country" banks who were originally merely capitalists (usually merchants with good cash flow from their trading activities) in possession of sufficient money hoards to be able to use them to buy, at a discount, the IOUs of their business associates.[28] This is implicit in Marx's

[26] See Ralph George Hawtrey, *A Century of Bank Rate* (London: Longmans, Green and Co., 1938), chapter VI.
[27] Karl Marx, *Capital*. Vol. II, in MECW (London: Lawrence & Wishart, 1997), 36: 473–7.
[28] Karl H. Niebyl, *Studies in the Classical Theories of Money* (New York: Columbia University Press, 1946), chapter 3.

analysis of money and interest, and later explicit in Kalecki's first exposition of capitalist financing.[29]

This inter-capitalist credit and debt is what distinguishes capitalist credit from its predecessors in usury and traditional moneylending in pre-capitalist societies, or the sovereign debt of the absolutist state within which merchant capitalist credit first emerged. His analysis of interest-bearing capital[30] shows that Marx was aware of the key distinguishing feature of capitalist credit—namely, that it redistributes money hoards among capitalists, rather than exploiting the rural poor or buying pensions from the state.[31] For Marx, this redistribution distinguishes capitalist credit from pre-capitalist redistribution among landowners or merchants. Furthermore, in a capitalist economy, money comes into exchange through the expenditure of capitalists' money on production, and not as a conventionally, or even legally, accepted token of value in exchange.

With the emergence of finance capital, the operations of banks as a credit club of capitalists become the foundation of monetary endogeneity. Capitalists have assets—including financial assets such as bills, bonds, shares, and government paper—that they can post as security of loans, and those loans create deposits.[32] It is this financially collateralized lending, rather than the provision of government reserves, as postulated by most post-Keynesians that makes the supply of credit determined by demand, or the ability of capitalists to provide collateral.

[29] Michal Kalecki, "An Essay on the Business Cycle Theory," in *The Collected Works of Michał Kalecki Volume I Capitalism: Business Cycles and Full Employment*, ed. Jerzy Osiatynski (Oxford: The Clarendon Press, 1933), 93–8.

[30] Marx, *Capital*, Vol. III, chapter XXI.

[31] It is the neglect of the distinction between capitalist credit and debt and pre-capitalist debt, and the income and balance sheet implications of that distinction, that confuses long-term (econometric) studies of debt, such as Carmen M. Reinhart, and Kenneth S. Rogoff, "This Time is Different: A Panoramic View of Eight Centuries of Financial Crises," NBER Working Paper No. 13882 (March 2008).

[32] Hartley Withers, *The Meaning of Money* (New York: Dutton, 1909); Dennis Holme Robertson, "Theories of Banking Policy," in *Essays in Monetary Theory* (London: P.S. King, 1940). "We have spoken of bankers and financiers as the makers of credit. But we have also recognized that the chief financial material out of which they make it is the stocks and shares and other certificates of value which represents the capital created by the saving and investing classes. It is thus the growth of the forms of saving which take these financial shapes that enables the increased credit to emerge from the financial factories. All such modern saving can furnish material for the creation of more credit." John Atkinson Hobson, *Gold Prices and Wages with an Examination of the Quantity Theory* (London: Methuen, 1924), 89.

It follows that within this kind of capitalist finance, we must test the relevance of Marx's theory of interest rather than in the financial system based on gold production of Marx's time. As a first approximation to reality, it is convenient, for the sake of simplicity, to leave aside the government and foreign sectors, and assume that workers are true proletarians, whose only asset is their labour power. This gives a "pure" capitalist economy in which the only banking is the "pure" capitalist credit club. Banks operate holding the deposits of capitalists and advancing loans to them. The profits of the banks are the margin between deposit and lending rates of interest multiplied by the value of the balance sheet of every bank, after deducting the operating costs of each bank. Bank profits are therefore unrelated to the level of the rate of interest itself.[33]

In this situation, the profits of the financial sector make no difference to profits overall in this capitalist economy: the margin between deposit and lending rates received by capitalists engaged in banking business is obtained at the expense of the profits of non-bank capitalists; the costs of banking business (premises, staff) constitute demand for the output of the non-financial sector, and in this way, returns to non-bank capitalists a part of their profit that those capitalists hand over to bank capitalists under that margin between borrowing and deposit rates of interest. In this sense, bank expenses may be subsumed under Investment spending (insofar as those expenses are a necessary part of investment) or Capitalists' Consumption (insofar as they are merely the discretionary extravagances that are nowadays associated with financial business) in Kalecki's well-known profits equation, based on Marx's schemes of reproduction in Volume II of *Capital*.[34]

---

[33] "The rate of interest that is paid on deposits is always somewhat lower than the rate charged by banks on loans. The difference between these two rates remunerates the bank ..." Knut Wicksell, *Interest and Prices: A Study of the Causes Regulating the Value of Money* (London: Macmillan, 1936), 139.

[34] The theory may be summarized as follows. In a closed economy, with no government, in a given period, total income (Y) is equal to the sum of profits plus wages $(W + P)$, which in turn, is equal to Consumption plus Investment $(C + I)$. $Y - C = I = $ Saving. Saving may be divided into the saving of workers (S_w) and the saving of capitalists (S_c). Similarly, Consumption may be divided into the consumption of workers (C_w) and the consumption of capitalists (C_c).

Profits are therefore equal to $S_c + C_c$. S_c is equal to total Saving or Investment minus $S_w(1 - S_w)$. Total Profits $(S_c + C_c)$ therefore equal to $I + C_c - S_w$. See Michal Kalecki, "The Short-term Rate of Interest and the Velocity of Cash Circulation," *Review of Economic Studies* 2 (1942).

Marx's rejection of the classical theory of interest, the link between interest and the gross profits of capital, may also be examined from the "capitalists" credit club point of view. As indicated earlier, a literal reading of Marx and the classics suggests that *current* interest is paid out of *current* profits. In fact, at any one time capitalists hold loans, and they also hold deposits and bank shares accumulated from past profits. As Kalecki was to point out, it is his ownership of money capital that makes a man with entrepreneurial ability into a capitalist.[35] It is out of the total accumulation of profits, rather than just the current accumulation of profits, that interest is paid. But the interest received by capitalists adds to their income from productive activities. In our "pure" capitalist economy, the total value of those deposits and bank shares is equal to the total value of the loans in the banking system. If rates of interest are zero, banks make no profit and the capitalists' net income is the profit that they make from production. If interest rates rise, the net income of the capitalists is unchanged: as a class, they now pay interest. But their interest income, including the dividends received on their bank shares, has also risen by the same amount. How do they pay that higher interest? They do so by using the deposits that they have in the banking system. In effect, the payment of interest requires a purely financial circulation of bank deposits, rather than the receipt of bank deposits from current production. This is the institutional nexus behind Kalecki's observation that the velocity of circulation of deposits varies in proportion to the rate of interest on money.[36]

What if the capitalists do not have enough deposits to pay a really exorbitant increase in interest rates? In a credit system, they can borrow more by pledging assets as security against loans, and this corresponds to an increase in their deposits. Providing that banks are accommodating, capitalists will borrow as much deposits as are necessary to maintain interest and debt payments. From those interest and debt receipts, they can repay debts.

It follows that in a financial capitalist system, current profits are not, as the Ricardian theory asserts, the sole source of the means of payment that capitalists have with which to settle their financial obligations. Capitalists have savings and may borrow against the assets that they possess. This can

---

It is easy to show that in the more complicated situation where banks earn money from intermediating household or workers' deposits and loans, the profits of banks make no difference to aggregate profits.

[35] Michal Kalecki, *Selected Essays on the Dynamics of the Capitalist Economy 1933–1970* (Cambridge: Cambridge University Press, 1971), 109.

[36] Kalecki The Short-term Rate of Interest and the Velocity of Cash Circulation".

be illustrated by considering the unlikely extreme (Grossman?) case, where aggregate profit is equal to zero, but interest remains stubbornly positive. Of course, this does not mean that no capitalists are making a profit, merely that the profits of some capitalists are balanced by the business losses of other capitalists. Any profits in the banking sector from the margin between lending and deposit rates would be at the expense of overall losses among non-bank capitalists.

In this situation of overall zero profits, capitalists still have deposits (from accumulated past profits and borrowing) and loans from the bank intermediaries. Interest on that borrowing can be paid from deposits held by capitalists who owe money. Capitalists with credit balances will, therefore, receive interest income. The higher the rate of interest, the higher will be the interest paid, and received by capitalists. Bank deposits will be redistributed from net debtor capitalists to net creditor capitalists. What happens when, as a result of successive deposit redistributions, net debtors start to run out of bank deposits to pay interest on their borrowing? In that case, providing they have assets to post as collateral, they can borrow to pay interest, or else borrow without security.[37] The expansion of loans increases also the supply of deposits. As new deposits are redistributed from net debtors to net creditors, the net creditors accumulate the new deposits, which the net creditors can use to repay their own loans. The only circumstance that can prevent the continuing servicing of financial liabilities in this way is not the failure to generate a profit in production and trade, but a refusal of banks to lend more to net debtors.

The classical theory of interest asserts that capitalists must engage in production and productive investment in order to generate the income that they must pay as interest. The theory does not hold because in a capitalist economy, capitalists are ultimately, through the intermediation of banks, indebted to each other and this implies that equivalent deposits must be in the system and some of those deposits will be available to make interest payments. With a sufficiently elastic credit system, capitalists may pay any amount of interest to each other, and will accordingly receive that same amount of interest (from which to pay interest in future). In practice,

---

[37] Nobuhiro Kiyotaki, and John Moore, "Credit Cycles," *Journal of Political Economy* 105, no. 2 (April 1997) present a model of credit cycles in which the only collateral is real or productive capital. Such a credit cycle, of course, then follows the investment cycle. The much more convenient and widespread use of financial assets as collateral extends the range and possibilities of the credit cycle far beyond the less financial investment cycle.

of course, the distribution of credits and debts are not the same, so the capitalists will be either net creditors or net debtors to each other. Interest and debt are thus ways of redistributing their income among capitalists. They do not require production or investment to generate the profits out of which interest may be paid.[38]

V. Conclusion

In Volume III of *Capital*, Marx put forward the elements of a critique of the classical theory of interest that regards interest as determined by the current rate of profit. This classical theory had been established by David Ricardo in his *Principles of Political Economy*. The elements of Marx's critique included the idea that the development of the credit system gave rise to larger concentrations of money capital that would tend to depress the rate of interest, a separate rate of interest on long-term loans, and a view that the average rate of interest is determined by the average rate of profit (other things being equal and over a longer period). It should be borne in mind that Marx was writing in a time of "classic capitalism," with entrepreneurs or functioning capitalists eternally in debt to money capitalists, and rarely playing the part of money capitalists. With finance capital, the money capitalist and the functioning capitalist are merged. It is only after Hilferding, and the discussion of "pure credit" in Wicksell and Schumpeter, that we can understand fully how capitalist interest involves the circulation of surplus value in the form of accumulated money profits. In finance capital, interest is disconnected from the rate of profit and represents the rate of exchange between different types of financing. To Marx, we owe the first systematic break from Ricardo's theory of interest, in which interest is determined by the rate of profit. Once capitalists have ownership of money "hoards," the rate of interest becomes disconnected from any current rate of profit in the economy.

---

[38] The process by which this happens in described in Jan Toporowski, "A Kalecki Fable on Debt and the Monetary Transmission Mechanism," London School of Economics, Financial Markets Group *Special Paper* No. 239 (August 2015). Wicksell, who conceded that capitalists hold bank deposits (Wicksell, *Interest and Prices A Study of the Causes Regulating the Value of Money*, 138–9), does not draw the logical inference from this that those capitalists then also receive interest on those deposits in addition to their income from production and trade.

BIBLIOGRAPHY

Barbon, Nicholas. *A Discourse of Trade*. London: Milbourn, 1690.

Engels, Fredrick. "Preface." In MECW. Vol. 37. London: Lawrence & Wishart, 1998.

Hawtrey, Ralph George. *A Century of Bank Rate*. London: Longmans, Green and Co., 1938.

Hilferding, Rudolf. *Finance Capital A Study of the Latest Phase of Capitalist Development*. London: Routledge and Kegan Paul, 1981.

Hobson, John Atkinson. *Gold Prices and Wages with an Examination of the Quantity Theory*. London: Methuen, 1924.

Kalecki, Michal. "An Essay on the Business Cycle Theory." In *The Collected Works of Michał Kalecki Volume I Capitalism: Business Cycles and Full Employment*, edited by Jerzy Osiatynski. Oxford: The Clarendon Press, 1933.

Kalecki, Michal. "The Short-term Rate of Interest and the Velocity of Cash Circulation." *Review of Economic Studies* 2 (1941): 97–9.

Kalecki, Michal. *Selected Essays on the Dynamics of the Capitalist Economy 1933–1970*. Cambridge: Cambridge University Press, 1971.

Kiyotaki, Nobuhiro and John Moore. "Credit Cycles." *Journal of Political Economy* 105, no. 2 (April 1997): 211–48.

Marx, Karl. *Theories of Surplus Value Part III*. Moscow: Progress Publishers, 1971.

Marx, Karl. *Capital*. Vol. II. In MECW. Vol. 36. London: Lawrence & Wishart, 1997.

Marx, Karl. *Capital*. Vol. III. In MECW. Vol. 37. London: Lawrence & Wishart, 1998.

Niebyl, Karl H. *Studies in the Classical Theories of Money*. New York: Columbia University Press, 1946.

Reinhart, Carmen M. and Kenneth S. Rogoff. "This Time is Different: A Panoramic View of Eight Centuries of Financial Crises." NBER Working Paper No. 13882 (March 2008).

Ricardo, David. *The High Price of Bullion: A Proof of the Depreciation of Bank Notes*. In *The Works and Correspondence of David Ricardo, Volume III, Pamphlets and Papers, 1809–1811*, edited by Piero Sraffa, 47–98. Cambridge: Cambridge University Press, 1951a.

Ricardo, David. *On the Principles of Political Economy and Taxation*. In *The Works and Correspondence of David Ricardo Volume I*, edited by Piero Sraffa with Maurice Dobb. Cambridge: Cambridge University Press, 1951b.

Robertson, Dennis Holme. "Theories of Banking Policy." In *Essays in Monetary Theory* London: P.S. King, 1940.

Schumpeter, Joseph A. *History of Economic Analysis*. New York: Oxford University Press, 1954.

Shackle, G. L. S. "Foreword." In *Value Capital and Rent*, by Knut Wicksell, 5–13. London: George Allen and Unwin, 1954.

Smith, Matthew. *Thomas Tooke and the Monetary Thought of Classical Economics*. Abingdon, UK: Routledge, 2011.

Toporowski, Jan. *Theories of Financial Disturbance: An Examination of Critical Theories of Finance from Adam Smith to the Present Day*. Cheltenham: Edward Elgar, 2005.

Toporowski, Jan. "A Kalecki Fable on Debt and the Monetary Transmission Mechanism." London School of Economics, Financial Markets Group Special Paper No. 239 (August 2015).

Wicksell, Knut. *Interest and Prices: A Study of the Causes Regulating the Value of Money*. London: Macmillan, 1936.

Withers, Hartley. *The Meaning of Money*. New York: Dutton, 1909.

Money, Power, and Capitalism: Marx's Theory of Money and the Contemporary State-Credit Standard

Ramaa Vasudevan

I. Introduction

The global financial crisis triggered a resurgence of interest in Marx's analysis of capitalist dynamics and the financial system. What is extraordinary is not simply the fact that Marx "predicted" capitalism's propensity to crisis, but more significantly, that the analytical framework he elaborated in the three volumes of *Capital* is supple enough to help comprehend the more complex world of contemporary capitalism. My focus here is on how Marx's ideas about money and finance help in comprehending the contemporary international financial system.[1]

---

[1] The approach of this chapter is influenced by the work of Suzanne de Brunhoff and Duncan Foley, in particular: Suzanne de Brunhoff, *Marx on money* (New York: Urizen Books, 1976); Suzanne de Brunhoff "Marx's Contribution to the Search for a Theory of Money," in *Marx's theory of Money: Modern Appraisals*, ed. by Fred Moseley (New York: Palgrave Macmillan, 2005); Duncan Foley and Suzanne de Brunhoff, "Karl Marx's Theory

---

R. Vasudevan (✉)
Department of Economics, Colorado State University, Fort Collins, CO, USA

© The Author(s) 2019   229
S. Gupta et al. (eds.), *Karl Marx's Life, Ideas, and Influences*, Marx,
Engels, and Marxisms, https://doi.org/10.1007/978-3-030-24815-4_11

While Marx's theory of money was integral to his analysis of capitalist dynamics, the rich potential of Marx's analysis of money and finance is only recently receiving the attention it deserves. One possible reason for this neglect is that the abstract theory of commodity money that Marx had put forward has been seen as largely irrelevant to contemporary capitalism where money is linked to state credit. The second reason is the challenge of building a coherent analysis of the credit system from the "disordered jumble of notes, comments and extract materials,"[2] which Engels pulled together in Part V of the third volume of *Capital*. However, even though Marx begins his analysis in terms of commodity money, the method and framework of analysis is robust enough to comprehend the evolution of the non-commodity forms of modern money. The full development of the consequences of his theory to the complex monetary and financial phenomena of today's world is a challenge that Marxist political economists need to confront.

Marx's abstract theory was not simply concerned with the existence of commodity money, but more significantly, *with how and why and by what means a commodity becomes money*. The analytical structure of Marx's theorization of money reflect both his materialist conception of history and the dialectical method of analysis he deployed to understand concrete phenomena. We can deploy this same approach to comprehending *how and why and by what means* credit money (and state-credit money, in particular) became the basis of the modern monetary system.

I begin by highlighting some aspects of the analytical approach that Marx deployed in theorizing money, and then, turn to the concrete analysis of financial markets and the emergence of state-credit money in the nineteenth-century England, as a prelude to comprehending the contemporary international monetary system.

of Money and Credit," in *A Handbook of Alternative Monetary Economics*, ed. Philip Arestis and Malcolm C. Sawyer (Northampton, MA: Edward Elgar, 2007); Duncan Foley, "On Marx's Theory of Money," *Social Concept* 1, no. 1 (1983); "Money in Economic Activity," in *The New Palgrave: Money*, ed. John Eatwell, Murray Milgate, and Peter Newman (London: Palgrave Macmillan, 1989); Duncan Foley, "Marx's Theory of Money in Historical Perspective," in *Marx's Theory of Money: Modern Appraisals*, ed. Fred Moseley (New York: Palgrave Macmillan, 2005). Ramaa Vasudevan, "The Significance of Marx's Theory," *Economic and Political Weekly* 52, no. 37 (2017) provides a review of the analytical structure of Marx's theory of money.

[2] Engels in the preface to Karl Marx, *Capital*, Vol. III (London: Penguin, 1981), 84.

II. Marx's Method

Before discussing the role of money in financing capitalist production, Marx set up a simple thought experiment to show how a product becomes a commodity, the commodity becomes exchange value, the exchange value of the commodity appears as its "immanent money property," and achieves a separate existence in the form of money. This thought experiment allows him to uncover the contradictions inherent in the money relation—contradictions that are wrapped up in the separate existence of money alongside commodities. Marx wrote,

> It is an inherent property of money to fulfill its purposes by simultaneously negating them; to achieve independence from commodities, to be a means which becomes an end, to realize exchange value of commodities by separating them from it; to facilitate exchange by splitting it; to overcome the difficulties of direct exchange of commodities by generalizing them; to make exchange independent of the producers in the same measure as producers become dependent on exchange.[3]

Thus, the money-form arises, in the first instance, from the contradiction between the dual existence of commodities as use value and as exchange value. This contradiction is further developed and displaced once the act of exchange is split into two mutually independent acts of purchase and sale. This separation between the acts of purchase and sale contains the latent possibility of crises.[4] The contradictory unity of use value and exchange value is reproduced in that between the flows of money and commodities. Marx's analysis of money thus contained the possibility of a divergence between the structure of demand and that of the concrete use values produced in the course of these flows, anticipating Keynes' postulation of the principle of effective demand.

Marx also pointed to a third level of contradiction, in *Grundrisse*. This arises when "the overall movement of exchange itself becomes separate from the exchangers." This is the sphere of commerce, concerned solely with exchange for the sake of exchange and not for consumption, which

---

[3] Karl Marx, *Grundrisse* (London: Penguin, 1973), 151.
[4] Peter Kenway, "Marx, Keynes, and the Possibility of Crisis," *Cambridge Journal of Economics* 4, no. 1, (1980); James Crotty, "The Centrality of Money, Credit and Financial Intermediation in Marx's Crisis Theory," in *Rethinking Marxism*, ed. Steven Resnick and Richard Wolff (New York: Autonomedia, 1985).

mediates the circulation of commodities produced under varied social relations. This is basis for the emergence of merchant capital, the oldest historical mode in which capital has an independent existence. Production for exchange and consumption is subsumed into the imperatives of commerce—"buying cheap in order to sell and only selling in order to buy again with the aim of acquiring money, not commodities." A new contradiction emerges "since production works directly for commerce and only indirectly for consumption, it must not only create but also be seized by this incongruency between commerce and exchange for consumption" and between the different laws and motives that govern commerce and the two extremities between which commerce is conducted.[5]

As the contradictions of the money form continue to unfold with the development of capitalism, the operations of the sphere of credit and finance also emerge as distinct from the sphere of commerce. The contradictions of the money form now appear in the disjunction between money's role as the universal equivalent and also as a particular commodity that is subject to particular conditions of exchange in its exchange with other commodities, "conditions which contradict its general unconditional exchangeability."[6] If posed in terms of a commodity-money standard, this points to the contradiction between the value of money as an expression of exchange value of all commodities, and its particular value as produced commodity.

More significant, these passages in the *Grundrisse* contain the core of Marx's argument of how the contradictions of the money form are displaced as money evolves with the development of capitalism to become both a general equivalent and a financial asset. These passages, also provide a road map for a path to integrating the concrete discussion of credit and finance in *Capital*, Volume III with the abstract theory of *Capital*, Volume I.[7] In this chapter, the purpose is to highlight how these passages also allow the extrapolation of the logical structure of Marx's argument to the investigation of the contemporary monetary system based on a state-credit standard—where the monetary liability of a state functions as money, both domestically and internationally.

[5] Karl Marx, *Grundrisse* (London: Penguin, 1973), 148–9.
[6] Ibid., 150–1.
[7] This argument is made in Vasudevan, "The Significance of Marx's Theory," *Economic and Political Weekly* 52, no. 37 (2017).

III. MARX ON CREDIT MONEY

The critical link in the evolution of the state-credit standard is money in its role as a means of payment—and as credit money—which is simply a tradable promise to pay. Marx investigated how money's function as a means of payment springs directly out of commerce. While credit money plays a limited role when capitalism is not yet developed, the credit economy develops on the basis of the monetary economy with the growth and spread of capitalism, and eventually comes to dominate and replace it.[8] Thus, Marx's theory of credit money is constructed as a secondary, more concrete layer of analysis. It is, however, critical to the analysis of capitalist dynamics, and the structure of his argument is meant to clarify the monetary roots of the credit system.

He draws an analogy between the relationship between the monetary system and the credit system, and that between Catholicism and Protestantism, saying that:

> The monetary system is essentially a Catholic institution, the credit system essentially Protestant... But the credit system does not emancipate itself from the basis of the monetary system any more than Protestantism has emancipated itself from the foundations of Catholicism.[9]

The forms of credit money in the early nineteenth century included bills of exchange (which originated as IOUs between traders and producers) and bank deposits (which were the liability of the banks). The credit system has become considerably more complex today. The forms of credit money too have evolved to include repos, and other forms of what is called shadow money today.[10] While the bills of exchange were promises to pay, backed by the private guarantees of financial institutions, repos are promises to pay, backed by a tradable collateral. Credit money is the logical and historical link between the monetary system and the financial system and is also, I will argue, key to the evolution of world money.

---

[8] Marx, *Capital*, Vol. III, chapter 25.

[9] Ibid., 727.

[10] Zoltan Pozsar, "Shadow Money: The Money View," Office of Financial Research Working Paper 14-04 (2014) provides an overview of contemporary shadow money. Ramaa Vasudevan, "Shadow Money in the Nineteenth Century," in "The Nineteenth Century: Is Marx Relevant for Understanding Contemporary Shadow Money," *Review of Political Economy* 30, no. 3 (2018) discusses modern shadow money through the lens of Marx's writings on the bill market of his time.

The forms of credit money, which emerged in the financing of trade, were the foundation of the capitalist financial system. The growing dominance of credit money in the financial system is fundamentally an expression of the separation of the sphere of finance and money-dealing from that of commerce that Marx alluded to in the *Grundrisse*. It contains the potential contradiction between money's value as a general equivalent and its particular valuation as an asset.

This contradiction is in concrete practice, expressed and resolved through the workings of the money market, where credit money and short-term paper are traded. In the early half of the nineteenth century, credit money in the form of bills of exchange played an important role in mediating inland trade in England. But by the latter half of the century, the sterling bill was the dominant instrument mediating international trade, and the bill market had matured into a buoyant well-developed money market. Proliferating bill trade created private monetary mechanisms at a time when note issue by the Bank of England was tied to gold reserves. These mechanisms played a crucial role in fostering liquidity independent of gold reserves.[11]

Marx had stressed that the mediation of this chain of payments by forms of credit money, like bills of exchange, does not do away with the need for cash payments in an absolute sense. In the historical context of the mid-nineteenth century, the credit money mechanisms of the bill market were, in the final analysis, anchored to Bank of England notes and gold reserves. The monetary system is a hierarchy of claims and liabilities. At each level of this hierarchical structure, there is a higher form of money—as a means of payment—that can extinguish debts at lower levels of the hierarchy.[12] Thus, bills of exchange had to be settled in terms of Bank of England notes, and Bank of England notes were ultimately settled through payment of gold.

There is thus, as Marx delineated, a contradiction inherent in the credit money system. As long as payments balance each other, it is merely functioning in the nominal form of a unit of account. However, when actual

---

[11] Ramaa Vasudevan, "From the Gold Standard to the Floating Dollar Standard: An Appraisal in the Light of Marx's Theory of Money," *Review of Radical Political Economics* 41, no. 4 (2009); Vasudevan, "Shadow Money in the Nineteenth Century" provide a fuller articulation of this argument.

[12] Perry Mehrling, "The Inherent Hierarchy of Money," in *Social Fairness and Economics: Essays in the Spirit of Duncan Foley*, ed. Lance Taylor, Armon Rezai and Thomas Michl (New York: Routledge, 2012).

payments have to be made, money is needed not in this nominal form, but in its form as money proper—the "universal commodity," thus precipitating a monetary crisis. Such monetary crises occur, Marx writes,

> where the ever-lengthening chain of payments, and an artificial system of settling them, has been fully developed. As the hart pants after fresh water, so pants his soul after money, the only wealth. In a crisis, the antithesis between commodities and their value form is raised to the level of an absolute contradiction.[13]

Developed capitalist countries replace money by credit operations or credit money. In times of pressure, once credit dries up, money confronts all other commodities as the only means of payment and true embodiment of value. So, at precisely the time that there is this "violent scramble for means of payments,"[14] it becomes harder to convert credit money into hard cash. In the context of the bill market of the nineteenth century that Marx was writing about, the crisis appears in the form of a demand for Bank of England notes, itself a form of credit money that was tied to gold reserves. Thus, the Bank of England came to play a critical role in restoring liquidity and re-establishing the terms of convertibility.

Such crisis occurred, for instance, in 1847 and 1857, and the Bank of England was compelled to periodically intervene to prop up the banking system. Marx characterized the Bank of England as "the biggest capital power in London" and the "centre of gravity of all commercial credit." Even so, its power is not absolute; it had to develop the tools and mechanisms for enforcing its will over the private channels of liquidity creation in periods of normalcy when the market was dominated by the private financial institutions—the large discount houses and joint stock banks.[15]

In particular, the Bank of England was constrained by the gold reserves in its vaults. Gold was needed to secure convertibility. But gold had another critical function in the nineteenth century. In the context of the International Gold Standard system, gold functioned as "world money" and was needed for the settlement of international payments. The breakdown in convertibility during the crises in 1847 and 1857 were further compounded by the outflow of gold. These breakdowns in convertibility,

---

[13] Karl Marx, *A Contribution to a Critique of Political Economy* (Chicago: International Library Publishing, 1972), 235.

[14] Ibid., 235.

[15] Vasudevan, "Shadow Money in the Nineteenth Century" elaborates this argument.

Marx argued, had far-reaching implications for the reproduction of the existing social relations. It is the threat to the underlying system of social relations that dictates the imperative need for central bank intervention to ensure the conditions for convertibility and protect the value of money.

We see the same compulsions operating today in the bailouts to banks after the financial crisis following the collapse of Lehman Brothers. At the heart of the collapse was the implosion of what has been called the shadow banking system—unregulated financial mechanisms of funding capital market through the contemporary equivalent of the bills of exchange, the repo.[16] The consequences of the breakdown in these mechanisms of liquidity and credit creation compelled massive interventions by the US Federal Reserve.

There is another aspect of Marx's discussion of monetary crisis and the drain of gold—which is his analysis of the contagion-like spread of balance of payments crisis from one country to another in succession—like volley-firing. Thus, a balance of payments crisis may begin in one country—a creditor country like England—but the drain of gold induced by this crisis and the ensuing bankruptcy of importers leads to distress sales of goods and securities and transmits the crisis to its trading partners.[17]

Marx recognized, much before John Maynard Keynes, the inherent deflationary bias of the gold standard system. The Bank of England dealt with such crisis by abandoning convertibility of sterling claims to gold in 1846, 1857, and 1866. But by the end of the century, for instance, during the Barings crisis of 1890, the Bank was able to weather monetary and financial crisis, without revoking its commitment to convertibility.[18] It did so by borrowing from countries like France, and special depositors like India and Japan. This was a development that Marx did not explicitly address or anticipate.

The historical evolution of the International Gold Standard after Marx's death suggests that countries like India and Japan provided a critical source of short-term credit when other advanced capitalist countries like France failed to lend to the Bank of England. The financial system centred in the City of London recycled these surpluses in the form of capital exports to

---

[16] Zoltan Pozsar et al., "Shadow Banking," *Federal Reserve Bank of New York Staff Report*, no. 458, 2010.

[17] Marx, *Capital*, Vol. III, 623–4.

[18] Vasudevan, "From the Gold Standard to the Floating Dollar Standard."

primary commodity exporters in Latin America and Australia that bore the brunt of convertibility crisis and destabilizing capital flows.[19]

Marx had recognized the elasticity that credit money provided to the monetary system. However, he did argue that in times of crisis, the limited stock of gold reserves with the Bank of England constrained its capacity to intervene in the bill market. But the parallel monetary mechanisms of the international bill market, and the asymmetric integration of less advanced countries, and Britain's colonial power, in effect, imparted a greater degree of elasticity and heft to the Bank of England's capacity to intervene in the financial markets. The Bank of England was, in the last decades of the century, able to exercise much greater control over the money market and maintain convertibility through its interventions in the money market even though it held a relatively small stock of gold reserves. In the process, the Bank of England also took on the mantle of the lender of last resort for the financial system, not just domestically but also internationally.[20] This role was embedded in the financial revolution that put the City of London at the hub of the international financial system. This process can be understood in terms of the separation and growing dominance of the sphere of finance from that of commerce alluded to in the passages in the *Grundrisse* that informed Marx's method. This process unfolded not just within national boundaries but also internationally across national borders.

IV. THE EVOLUTION OF A STATE-CREDIT STANDARD

The concrete history of Bank of England interventions since the 1890s also reveals how the contemporary state-credit standard evolved out of the state and central bank's attempt to manage and regulate these private money markets. Increased treasury operations in this period helped bolster the Bank of England's control over the bill market. With the introduction of the treasury bill at the end of the nineteenth century, short-term claims on the state also came to play a greater role in the money market. In the process, gold was, over time, replaced by the monetary liability of the British state at the top of the monetary hierarchy, and the money market became linked more closely to the Bank of England's management of public debt.[21]

---

[19] This argument is put forward in ibid.
[20] See ibid.
[21] Vasudevan, "Shadow Money in the Nineteenth Century."

The issue of public debt also generates a parallel sphere of financial transactions, which fostered the growth of financial dealers and speculators. The liabilities of the state, functioning in the hands of the creditors, as a liquid asset that can be sold and resold multiple times engender further growth in the financial system. What the buyers of public debt lend is transformed into tradable assets, which can be sold and resold multiple times, to function as money. It thus represents the creation and transfer of wealth to those who hold this debt, fostering the growth of "stock exchange gambling and a modern bankocracy."[22] Public debt breeds speculation and the concentration of wealth. This connection between public debt and the growth and centralization of wealth with the development and evolution of the financial system underscored why "public credit becomes the credo of capital," marking "the capitalist era with its stamp."[23]

This is apparent in the confounding process through which the accumulation of debts appears as an accumulation of capital. To use Marx's evocative words,

> As with a stroke of the enchanter's wand, it endows unproductive money with the power of creation and thus turns it into capital, without forcing it to expose itself to the troubles and risks inseparable from its employment in industry or even in usury.[24]

And so, it would appear that a nation becomes the richer the more deeply it is in debt.

There is thus a deep nexus between public debt and private finance. This nexus has become more entrenched through the twentieth century. Public debt is both the anchor and the basis of expansion of the contemporary capitalist financial system. The growth of capitalist financial system, Marx wrote,

> develops the motive of capitalist production, enrichment by exploitation of others labour, into the purest and most colossal system of gambling and swindling and restricts even more the already small number of exploiters of social wealth.[25]

[22] Karl Marx, *Capital*, Vol. I (London: Penguin, 1976), 919.
[23] Ibid.
[24] Ibid.
[25] Marx, *Capital*, Vol. III, 572.

The structural implications of the rise to dominance of finance for growing inequality and the concentration are of course of profound significance in the contemporary world. The implication of the state in the mechanisms of financial markets—through monetary policy interventions and bank bailouts—also highlights how the power of the state has become crucial to preserving this dominance and buttressing the resilience of the financial system. At the same time, the management of rising public debt is increasingly holding the state hostage to finance, through what has been called the doom loop.[26] The gambles of the financial system keep getting larger, threatening the functioning of the capitalist financial system. This necessitates even larger interventions by the state and the central banks to restore the financial system. The stranglehold of finance thus becomes even more powerful.

The money market where short-term bills are traded is a critical terrain where the connection between the financial system and state credit is established. The liquidity of the private sterling bill derived from the implicit back-stop that the Bank of England provided to the Discount Houses. However, with the introduction of the treasury bill and increasing recourse to this instrument in the money market after 1890, the money market began to trade directly in short-term claims of the state. These claims came to be regarded as close substitutes to "hard cash" or gold precisely because they were promises to pay of the state. The treasury bill has thus emerged as a critical anchor for the money market in the twentieth century. The credit-money system that had originated in private commercial transactions embedded in a system of private guarantees established an instrument that was directly secured by the power and prestige of the state. This has profound implications for the resilience of the financial system and the evolving nexus between the state and private finance.

The evolution of the financial system in the advanced capitalist world after the Great Depression and the Second World War ushered in a period where the state played an even greater role in regulating the channels of private liquidity and the financial system.

---

[26] Andrew G. Haldane and Piergiorgio Alessandri, "Banking on the State," Paper Presented at the Federal Reserve Bank of Chicago Twelfth Annual International Banking Conference (2009).

V. State, Private Finance, and World Money

While Marx planned to introduce the world market only after elaborating his investigation of competition and the redistribution of surplus value among its different claimants, world trade and commerce are, in fact, the historic presupposition for the emergence of capitalism. Merchant capital, which existed before the spread of capitalist social relations, can be seen as "the oldest historical mode in which capital has an independent existence."[27] The wealth of the merchant capital "always exists as money wealth, and his money always functions as capital," and the operations of trade, separate from that of production, become a means of increasing wealth.[28] Even before merchant capital subjected production in different regions and spheres to its control, it imparted to these spheres a greater orientation towards trade, transforming products into commodities: "It expands its scope, diversifies it, and renders it cosmopolitan, developing money into world money."[29]

Historically, money's role as world money arises with the development of the world of market and the extension of the international division of labour. While no fundamentally new functions arise in the course of international circulation of commodities that have not arisen in the course of domestic circulation, the settlement of international payments with a transfer of world money becomes the means by which wealth is transferred from one nation to another, and is redistributed internationally. In its role as world money, money serves as an embodiment of social power internationally.

Thus, the acquisition of power in the mercantilist period of nascent capitalism was associated with the accumulation of wealth in the form of money—more specifically, as world money. When bullion served as world money, trade surpluses led to the accumulation or reserves in the creditor country while deficit countries were faced with an outflow of reserves and indebtedness. Marx wrote of the early period of capitalist development, that:

> the transformation of feudal agricultural societies into industrial societies, and the resulting industrial struggle among nations on the world market, involves an accelerated development capital which cannot be attained in a so called natural way but only by compulsion...by the accelerated production of the conditions of the capitalist mode of production.[30]

[27] Marx, *Capital*, Vol. III, 442.
[28] Ibid., 443.
[29] Ibid., 449.
[30] Ibid., 920.

The modes of accelerating the transformation include taxes, protective duties, the forcible expropriation of independent direct producers, and the concentration of capital. Thus,

> the mercantile system is not a mere slogan in the mouths of its spokesmen. Under the pretext of being concerned only with the wealth of the nation and the sources of assistance for the state, they actually declare the interests of the capitalist class, and enrichment in general, are the final purpose of the state, and proclaim bourgeois society as against the old supernatural state. At the same time, however, they show their awareness that the development of the interest of capital and the capitalist class, of capitalist production, has become the basis of a nation's power and predominance in modern society.

With the development of capitalism, merchant capital loses its separate existence and appears as a particular moment or function of capital. Marx further outlines how merchant capital separates into the distinct categories of commercial capital and money-dealing capital, which appear as specialist functions and forms of capital in the sphere of circulation. The former mediates the trade of commodities, while the latter performs the technical operations associated with commerce and monetary circulation.[31]

The circulation of credit money, which emerged as a way of financing trade, breeds financial intermediaries whose primary function is the mediation of these credit transactions. Thus, even though money-dealing capital arises as a specialized function of merchant capital, it becomes an integral part of, and is further transformed by, the development of capitalism. The banking system evolved out of the money-dealing capital once "borrowing and lending, and the management of interest-bearing capital, emerge as a special function of money-dealing capital."[32]

Interest-bearing capital, which is also an antediluvian form of capital, like merchant capital, gets transformed under capitalism, and manifests the capitalist "relationship in its most superficial and fetishized form as a 'mysterious and self-creating' source of its own increase, independent of production and circulation."[33] Unlike commercial credit that is advanced to enable the exchange of commodities, it constitutes an advance of money between capitalists for the finance of capitalist production. The advance of money capital allows interest-bearing capital to claim a share of the surplus

---

[31] Ibid., chapter 19, 20.
[32] Ibid., 528.
[33] Ibid., 516.

value created in production as interest. Marx develops the category of interest-bearing capital further into the categories of loanable capital and bank capital. The former involves not just the lending of funds owned by the lender, but more fundamentally, the collection and recycling of idle funds.[34] Bank capital is not simply mobilizing idle funds, it expands loanable capital through the creation of special liabilities—claims of money that act like money that act as claims on money. The evolution of commercial banking and investment banking can be understood through the lens of Marx's analysis.

Thus, commercial banking expands monetary circuits though the doubling of money and claims on money, while investment banking, in a parallel manner, involves the doubling of industrial capital and securities.[35] But, unlike the money claims that commercial banking issues, the securities the investment bank deals with are not claims on money, but on future streams of income that have to be exchanged with money. Banking profits accrue from market-making activity that exploits bid-ask spreads on the traded securities.

The accumulation of funds in the banking system can thus grow in step or even more rapidly than the scale of reproduction processes.[36] The expansion of credit enables an expansion in the scale of production and the extraction of surplus value. It also accelerates the development of technology and the creation of the world market.

As the scope of the financial system extends beyond national boundaries to embrace all parts of the global economy, the emerging global networks of the financial system become the engine that mobilizes and centralizes funds on a global scale. The system serves to draw surpluses (and revenues) from across the world, under its control, making profit by lending it further to capitalists in other parts of the global economy.

It has been argued that the International Gold Standard was in effect a British Pound-sterling standard, with the sterling bill being used increasingly to finance trade and international transactions. The Bank of England was able to calibrate international liquidity through its manipulation of the discount rate, despite its relatively small reserves of gold, because it

---

[34] Costas Lapavitsas, "Two Approaches to the Concept of Interest-Bearing Capital," *International Journal of Political Economy* 27, no.1 (1997).

[35] This argument is elaborated in Duncan Lindo, "Political Economy of Financial Derivatives: A Theoretical Analysis of the Evolution of Banking and Its Role in Derivatives Markets" (PhD Thesis, SOAS, 2013).

[36] Marx, *Capital*, Vol. III, chapters 31, 32.

could draw on surpluses from the colonies and other countries on the periphery, and shift the burden of adjustment and crises to these countries. While the international acceptance of sterling bills and the City of London's pivotal role in international financial markets did impart elasticity to the International Gold Standard beyond what the limited gold reserves of the Bank of England would allow, the system was, in the final analysis, based on gold.

In fact, it was only with breakdown of the post-war Bretton Woods system and the floating of the dollar that world money was finally delinked from gold. With this development, the monetary liability of the US became the basis for the international financial system and the modern international monetary system evolved to a state-credit standard hinged on the dollar. Marx's method, which investigates the emergence and eventual dominance of credit money domestically, also allows the discovery of the logical and historical path by which an international state-credit standard developed.

A few aspects of the evolution of an international state-credit standard are worth emphasizing. First, the pattern by which wealth is transferred from deficit countries to the surplus countries, the consequent re-ordering of power internationally as the reserves of world money are redistributed, undergoes a change with this evolution. The international acceptance of the monetary liability of a state as world money transforms the nation-state to a borrower of last resort, creating liquidity by acting like banks do when they borrow short and lend long.[37] While the country issuing world money needs to sustain balance of payments deficits in order to generate international liquidity, such deficits do not imply a loss of social power on the international arena, but rather its opposite. The pattern of deficits, the drain of reserves, and outflow of wealth no longer applies to the nation-state issuing world money. The dominant country can evade the consequences of debt-deflationary crises that Marx saw as inherent to the functioning of world money when it was still tied to gold. The constraint on its capacity to intervene and create liquidity is not the stock of its foreign reserves holdings, but its capacity to borrow internationally.

Second, in acting as the banker to the world, the dominant nation-state issuing world money also centralizes and recycles surpluses from and to the periphery (and rival nation-states). The foreign assets are thus being

---

[37] Vasudevan, "From the Gold Standard to the Floating Dollar Standard."

accumulated on the basis of wealth and money stocks appropriated from creditor countries that hold the monetary liability of this state. The ease of access to credit for the dominant country, which is key to the functioning of the state-credit standard, is also the basis of the exorbitant privilege that the country appropriates, from the difference on the return on its monetary liability (the interest paid on foreign holdings of treasury bills), and the returns on its accumulation of foreign assets (the income it receives from its investments abroad).[38]

Third, there is a network externality associated with the use of world money. As more countries use a particular world money to settle international transactions, it becomes further entrenched as a liquid and safe universal equivalent and embodiment of wealth in the abstract. When a dominant country's currency—the monetary liability of its state—performs the role of world money, this network externality serves to further preserve and extend this disproportionate dominance in the international financial system.

Thus, the state-credit standard reflects and perpetuates the asymmetric exercise of power and dominance by the nation-state that issues this world money. It also places the burden of calibrating international liquidity and ensuring stability of international financial system on this dominant state.

VI. Conclusion

The emergence of the floating dollar standard after the dismantling of the end of the Bretton Woods system ushered in a period when developing countries were increasingly integrated to the international financial system. Neo-liberalism was espoused and advocated as a tool to sustain the dollar's role as world money and reinforce the dominance of the US. The rise to dominance of finance, along with the profusion of financial assets, has been integral to the workings of the floating dollar standard. These mechanisms of dollar liquidity have, at the same time, engendered growing global imbalances (due to growing US trade deficits), profound inequality, and concentration of wealth, and have been fuelling increasing financial fragility.

---

[38] Pierre-Olivier Gourinchas and Hélène Rey, "From World Banker to World Venture Capitalist: US External Adjustment and the Exorbitant Privilege," NBER Working Paper 11563 (Cambridge, MA: National Bureau of Economic Research, 2005).

The crisis triggered in the wake of the collapse of Lehman Brothers reflected some of the tensions and vulnerabilities of the system based on the dollar standard. While the crisis was, in a very fundamental sense, a crisis of dollar hegemony, the power of finance and the dominance of the dollar remains entrenched a decade after the crisis. In fact, the financial sector in the US has become even more concentrated in the wake of the crisis, and has launched a concerted push back against regulations. Investment banking is also witnessing a resurgence. The casino of finance seems to be back in business. The expanding balance sheets of central banks reflects how deeply they have been implicated in shoring up the financial system.

While the history of the last century is testimony to the growing capacity of the state to act as the lender of last resort for financial system and ensure its resilience after each crisis, the growing scale of the casino and its consequence for growing inequality suggests that Marx's caution about the limits to the power of the state has resonance today. The evolution of world money based on an international state-credit standard expanded the capacity of the state and central bank at the centre of the international financial system to manage to financial system. This power is, however, not absolute.

BIBLIOGRAPHY

Crotty, James. "The Centrality of Money, Credit and Financial Intermediation in Marx's Crisis Theory." In *Rethinking Marxism*, edited by Steven Resnick and Richard Wolff, 45–8. New York: Autonomedia, 1985.

de Brunhoff, Suzanne. *Marx on Money*. New York: Urizen Books, 1976.

de Brunhoff, Suzanne. "Marx's Contribution to the Search for a Theory of Money." In *Marx's Theory of Money: Modern Appraisals*, edited by Fred Moseley, 209–22. New York: Palgrave Macmillan, 2005.

Foley, Duncan. "On Marx's Theory of Money." *Social Concept* 1, no. 1 (1983): 5–19.

Foley, Duncan. "Money in Economic Activity." In *The New Palgrave: Money*, edited by John Eatwell, Murray Milgate and Peter Newman, 248–62. London: Palgrave Macmillan, 1989.

Foley, Duncan. "Marx's Theory of Money in Historical Perspective." In *Marx's Theory of Money: Modern Appraisals*, edited by F. Moseley, 36–50. New York: Palgrave Macmillan, 2005.

Foley, Duncan and Suzanne de Brunhoff. "Karl Marx's Theory of Money and Credit." In *A Handbook of Alternative Monetary Economics*, edited by Philip Arestis and Malcolm C. Sawyer, 188–204. Northampton, MA: Edward Elgar, 2007.

Gourinchas, Pierre-Olivier and Hélène Rey. "From World Banker to World Venture Capitalist: US External Adjustment and the Exorbitant privilege." NBER Working Paper 11563. Cambridge, MA: National Bureau of Economic Research, 2005.

Haldane, Andrew G. and Piergiorgio Alessandri. "Banking on the State." Paper Presented at the Federal Reserve Bank of Chicago Twelfth Annual International Banking Conference, 2009.

Kenway, Peter. "Marx, Keynes, and the Possibility of Crisis." *Cambridge Journal of Economics* 4, no. 1 (1980): 23–36.

Lapavitsas, Costas. "Two Approaches to the Concept of Interest Bearing Capital." *International Journal of Political Economy* 27, no. 1 (1997): 85–106.

Lindo, Duncan. "Political Economy of Financial Derivatives: A Theoretical Analysis of the Evolution of Banking and Its Role in Derivatives Markets." PhD Thesis, SOAS, University of London, 2013.

Marx, Karl. *A Contribution to a Critique of Political Economy*. Chicago: International Library Publishing, 1972.

Marx, Karl. *Grundrisse*. London: Penguin, 1973.

Marx, Karl. *Capital*. Vol. I. London: Penguin, 1976.

Marx, Karl. *Capital*. Vol. III. London: Penguin, 1981.

Mehrling, Perry. "The Inherent Hierarchy of Money." In *Social Fairness and Economics: Essays in the Spirit of Duncan Foley*, edited by Lance Taylor, Armon Rezai, and Thomas Michl, 394–404. New York: Routledge, 2012.

Pozsar, Zoltan. "Shadow Money: The Money View." Office of Financial Research Working Paper 14-04, 2014. Available at https://papers.ssrn.com/sol3/papers.cfm?abstract_id=2476415.

Pozsar, Zoltan, Adam Ashcraft, and Hayley Boesky. "Shadow Banking." Federal Reserve Bank of New York Staff Report No. 458, 2010.

Vasudevan, Ramaa. "From the Gold Standard to the Floating Dollar Standard: An Appraisal in the Light of Marx's Theory of Money." *Review of Radical Political Economics* 41, no. 4 (2009): 473–91.

Vasudevan, Ramaa. "Quantitative Easing Through the Prism of the Barings Crisis in 1890: Central Banks and the International Money Market." *Journal of Post-Keynesian Economics* 37, no. 1 (2014): 91–114.

Vasudevan, Ramaa. "The Significance of Marx's Theory of Money." *Economic and Political Weekly* 52, no. 37 (2017): 70–82.

Vasudevan, Ramaa. "Shadow Money in the Nineteenth Century: Is Marx Relevant for Understanding Contemporary Shadow Money." *Review of Political Economy* 30, no. 3 (2018): 461–83.

Marx as Evolutionary and Some "Revisionist" Implications

Samuel Hollander

I. Introduction

The term "revolution" suggests violent overturn, and the view of Marx as "revolutionary" is not only standard textbook fare filtering through to popular opinion, but also often found in authoritative professional accounts, as by Isaiah Berlin, who unconditionally asserted that Marx "was, all his life, a convinced and uncompromising believer in a violent working class revolution."[1] Some formulations do not specify that violence is intended by the attribution to Marx, but such a reading is invited. Thus, according to a recent contributor to the *New York Review of Books*, "[w]ith the rise of totalitarian fascism in the 1930s, the Frankfurt School lost confidence in the ability of workers to mount a revolution against monopoly capitalism and the states sustaining it, as Marx predicted they would. It regarded workers as paralyzed by conformist tendencies and

---

[1] Isaiah Berlin, *Karl Marx: His Life and Environment*, 4th ed. (Oxford: Oxford University Press, 1978), 189.

S. Hollander (✉)
University of Toronto, Toronto, ON, Canada

© The Author(s) 2019   247
S. Gupta et al. (eds.), *Karl Marx's Life, Ideas, and Influences*, Marx,
Engels, and Marxisms, https://doi.org/10.1007/978-3-030-24815-4_12

unable to discern the source of their grievances in the capitalist system."[2] Of particular interest is the presumption of violence by Eric Hobsbawm when he refers to "the actual revolution, in the sense of the (presumably violent) transfer of power … [which] would in turn initiate a lengthy process of post-revolutionary transition."[3]

Needless to say, the secondary literature yields conflicting opinions. Thus, Joseph Schumpeter refers to "the grand vision of an imminent evolution of the economic process—that, working somehow through accumulation, somehow destroys the economy as well as the society of competitive capitalism and somehow produces an untenable social situation that will somehow give birth to another type of social organization," which he finds "constitutes Marx's claim to greatness as an economic analyst."[4] Yet, when discussing Darwin, Schumpeter makes no mention of Marx's own description of *Capital* as demonstrating "in the social context the same gradual process of evolution that Darwin demonstrated in natural history."[5] Stedman Jones attributes a methodological parallel with "Darwinism" but specifically to Engels.[6] Returning now to the main issue—evolution or revolution—Mandell Bober makes the valid point that we are obliged to turn "to direct evidence in Marx's utterances," since "the dialectic cannot inform us whether the future social synthesis will be achieved by a revolutionary cataclysm or by a peaceful transition."[7] A grave deficiency indeed. In any event, he finds that "up to the early 1850's it seems that Marx and Engels put great stress on violence, almost giving the impression of relishing it; while from the 1860's on they begin to allow that at least in certain countries, a peaceful method, the ballot, may be both available and preferable." I shall have this reading in mind as my argument proceeds.

[2] Samuel Freeman, "The Headquarters of Neo-Marxism," *New York Review of Books* 64, no. 5 (23 March 2017): 63.

[3] Eric Hobsbawm, *How to Change the World: Reflections on Marx and Marxism* (New Haven and London: Yale University Press, 2011), 65.

[4] Joseph A. Schumpeter, *History of Economic Analysis* (London: George Allen and Unwin, 1954), 441.

[5] Karl Marx, "Marx to Engels, 7 December 1867," in MECW (New York: International Publishers, 1987), 42: 494.

[6] Gareth Stedman Jones, *Karl Marx: Greatness and Illusion* (London: Allen Lane, 2016), 563–4, 566–7.

[7] Mandell M. Bober, *Karl Marx's Interpretation of History* (New York: Norton, 1965), 262.

The perspective on Marx as "revolutionary" in the violent sense, I find unconvincing and I shall review the evidence for this conclusion. The repeated use of "somehow" by Schumpeter in singing the praises of Marx as "evolutionist" certainly suggests the need to tighten up this side of the argument. I shall maintain that while Marx was no less "evolutionary" than, say, John Stuart Mill, his version of evolution, insofar as it relates to prominent features of advanced capitalism, implies a powerful "laissez-faire" bias in two senses: a concern lest reformist measures to correct perceived injustices in the going system assure its permanence, halting the allegedly necessitarian process of transmutation in its tracks; and a warning against *premature* action to transform systems. Much of this is well known and ought to have sufficed to render inappropriate the designation of Marx himself as a "revolutionary"—"conservative" would be a far more accurate designation. Less well known, and strongly reinforcing his laissez-faire reasoning, is Marx's sophisticated appreciation of the operation of the free-market pricing system. This, I shall demonstrate.

I then carry the story further, with an eye to Marx's evolutionism beyond developments within advanced capitalism. There is the *proletarian takeover*, which might, for Marx, occur by way of democratic voting enabled by extensions of the franchise accorded by the capitalist state in response to pressures generated by capitalist development. Here, I take issue with Hobsbawm, who attributes this allegedly "revisionist" abandoning of "the old insurrectionary perspectives" to Engels alone, and late in the day, in his 1895 Introduction to Marx's "The Class Struggles in France."[8]

And there is *the stage following a proletarian political takeover*, which includes allowance for a residual capitalist sector in the first post-capitalist stage, for income inequality, and even for compensation of expropriated property owners. Here, I elaborate Hobsbawm's recognition (noted above) of the proletarian revolution as initiating a transition period of "uncertain and doubtless variable length, while capitalist society is gradually transformed into communist society."[9] To my mind, these three themes in conjunction render the evolutionist perspective overwhelming.

I do not doubt that Marx himself must ultimately be held responsible for being understood as positing a "cataclysmic vision of the overthrow of

[8] Hobsbawm, *How to Change the World*, 67.
[9] Ibid., 57.

capitalism by an uprising of the proletariat."[10] After all, there is the famously dramatic affirmation in the *Manifesto of the Communist Party*: "The Communists disdain to conceal their views and aims. They openly declare that their ends can be attained only by the forcible overthrow of all existing social conditions,"[11] and in *Capital* itself: "Force is the midwife of every old society pregnant with a new one."[12] My contention is that in neither case does Marx follow through with respect to a violent transition from advanced capitalism. The choice of subtitle—*A Critique of Political Economy*—and the theme of non-wage income as "exploitation" were certainly intended as weapons for the proletariat, but not *necessarily* to the end of achieving an institutional "revolution" by violent means. I do not, however, argue that Marx excluded the possibility of violent revolution under any circumstances, but rather that he dismissed such an outcome in Britain and the United States; and I certainly do not propose a re-evaluation of his ideal—the replacement of the capitalist exchange system by a central control economy dispensing entirely with the price mechanism, for Marx, of course, abhorred labour's "dependency" upon capital and all this implied for its behavioural and moral development, and in addition, perceived an enormous siphoning off of wealth to middlemen under capitalist arrangement. These objections he sought to undermine by his "Critique of Political Economy."

In what follows, I first elaborate my three-fold Marxian evolutionary theme, relating to progress within advanced capitalism, the communist takeover, and the first stage of communism (section "The Evolutionary Theme Elaborated"). An account then follows of the full extent of Marx's laissez-faire "conservatism," including not only fear of reformist measures by the capitalist state, but the less familiar technical arguments for non-intervention based on the operation of the price mechanism (section "Marx as laissez-faire Conservative: The Economic Dimension"). Now, reform implied that the evolutionary process might not take the path of undermining capitalism, but, to the contrary, might guarantee capitalism's survival; and as I go on to show (section "Aspects of Marx's "Revisionism" and Implications for the Implementation of a Proletarian Programme"), Marx came to recognize the positive impact of contemporary factory

---

[10] Jacob S. Schapiro, "Comment," *Journal of the History of Ideas* 10, no. 2 (1949): 304.

[11] Karl Marx and Frederick Engels, *Manifesto of the Communist Party*, in MECW (New York: International Publishers, 1976), 6: 519.

[12] Karl Marx, *Capital*, Vol. I, in MECW (New York: International Publishers, 1996), 35: 739.

reform and, more generally, even saw some potential for real-wage increase, tendencies which—together with national character and even nationalism—might account for a growing suspicion that the working classes in Britain would be unwilling to implement a "proletarian" programme *even when in a position to do* so as a result of universal (male) suffrage accorded by the capitalist state—that the evolutionary transition to communism might be brought to a premature halt.

II. The Evolutionary Theme Elaborated

II.1. Evolutionary Processes within Capitalism

As I have intimated, Marx represented *Capital* as "demonstrat[ing] that present society, economically considered, is pregnant with a new, higher form … showing in the social context the same gradual process of evolution that Darwin demonstrated in natural history," and he cautioned in the preface that "even when a society has got upon the right track for the discovery of the natural laws of its movement—and it is the ultimate aim of this work, to lay bare the economic laws of motion of modern society—it can neither clear by bold leaps, nor remove by legal enactments, the obstacles offered by the successive phases of its normal development."[13] The evolutionary theme is nicely outlined in the *Economic Manuscript of 1861–63*: "Just as one should not think of sudden changes and sharply delineated periods in considering the succession of the different geological formations, so also in the case of the creation of the different economic formations of society."[14] The principle is applied to the dissolution of capitalism: "This is an essentially different conception from that of the bourgeois political economists, themselves imprisoned in capitalist preconceptions, who are admittedly able to see how production is carried on *within* the capital-relation, but not how this *relation* is itself produced, and how at the same time the material conditions for its dissolution are produced within it, thereby removing its *historical justification* as *a necessary form* of economic development, of the production of social wealth."[15]

---

[13] Marx, *Capital*, Vol. I, 9.
[14] Karl Marx, *Economic Manuscript of 1861–63*, in MECW (New York: International Publishers, 1991), 33: 442.
[15] Karl Marx, *Economic Manuscript of 1861–63*, in MECW (New York: International Publishers, 1994), 34, 466.

I turn now to the specific processes envisaged as at play within capitalism setting the stage for a transition to communism. Observations in the third volume of *Capital*, composed probably in the 1860s, relate to the joint-stock company—"the ultimate development of capitalist production"[16]—as a transitional form from private to social organization: "The capital, which in itself rests on a social mode of production and presupposes a social concentration of means of production and labour power, is here directly endowed with the form of social capital (capital of directly associated individuals) as distinct from private capital, and its undertakings assume the form of social undertakings as distinct from private undertakings. It is the abolition of capital as private property within the framework of the capitalist mode of production itself." An earlier comment refers to *"[s]hare* capital as the most perfected form (turning into communism) together with all its contradictions"[17]

The part played by credit is much emphasized in the third (posthumous) volume of *Capital*, and also with respect to the growth of cooperatives; and the formulation is one of the best I know of Marx's evolutionary orientation confirming his own designation of *Capital* as "Darwinian":

> The cooperative factories of the labourers themselves represent within the old form the first sprouts of the new, although they naturally reproduce, and must reproduce, everywhere in their actual organization all the shortcomings of the prevailing system. But the antithesis between capital and labour is overcome within them, if at first only by way of making the associated labourers into their own capitalists, that is, by enabling them to use the means of production for the employment of their own labour. They show how a new mode of production naturally grows out of an old one, when the development of the material forces of production and of the corresponding forms of social production have reached a particular state. Without the factory system arising out of the capitalist mode of production, there could have been no cooperative factories. Nor could these have developed without the credit system arising out of the same mode of production. The credit system is not only the principal basis for the gradual transformation of capitalist private enterprises into capitalist stock companies, but equally offers the means for the gradual extension of cooperative enterprises on a more or less national scale. The capitalist stock companies, as much as the cooperative factories, should be considered as transitional forms from the

[16] Marx, *Capital*, Vol. III, in MECW (New York: International Publishers, 1998), 37: 434.
[17] Karl Marx, "Marx to Engels, 2 April 1858," in MECW (New York: International Publishers, 1983), 40: 298.

capitalist mode of production to the associated one, with the only distinction that the antagonism is resolved negatively in the one, and positively in the other.[18]

Cooperatives alone, be it noted, were clearly regarded by Marx as insufficient to assure a smooth transition from capitalism, but only as contributing to that outcome. Marx also refers to the growth of monopoly, which "requires state interference"[19]—a theme expanded by Engels with an eye to prospective nationalization of industry by the capitalist state.[20]

Apart from the foregoing applications of the principle of Historical Materialism are tendencies emanating from capitalist development relating to *proletarian character* itself: "Modern industry, indeed, compels society, under penalty of death, to replace the detail-worker of to-day, crippled by life-long repetition of one and the sane trivial operation, and thus reduced to the mere fragment of a man, by the fully developed individual, fit for a variety of labours, ready to face any change of production, and to whom the individual social functions he performs, are but so many modes of giving free scope to his own natural and acquired powers."[21] The circumstance that modern industry forces the predominance of technical and vocational training is one significant feature: "one step already spontaneously taken towards effecting this revolution is the establishment of technical and agricultural schools, and of *écoles d'enseignement professionnel*, in which the children of the workingmen receive some little instruction in technology and in the practical handling of the various implements of labour."[22] At least by implication, the proletariat would become increasingly competent to undertake the tasks required of it in any post-capitalist arrangement—however that might be achieved.

I should briefly note here the so-called Russian option sometimes attributed to Marx entailing a transition to communism based upon the peasant commune (the *obshchina*), rather than upon capitalist development. If taken seriously, this alternative would undermine the entire perception of communism *requiring* a preliminary stage of advanced capitalism, in line with the celebrated principle stated in the Preface to *Capital*, whereby the "natural laws of capitalist production" entail "tendencies working with

[18] Marx, *Capital*, Vol. III, 438.
[19] Ibid., 436.
[20] Frederick Engels, *Anti-Dühring: Herr Eugen Dühring's Revolution in Science*, in MECW (New York: International Publishers, 1987), 25: 264–5.
[21] Marx, *Capital*, Vol. I, 490–1.
[22] Ibid., 491.

iron necessity towards inevitable results," such that "[t]he country which is more developed industrially only shows, to the less developed, the image of its own future."[23] There could be no transition to communist organization based directly on the rural commune.

II.2. The Acquisition of Proletarian Control

By a "Communist Revolution," Marx referred specifically to the acquisition and maintenance of *political* power by the proletariat. Thus, he avers in his objections of 1875 to the Gotha Programme that "[b]etween the capitalist and communist society lies the period of the revolutionary transformation of the one into the other," corresponding to which there "is also a political transition period in which the state can be nothing but *the revolutionary dictatorship of the proletariat*."[24] The term "revolution," it may seem, might legitimately be retained since there is no conflict with those evolutionary processes occurring *within* capitalism; on the contrary, the communist takeover occurs only when the time is ripe. But the following considerations relating to the character of the "revolution" itself require attention.

Recall from our Introduction that the *Manifesto of the Communist Party* closes with a declaration that the communists "openly declare that their ends can be attained only by the forcible overthrow of all existing social conditions." But this is misleading—unless what is intended is "forcible overthrow" *after* having achieved power by legal means—since from the 1840s, Marx and also Engels had recognized the potential of constitutional reform enhancing proletarian political power. In the *Principles of Communism*, upon which the *Communist Manifesto* was based, Engels had recognized the possibility of achieving political control by constitutional means,[25] while the *Communist Manifesto* itself: (a) describes the impact of modern industrial development on the proletariat, whose quantitative expansion and coherence are reflected in unionization extending increasingly to the national level, and the establishment of a workers' party; (b) expresses hostility towards a variety of "critical-utopian" socialists of the day for "violently oppos[ing] all political action on the part of the working class"; and (c) supports constitutional reform measures proposed by the

---

[23] Ibid., 9.

[24] Marx, *Critique of the Gotha Programme*, in MECW (New York: International Publishers, 1989), 24: 95.

[25] Frederick Engels, *Principles of Communism*, in MECW (New York: International Publishers, 1976), 6: 350.

Chartists in England, the Agrarian Reformers in America, and the Social Democrats in France.[26] Support for the Chartists is found in *The Poverty of Philosophy* of 1847[27]; and particularly significant as a sort of retrospective evaluation after the failed revolutionary attempts of 1848 is a paper entitled "The Chartists" of 1852, which perceives universal suffrage as synonymous with proletarian political power: "the carrying of Universal Suffrage in England would ... be a far more socialistic measure than anything which has been honoured with that name on the Continent. *Its inevitable result, here, is the political supremacy of the working class.*"[28] Needless to say, the achievement of universal suffrage should be seen as part of the evolutionary process, the capitalist state being obliged to offer such a concession from fear of its own creation—the proletariat.

Recognition dating back to the 1840s of the possibility of a peaceful transition to the proletarian dictatorship throws into question Bober's focus on the early 1860s as marking a distinct shift away from "violence" as sine qua non. Stedman Jones implicitly sides with Bober when he refers to Marx's "belittlement" in the 1840s and early 1850s (as in the *Eighteenth Brumaire*) "of the significance of manhood suffrage and the democratic republic," his "hostility towards political democracy and universal suffrage," his "refusal to think of universal suffrage as anything other than a pathological symptom," and his "suspicion about demands for manhood suffrage.... He was still prone to dismiss universal suffrage as an illusion."[29] What then comes of the potentiality of constitutional reform measures that I have cited from the *Communist Manifesto* with respect to Britain, America, and France and from "The Chartists" of 1852 referring specifically to Britain? Are they to be simply dismissed? I suggest that the apparent contrast reflects Marx's opposition to universal suffrage as a strictly liberal principle of "one man one vote," but approval that provided the *inevitable result* would indeed be *the political supremacy of the working class*—namely, a communist dictatorship. As I shall presently confirm, neither Marx nor Engels would have countenanced a democratic system that allowed the replacement of a proletarian majority or, worse still, a situation where so-called proletarians opted for bourgeois policies.

[26] Marx and Engels, *Manifesto of the Communist Party*, 493, 517–18.
[27] Karl Marx, *The Poverty of Philosophy: Answer to the "Philosophy of Poverty" by M. Proudhon*, in MECW (New York: International Publishers, 1976), 6: 210.
[28] Karl Marx, "The Chartists," in MECW (New York: International Publishers, 1979), 11: 335–6; Marx's emphasis.
[29] Stedman Jones, *Karl Marx*, 307, 337, 342, 550.

When we move forwards to the violent events in France of 1870, we find Marx in *The Civil War in France* (1871) criticizing the Commune for inadequate ruthlessness, complaining, for example, that reprisals had at one stage been merely an "empty threat."[30] And if we left the matter there, we might perhaps better understand Marx's reputation as the "Red Terrorist Doctor." But the matter is not so simple. Allowance must surely be made for the vicious conduct of the opposing government forces working hand in hand with the Prussians which, to my mind, largely justifies Marx's reading of the Communards as acting defensively. As for matters of principle, Marx goes on to admit candidly that "the working class cannot simply lay hold of the ready-made State machinery, and yield it for its own purposes."[31] The evolutionary processes at play could not be bypassed: "The working class did not expect miracles from the Commune. They had no ready-made utopias to introduce *par décrét du peuple*. They know that in order to work out their own emancipation and along with it that higher form to which present society is irresistibly tending by its own economic agencies, they will have to pass through long struggles, through a series of historical processes, transforming circumstances and men. They have no ideals to realize, but to set free elements of the new society with which old collapsing bourgeois society itself is pregnant."[32]

On various occasions in the early 1870s, Marx distinguishes between countries with respect to violent revolution, as Bober and others correctly note. All depended on the ruling circumstances. An interview accorded to *The World* newspaper—only a few weeks after composition of *The Civil War in France*—conveys the point in question: "In England ... [i]nsurrection would be madness where peaceful agitation would more swiftly and surely do the work."[33] This perspective on the English case is represented by Stedman Jones as a "revised position,"[34] whereas I have documented earlier indications of the same orientation. As for France, Marx opines in the interview that "a hundred laws of repression and a mortal antagonism between classes seem to necessitate the violent

[30] Karl Marx, *The Civil War in France*, published anonymously as the *Address of the General Council of the International Working-Men's Association*, in MECW (New York: International Publishers, 1986), 22: 327.

[31] Ibid., 328.

[32] Ibid., 335.

[33] Karl Marx, "Record of Interview with *The World* Correspondent," in MECW (New York: International Publishers, 1986), 22: 602.

[34] Stedman Jones, *Karl Marx*, 551.

solution of social war," contrasting with *The Civil War in France,* but one notes that Marx expresses himself tentatively. At the 1872 Hague Congress of the International, he expressly allows the possibility of a peaceful transition to communism in the English, American, and possibly Dutch cases, but considers inevitable resort to "force" in "most" Continental states without specific mention of France:

> We know that the institutions, customs and traditions in the different countries must be taken into account; and we do not deny the existence of countries, like England and America, and if I knew your institutions better I might add Holland, where the workers may achieve their aims by peaceful means. That being true we must also admit that in most countries on the Continent it is force which must be the lever of our revolution; it is force which will have to be resorted to for a time in order to establish the rule of the workers.[35]

Needless to say, to allow that in most Continental countries, "force ... must be the lever of our revolution" conflicts radically with the evolutionary principle laid down in the Preface to *Capital,* whereby "the country which is more developed industrially only shows, to the less developed, the image of its own future."

A word is in order here regarding a circular letter of September 1879 sent to leaders of the Social Democratic party by Engels, and also signed by Marx, lambasting as "too moderate" a trio of Zürich journalists, including Eduard Bernstein, proposing a new party newspaper which would be opposed to "political radicalism" and would "adopt a line that is socialist in principle."[36] By calling for "an influx of supporters from the ranks of the educated and propertied classes," especially as Reichstag members,[37] the trio also apparently denied the merits of "a workers" party," whereas the *Communist Manifesto* only tolerated entry of people from the ruling class, subject to their commitment to the "militant proletariat."[38] And they culpably applauded the Party for "showing that it does not wish to pursue the path of forcible, bloody revolution, but rather ... to tread the path of legal-

---

[35] Karl Marx, "On the Hague Congress," in MECW (New York: International Publishers, 1988), 23: 255.

[36] Karl Marx and Frederick Engels, "Circular Letter, 17–18 September 1879," in MECW (New York: International Publishers, 1991), 45: 401.

[37] Ibid., 403.

[38] Ibid., 407.

ity, i.e. of reform."[39] But we must be cautious. Engels and Marx were *not*, by all this, engaging in a call to arms and revolution. For they admitted that Social Democratic voters "have sense enough not to break their heads against a wall and attempt a 'bloody revolution' with the odds of one to ten," but insisted only that all options should be left open, and that Social Democrats not "deny themselves all chance of exploiting some violent upheaval abroad, a sudden wave of revolutionary fervour engendered thereby." A mild alternative is also proposed when responding to the Zürich trio's declaration that while they had no wish "to relinquish our party and our programme ... we shall have enough to do for years to come if we concentrate our whole strength, our entire energies, on the attainment of certain immediate objectives which must in any case be won before there can be any thought of realizing more ambitious aspirations,"[40] which is of course Bernstein's trademark philosophy. As an alternative, the Engels-Marx letter merely proposed participation in "polemic," that is in "resolute political opposition ... laying stress on ambitious goals which are calculated to frighten off the bourgeoisie," and "attainable anyway in our own generation," rather than have the party "devote all its strength and energies to those petty-bourgeois stop-gap reforms which provide new props for the old social order and which might, perhaps, transform the ultimate catastrophe into a gradual, piecemeal and, as far as possible, peaceable process of dissolution"[41] One notes that there is no positive rejection here of "petty-bourgeois stop-gaps reforms," only the importance of supplementing such steps by "polemic" to assure against the dangers posed by reform.

II.3. The First Stage of Communism

A third consideration is the extension of the evolutionary dimension beyond the acquisition of proletarian control of the state. Needless to say, the state itself—necessarily a repressive set of institutions as the term "dictatorship" implies—is a capitalist residue which, Marx affirmed in *The Civil War in France*, would ultimately have to be destroyed,[42] or—as Engels never tired of insisting—would die out naturally in the course of

---

[39] Ibid., 404.
[40] Ibid., 405.
[41] Ibid., 406.
[42] Berlin, *Karl Marx*, 257.

time.[43] But beyond this general consideration, there are several more specific instances of capitalist residue.

Firstly, in an initial phase, after acquisition of proletarian control, a capitalist sector is to be retained—and this for an unspecified period. As expressed in the *Manifesto of the Communist Party*, while the immediate end of the revolution was to seize the state, the proletariat "centralis[ing] all instruments of production" as well as credit, and the means of communication and transport, "in the hands of the State," nevertheless "the proletariat will use its political supremacy to wrest, *by degrees*, all capital from the bourgeoisie."[44] The same caution is implied by the function here accorded the revolutionary dictatorship in *extending* "factories and instruments of production owned by the State." A gradual dismantling of the private property system is a conspicuous feature of Engels's *Principles of Communism*.[45]. It would, of course, entail fine judgement to specify the rate at which the capitalist sectors might be safely dismantled by the communist regime, with reliance implicitly placed on the ability of the new administration not to compromise the performance by what remained of the traditional sectors in creating or maintaining the capacity required to assure the successful implementation of a communist programme.[46]

Secondly, there is an affirmation by Engels that his own and Marx's support for "cooperatives" applied only to a transitional arrangement,[47] which implies that even *competing* cooperatives would have been acceptable, along with a capitalist sector in the initial stage of communism, since *centrally controlled* cooperation was part of the permanent "common" plan, as Marx insisted in the *Civil War in France*.[48]

Thirdly, the initial stage of communism would entail wage *inequality* reflecting differential physical and mental abilities, Marx in the *Critique of the Gotha Programme* (1875) vividly explaining that "we are dealing here with a communist society, not as it has *developed* on its own foundations,

---

[43] Samuel Hollander, *Friedrich Engels and Marxian Political Economy* (Cambridge: Cambridge University Press, 2011), 323–4.

[44] Marx and Engels, *Manifesto of the Communist Party*, 504–5; emphasis added.

[45] Engels, *Principles of Communism*, 349–50; see Hollander, *Friedrich Engels*, 324.

[46] This raises the issue of the productivity of the traditional compared with joint-stock arrangement, especially with regard to innovation. Here, we should take note of Marx's recognition of complex decision-making by the *owner-entrepreneur* regarding innovation in the face of uncertainty. On this issue, see Samuel Hollander, *The Economics of Karl Marx: Analysis and Application* (Cambridge: Cambridge University Press, 2008), 438–43.

[47] Hollander, *Friedrich Engels*, 149–50, 166.

[48] Marx, *The Civil War in France*, 335.

but, on the contrary, just as it *emerges* from capitalist society, which is thus in every respect, economically, morally, and intellectually, still stamped with the birth-marks of the old society from whose womb it emerges."[49] Only in some "utopian" phase of communism would the principle "From each according to his abilities to each according to his needs" apply; by contrast, his labour certificate scheme, a prime feature of his proposed centrally organized system, recognized natural differentials between individuals with regard to "talent": "But one man is superior to another physically or mentally and so supplies more labour in the same time, or can work for a longer time; and labour, to serve as a measure, must be defined by its duration or intensity.... *It is, therefore, a right of inequality.*"[50] The correction on grounds of justice of what has been termed "luck inequality"—pay differentials reflecting fortuitous differences in ability, both mental and physical—would apply only in some distant and indistinct utopian phase of communism. Of Marx's position, Friedrich Hayek had no inkling when he insisted that "from the fact that people are very different it follows that, if we treat them equally, the result must be inequality in their actual position, and that the only way to place them in an equal position would be to treat them differently."[51]

Finally, there is the matter of compensation for expropriated property. Joseph Persky refers specifically to J.S. Mill's advocating compensation rather than confiscation in his land reform programme, implying that such a recommendation would be completely foreign to Marx,[52] whereas when discussing expropriation of big landed proprietors, once "our Party is in possession of political power," Engels recalled in 1894 that "[w]e by no means consider compensation as impermissible in any event; Marx told me (and how many times!) that in his opinion we would get off cheapest if we could buy out the whole lot of them" and "[w]hether this expropriation is to be compensated for or not will to a great extent depend not upon us but the circumstances under which we obtain power."[53] I see no evident reason why the same allowance cannot be applied to residual capitalist industrial ventures.

[49] Marx, *Critique of the Gotha Programme*, 85–6.

[50] Ibid., 86–7.

[51] Friedrich Hayek, *The Constitution of Liberty* (Chicago: University of Chicago Press, 2011), 149–50.

[52] Joseph Persky, *The Political Economy of Progress: John Stuart Mill and Modern Radicalism* (Oxford: Oxford University Press, 2016), 182–3.

[53] Frederick Engels, "The Peasant Question in France and Germany," in MECW (New York: International Publishers, 1990), 27: 500.

III. Marx as Laissez-Faire Conservative:
The Economic Dimension

Marx's evolutionary perspective implies, in and of itself, that reformist interventionism threatens the developmental process, and thus the transition from capitalism to communism. The *Manifesto of the Communist Party* refers to "Conservative, or Bourgeois Socialism," alluding to "a part of the bourgeoisie [which] is desirous of redressing social grievances, in order to secure the continued existence of bourgeois society."[54] In a variation of the theme appearing in *The Class Struggles in France 1848–50*, Marx opposed reformist measures designed to *forcibly stem the growth of capital*, that is to prevent the evolution of the system.[55] As Mises put the matter, Marx regarded reform measures as "not progressive, but reactionary."[56] But we need not turn to Mises, since Engels himself admitted "a conservative side" to the evolutionary process, recognizing "that definite stages of cognition and society are justified for their time and circumstances."[57] In these terms, Engels had condemned the Ten-Hours Bill as "reactionary."[58] Marx was famously to revise his view when it came to factory legislation—a matter I shall touch on presently.

Marx's case for non-intervention extends beyond a fear of the consequences of reform and improving living standards. His laissez-faire reasoning has a positive dimension, namely a sophisticated appreciation of the operation of the free-market pricing system, a matter not sufficiently appreciated by those commentators who take for granted that he must necessarily have favoured interventionism.[59] In fact, Marx silently allied himself with contemporary conservative opponents of reformist state intervention, and also to some degree with Friedrich Hayek in our own day. Consider, first, an application by Marx of price-theoretical principles to income-redistribution proposals, as by James Mill, entailing state

[54] Marx and Engels, *Manifesto of the Communist Party*, 513.
[55] Karl Marx, *The Class Struggles in France*, in MECW (New York: International Publishers, 1978), 10: 126.
[56] Ludwig von Mises, *Planning for Freedom* (South Holland, IL: Libertarian Press, 1980), 29.
[57] Frederick Engels, *Ludwig Feuerbach and the End of Classical German Philosophy*, in MECW (New York: International Publishers, 1990), 26: 360.
[58] Frederick Engels, "The Ten Hours Question," in MECW (New York: International Publishers, 1978), 10, 271–6; 288–300.
[59] Murray Rothbard, *Economic Thought before Adam Smith: An Austrian Perspective on the History of Economic Thought* (Aldershot: Edward Elgar, 1995), xii, 530.

confiscation of rent. The point in question for Marx is that confiscation would require in practice land-valuation indexes ("cadastres"), whereas these could not be taken as settled once and for all because of continuous disturbances in technical and market conditions. Thus, regarding technology: "rent could not be the invariable index of the degree of fertility of the land, since every moment the modern application of chemistry is changing the nature of the soil and the geological knowledge is just now in our days beginning to revolutionize all the old estimates of relative fertility."[60] There were, for example, instances when "rent proper is wiped out by the competition of new and more fertile soils" or when hitherto scarce improvements lose their value on becoming "universal owing to the development of agronomy."[61] But beyond this, and even in the absence of changing technology, "fertility is not so natural a quality as might be thought [but] is closely bound up with the social relations of the time. A piece of land may be very fertile for corn growing, and yet the market price may induce the cultivators to turn it into an artificial pastureland and thus render it infertile."[62] The state, in brief, lacked the changeable detailed knowledge required for the proposed reform, a more "Austrian" conclusion than which it would be difficult to imagine.

It was also Marx's methodological position that the entire issue of "distributive justice," above all complaints of "unfairness" directed at capitalist income arrangements, was rendered irrelevant by the fact that the distribution pattern is the *necessary* outcome of the "mode of production."[63] In these terms, Marx objected to the option of reform *within* capitalist arrangement to correct allegedly gross distributional defects as proposed by the 1875 Gotha Programme: Is not "present-day distribution … the only 'fair' distribution on the basis of the present-day mode of production?"[64] And he denied Adolphe Wagner's attribution to him in 1879 of the view that profit was "a *deduction from*, or *robbery of*, the worker."[65] Indeed, by ignoring the economic role of income inequality a redistributive programme implied the undermining of productive capacity and the very ability to produce a surplus. So far was this argument carried

---

[60] Marx, *The Poverty of Philosophy*, 203.

[61] Ibid., 205.

[62] Ibid., 204.

[63] Hollander, *The Economics of Karl Marx*, 390–6, 403.

[64] Marx, *Critique of the Gotha Programme*, 84.

[65] Karl Marx, "Notes on Wagner's *Lehrbuch der Politischen Oekonomie*," in MECW (New York: International Publishers, 1989), 24: 535.

that in manuscript notes of 1879, Marx protested that he was falsely represented as maintaining that profit was "a deduction from, or robbery of, the worker," whereas in fact, "the capitalist is a necessary functionary of capitalist production [who] enforces the production of surplus value, thus first helping to create what is to be deducted" from the labourer.[66] Already in *Poverty of Philosophy*, Marx had insisted against Proudhon upon the necessity in a private property society of "classes which profited and classes which decayed"—the latter implying the immiseration of labour—as a condition for "the development of productive forces" and the generation of surplus.[67]

IV. Aspects of Marx's "Revisionism" and Implications for the Implementation of a Proletarian Programme

Consider next Marx's affirmation in 1864 that the expansion of the British cooperative movement during 1848–64 was "excellent in principle, and … useful in practice."[68] This perhaps intimates potential for improvement in labour's condition, but is qualified since cooperation, because "kept within the narrow circle of the casual efforts of private workmen," was unable "to arrest the growth in geometrical progression of monopoly, to free the masses, [or] *even to perceptibly lighten the burden of their miseries.*"[69] To have positive effects of this order, "co-operative labour ought to be developed to national dimensions, and consequently, to be fostered by national means," whereas this extension would never be countenanced by "the lords of land and the lords of capital [who] will always use their political privileges for the defence and perpetuation of their economical monopolies." *Never be countenanced?* Yet Marx himself in the same Inaugural Address had *retracted* this sort of argument in relation to reactionary hostility towards *factory legislation*, referring to the "immense physical, moral, and intellectual benefits hence accruing to the factory operatives [which] are now acknowledged on all sides" and which proved the fallacy of middle-class predictions "that any legal restriction of the hours of labour

---

[66] Hollander, *The Economics of Karl Marx*, 386–7.

[67] Marx, *Poverty of Philosophy*, 158–9. The celebrated proposal for a "heavy progressive or graduated income tax" (*Manifesto of the Communist Party*, 505), be it noted, relates to the weakening of remnants of capitalism *after* the communist takeover and is not part of a reformist redistributive programme pertaining to the existing system.

[68] Karl Marx, "Inaugural Address of the Working Men's International Association," in MECW (New York: International Publishers, 1985), 20: 11–12.

[69] Ibid., 12; emphasis added.

must sound the death knell of British industry"—as if that had not been his own earlier contention; it was in fact, "the first time that in broad daylight the political economy of the middle class had succumbed to the political economy of the working class," namely "the blind rule of the supply and demand laws" to "social production controlled by social foresight."[70] *Capital* itself refers to the "physical and moral regeneration" of the factory workers, reformist legislation perceived as a feature of the *evolutionary* process entailing an increasingly powerful working class generated by the capitalist developmental process itself.[71] Bear in mind also Marx's inclusion in the Preface to *Capital* of social welfare legislation as one of his "tendencies working with iron necessity towards inevitable results."[72] That the "factory magnates," especially after 1860, were becoming increasingly "reconciled to the inevitable" because of modern industrial development,[73] provides a new twist to the evolutionary processes at play in advanced capitalism, and promises to undermine Marx's "conservatism" in a major way.

A related index of Marx's "revisionism" is provided by a remarkable pronouncement in the third volume of *Capital* regarding technological unemployment, implying that the capitalist state would, under some conditions, take measures to check the rate of innovation for fear of the proletarian response: "a development of productive forces which would diminish the absolute number of labourers, i.e., enable the entire nation to accomplish its total production in a shorter time span, would cause a revolution, because it would put the bulk of the population out of the running."[74] We recall too, Marx's presumption that the state would intervene to control monopoly.

Let us look now at the notion of "absolute immizerization" of labour inducing proletarian dissatisfaction and enthusiasm for institutional change. In a Report to the General Council of the International of June 1865, Marx declared that unions could not reverse "the general tendency of capitalist production ... not to raise, but to sink the average standard of wages"; at best, the working class are capable of "retarding the downward

[70] Ibid., 10–11.
[71] Marx, *Capital*, Vol. I, 300, 412.
[72] Ibid., 9–10.
[73] Ibid., 300.
[74] Marx, *Capital*, Vol. III, 262.

movement, but not changing its direction."[75] In "Instructions," drawn up in August 1866 relating to the International, he emphasized primarily their role as a political training ground, acting "as organized agencies for superseding the very system of wages labour," and only secondarily as "counteracting capitalists" bargaining advantage by restricting competition between individual labourers.[76] And shortly thereafter (3 July 1871), Marx found that little had been accomplished regarding improved standards by purely *national* working-class organizations—unions as well as cooperatives: "The working classes remain poor amid the increase of wealth, wretched amid the increase of luxury. Their material privation dwarfs their moral as well as their physical stature."[77] Indeed, the principle whereby "[t]he country which is more developed industrially only shows, to the less developed, the image of its own future" is applied in *Capital* to predict ultimately falling wages in the United States: "Capitalist production advances there with giant strides, even though the lowering of wages and the dependence of the wage worker are yet far from being brought down to the normal European level."[78] Nonetheless, in the 1871 interview, Marx allowed at least the *potential* for real-wage improvement as a result of international cooperation: "Formerly, when a strike took place in one country, it was defeated by the importation of workmen from another. The International has nearly stopped all that."[79] Furthermore, Marx might have allowed better prospects in the British case were it not for the special feature of Irish immigration.[80] As for improvements in welfare more generally, Marx, in the 1879 circular letter, did not oppose "stop-gap" reforms, and in 1880, approved French reforms extending to Monday holidays, minimum wages, non-discriminatory pay between the sexes, and employer contributions to insurance.[81] As with British factory legislation, Marx's non-interventionist "conservatism" seems to be weakening.

[75] Karl Marx, "Value, Price and Profit," in MECW (New York: International Publishers, 1985), 20: 148–9.

[76] Karl Marx, "Instructions for the Delegates of the Provisional General Council," (New York: International Publishers, 1985), 20: 191.

[77] Marx, "Record of Interview with *The World* Correspondent," 602.

[78] Marx, *Capital*, Vol. I, 760.

[79] Marx, "Record of Interview with *The World* Correspondent," 602.

[80] Karl Marx, "Marx to S. Meyer and A. Vogt, 9 April 1870," in MECW, vol. 43, 474–5.

[81] Marx, "Preamble to the Programme of the French Workers" Party," in MECW (New York: International Publishers, 1989), 24: 340–1.

The dilemma created for Marx of course is that improved conditions of work and pay threaten to compromise labour's readiness to adopt a truly "proletarian" stance, the 1879 letter intimating this concern by referring to stop-gap reform as providing "new props for the old social order." Recourse might always be made to the standard repost that any improvement is a *secondary* matter so long as the wages system itself remained untouched—"Even ... the most rapid possible growth of capital, however much it may improve the material existence of the worker, does not remove the antagonism between his interests and the interests of the bourgeoisie, the interests of the capitalist."[82] But this assurance does not efface Marx's expressed doubts regarding contemporary proletarian "class consciousness," which could only be aggravated by improvement in labour's well-being. We encounter his concerns in discussion with Engels regarding the American Civil War when he complained of "the sheeplike attitude of the working men in Lancashire.... Of late, England has made more of an ass of itself than any other country, the working men by their servile Christian nature, the bourgeois and aristocrats by the enthusiasm they have shown for slavery in its most direct form."[83] The following year, again to Engels, Marx refers to "what seems to be a bourgeois contagion" affecting English workers.[84]

Class consciousness was also undermined by working-class *nationalism* manifested in hostility towards the Irish, which encouraged the worker to feel at one with the aristocrats and capitalists against a common enemy.[85] And we have encountered Marx's disappointment with the "servile Christian nature" attributed to working men, which introduces the role of national character. His concern is expressed particularly clearly in his Report to the General Council of the International of June 1865, complaining that while a well-trained, self-conscious, militant proletariat was essential to assure the pressures required for the demise of capitalism, British unions were not filling the bill: "They fail generally from limiting themselves to a guerilla war against the effects of the existing system,

[82] Karl Marx, *Wage Labour and Capital*, in MECW (New York: International Publishers, 1977), 9: 220–1.

[83] Karl Marx, "Marx to Engels, 17 November 1862," in MECW (New York: International Publishers, 1985), 41: 430.

[84] Karl Marx, "Marx to Engels, 9 April 1863," in MECW (New York: International Publishers, 1985), 41: 468.

[85] Karl Marx, "Marx to Kugelmann, 29 November 1869," in MECW in MECW (New York: International Publishers, 1988), 43: 390.

instead of simultaneously trying to change it, instead of using their organised forces as a lever for the final emancipation of the working class, that is to say, the ultimate abolition of the wages system."[86] Indeed, at the London conference of the International in September 1871, Marx represented trade unions as "an aristocratic minority."[87]

To be especially noted is the fact that several of the expressions of concern are found after the passage of Disraeli's 1867 Reform Act, which doubled the (adult male) electorate. The implications are grave if we recall the affirmation in "The Chartists" of 1852 that the "inevitable result" of Universal Suffrage" would be "the political supremacy of the working class"—the Revolutionary Dictatorship of the Proletariat no less. *This was no longer taken for granted.* Marx's expressed concerns with proletarian class consciousness implied that a working-class parliamentary majority might be unwilling to implement a communist programme, or even that a working-class electorate might choose to replace the Proletarian Party at the polls, bringing to a dead halt the entire evolutionary process relied upon to assure the transition to communism. A paper of 1878 introduces a further limitation created by *public opinion*, namely that a proletarian Parliamentary majority in Britain and America "could, by lawful means, rid themselves of such laws and institutions as impeded their development, though they could only do so insofar as society had reached a sufficiently mature development."[88] All of this seems to have passed Duncan by, for he ascribes recognition of the unwillingness of the proletariat to confirm to Marx's expectations of them specifically to Bernstein, writing of Bernstein as "alter[ing] the inherited Marxist categories to accord with what seems to him to be existing facts."[89]

Engels confirms the seriousness of the matter. The economic prosperity in the 1850s and the collapse of the Chartist movement suggested to him that "the English proletariat is actually becoming more and more bourgeois"[90]; indeed, that "the English proletarian has declared himself in

[86] Marx, "Value, Price and Profit," 149.

[87] Karl Marx, "Speech on Trades Unions at London Conference of the International Working Men's Association," in MECW (New York: International Publishers, 1986), 22: 614.

[88] Karl Marx, "Parliamentary Debate on the Anti-Socialist Law," in MECW (New York: International Publishers, 1989), 24: 248.

[89] Graeme Duncan, *Two Views of Social Conflict and Social Harmony* (Cambridge: Cambridge University Press, 1973), 304.

[90] Frederick Engels, "Engels to Marx, 7 October 1858," in MECW (New York: International Publishers, 1983), 40: 344.

full agreement with the dominancy of the bourgeoisie."[91] And some 15 years after the Reform Act, Engels lamented labour's failure, as evidenced by trade union policy, to take advantage of the opportunities offered by the enfranchisement of "the greater portion of the organized working class" to advance measures designed to undermine the "wage system" itself.[92] The prospect for the mutation of capitalism is a grim one indeed.

VI. Concluding Remarks

The evolutionary processes discernible in Marx's analysis discussed in this chapter relate to progress within capitalism, the acquisition of proletarian control, and the initial stage of communism. The most contentious issue is surely the *transition* to communism, particularly its "revolutionary" character. This chapter commenced by referring to a loss of confidence by the Frankfurt School in the 1930s in the ability of workers to mount a revolution against monopoly capitalism, as Marx allegedly predicted they would, since workers had become paralysed by conformist tendencies. But what we have shown is that Marx himself, half a century before the rise of fascism, feared that the British proletariat might be seduced by bourgeois ideology, wholly undermining the evolutionary processes generated by capitalist development, in effect thwarting the logic of historical material- ism. His expressions of doubt sometimes occur in private correspondence and would not therefore have been common knowledge, but by no means all of them, as in his Report to the General Council of the International of June 1865 and at the London conference of the International in September 1871. English working-class *nationalism* and the general state of public opinion were two of the complicating issues, as we have seen. But beyond this, there was a far broader concern relating to the threats to international working-class cooperation created by nationalist sentiment on the Continent. For Marx warned on 23 July 1870 regarding the Franco- Prussian War: "If the German working class allow the present war to lose its strictly defensive character and to degenerate into a war against the French people, victory or defeat will prove alike disastrous."[93] He judged

[91] Frederick Engels, "Engels to Marx, 8 April 1863," in MECW (New York: International Publishers, 1985), 41: 465.
[92] Frederick Engels, "Trades Unions," in MECW (New York: International Publishers, 1989), 24: 386–7.
[93] Karl Marx, "First Address of the General Council of the International Working Men's Association on the Franco-Prussian War," in MECW (New York: International Publishers, 1986), 22: 6.

that "the principles of the International are … too widely spread and too firmly rooted amongst the German working class to apprehend such a sad consummation," but the *possibility* of a "sad consummation" as a result of extremist nationalism is clearly recognized or else there would have been no need for the warning. Marx's worst fears were tragically to materialize, the term "sad consummation" scarcely capturing the bloodbath that was to occur.

BIBLIOGRAPHY

Berlin, Isaiah. *Karl Marx: His Life and Environment.* 4th ed. Oxford: Oxford University Press, 1978.

Bober, M. M. *Karl Marx's Interpretation of History.* New York: Norton, 1965.

Duncan, Gareth. *Two Views of Social Conflict and Social Harmony.* Cambridge: Cambridge University Press, 1973.

Engels, Frederick. *Principles of Communism.* In MECW. Vol. 6, 341–57. New York: International Publishers, 1976.

Engels, Frederick. "The English Ten Hours Bill." In MECW. Vol. 10, 288–300. New York: International Publishers, 1978a.

Engels, Frederick. "The Ten Hours Question." In MECW. Vol. 10, 271–6, New York: International Publishers, 1978b.

Engels, Frederick. *Anti-Dühring. Herr Eugen Dühring's Revolution in Science.* In MECW. Vol. 25, 1–309. New York: International Publishers, 1987.

Engels, Frederick. "Trades Unions." In MECW. Vol. 24, 382–8. New York: International Publishers, 1989.

Engels, Frederick. *Ludwig Feuerbach and the End of Classical German Philosophy.* In MECW. Vol. 26, 353–98. New York: International Publishers, 1990a.

Engels, Frederick. "The Peasant Question in France and Germany." In MECW. Vol. 27, 481–502. New York: International Publishers, 1990b.

Freeman, Samuel. "The Headquarters of Neo-Marxism." *New York Review of Books* 64, no. 5 (23 March 2017): 63.

Hayek, Friedrich. *The Constitution of Liberty.* Chicago: University of Chicago Press, 2011.

Hobsbawm, Eric. *How to Change the World: Reflections on Marx and Marxism.* New Haven and London: Yale University Press, 2011

Hollander, Samuel. *The Economics of Karl Marx: Analysis and Application.* Cambridge: Cambridge University Press, 2008.

Hollander, Samuel. *Friedrich Engels and Marxian Political Economy.* Cambridge: Cambridge University Press, 2011.

Marx, Karl. *The Poverty of Philosophy. An Answer to the "Philosophy of Poverty" by M. Proudhon.* In MECW. Vol. 6, 105–212. New York: International Publishers, 1976.

Marx, Karl. *Wage Labour and Capital*. In MECW. Vol. 9, 197–228. New York: International Publishers, 1977.

Marx, Karl. *The Class Struggles in France, 1848 to 1850*. In MECW. Vol. 10, 45–145. New York: International Publishers, 1978.

Marx, Karl. "The Chartists." In MECW. Vol. 11, 133–41. New York: International Publishers, 1979.

Marx, Karl. "Inaugural Address of the International Working Men's Association." In MECW. Vol. 20, 5–13. New York: International Publishers, 1985a.

Marx, Karl. "Instructions …for the delegates of the General Council of the International." MECW. Vol. 20, 185–94. New York: International Publishers, 1985b.

Marx, Karl. "Value, Price and Profit. A Report to the General Council of the International." In MECW. Vol. 20, 101–49. New York: International Publishers, 1985c.

Marx, Karl. *The Civil War in France*. In MECW. Vol. 22, 307–59. New York: International Publishers, 1986a.

Marx, Karl. "First Address of the General Council of the International Working Men's Association on the Franco-Prussian War." In MECW. Vol. 22, 3–8. New York: International Publishers, 1986b.

Marx, Karl. "Interview with *The World*." In MECW. Vol. 22, 600–6. New York: International Publishers, 1986c.

Marx, Karl. "Speech on Trades Unions at the London Conference of the International Working Men's Association." In MECW. Vol. 22, 614–15, New York: International Publishers, 1986d.

Marx, Karl. *Economic Manuscripts*. In MECW. Vols. 30–34. New York: International Publishers, 1988–1994.

Marx, Karl. "On the Hague Congress." In MECW. Vol. 23, 254–6. New York: International Publishers, 1988.

Marx, Karl. *Critique of the Gotha Programme*. In MECW. Vol. 24, 81–99. New York: International Publishers, 1989a.

Marx, Karl. "Marginal Notes on Wagner's *Lehrbuch der Politischen Oekonomie*." In MECW. Vol. 24, 531–59. New York: International Publishers, 1989b.

Marx, Karl. "Parliamentary Debate on the Anti-Socialist Law. Outline of an Article." In MECW. Vol. 24, 240–50. New York: International Publishers, 1989c.

Marx, Karl. "Preamble to the Programme of the French Workers' Party." In MECW. Vol. 24, 340–1. New York: International Publishers, 1989d.

Marx, Karl. *Capital*, Vol. I. In MECW. Vol. 35. New York: International Publishers, 1996.

Marx, Karl. *Capital*, Vol. III. In MECW. Vol. 37. New York: International Publishers, 1998.

Marx, Karl and Frederick Engels. *Correspondence*. In MECW. Vols. 38–46. New York: International Publishers, 1982–1992.

Mises, Ludwig von. *Planning for Freedom*. South Holland, IL: Libertarian Press, 1980.

Persky, Joseph. *The Political Economy of Progress: John Stuart Mill and Modern Radicalism*. Oxford: Oxford University Press, 2016.

Rothbard, Murray. *Economic Thought Before Adam Smith: An Austrian Perspective on the History of Economic Thought*. Aldershot: Edward Elgar, 1995.

Schapiro, Jacob S. "Comment." *Journal of the History of Ideas* 10, no. 2 (April 1949): 303–4.

Schumpeter, Joseph A. *History of Economic Analysis*. London: George Allen and Unwin, 1954.

Stedman Jones, Gareth. *Karl Marx: Greatness and Illusion*. London: Allen Lane, 2016.

Marx's Ideas and Conceptions of Socialism in the Twenty-First Century

Tian Yu Cao

I. Introduction: How to Interpret Marx's Conception of Socialism

The collapse of the Soviet model, along with the decline of Keynesianism since the 1970s, has posed a serious challenge to socialists: Is it still possible to conceive a theoretically coherent and practically viable economic model in which the socialist principle of no-alienation[1] is not compromised by the concerns of productivity and efficiency? What would be the necessary conceptual resources for this endeavour? It seems that in the last three decades, all the available or conceivable conceptual resources have

[1] In this chapter, the notion of non-alienation is understood broadly: objectively, it means no exploitation, no dominance, self-governing, freedom, equality, justice; subjectively, communal solidarity, creativity, etc. For a critical review of the debate on the centrality of the no-alienation principle in the conception of socialism and other issues related with market socialism between Gerald Allan Cohen and David Miller, see David Miller, "Our Unfinished Debate About Market Socialism," *Politics, Philosophy & Economics* 13, no. 2 (2014): 119–39. This chapter intends to indirectly address their concerns from an institutional rather than individualistic-moral-psychological perspective.

T. Y. Cao (✉)
Boston University, Boston, MA, USA

© The Author(s) 2019
S. Gupta et al. (eds.), *Karl Marx's Life, Ideas, and Influences*, Marx,
Engels, and Marxisms, https://doi.org/10.1007/978-3-030-24815-4_13

been exhaustively tried, but the challenge remains. In this chapter, a suggestion is made that in taking up the challenge, some of Marx's ideas should be taken as more than instructive and inspiring; in fact, they have provided conceptual foundations for a socialist economic model that is both coherent and viable.

Some sceptics may raise their eyebrows. Is Marx still relevant in this endeavour? Is it not true that Marx's ideas were responsible for the failure of the Soviet model, whose guiding principles—the state ownership of the means of production and central planning—were directly taken from Marx's teaching? It sounds true, but not quite. It was only the Soviet interpretation of Marx's conception of the two pillars of socialism—"social property" and "conscious social regulation"—articulated in his *Critique of the Gotha's Program*,[2] Marx's most mature conception of what a socialist society should be like. However, there can be a different interpretation that, it can be argued, is truer to the spirit of Marx's conception of socialism.

The grounds for an alternative interpretation are provided by two of Marx's fundamental ideas about post-capitalist society. One is the idea of "the republican association of free and equal producers,"[3] concerning the fundamental organization in any post-capitalist society: in its first phase, what we commonly call socialist society, as well as its high phase, a truly communist society. The other is the idea of "equal right,"[4] which concerns exclusively the economic foundation of the socialist, but not the communist, society.

The meaning of the first idea is clear-cut in its social and political aspects: a firm rejection of statism. Its meaning in the economic aspect, however, depends on the economic situation of the post-capitalist society: in a communist society, it means "from each according to his ability, to each according to his needs!"[5] While in a socialist society, it can only mean the exchange of equal labours.[6] And this is directly linked to Marx's second idea, whose non-statist implications to his conception of the two pillars of socialism deserve serious explorations.

---

[2] Karl Marx, *Critique of the Gotha's Program*, in MECW (New York: International Publishers, 1989), 24: 75–99.

[3] Karl Marx, "Instructions for the Delegates of the Provisional General Council," in which Marx used the phrase of "the republican and beneficent system of the association of free and equal producers," in MECW (New York: International Publishers, 1985), 20: 190.

[4] Karl Marx, *Critique of the Gotha's Program*, in MECW (New York: International Publishers, 1989), 24: 86.

[5] Ibid., 87.

[6] Ibid., 86.

II. THE TWENTY-FIRST-CENTURY CONTEXT: FINANCIAL CAPITALISM GLOBALIZED

Before proceeding with the explorations, it is critical to note that socialism is not a doctrinaire design, but can only be the outcome of the struggles and movement of the working classes in response to their capitalist conditions of existence. The fundamental condition for workers' existence in the contemporary era of globalization is the financialization of economic life and the dominance of financial capital. Although Marx's focus was on the primacy of production, he also saw capitalist dynamics as being deeply entwined with finance. Financial capital is what Marx called moneyed capital that functions as an external agent providing the finance that launches the circuit of capital. Since the 1980s, non-financial enterprises, banks, and even working-class households in the advanced capitalist world have become increasingly implicated in the web of finance, the so-called financial inclusion. The discipline imposed by finance on production has bred the strategy of rationalize, retrench, and outsource, leading to greater concentration and centralization of all spheres of production on the one hand, and the growth of inequality and concentration of wealth on the other.

The role of financial capital, just as the role of one of its special forms, the credit system, as Marx indicated, has a dual character.[7] One the one hand, it makes possible that the expansion of individual capitalist enterprises need not be limited to the reinvestment of their retained earnings, and thus accelerates the expansion of the scale of production; for the same reason, it also accelerates the development of technology and the creation of the world market. That is, it is crucial to the expansion and development of capitalism. On the other hand, since it is driven by the capitalist impulse to make a profit, it also accelerates the violent outbreak of contradiction and crisis. Marx's verdict was that credit system, or financial capital in general, as the principal lever of overproduction and excessive speculation,

> develops the motive of capitalist production, enrichment by exploitation of others' labour, into the purest and most colossal system of gambling and swindling and restricts even more the already small number of exploiters of social wealth.[8]

---

[7] Karl Marx, *Capital*, Vol. III, in MECW (New York: International Publishers, 1998), 37: 397–439.
[8] Ibid., 439.

What should be stressed here is that in criticizing all the evil motivations and evil consequences of financial capital, Marx's sharp insights into its dual and contradictory nature should not be forgotten: underneath all the evils, there is a rationale for it to emerge in the historical development of capitalism. The ground on which financial capital is premised is the rational and productive separation of management from ownership of working conditions (or capital in its generalized sense). The bearings on conceiving socialism of workers' experience with contemporary financial capitalism will be seen clearer when the evolution of economic formations is examined in Sect. V from Marx's perspective of socializing economic activities.

III. Socialism and the Law of Value

The best place to begin exploring the implications of Marx's idea of "equal right" to his conception of socialism is his frequently quoted claim:

> What we have to deal with here is a communist society, not as it has developed on its own foundations, but, on the contrary, just as it emerges from capitalist society; which is thus in every respect, economically, morally, and intellectually, still stamped with the birthmarks of the old society from whose womb it emerges. Accordingly, the individual producer receives back from society—after the deductions have been made—exactly what he gives to it. What he has given to it is his individual quantum of labour.[9]

That is, in a socialist society, "a given amount of labour in one form is exchanged for an equal amount of labour in another form."[10] This means "the same principle prevails as that which regulates the exchange of commodities, as far as this is exchange of equal values."[11]

Essentially, what Marx said here is that *the law of value will still be operative in a socialist society*, although there are restrictions: nothing but labour can enter into exchange, and nothing can pass to the ownership of the means of production.

Considering the central place of the law of value occupies, in history and at present, in the understanding of socialism, a careful examination of the concept of value is mandatory.

---

[9] Marx, *Critique of the Gotha's Program*, 85–6.
[10] Ibid., 86.
[11] Ibid.

Marx's classical formulation was this: the value of a commodity was created by socially necessary labour for its production. But how the value is determined, or what kind of social process through which the value is formed, is an interesting yet not properly understood question, which has implications to the way of understanding the notions of value, market, and their relationship. A proper understanding of these issues will shed some light on an alternative model of a socialist economy.[12]

To clear the way to understand the social process through which value is formed, *a non-social but naturalistic view* about value has to be rejected. According to this naturalistic view, the amount of socially necessary labour can be measured by the natural scale of *time* the labourer spent on its production. The reason for rejection is simple: socially necessary labour is an *abstraction* of concrete natural (physical or mental) labour; in its essence, socially necessary labour is not concrete labouring action anymore, but what is *necessary* to create *what is socially needed, judged by society*, which thus can only be evaluated by society *through social processes*. For this reason, it cannot be measured by *the natural scale of labouring time*, but can only be measured by *its social scale, whose form is, ultimately, money*.

Another misleading thesis should also be revised. The thesis claims that abstract labour creates value. The thesis seems to presume the existence of abstract labour prior or simultaneous to the value it creates. But this is unreasonable. Human activities in production are always concrete, they become value (socially necessary labour) only through a social-economical process of abstraction, not because they involve the exercise of some *general and thus "abstract" human physical and mental energy and effort*, which remain to be *natural-individual rather than social*, and thus have nothing to do with "socially necessary labor" until it is socialized through certain social processes. So, it is correct to say that "value is the abstraction of concrete labour thorough social processes," but improper to claim that "abstract labour creates value."[13]

---

[12] The analysis and understanding of value, market and socialism underlying this chapter is mainly taken from the late Chinese Marxist economist Zili Lin, *On the Socialist Economy: China's Economic Reform* (Beijing: Economic Science Publisher, vol. 1, 1985; vol. 2, 1986; vol. 3, 1994), passim. His most important theoretical works were selected and translated into English, Zili Lin, "Going towards the Market," special issue, *Chinese Economic Studies* 27 (1994): 27.

[13] Zili Lin, "New Theory of Value—Renewal of Classical Theory of Value" in "Going towards the Market," special issue, *Chinese Economic Studies* 27 (1994): 58.

The gravest defect of this widespread but misleading thesis is that it excludes from the process of abstraction *the adaptability or utility of different concrete labours to social demand*. The exclusion betrays its untenable presumption that social supply and demand are always in balance, which frequently turns out not the case. Surely concrete labour not needed by society cannot be recognized as a socially necessary labour. So the exclusion of utility from value formation is *practically impossible* unless the abstraction of labour (the ascription of value to concrete labour) is achieved by an authority's direct evaluation in a closed economy rather than through open yet indirect social process of labour exchanges, or market transactions. Theoretically, the exclusion renders the labour theory of value unable to explain the formation and function of price that is closely related to utility. Of course, price frequently deviates from value, but when external factors such as monopoly, non-economic interventions, and market failures are absent—that is, in a fully competitive and complete market—the deviation is insignificant.

In examining the value formation, which is premised on an understanding of commodity exchange, another relevant claim should be rejected. The claim says that commodity exchange is the result of the division of labour and the rise of private ownership. But the lack of commodity exchange in both privately owned feudal manor and public ownership-based command economy shows that ownership itself is irrelevant to commodity exchange; it also shows that the very existence of division of labour in both these circumstances does not by itself dictate the need for commodity exchange as a way of coordination; the required coordination could be done in a direct way. Then what is crucial for the emergence of commodity exchange or market exchange? It can be argued that a combination of three factors is crucial for market exchange.

The first factor is the existence of different economic subjects who possess different products, which are the materialized forms of different labours. The difference among labours means the difference in kind (fishing differs from shoe-making) and in quality (skilled or not); it also involves different material, technological, and organizational conditions under which labours are performed. How could these different labours be coordinated or exchanged between different economic subjects? Here come the other two factors. If there is a direct knowledge of social demand for various different labours obtainable by each and all providers, then there is no need for market exchange, although non-market coordination would still be very difficult. But the lack of such kind of direct knowledge makes any non-market coordination impossible. The third factor is the lack of a unified measurement through which different labours can be directly measured and compared. A combination of these three factors would render market transactions inevitable for the socially necessary coordination of various labours, even in a society of public ownership.

Central to this argument is the notion of adaptability of labour to social demand. Since whether or not and how good certain particular labour meets social demand could not be measured directly, all the differences involved in different labours have to be converted or abstracted to a unified measurement, without which no proper coordination or exchange would be possible. Yet *the abstraction itself could only be achieved through a trial-and-error process of labour exchange*—namely through market transactions or market evaluations. The result of abstraction based on the adaptability of labour to demand is the formation of price. Then what is value? *Value is the essence of price, the socially necessary labour, which explains the formation and function of price.*

The notion of socially necessary labour, accordingly, expresses not only the quantity but also the quality and the kind of a specific labour performed under specific material, technological, and managerial conditions that meets specific social demand, and thus is at the same time *an expression of social demand*. Precisely because the supply-demand interaction affects the formation of labour abstraction, that is, *value is formed through the process of price formation, value can regulate supply and demand* and bring a roughly balanced relationship between the two in a fully competitive and complete market system. That is, the measurement of value formed in market competition evaluates the economic behaviour of producers. The evaluation exerts severe pressures on producers, forces them to adapt their labour to social demand, to reduce cost and speed turnover, resulting in structural improvement and efficient growth of the whole economy.

Running an economy is to solve two problems: the allocation of labour and the exchange of labour. The former refers to economic structure, the latter affects efficiency. The historical inevitability of market economy lies in the fact that because the three factors discussed above always exist, only such an economy could offer relatively effective solutions to the two fundamental economic problems.

The task of a proper theory of value is to offer a proper understanding of the underlying rationale for the workings of a market economy in terms of value formation. But the classical theory of value without taking into consideration labour's adaptability to social demand failed precisely around these two problems: overlooking the adaptability of particular labours to social demand is to neglect the key fact that the structure of social demand cannot be directly known and grasped; overlooking the differences between different labours is to ignore the difficulty, and indeed impossibility of directly measuring labour. The hidden assumption of classical theories is that labour can be directly measured, allocated, and exchanged. Theoretically, it is untenable and was sharply criticized by Nikolai Ivanovich Bukharin at the early stage of the Soviet economy.[14] Practically, its implications are disastrous, as was vindicated by Russia's War Communism (1918–21) and by other experiments on command economy afterwards.

IV. MARKETS: THEIR CONSTITUTIONAL CORE AND CONTEXTUAL REALIZATIONS

The above understanding of value offers a perspective from which we may take the rise of the market as the rise of a mechanism for socializing economic activities, and the rise of the product market as the first step in this direction. It is historically necessary and inevitable because it is the only way to address two key questions in any economy in which three factors exist: the structural balance and efficiency.

To be sure, in historically emerged markets, markets' negative potentials have been in full display: polarization, inequality, and class division; not self-regulating, thus anarchy and periodic convulsions, monopoly, and manipulation; nurturing a culture of greed, fear, and other forms of alienation and destruction. Yet markets' negativities should not blind economic thinkers from realizing and recognizing markets' constitutive core, *competitive equal exchanges*, which has great positive potentials, and thus should be preserved in a socialist economy.

More important, however, is the embeddedness of markets in society. Since the operation of a market cannot be detached from its context: legal and regulative institutions for legitimating and regulating productive, trading, tax, environmental and financial activities in relevant markets, and cultural norms, bounds, and values that condition and constraint markets, it is arguable that the nature of a market is subordinated to and even constituted and dictated by the nature of the context in which the market is embedded. Thus if the legal-political institutions and cultural norms are capitalist in

---

[14] Nikolai Ivanovich Bukharin, "Notes of an Economist (the Beginning of the New Economic Year)," *Economy and Society* 8, no. 4 (1979).

nature, then markets operating in such a context can only be an integrated part of capitalism with all its negative consequences that the market-critics frequently cite. But in a context in which a set of socialist political-legal institutions, cultural legitimization, and regulatory regimes is firmly established and installed, markets embedded in such a socialist context will be socialist in nature. At the minimum, the socialist context can prevent the existent markets' logic, inherited from historically emerged markets, of chasing profit from colonizing the political, social, and cultural spheres, as Jürgen Habermas hoped for. At the maximum, the socialist context can constrain historical markets' logic by a renewed logic of reciprocity, redistribution, and communality with a socialist rather than pre-capitalist Polanyian character in organizing economic activities, so that social inclusion can be promoted, political participation can be encouraged, and consumer culture can be replaced by a communal and humanist culture.

To be sure, in a socialist society, in areas where social demand can be known, or there are market failures or natural monopolies or vital national interests, central planning as a way of social coordination is feasible and desirable, and thus should be the guiding principle without conceding to marketization. More importantly, the core task for a socialist government's regulation in areas where market is allowed to play a fundamental role is to make sure that no forms of monopoly in capital and information is allowed, and *all institutional designs and government policies should aim at universal and equal access to capital and information for all citizens.*

With these caveats in mind, it is clear that the market mechanism, as a mode of production and coordination, or a mode of allocation and a form of operation is compatible with socialism and cannot be categorically equated with capitalism. Capitalism is a regime of endless capital accumulation through profit-chasing by private owners of capital, while the market mechanism is compatible with various social systems, depending on the context in which it is embedded and operating. Since the market mechanism does not depend on private ownership and is not intrinsically contradictory with public (communal, regional, or national) property, the capitalist markets based on private ownership can only be viewed as a historically emerged (and somewhat alienated) form of market. In contrast, a socialist market is premised on the abolition of closed private property through an equal and universal access to social property or social capital (capital is generally understood as the conditions of production), mediated by a socialist capital market that is supported and protected by socialist political power and legal institutions, and is guided by socialist cultural norms.

V. MARKETS AND THEIR EVOLUTION: FROM PRODUCT MARKETS TO LABOUR MARKETS AND CAPITAL MARKETS

The notion of "socialization" as Marx's organizing concept in his theoretical framework is crucial for understanding the market's compatibility or even constitutive necessity to socialism. From a very general and historical perspective, Marx cultivates an idea that in the historical development of human economic activities, there is a general tendency of moving from closed or autarkic economies towards more and more open or socialized economies. That is, production and demand are more and more socially defined. The socialization can be achieved through mechanisms of market or planning or a combination of both. But for the reasons mentioned above, the market generally is relatively more efficient (and under certain conditions, even is indispensable) for socialization, except for some well-defined areas in a socialist context. The emergence of the product market, the labour market, the capital and financial markets, accordingly, can be viewed as representing different levels of socialization, and each level features a historical epoch.

Thus, the emergence of the wage-labour system features a transition from the closed feudal economy to an open capitalist economy, in which labourers are freed from personal attachment and non-economic coercion. As a result, the labour resource can be more efficiently allocated than before.

But the wage system is not part of a fully developed integral market since the transactions that happen in the labour market are not equal exchanges of labour. Of course, Marx claimed that labour market transactions were equal exchanges, the exploitation occurred only in the process of production in which surplus labour was appropriated without compensation as a source of profit. But if the following facts are taken seriously into full consideration, then a different view of the labour market may be more reasonable.

First, what a capitalist buys and a labourer sells in the labour market actually is not labour power, but rather a certain concrete labour, with certain quantity, a certain kind, a certain quality, a certain level of skill, performed under certain labour conditions, to be delivered later as the hiring contract specifies. Second, such a concrete labour as a commodity has a value that is constituted by the social process of abstraction mentioned in Sect. III. Third, once this is clarified, the unequal nature of the labour market transactions is not difficult to see. Obviously, no capitalist pays the full value of the concrete labour he buys; otherwise, no profit would be possible. What a capitalist pays can only be the remainder of the full value of the concrete labour a worker sells with the subtraction of a rent the capitalist claims for offering the worker the opportunity of performing his labour—namely, for providing the worker the working conditions so that the worker can perform and sell his labour to the capitalist. The rent is also determined by the market, the market of capital. Through competitions in capital markets, the rent will reach an equilibrium, the average rate of profit, the same amount of capital gets the same amount of profit or rent for its being used for a certain period of time.

At a very abstract level, some Marxist economists argued that the tendency in the evolution of the wage system was towards a labour market of equal exchange.[15] But the realization of the tendency, according to this argument, premised on the socialization of capital, which in fact, would feature a new historical epoch and characterize the transition from capitalism to socialism. Capitalism is characterized by the separation of workers from the means of production, which is monopolized by private owners, who thereby control workers, demand and receive rent, and thus make equal exchange in labour market impossible.

Yet the state ownership of the means of production (nationalization) is not a solution to the monopoly of capital and the separation of workers from working conditions, neither is it a proper form of socializing capital. In fact, the closed, monopolized ownership by the state blocks ways to an integral market of capital, and thus undermines the very ground for universal access by workers to capital. This institutional arrangement makes the removal of workers' separation from the working conditions virtually impossible, thus undermining the economic foundation for socialism. In line with Marx's idea of a post-capitalist "socialized individual ownership" by free producers organized in free associations, the desirability of open and universally accessible character of social capital entails a call for capital markets, whose nature is critically conditioned by the context in which these markets are embedded and operating.

The transition from monopolized (closed) to socialized (open and universally accessible) capital is a long historical process, critically relying on the separation of operating- (use- and managing- and controlling) right from ownership of capital. However, the separation of ownership from the actual operation of capital, or the property rights of capital, or the property rights of all kinds of working conditions, is a commonplace in modern

[15] Lin, *On the Socialist Economy* and "Going towards the Market," passim.

organization of production, service, circulation, and finance. This is especially true in the era of globalization. In fact, the separation has provided the ontological foundation for financial capitalism, although the implication of the separation for socialism is yet to be explored.

The economic meaning of *ownership* of capital that is separated from its actual *operation (use, management, and control)* is largely reduced to the income derived thereby. This causes the principal-agent problem, but the fact that formal ownership alone cannot promise full control and appropriation of the residual is beyond dispute. In addition, even the formal ownership itself has mostly shifted from individuals to investment institutions, such as pension funds, indicating that the boundary between private and social capital has already been somewhat blurred.

With regard to the transition discussed above, Marx's comments on the capital involved in joint stock companies, which are the result of the capital market involving an interplay between fictitious and real capitals, are illuminating:

> [The capital] is here directly endowed with the form of social capital, and its undertakings assume the form of social undertaking as distinct from private undertakings. It is the abolition of capital as private property within the framework of capitalist production itself, ...and the abolition of the capitalist mode of production within the capitalist mode of production itself, and hence a self-dissolving contradiction, which prima facie represents a mere phase of transition to a new form of production.[16]

What Marx said here, with some modification, can also be said to capital markets and financial markets in general. The developments of capital and financial markets in scope and depth in the last four decades have gone far beyond what was conceptualized by Marx, but the persuasiveness of Marx's insights into the dual and dialectic character of these developments remains the same.

---

[16] Marx, *Capital*, Vol. III, 434, 436. On page 434, Marx said: "The capital, which in itself rests on a social mode of production and presupposes a social concentration of means of production and labour power, is here directly endowed with the form of social capital (capital of directly associated individuals) as distinct from private capital, and its undertakings assume the form of social undertakings as distinct from private undertakings. It is the abolition of capital as private property within the framework of the capitalist mode of production itself." On page 436, Marx said: "This is the abolition of the capitalist mode of production within the capitalist mode of production itself, and hence a self-dissolving contradiction, which prima facie represents a mere phase of transition to a new form of production."

If the separation of operation from formal ownership of capitals, or the separation of functioning capital from money capital and fictitious capital, is the key to socialize capital (or property rights of working conditions in general, including capital, land and natural resources, social and intellectual resources), then it should be applicable to both private and public ownership (except for some special areas noted above), such as collectively owned land and state property. This is the only way leading to a complete and healthy capital market. Such a complete capital market surely is a desirable structure for socializing capital, namely, for providing individually dispersed associated producers a universally equalized access to all kinds of capitals, regardless of their formal ownership. For this reason, thus defined capital market is a necessary institutional basis for labour's liberation from the control of closed (capitalist or state) ownership. If such socialization realized through capital markets can be viewed as a strategic alternative to privatization in replacing statist socialism, then a complete socialization of product, labour, capital, land, management, knowledge, and other human and natural resources, and even risks involved in economic activities, realized in relevant markets, should be duly recognized as constitutive to the economic foundation of socialism.

VI. MARKETS AND SOCIALIST ECONOMY

Once the theoretical ground for understanding the market as a way of realizing Marx's fundamental idea of socializing economic activities is cleared, it becomes possible to argue that the market mechanism is compatible and even constitutively necessary to socialism; it is more than just an interim expedient at the primary stage of socialism.[17]

This argument proceeds in three steps. First, it was argued that socialism should be dissociated from its historical statist (Soviet or Keynesian) models and defined only by its basic principles: no-alienation (which provided the moral-political justification for socialism to replace capitalism), and efficiency (which provided the economic justification for the replacement). Second, it was stressed that institutionally, although public ownership and central planning in a socialist society would keep their important roles, their roles would be demoted from foundational and their foundational places would be occupied, respectively, by social ownership mediated by capital markets, and by market coordination dictated by the law of value, whose grounding role was duly recognized and stressed by Marx in

---

[17] Lin, *On the Socialist Economy: China's Economic Reform* and "Going towards the Market."

his *Critique of the Gotha Program*. Third, and decisively, it demanded that enough strategic and constitutive moves should be conceived and implemented to develop a socialist market that could avoid the negative effects of historically developed capitalist markets, while preserving its positive core, that is, competitive equal exchanges. The underlying idea in the argument was to radically transform the market's fundamental ontology and the context in which the market operates.

More specifically, the market players should not be selfish individuals blindly chasing for private interests. Rather, these market players should be various communities (enterprises, trade unions, banks, investment institutions, etc.). These communities should be able to manage and use, but do not have to own, their working conditions, which could be acquired from social pool of capital through capital markets, in an autonomous way. Internally these communities should be organized as republican associations of free producers or workers, as was conceived by Marx in his *Critique of Gotha Program*. That is, these republican associations as market players should be organized in democratic ways for decision-making on economic issues (most important among them are the income level of capital owners and managers, hiring and firing, distribution of accumulation and consumption), and political issues (most important among them is the power distribution within the community), guided, culturally, by socialist values and norms (e.g., equality, communal solidarity and justice; human needs rather than consumption and possession). Externally, in addition to market relations with other market players, they are subject to democratically organized socialist government's regulations at relevant levels, also guided by socialist values and norms.

These Marxian associations, new kind of market players,[18] have provided the only institutional setting in which moral incentives would flourish and dominate human's psyche and behaviour, which Ernesto Che Guevara and many others took as the decisive factor for socialism.[19] Without this institutional setting, Ernesto Che Guevara, Gerald Cohen, and numerous others' moralistic-idealist conceptions of socialism would be groundless.

---

[18] For a brief description and discussion of a few, so far, real-life examples of the new kind of market players (an ideal type), which did not have all the defining features of the ideal type and were already in the process of corrupting, see Tian Yu Cao, "Land Ownership and Market Socialism in China," in *The Land Question—Socialism, Capitalism, and the Market*, ed. Mahmood Mamdani (Makerere Institute of Social Research Book Series, 2015).

[19] Quoted from Ernesto Che Guevara, "Socialism and man in Cuba," *The Che Reader*, ed. David Deutschmann (Melbourne: Ocean Press, 2005), 212–30.

In order to avoid the communitarian trap of exclusiveness and distinguish itself from the anarchic syndicalism, in this model, all newcomers getting into an association through labour markets should automatically enjoy full membership of the association and the related inalienable membership rights.[20]

With the changed players and the changed institutional contexts, the underlying logic of the socialist market will be radically different from that of the capitalist market. While competitions and incentives remain the core of the market for effective information processing that is necessary for efficiency, the motivations and goals are no longer focused on an exclusive and infinite accumulation of capital through chasing profits, but rather on reciprocity and communal-regional-national balanced economic developments for meeting human needs. Thus the result of market activities would not be polarization, class division and exclusion, but rather inclusion, trust, personal empowerment in free choice (in consumption, employment, expressions) and in decision-making.

With these foundational changes, the labour market will no longer be a mechanism through which workers are exploited, but rather a mechanism through which workers' freedom is realized: Workers entering an enterprise will enjoy full membership rights equal to all other members, not as employees; those fired or voluntarily leave the enterprise will have unconditional basic income to rely on, and will have the right to receive self-chosen training for re-entering a preferable enterprise; these retraining opportunities should be offered by regional or national government funded by regional or national pool of social capital.

Similarly, the capital and financial markets will no longer be places for speculations leading to volatility, but rather for effective use of capital (in various forms of property rights of working conditions) through value discovery, which is a great help in structural adjustments and various innovations, and thus facilitates the change of government's function from administrative planning to regulations.

A conclusion can be reached, which is that markets are not only compatible with socialism. But rather, in terms of their subjects (communities in which workers and all other members enjoy equal status and rights stipulated and protected by a socialist constitution) and in terms of the socialist commons (socially usable resources: assets, knowledge, and activities) realized through capital and financial markets, markets provide a desirable, feasible, and indispensable mechanism, and serve as the economic foundation for realizing socialist principles: no-alienation and efficiency.

[20] Cao, "Land Ownership and Market Socialism in China."

VII. The Necessity of Politics

This market-based conception or model of socialism is underlain by the fundamental assumption of the embeddedness of markets in their social-political-legal-cultural settings, and thus is critically premised on workers' socialist political will and political power. Their inalienable republican rights within associations, which is constitutive for these associations to be the new kind of market players, and without (regionally and nationally), have to be clearly stipulated in the constitution and protected by legal institutions. Also, to be clearly stipulated in the constitution and protected by legal institutions is the equal and universal access by all associated citizens to capital, information, and services, which is crucial for the capital market to become a mechanism for creating the socialist commons. Workers' socialist political will and political power are decisive also because the coordination and regulation of markets have to be guided by the socialist political will and carried out by the socialist political power structure.

Then the crucial question remains: How can such a socialist political will and such a socialist political power structure emerge from today's capitalist environment? But this practical and strategic issue is beyond the scope of this chapter and has to be properly addressed on other occasions.

Bibliography

Bukharin, Nikolai Ivanovich. "Notes of an Economist (The Beginning of the New Economic Year)." *Economy and Society* 8, no. 4 (1979): 473–500.

Cao, Tian Yu. "Land Ownership and Market Socialism in China." In *The Land Question—Socialism, Capitalism, and the Market*, edited by Mahmood Mamdani, 77–94. Makerere Institute of Social Research Book Series, 2015.

Guevara, Ernesto Che. "Socialism and Man in Cuba." In *The Che Reader*, edited by David Deutschmann, 212–30. Melbourne: Ocean Press, 2005.

Lin, Zili. *On the Socialist Economy: China's Economic Reform*. Vol. 3. Beijing: Economic Science Publisher, 1985–1994.

Lin, Zili. "Going Towards the Market." Special issue, *Chinese Economic Studies* 27 (1994): 1–208.

Marx, Karl. *Critique of the Gotha's Program*. In MECW. Vol. 24, 81–99. New York: International Publishers, 1989.

Marx, Karl. *Capital*. Vol. III. In MECW. Vol. 37. New York: International Publishers, 1998.

Miller, David. "Our Unfinished Debate about Market Socialism." *Politics, Philosophy & Economics* 13, no. 2 (2014): 119–39.

Marx's Metaphysics of Human Labour in the Light of Sraffa: Labour Theory of Value Reconsidered

Ajit Sinha

I. Labour as the Ultimate Cause of Value in Classical Economics

In this chapter, I analyse the foundations of Marx's analysis of a capitalist economy in terms of labour time to locate the root cause of Marx's problem of relating values to prices and surplus values to profits, and then, show how Sraffa succeeds in solving the problem by liberating Marx from his metaphysics of "human labour."

The idea of measuring commodities in units of labour time is, however, not originally Marx's. It was used in earnest by Adam Smith,[1] who wanted to find a standard of measure for the values of commodities so that the *real* wealth of a nation could be compared over periods of time, independently of fluctuations in the prices of commodities. He thought that if the

---

[1] Adam Smith, *An Inquiry into the Nature and Causes of the Wealth of Nations*, Vol. I (Indianapolis: Library Fund, 1981).

A. Sinha (✉)
Azim Premji University, Bengaluru, India

© The Author(s) 2019
S. Gupta et al. (eds.), *Karl Marx's Life, Ideas, and Influences*, Marx, Engels, and Marxisms, https://doi.org/10.1007/978-3-030-24815-4_14

ultimate cause of value could be discovered, then that could provide us with the standard that will remain invariant in the face of apparent changes in prices. This led Adam Smith to think of man's primordial state when he must have had to act *directly* against nature to wrest his basic needs of survival from it. For Adam Smith, this primordial act of man against nature is both an act of *production* as well as an act of *exchange*. Expenditure of labour in the process of production is also a sacrifice in terms of "toil and trouble," which is a payment of price for the product appropriated from nature. Thus, all prices or all economic values must be measured by this "originary" or the ultimate price, which measures the "real" value of the commodity as opposed to the "nominal" value measured by the money-commodity, such as gold or silver. After having determined the standard of measure of values of commodities in a commodity's ability to command certain length of time of the labourer or his "sacrifice of labour," Adam Smith developed a theory of value in terms of accounting of the income generated in production by "adding up" wages, profits, and rent, which he considered were known data at any given point of time.

Ricardo[2] rejected Adam Smith's "adding up" theory of value on the grounds that the value of total income must be fixed independently of how it is cut between various recipients of it. From this point of view, Adam Smith's explanation of why labour is the ultimate cause of value also becomes problematic—if labour as "sacrifice" is the cause of value of the commodity, then a change in the cause must result in a change in the effect, and thus a fall in the real wage—which implies an increase in the sacrifice to acquire a commodity for the labourer—must lead to an increase in the value of the commodity. This contradicts Ricardo's proposition that the size of the total must be independent of how it is cut for different recipients. Therefore, Ricardo removed the *subjective* interpretation of labour and proposed an alternative hypothesis that labour is the ultimate cause of value not because of the subjective aspect of the "sacrifice" by the labourer as a payment of price for the good received, but because labour in the act of production is an *objective input* and since all other inputs of production can be reduced to labour in the final analysis, it is the ultimate cause of value. From this perspective, Ricardo needed to show that changes in prices of commodities must, in the final analysis, be explained solely by showing changes in the labour input required to produce the commodities.

---

[2] David Ricardo, *Principles of Political Economy and Taxation* (Cambridge: Cambridge University Press, 1951).

But Ricardo had to admit that in a general case, when the technique of producing commodities are such that their ratios of direct to indirect labour inputs are not equal, then changes in wages can have an independent effect on prices, that is, prices can change without any changes in their labour inputs, thus violating the fundamental proposition that labour is the ultimate cause of value.[3]

II. Surplus Value and Marx's Metaphysics of Human Labour

Marx had a fair inkling that Adam Smith's (and also Ricardo's) idea that in the final analysis, all production can be reduced to man's direct labouring activity against nature may be logically flawed since it may not be possible to reduce the material means of production to zero as one goes back and back in the production chain to draw a long series of labouring activity pure and simple. In *Capital* Volume II, Marx wrote:

> The statement that the entire price of commodities is either "immediately" or "ultimately" resolvable in v + s [wages + surplus] would only cease to be an empty subterfuge if Smith could demonstrate that the commodity products whose price is immediately resolved into c (the price of the means of production consumed) + v + s are finally compensated for by commodity products which entirely replace these "consumed means of production", and which are for their part produced simply by outlay of variable capital [wage advances only], i.e., capital laid out on labour-power. The price of these latter commodities would then immediately be v + s. And in this way the price of the former, too, c + v + s, where c stands for the component of constant capital, would be ultimately resolvable into v + s. Adam Smith himself did not believe he had given such a proof.[4]

Marx's fundamental attack on political economy was that neither Adam Smith nor Ricardo could explain the source of profits. Both Adam Smith and Ricardo take profits as a given income category in a bourgeois economy. Adam Smith's argument that profit is a return on "risk taking" can be a reasonable explanation for differential rates of interest on capital due

[3] For my detailed analysis of Adam Smith's and Ricardo's theories of value, see Ajit Sinha, *Theories of Value from Adam Smith to Piero Sraffa* (London: Routledge, 2018) and *Essays on Theories of Value in the Classical Tradition* (Cham: Palgrave Macmillan, 2019).

[4] Karl Marx, *Capital*, Vol. II (London: Penguin Classics, 1992), 450.

to differential risks involved in different industries, but it cannot be an explanation for the origin of profits since "risk" does not produce anything. Ricardo also takes a positive rate of profits as given and only analyses how it is affected by changes in the value of wages. So, one of the fundamental projects that Marx takes up in *Capital* was to explain the source of profits.

To answer the question, where do profits come from?, Marx first claims that "[t]he wealth of societies in which the capitalist mode of production prevails appears as an 'immense collection of commodities'; the individual commodity appears as its elementary form. Our investigation, therefore, begins with the analysis of the commodity."[5] He argues that an economic good takes a commodity form if it is produced for exchange against some other good. He then posits that a relation of exchange is a relation of equality, and asks the question: if one-quarter of corn exchanges against one quintal of iron, then what could be the common substance in the two highly disparate use values that must be present in equal amount in the two commodities? His answer is that the "common substance" can be nothing else than the fact that both are "products of labour." And therefore, exchange of commodities represents exchange of equal labour. But of course, the labour of an ironsmith is qualitatively as different from the labour of a farmer as iron is different from wheat. Marx argues that though it is true that "concrete labours" of an ironsmith and a farmer are qualitatively different, nevertheless, underneath them lies expenditure of undifferentiated human energy that can be calculated by a clock.

Leaving aside the problematic nature of Marx's "deduction" or "discovery" of exchange of equal undifferentiated labour residing underneath the exchange of commodities,[6] it is curious that Marx argues this, knowing well from his readings of Ricardo that such a "deduction" would be incorrect for the most general case of capitalist economies. As a matter of fact, Marx had already worked out his solution to the "transformation problem" in his manuscripts of the early 1860s and therefore was well aware that the results of his "deduction" were incorrect—he gives a hint of it at the end of Chapter 5 in a footnote: "How can we account for the origin of capital on the assumption that prices are regulated by the average price, i.e., ultimately by the value of the commodities? I say 'ulti-

[5] Karl Marx, *Capital*, Vol. I (New York: Vintage, 1977), 125.
[6] See Ajit Sinha, *Theories of Value from Adam Smith to Piero Sraffa* (London: Routledge, 2018) for a discussion on this point.

mately' because average prices do not directly coincide with the values of the commodities."[7] Thus, it would be fair to interpret that the "deduction" of equal labour in exchange for the exchange of commodities is a supposition. Marx, at this stage of analysis, could be implicitly assuming an equal ratio of direct to indirect labour time for all the industries, or at least, we can make sense of it by making that assumption.

The strategy Marx employs is to argue that a commodity in a barter exchange relation appears as C_1–C_2, which represents equal undifferentiated labour. By introducing money-commodity as a means of transaction, we can expand the relation of exchange to C_1–M–C_2, which does not change the nature of the relation. However, in a capitalist economy, he argues, a capitalist is not interested in selling a commodity to buy another commodity for consumption. His interest is to invest money as capital to withdraw more money at the end of the circuit. Thus, a circuit of capital in the sphere of exchange begins with a single capitalist starting with some money capital M, exchanging it for some commodities C, and then exchanging C back for money M. If both the M, before and after the exchanges, remain equal, then the whole process would appear to be a mad exercise. Thus, for this circuit to have any meaning for the capitalist, the terminal M must be quantitatively larger than the initial M; in other words, the circuit must be of the form M–C–M', M' > M. The problem Marx poses to himself is: if equal labour-values exchange in the commodity sphere, then where does the difference between M' and M come from?

> The transformation of money into capital has to be developed on the basis of the immanent laws of exchange of commodities, in such a way that the starting-point is the exchange of equivalents. The money-owner, who is yet only a capitalist in larval form, must buy his commodities at their value, sell them at their value, and yet at the end of the process withdraw more value from circulation than he threw into it at the beginning. His emergence as a butterfly must, and yet must not, take place in the sphere of circulation. These are the conditions of the problem. *Hic Rhodus, hic salta!*[8]

One of Marx's central criticisms of political economy was that both Adam Smith and Ricardo did not understand the true nature of wage as an income category. They treated wage as a price paid to the labourer for the labour services performed. Marx argues that wage as a specific form of

---

[7] Marx, *Capital*, Vol. I, 269f24; (emphasis added).
[8] Ibid., 268–9.

income for the labouring class is the *differentia specifica* of capitalism. In capitalism, workers, de jure, appear as independent commodity owners exchanging commodities with other independent commodity owners. But the commodity they sell to the capitalists in exchange for wages is not the labour services as such, but rather their capacity to work, which Marx called labour-power. And the value of the labour-power is determined by the same principle as the value of any other commodity, that is, by the labour time it takes to (re)produce the labourer's capacity to work. Thus, in this specific exchange, a specified wage basket of commodities stands on one side and the labour-power stands on the other. However, one peculiarity of this particular commodity, the labour-power, is that its consumption or use in the production process adds to the value of the raw materials and other such that it works on. Another peculiarity of this particular commodity is that the workers' capacity to work is quite elastic—an average worker can or can be made to work any number of hours below a certain natural maximum in a day. In a capitalist economy, it so happens that the technique of production has become so productive that the wage basket needed to (re)produce the worker's capacity to work is produced in much less labour time than the maximum limit to which a worker can work in a day, and therefore the capitalists are able to stretch the working day beyond the labour time needed to produce the wage basket. In other words, workers give more labour time in the process of production than they receive in return as their wages. Thus the value they add in the process of production is higher than the value they take away as wages. This difference represents "surplus value," which is the source of profits.

Thus, the total value of a commodity has three components—the first component is the constant capital (c), which is the value of raw materials and means of production used up in the process of production plus the fresh labour added by the labourers, which in turn has two components—variable capital (v), which is the value of the wage goods that workers receive and the other is the surplus value (s), which is the extra labour time the worker is made to work over and above the labour time needed to produce the wage basket. In other words, if value of one ton of iron is λ_i then $\lambda_i = c_i + v_i + s_i$, where c_i stands for the value of the raw materials and used-up machines and other such in the production of one ton of iron, and v_i and s_i, respectively, stand for the value of wage goods received by the workers in producing one ton of iron and the difference between the total labour time worked by the workers to produce one ton of iron and the value of the wages received by them.

Now, let us analyse the three components of λ_i separately. How do we determine c_i? It appears that to determine the value of a commodity, one needs to already know the value of other commodities that it uses as its raw materials and other means of production. In Adam Smith's and Ricardo's conceptual framework, one could go back and back in the chain of production of means of production till one hits upon a stage where labour all alone produced the first means of production. But as we have seen above, Marx had rejected this conceptual framework. One way to get out of this circle would be to argue that the value of all the commodities that directly or indirectly go into the production of iron are determined simultaneously. So let us borrow Sraffa's example of an economic system given by:

90 t. iron + 120 t. coal + 60 qr. wheat + 3/16 labour → 180 t. iron

50 t. iron + 125 t. coal + 150 qr. wheat + 5/16 labour → 450 t. coal

40 t. iron + 40 t. coal + 200 qr. wheat + 8/16 labour → 480 qr. wheat

Let us say that the unknown labour-values of iron, coal, and wheat are given by λ_i, λ_c, and λ_w, respectively. Since the units of labour-values are the same as the unit of direct labour, they can be added to each other. Given Marx's proposition that total value of a commodity is determined by the value of the constant capital plus the direct labour time used in its production, we can convert the above description of a system of production to a set of simultaneous equations such as:

$$
\begin{array}{l}
90\lambda_i + 120\lambda_c + 60\lambda_w + 3/16 \text{ labour} = 180\lambda_i \\
50\lambda_i + 125\lambda_c + 150\lambda_w + 5/16 \text{ labour} = 450\lambda_c \\
40\lambda_i + 40\lambda_c + 200\lambda_w + 8/16 \text{ labour} = 480\lambda_w \\
\hline
180\lambda_i + 285\lambda_c + 410\lambda_w + 1 \text{ labour} = 180\lambda_i + 450\lambda_c + 480\lambda_w
\end{array}
\tag{1}
$$

These three equations will solve for values of λ_i, λ_c, and λ_w in terms of labour time along with the value of the net output $(165\lambda_c + 70\lambda_w) = 1$ labour. Now, to understand the nature of Marx's proposition that equal values exchange, let us change the unknowns from labour-values to prices such as p_i, p_c, and p_w. Since the unit of prices is not in terms of labour time, we will have to convert direct labour units to its counterpart in terms of price, which would be its income or wages.

$$90p_i + 120p_c + 60p_w + 3/16(165p_c + 70p_w) = 180p_i$$
$$50p_i + 125p_c + 150p_w + 5/16(165p_c + 70p_w) = 450p_c$$
$$40p_i + 40p_c + 200p_w + 8/16(165p_c + 70p_w) = 480p_w$$
$$\overline{180p_i + 285p_c + 410p_w + 1(165p_c + 70p_w) = 180p_i + 450p_c + 480p_w} \quad (2)$$

The solutions for ps will confirm Marx's proposition that $\lambda_i / \lambda_c = p_i / p_c$, $\lambda_i / \lambda_w = p_i / p_w$, and $\lambda_c / \lambda_w = p_c / p_w$. It should, however, be noted that this result is contingent on the assumption that labourers receive their share of total net income in the same proportion as their share of the expenditure of labour time in the total expenditure of direct labour time in the economy. If that were not so, for example, suppose coal workers received higher income per unit of expenditure of labour, then the ratios of ps will deviate from the ratios of λs, and thus, Marx's proposition will no longer be true. Now, so long as we assume that all the three kinds of labour are unskilled or simple labour of equal intensity, then, as Adam Smith and Ricardo had argued, a rational calculation on the part of iron and wheat workers will make them move from the iron and wheat industries to the coal industry, bringing down coal prices vis-à-vis iron and wheat, and therefore bringing the ratio of ps in conformity with the ratios of λs, and so, the law of value must prevail in the long run. However, let us suppose that the work of a coal miner is more intense than the work of an ironsmith or a farmer. In that case, the coal miner must receive a higher return per unit of labour than the other two workers, otherwise coal mining will disappear in the long run. In this case, whatever differential returns that get established in the society for the coal miners will determine the ratios of ps; and for Marx's proposition to hold, one will have to change the values by counting every unit of the coal miner's labour by as higher a proportion as its share in total income. In other words, *the measure of labour time itself must become contingent on how the income (or the net output) is distributed among the workers—it is the prices that determine values!* Marx admits that in the real world, the differentials in returns to labour have very little to do with the actual expenditure of human energy:

More complex labour counts only as *intensified*, or rather *multiplied* simple labour, so that a smaller quantity of complex labour is considered equal to a larger quantity of simple labour. Experience shows that this reduction is constantly being made. A commodity may be the outcome of most complicated labour, but through its *value* it is posited as equal to the product of simple labour. The various proportions in which different kinds of labour are reduced to simple labour as their unit of measurement are established by a social process that goes on behind the backs of the producers; these proportions therefore appear to the producers to have been handed down by tradition.[9]

The distinction between higher and simple labour, "skilled labour" and "unskilled labour", rests in part on pure illusion or, to say the least, on distinctions that have long since ceased to be real, and survive only by virtue of a traditional conventions[10];

Hence, the measure of labour time and consequently the values of commodities are determined by the conventional differentials in returns to various kinds of labour.

Up till now, we have been assuming that all the net income generated in the economy is appropriated by the labourers themselves as returns to their labour inputs in production and hence the material means of production have not yet become "capital" in Marx's sense. But once we push down the returns to the labourers from 100% of total income to less than 100%, then a surplus income emerges. Till now, we have homogenized heterogeneous labour by taking the income differentials as the multiplication factors for measuring homogeneous labour. In the current context, the same principle translates into measuring direct labour inputs by equating one-to-one their proportion of wage bill to the total wage bill in the economy, with their proportion of direct labour input to the total direct labour input in the economy. Now, the surplus that has emerged needs to be accounted for as "profits on capital." Ricardo had already established that if the indirect-to-direct labour ratios (or in Marx's case, c/v, since $c/(v+s) = (c/v)/(1+s/v)$, given that it is assumed that s/v are equal, the proposition boils down to equality or inequality of c/v) are equal across industries, then a percentage decline in wages across industries would generate equal percentage returns on capital across industries, given the measure of capital on the basis of the old prices, and therefore there will be no

[9] Ibid., 135.
[10] Ibid., 305f19.

rational reason for prices to change; but if the ratio of direct to indirect labour (or c/v) is not equal across industries, which is the general case, then industrial returns to capital will be unequal, given the measure of capital on the basis of the old prices. In Marx's terms, when surplus value emerges, then, on the basis of the old prices, the industrial rate of profits must be given by: $r_j = s_j / \left(c_j + v_j \right) = \left(s_j / v_j \right) / \left(c_j / v_j + 1 \right)$, where "$j$" represents the industry. Since s_j / v_j is assumed to be equal for all industries, unequal c_j / v_j would result in unequal r_j. This, Marx maintained, following Smith and Ricardo, cannot be a stable position in the long run as rational calculation by capitalists would generate movement of capital from low profits industries to high profits industries, forcing prices to readjust by relatively raising the exchange ratios of low profits industries compared to high profits industries. Ricardo had understood that once this happens, then capital can no longer be measured by the old prices, and so he had to give up the project of determining prices and the rate of profits and concentrate on analysing only *changes* in those variables. Marx also poses the problem in desperate terms: "it might seem that we must abandon all hope of understanding these phenomena,"[11] but then goes on to provide a solution for the determination of new set of prices and the equal rate of profits in the system.

Marx's solution to this problem was simple, but unfortunately incorrect. He correctly reckons that if all industries must receive an equal rate of profits, then it must be the average rate of profits of the system. He, however, proposes to derive the average rate of profits from the given labour-value magnitudes by dividing the aggregate surplus value in the system by the aggregate of constant plus variable capitals in the system. In other words, if $\Sigma s_j = S$ and $\Sigma \left(c_j + v_j \right) = \left(C + V \right)$, where $j = 1, \ldots, n$, then Marx's average rate of profits (r) is given by $S / \left(C + V \right)$. After calculating the average rate of profits (r), he applies this rate of profits to mark up the values of each industry's constant plus variable capital by the average rate of profits to derive the "price of production" of each commodity. In other words, the price of production for each commodity is given by: $\left(c_j + v_j \right)\left(1 + r \right) = \left(c_j + v_j \right) \left\{ \left(C + V + S \right) / \left(C + V \right) \right\}$. It is evident from the above equation that $\Sigma \left(c_j + v_j \right)\left(1 + r \right) = C + V + S$ and $\Sigma \left(c_j + v_j \right) r = S$. In other words, total prices of production is equal to total labour-values and

---

[11] Karl Marx, *Capital*, Vol. III (London: Penguin Classics, 1991), 252.

total profits is equal to total surplus values. Marx's contention is that in a competitive capitalist economy, commodities do not exchange in proportion to their labour-values, but rather in proportion to their prices of production. But this in itself does not invalidate the basis of his analysis of capitalism in terms of labour-values and its three main components, since the average rate of profits and the prices of production are derived from value magnitudes and cannot be derived otherwise; and given the results that the sum of the prices of production is proportional to the sum of values, and the sum of profits is proportional to the sum of surplus values, it stands as a proof that the source of profit is surplus value. The competitive mechanism of the capitalist system only succeeds in obscuring this fundamental truth by a reallocation of the total surplus values among the capitalists through the price mechanism; but the nature of the fundamental relation between the capitalists and the workers, analysed on the basis of labour-values of commodities, remains intact at the level of the system as a whole:

> The price of production includes the average profit. And what we call price of production is in fact the same thing that Adam Smith calls 'natural price', Ricardo 'price of production' or 'cost of production', and the Physiocrats 'prix nécessaire', though none of these people explained the difference between price of production and value. We call it the price of production because in the long term it is the condition of supply, the condition for the reproduction of commodities, in each particular sphere of production. We can also understand why those very economists who oppose the determination of commodity value by labour time, by the quantity of labour contained in the commodity, always speak of the prices of production as the centres around which market prices fluctuate. They can allow themselves this because the price of production is already a completely externalized and *prima facie* irrational form of commodity value, a form that appears in competition and is therefore present in the consciousness of the vulgar capitalist and consequently also in that of the vulgar economist.[12]

This clearly does not solve the problem, however. Since the ratios of prices of production are not equal to the ratios of labour-values any more, the measure of capital on the basis of their labour-values becomes illegitimate, and hence Marx's determination of the average rate of profits of the

---

[12] Ibid., 300.

system is not the correct average. In other words, Ricardo's problem remains unsolved. We still do not have the determination of either prices or the average rate of profits. Marx apparently was well aware of it as he goes on to admit:

> The development given above also involves a modification in the determination of a commodity's cost price. It was originally assumed that the cost price of a commodity equaled the *value* of the commodities consumed in its production. But for the buyer of a commodity, it is the price of production that constitutes its cost price and can thus enter into forming the price of another commodity. As the price of production of a commodity can diverge from its value, so the cost price of a commodity, in which the price of production of other commodities are involved, can also stand above or below the portion of its total value that is formed by the value of the means of production going into it. *It is necessary to bear in mind this modified significance of the cost price, and therefore to bear in mind too that if the cost price of a commodity is equated with the value of the means of production used up in producing it, it is always possible to go wrong.*[13]

It is curious that even though Marx rejected the classical idea of deriving labour as the ultimate factor of production by reducing production to man's direct labour against nature and consistently criticized Adam Smith and Ricardo in his *Theories of Surplus Value* for reducing all capital to only wage advances and forgetting the material means of production in their inquiry of the rate of profits, he nevertheless throughout maintains that commodities are "products of labour." As a matter of fact, Marx from a very early stage had rejected the idea of starting the analysis of production from the imagined primordial relation between man and nature. In his *Economic and Philosophic Manuscripts of 1844*, Marx wrote: "Do not let us go back to a fictitious primordial condition as the political economist does, when he tries to explain. Such a primordial condition explains nothing"[14] and one year later, in *The German Ideology*, Marx and Engels wrote: "The premises from which we begin are not arbitrary ones, not dogmas, but real

---

[13] Ibid., 264; emphasis added.
[14] Karl Marx, *The Economic and Philosophic Manuscripts of 1844* (New York: International Publishers, 1964), 107.

premises from which abstraction can only be made in the imagination. ... These premises can thus be verified in a purely empirical way."[15]

However, by the time we get to the "Introduction" to the *Grundrisse*,[16] which was written in 1857, Marx appears to question the idea of the beginning of analysis from empirical givens. Here, Marx seems to suggest that beginning with a concrete empirical reality may be a false beginning. He argues that a quick reflection on such concrete reality as "population" makes it clear that it is a chaotic whole unless it is understood in terms of more abstract categories such as classes, which in turn rest on further abstract categories such as capital and wage labour and so on. Thus, starting from the most abstract categories and building up to the understanding of concrete reality is "obviously the scientifically correct method." Marx further argues that the theoretical construct of building up from most simple or abstract categories to the concrete empirical whole does not represent some sort of real historical unfolding, as Hegel thought. On the contrary, it is the state of development of the current stage of society in which the theoretician finds himself embedded is what determines his ability for abstraction—the more complex and advanced a society is, the more clearly it can see the abstractions. Hence, Adam Smith and Ricardo, who were situated in late eighteenth- and early nineteenth-century Scotland and England, could see labour as such as an abstract category because the society in which they were embedded had become highly manufacturing oriented, with extensive division of labour and free movements of workers from one branch of production to another. Whereas, the Mercantilists' and Physiocrats' visions were constrained by the predominance of one kind of specific labour such as commercial or agricultural, which did not allow them to see the abstract aspect of labour in general.

Though the "Introduction" was drafted to be the Introduction of *A Contribution to the Critique of Political Economy* published in 1859, Marx decided not to include it in the publication since he thought it "anticipated the results which still had to be substantiated" and replaced it with a relatively brief "Preface." In the Preface, on the question of the beginning, he simply states that "the reader who really wishes to follow

---

[15] Karl Marx and Frederick Engels, *The German Ideology* (New York: International Publishers, 1991), 42.

[16] Karl Marx, *Grundrisse* (Middlesex: Pelican Books, 1973).

me will have to decide to advance from the particular to the general."[17] Instead of any elaboration on the question of "scientific method" and of "beginning" of analysis, we find in this brief Preface a general statement of historical materialism, which he presents as "the guiding principles of his studies":

> In the social production of their existence, men inevitably enter into definite relations, which are independent of their will, namely relations of production appropriate to a given stage in the development of their material forces of production. The totality of these relations of production constitutes the economic structure of society, the real foundation, on which arises a legal and political structure and to which correspond definite forms of social consciousness. The mode of production of material life conditions the general process of social, political and intellectual life. It is not the consciousness of men that determines their existence, but their social existence that determines their consciousness.[18]

Here, we find that the object of analysis is no longer characterized as "concrete whole" such as "population," "nation state," and so on, but rather a mode of production, a theoretical construct of a stage in human history, the foundations of which are determined by how men relate to each other through their labour. Thus, the subject matter of economic analysis is defined by *human labour*—it is the ensemble of human relations in the act of production of their material conditions of existence. We find a continuation of this theme in *Capital* published in 1867. In fact, *Capital* was supposed to be in "continuation" of *A Critique* and the first chapter of the first edition of *Capital* was supposed to be a summary of it. In the "Preface" to the first edition of *Capital*, Marx proclaims that "What I have to examine in this work is the capitalist mode of production, and the relations of production and forms of intercourse [*Verkehrsverhältnisse*] that correspond to it."[19]

It appears that Marx's notion of "human labour" as the "substance" of value is based on the idea of a mode of production as an ensemble of human relations mediated through *human labour*—the play is all about human labour—this is Marx's fundamental metaphysics. In capitalism,

---

[17] Karl Marx, *A Contribution to the Critique of Political Economy* (New York: International Publishers, 1970), 19.

[18] Ibid., 20–1.

[19] Marx, *Capital*, Vol. I, 90.

humans relate to each other through their labour at two levels. First of all, there is extensive division of human labour in society, which is regulated through the market mechanism of commodity exchange—it is the impersonal market that regulates the social division of labour. Thus, underneath the relations of commodities lies the proportion of total labour allocated to the production of various commodities. The other relation of production of a capitalist economy is that the labourers do not appropriate their products but sell their capacity to work as a commodity to the capitalist for a wage (or a bundle of commodities). This again is regulated by the market and is represented by the proportion of total labour allocated to producing the total wage basket. Now, if the total labour allocated to producing the total wage basket is less than one, then the rest of the total labour must be allocated to producing commodities that are appropriated by the non-working class—in this case, the capitalists. This must also be represented by the proportion to total labour allocated to producing the commodities appropriated by the capitalists—this proportion of the total labour is surplus value, which is appropriated by the capitalists as profits. The source of the surplus value, however, can only be explained when we "leave this noisy sphere [market for commodity exchange], where everything takes place on the surface and in full view of everyone, and follow them [the capitalist and the worker] into the hidden abode of production, on whose threshold there hangs the notice 'No admittance except on business'."[20]

The conflict between Marx's *metaphysics* and *physics* of production explains the discrepancy between Marx's reasoning and his mathematics. From a purely scientific point of view, the *human contribution* to production is nothing but a contribution of mechanical energy, which in essence, is no different from animal's energy or even energy contributed by machines in the process of production. As horses or bullocks could be replaced by tractors in agriculture, humans can also be replaced by mechanical machines and robots once they become cheaper to employ than humans. This does not mean that such technical changes must lead to a fall in the surplus production—if that was the case, then such labour-replacing techniques will not be introduced in the first place. This brings us to inquire into the nature of surplus. According to the first law of thermodynamics, the total energy in the universe is constant; thus, no surplus can be produced in the universe as a whole. However, if we restrict a domain within the universe and create an "inside" and "outside," then a

---

[20] Ibid., 279–80.

surplus can be produced in the "inside" domain by taking energy from outside. One can think of economic production as conversion of "outside" energy of nature, which is freely available, and thus, has no economic value, to a form of energy that has economic value—this was fundamentally the approach the Physiocrats took in defining surplus output. Thus, surplus production in the field of economics is simply an aspect of the technique of production—all that is needed for surplus to be produced is that the total economic values of all the inputs used up should turn out to be less than total economic value of all the outputs produced—that is why wine maturing in the cellar or crops growing in the fields add to the surplus. Marx's idea that only human labour adds economic value in the process of production unwittingly harks back to the classical notion of labour being the ultimate cause of value.

III. SRAFFA: FROM MARX'S METAPHYSICS OF HUMAN LABOUR TO PHYSICS OF PRODUCTION

Sraffa[21] stays clear from all the humanist moorings of classical economics and Marx. The revolution of the 1870s that swept economics had rejected the classical idea that labour is the ultimate cause of value. Instead, they argued that the ultimate cause of value is scarcity, which is fundamentally a subjective condition of the intensity of our desire for something in relation to its availability. If something is not freely available in the amount that will satiate us, then we are willing to pay a price for it, which can be a sacrifice of our comfort or sacrifice of anything that we possess which has positive utility for us—there is nothing special about loss of comfort or leisure (i.e., labour) as a sacrifice for acquiring something of value. In this context, forgoing consumption is no different from forgoing comfort or leisure, and therefore, if forgoing comfort or leisure (i.e., labour) must receive a return for it (i.e., wages), then forgoing consumption, which is how capital investment can be interpreted, must also receive a return as profits. Now the question is, how do we measure the sacrifice of consumption? Let us suppose a farmer "A" sacrifices one quintal of consumption of wheat just harvested and uses it as seed for production of wheat in the next harvest cycle and another farmer "B" sacrifices one quintal of wheat to use as seed for production of wheat, and then another harvest cycle to turn it

---

[21] Piero Sraffa, *Production of Commodities by Means of Commodities* (Cambridge: Cambridge University Press, 1960).

into bread. Should the two farmers receive the same return on their equal sacrifice of consumption of one quintal of wheat? The answer is no; because farmer "B" has sacrificed one quintal of wheat for two time periods whereas farmer "A" has done it only for one. Therefore, farmer "B" must receive a higher profit. What we have noticed here is that the notion of sacrifice of consumption has a time dimension as the notion of labour. This gave rise to the idea that capital could also be measured in the time dimension as "time of waiting" by going back and back in the production cycle of any commodity till we hit upon the primordial state. This was the approach taken up by Jevons,[22] Menger,[23] Böhm-Bawerk,[24] and Wicksell[25] and had become highly influential in the profession as the alternative to the classical (and Marx's) explanation of profits in terms of some kind of deduction from what legitimately belonged to the workers. In the late 1920s, Sraffa had set himself a task of demolishing the theories that rooted economic calculations or the cause of prices and profits in human subjectivity or human psychology. But the successful destruction of it would also amount to the destruction of the old labour theory of value as they are the two sides of the same coin.

Sraffa soon realized that in a commodity producing society where means of production are produced by separate industries and bought and sold by each other in the manner as any final or consumption goods are, then it is impossible to trace back production of any commodity to its primordial state—production of commodities is always by means of commodities. No matter how far back we go in the chain of production, some *commodity residue* will always remain—the road to the primordial stage is theoretically blocked forever. Though it is true that by going back and back in the production chain one can always reduce the commodity residue to negligible proportion, and thus ignore it in the calculation of a long chain of labouring activity, it so happens that at what stage the commodity residue becomes negligible depends upon the rate of wages—if wages are relatively high, then the commodity residue will become negligible more quickly than when wages are comparatively low; and if wages are zero, then the commodity residue will never become negligible. This

---

[22] W.S. Jevons, *The Theory of Political Economy* (New York: Kelly & Millman, Inc., 1957).

[23] Carl Menger, *Principles of Economics* (Auburn: Ludwig von Mises Institute, 2007).

[24] Eugen von Böhm-Bawerk, *Capital and Interest*, Vols. 1–3 (Illinois: Liberation Press, 1959).

[25] Knut Wicksell, *Lectures on Political Economy, Vol. I: General Theory* (London: George Routledge and Sons, Ltd., 1934).

reveals a fundamental mistake in understanding the relationship between wages and profits when we root our theory of production in the idea of primordial relation of man to nature—if we could reduce the production chain to the primordial stage, then we could reduce all capital investment to a long series of only wage advances, and in this case, if wages go to zero, then the rate of profits must become infinity; however, if there must remain a commodity residue, no matter how far back we go in the production chain, then when wages go to zero, the rate of profits must reach a finite maximum. This theoretical insight had a momentous implication for Sraffa's theory—later, Sraffa credited Marx for this insight:

> The notion of a Maximum rate of profits corresponding to a zero wage has been suggested by Marx, directly through an incidental allusion to the possibility of a fall in the rate of profits 'even if the workers could live on air'; but more generally owing to his emphatic rejection of the claim of Adam Smith and others after him that the price of every commodity 'either immediately or ultimately' resolves itself entirely (that is, to say, without leaving any commodity residue) into wage, profit and rent—a claim which necessarily presupposed the existence of 'ultimate' commodities produced by pure labour without means of production except land, and which therefore was incompatible with a fixed limit to the rise in the rate of profits.[26]

The fact that there always remains a commodity residue rules out the possibility of conceptualizing industries as independent silos which produce all their means of production themselves and only exchange their final commodities or consumption goods. Once the idea of independence of industries is rejected, we realize that social production relies on a complex web of interconnected industries that produce at least one good that goes directly or indirectly into the production of all goods. An interconnected web of all such "basic goods" form a social system of production, where removal of one such industry would amount to complete cessation of the whole economy. It is in this context that we can understand why the industries get structurally constrained such that its productivity or the maximum rate of profits of the system becomes a physical property of the system of production.

Sraffa's theoretical story begins with a subsistence system, which is similar to Adam Smith's "early and rude state of society" or Marx's "simple commodity production." The characteristic of this system is that it pro-

---

[26] Piero Sraffa, *Production of Commodities by Means of Commodities* (Cambridge: Cambridge University Press, 1960), 94.

duces outputs exactly equal to what it uses as inputs—there is no net output production in the sense that all the income received by the labourers appear as necessary consumption similar to feed for the horses. So, suppose such a system is given by:

90 t. iron + 120 t. coal + 60 qr. wheat → 180 t. iron
50 t. iron + 125 t. coal + 150 qr. wheat → 285 t. coal
40 t. iron + 40 t. coal + 200 qr. wheat → 410 qr. wheat
_____
180 t. iron + 285 t. coal + 410 qr. wheat → 180 t. iron + 285 t. coal + 410 qr. wheat

In price terms, this system can be represented by:

$$90p_i + 120p_c + 60p_w = 180p_i$$
$$50p_i + 125p_c + 150p_w = 285p_c$$
$$40p_i + 40p_c + 200p_w = 410p_w$$
$$\overline{180p_i + 285p_c + 410p_w = 180p_i + 285p_c + 410p_w} \qquad (3)$$

The condition of "subsistence" that the aggregate of all inputs must be equal to outputs reduces this system of equations to only two independent equations, and thus, given any commodity as the measuring standard, say $p_w = 1$, we can uniquely determine the values of p_i and p_c. Thus, the exchange ratios that will ensure the historical viability of this system is uniquely and completely determined by the objective input-output data—no more information from outside is needed. Now, let us suppose this system becomes more productive and it produces more output than what it uses as inputs, such as:

$$90p_i + 120p_c + 60p_w \rightarrow 180p_i$$
$$50p_i + 125p_c + 150p_w \rightarrow 450p_c$$
$$40p_i + 40p_c + 200p_w \rightarrow 480p_w$$
$$\overline{180p_i + 285p_c + 410p_w \rightarrow 180p_i + 450p_c + 480p_w} \qquad (4)$$

Now the constraint of the aggregate equation of the subsistence system no longer holds, and therefore, technically we do not have an equation system any more. We have three independent inequalities with only two unknowns—the excess values of outputs must somehow be accounted for on the left hand side to turn it into a system of equations again. In this case, we do not know what exact ratio in which the three commodities must exchange, there can be several exchange ratios that can allow for this system to get back its original means of production to reproduce itself. It was at this stage that classical economists and Marx thought that they needed extra information from outside the equations and introduced the idea of market mechanics and rational behaviour on the part of the agents, which leads to adjustment of supplies with demands in such a way that the system comes to rest when each unit of capital receives equal returns. Thus, on the basis of this extra information, one can introduce one more unknown in the system as the rate of profits such that:

$$
\begin{aligned}
(90p_i + 120p_c + 60p_w)(1+r) &= 180p_i \\
(50p_i + 125p_c + 150p_w)(1+r) &= 450p_c \\
(40p_i + 40p_c + 200p_w)(1+r) &= 480p_w \\
\hline
(180p_i + 285p_c + 410p_w)(1+r) &= 180p_i + 450p_c + 480p_w
\end{aligned} \tag{5}
$$

Now we can solve for the relative prices and the rate of profits simultaneously.

Sraffa rejects this approach.[27] The assumption of rational behaviour by the agents turns the system into a mechanism where supplies adjust to demands to bring about equal returns to factors and this requires knowledge of how changes in inputs relate to changes in outputs for every industry on the side of supply and consumers' subjectivities on the side of demand. Sraffa was of the opinion that the analyst does not have access to such data. He argues that instead of making any assumption about human behaviour and the technique of production, one may stick to the data available after the "harvest" without asking the question: why people did what they did or how people will behave if the system is not in "equilibrium" of demand and supply? He succeeded in showing that there is enough information in this system of equations to not only determine the unique set of prices and the rate of profits, but also to establish, what he considered, the fundamental propositions of classical economics and Marx that can stand as an alternative to the economics rooted in human subjectivity.

Let us rewrite the equation system (5) without assuming that rate of profits across industries are equal:

---

[27] For a detailed analysis of my reinterpretation of Sraffa, see Ajit Sinha, *A Revolution in Economic Theory: The Economics of Piero Sraffa* (Cham: Palgrave Macmillan, 2016).

$$\left(90p_i + 120p_c + 60p_w\right)\left(1 + r_i\right) = 180p_i$$
$$\left(50p_i + 125p_c + 150p_w\right)\left(1 + r_c\right) = 450p_c$$
$$\left(40p_i + 40p_c + 200p_w\right)\left(1 + r_w\right) = 480p_w$$
$$\overline{\left(180p_i + 285p_c + 410p_w\right)\left(1 + R\right) = 180p_i + 450p_c + 480p_w} \qquad (6)$$

where r_is represent the industrial rate of profits and R stands for the average rate of profits of the system as a whole. Clearly, the average rate of profits of this system is given by (165 t. coal + 70 qr. wheat)/(180 t. iorn + 285 t. + 410 qr. wheat). This ratio is mathematically undefined because it is a ratio of disproportionate heterogeneous goods. It appears that the average rate of profits cannot be found without the knowledge of prices, which is supposed to homogenize these two collections of heterogeneous goods. We, however, know that multiplying any equation by a constant does not change the information set of the equation system in any way. So, let us multiply the equation for iron industry by 4/3 and the equation for coal industry by 4/5. This turns our equation system (6) to:

$$\left(120p_i + 160p_c + 80p_w\right)\left(1 + r_i\right) = 240p_i$$
$$\left(40p_i + 100p_c + 120p_w\right)\left(1 + r_c\right) = 360p_c$$
$$\left(40p_i + 40p_c + 200p_c\right)\left(1 + r_w\right) = 480p_w$$
$$\overline{\left(200p_i + 300p_c + 400p_w\right)\left(1 + R*\right) = 240p_i + 360p_c + 480p_w} \qquad (6')$$

Sraffa called this system of equations the Standard system, and proved that there always exists one and only one set of multipliers (such as 4/3, 4/5, 1) that will convert any given system of equations to its Standard counterpart. Now the average rate of profits of the Standard system, that is, $R*$, can be found out without the knowledge of prices. The ratio $\left(40 \text{ iron} + 60 \text{ coal} + 80 \text{ wheat}\right) / \left(200 \text{ iron} + 300 \text{ coal} + 400 \text{ wheat}\right)$ must always be equal to 1/5 or 20% no matter what prices happen to be, as this ratio is a collection of heterogeneous goods collected in the same proportion. Since the systems of Eqs. (6) and (6′) are mathematically equivalent as (6′) is only a rescaled system of (6), their mathematical properties must remain the same. Therefore, the systemic average rate of profits of the system derived from (6′) must also apply to the equation system (6), that is, $R = R*$. Now, if the industrial rate of profits are not equal, then some will be greater than the average and some will be smaller than the average. Let us call $r_i = (R + e_i)$, $r_c = (R + e_c)$ and $r_w = (R + e_w)$. Thus we can write our equation system (6) as:

$$
\begin{aligned}
(90p_i + 120p_c + 60p_w)(1 + R + e_i) &= 180p_i \\
(50p_i + 125p_c + 150p_w)(1 + R + e_c) &= 450p_c \\
(40p_i + 40p_c + 200p_w)(1 + R + e_w) &= 480p_w \\
\hline
(180p_i + 285p_c + 410p_w)(1 + R) &= 180p_i + 450p_c + 480p_w
\end{aligned}
\tag{7}
$$

By definition,
$$
\left\{ \begin{aligned}
&(90p_i + 120p_c + 60p_w)e_i + (50p_i + 125p_c + 150p_w)e_c \\
&+ (40p_i + 40p_c + 200p_w)e_w
\end{aligned} \right\} = 0.
$$

Without loss of generality, let us assume that $e_i > 0$ and e_c and $e_w < 0$. Now, again rescale the equation system back to its Standard counterpart by multiplying iron-equation by $4/3$ and coal-equation by $4/5$. We obtain:

$$
\begin{aligned}
(120p_i + 160p_c + 80p_w)(1 + R + e_i) &= 240p_i \\
(40p_i + 100p_c + 120p_w)(1 + R + e_c) &= 360p_c \\
(40p_i + 40p_c + 200p_w)(1 + R + e_w) &= 480p_w \\
\hline
(200p_i + 300p_c + 400p_w)(1 + R') &= 240p_i + 360p_c + 480p_w
\end{aligned}
\tag{7'}
$$

We should expect the average rate of profits of equation system (7'), that is, R', to be greater than R simply because we have increased the total weight of the iron industry in the system, which has a higher rate of profits than the average R. However, from inspection, we can see that $R' = R* = 20\%$. And since we have already established that $R* = R$, it follows that all the es must be equal to zero. In other words, all the industrial rates of profit must be equal and equal to $R*$, that is, $r_i = r_c = r_w = R = R*$. Now we can plug the value of $r_i = r_c = r_w = R = R* = 20\%$ into equation system (6) and solve for prices. Thus we do not need the market mechanics and rational human behaviour to solve for prices in this case either—the required information to solve for the equation system could be found out by rearranging the data. In other words, the condition of a uniform industrial rate of profits is a structural property of the equation system.

Now let us introduce labour in the system explicitly and draw out a complete structural relation of any given system of production. We go back to Sraffa's original example of a three-commodity economy:

90 t. iron + 120 t. coal + 60 qr. wheat + 3/16 labour → 180 t. iron

50 t. iron + 125 t. coal + 150 qr. wheat + 5/16 labour → 450 t. coal

40 t. iron + 40 t. coal + 200 qr. wheat + 8/16 labour → 480 qr. wheat

This can be represented in price terms as:

$$
\begin{aligned}
(90p_i + 120p_c + 60p_w)(1+r) + 3/16 \ w &= 180p_i \\
(50p_i + 125p_c + 150p_w)(1+r) + 5/16 \ w &= 450p_c \\
(40p_i + 40p_c + 200p_w)(1+r) + 8/16 \ w &= 480p_w \\
\hline
(180p_i + 285p_c + 410p_w)(1+r) + w &= 180p_i + 450p_c + 480p_w
\end{aligned} \tag{8}
$$

Converting it to its Standard counterpart, we get:

$$
\begin{aligned}
(120p_i + 160p_c + 80p_w)(1+r) + 4/16 \ w &= 240p_i \\
(40p_i + 100p_c + 120p_w)(1+r) + 4/16 \ w &= 360p_c \\
(40p_i + 40p_c + 200p_w)(1+r) + 8/16 \ w &= 480p_w \\
\hline
(200p_i + 300p_c + 400p_w)(1+r) + w &= 240p_i + 360p_c + 480p_w
\end{aligned} \tag{8'}
$$

Now, let us normalize our Standard net output to one, that is, put $(40p_i + 60p_c + 80p_w) = 1$, and call it the Standard commodity, which is our money-commodity. If wages are given in terms of this money-commodity, that is, as a proportion of the Standard net output, then we can derive the average rate of profits of this system for all the values of wages starting from zero to its maximum value $(40p_i + 60p_c + 80p_w)$, because the ratio of total profits to total capital remains in the Standard proportion and therefore can be determined without the knowledge of prices. This gives us a relationship between wages and profits, which is given by: $r = R*(1-w)$, where w is given in terms of the Standard net output and $R*$, which we have already derived from equation system (6'), is the maximum rate of profits of the system—it is the ratio of net output to total capital or the productivity of the system. This relationship between the productivity of the system and the rate of profits and wages is derived on the basis of the objective data without any knowledge of prices. Thus it is the fundamental structural property of the equation system. Since the Standard system is only a rescaled system of the actual system of observation, they are

algebraically equivalent systems, and therefore, the mathematical properties of the two systems must be identical too. In other words, the relationship $r = R*(1-w)$ must also hold for the observed system, if the wages
and prices in the observed system are measured by the Standard commodity as the chosen money-commodity. What we directly observe in the
Standard system in terms of physical data must show up to be true in the
empirical system in terms of its calculations in prices:

> Such a relation is of interest only if it can be shown that its application is not
> limited to the imaginary Standard system but is capable of being extended
> to the actual economic system of observation. ... But the actual system con-
> sists of the same basic equations as the Standard system, only in different
> proportions; so that, once the wage is given, the rate of profits is determined
> for both systems regardless of the proportions of the equations in either of
> them. Particular proportions, such as the Standard ones, may give transpar-
> ency to a system and render visible what was hidden, but they cannot alter
> its mathematical properties. ... The same rate of profits, which in the
> Standard system is obtained as a ratio between *quantities* of commodities,
> will in the actual system result from the ratio of aggregate *values*.[28]

When we move wages from zero to their maximum value, we find that
as wages and the rate of profits change, the set of prices change too. But
these prices change only to ensure that for every given w, prices adjust in
such a way that the structural property of the equation system,
$r = R*(1-w)$, is satisfied throughout—that is, prices play the role of
accounting for the distribution of income, which is determined independently of prices. Notice that when all the income goes to wages, then the
value of the net Standard output is equal to the value of the net output of
the observed system $\{(40p_i + 60p_c + 80p_w) = (165p_c + 70p_w)\}$, since in this
case the prices would be proportional to labour-values and both the systems use the same technique and one unit of labour to produce their
respective net outputs. For any other rate of wages, the values of observed
net output will not be equal to the value of the Standard net output.
However, the ratios of net output to total capital will remain constant with
respect to changes in prices throughout the variations of wages from zero
to its maximum value, as $R*$ is determined independently of prices.

In some sense, given wages, the average rate of profits determined by
the Standard system gives us the multiplication factor for homogenizing
capital, which appears to us as a heterogeneous collection of commodities.

[28] Ibid., 22–3.

As we have seen above, the procedure of homogenization of labour is dependent on the available objective data—it is simply a processing of proportions of total wage bills paid in various industries as proportions of total undifferentiated labour utilized in those industries. Similarly, homogenization of capital requires us to measure capital in such a way that profits received by capital turn out to be equal for every unit of capital in the system—that is, a return on the value of iron in each industry must be equal to a return on the value of coal and wheat when they are used as capital. This is possible only if returns on values of all commodities used as capital turns out to be equal to the average rate of profits of the system as a whole. The Standard average is the only average that can be distributed equally across the industries.

IV. Some Concluding Remarks

So, in the light of the above analysis, what are the aspects of classical and Marxian economics we must reject and aspects we rehabilitate? It is quite clear that Sraffa establishes that "profit is a non-price phenomenon." This is what Sraffa believed was the central aspect of classical economics and Marx. Adam Smith had clearly stated that wages and the rate of profits are determined in the dynamic context of history, and for any point of time, they are given "norms" and prices are determined by "adding up" the given distributional variables. In other words, it is the distribution of income that determines prices. In a letter to McCulloch, dated 13 June 1820, Ricardo wrote: "After all, the great questions of Rent, Wages, and Profits must be explained by the proportion in which the whole produce is divided between landlords, capitalists, and labourers, and which is not essentially connected with the doctrine of value."[29] In Sraffa's interpretation,[30] Ricardo had started off with the proposition that "it is the profits of the farmer that regulate the profits of all other trades," implying that in agriculture, both inputs and outputs can be treated as a single commodity—"corn." In this case, the rate of profits could be determined in physical terms independently of prices, and thus prices of all other commodities must adjust in such a way that all industries receive the same rate

---

[29] David Ricardo, *Works and Correspondence of David Ricardo*, Vol. VIII (Cambridge: Cambridge University Press, 1952), 194.
[30] Piero Sraffa, "Introduction", In *Works and Correspondence of David Ricardo*, Vol. I (Cambridge: Cambridge University Press, 1951).

of profits. It was the criticism by Malthus, who argued that "in no case of production, is the produce exactly of the same nature as the capital advanced. Consequently, we can never properly refer to a material rate of produce," that led Ricardo to abandon his "corn model" for the determination of the rate of profits and move to a general labour theory of value. Marx's theory of surplus value and his derivation of the rate of profits prior to the derivation of prices of production was also designed to show that profit is a non-price phenomenon. Sraffa's method of deriving the system's average rate of profits independently of prices, and then applying them to production equations to derive the prices follows Marx's procedure almost step by step, except that instead of deriving the production equations in terms of labour-values from the empirical input-output data, Sraffa derives the equations of his Standard system from the same input-output data. As Sraffa explains:

> There are besides, many possible applications {of the Standard commodity}, which I have not mentioned in the book, in problems discussed by Marx. Take, e.g. the determination of a general rate of profits, from the rate of surplus value: Marx takes an average of the rates of profits obtained in the production of the different commodities on the basis of 'values', and gets, as he acknowledges, an *approximately* correct result. An exact result could however be obtained by taking, instead of a simple average, a weighted average: & it can be shown that the appropriate weights can be derived directly from the proportions in which the comm{odities} enter the 'St{andard} com{modity}'.[31]

However, with the rejection of humanism of any kind, Sraffa removes the specificity of both the *human labour* and *rational human behaviour* from the centre of economic analysis. The importance of commodity residue as a central structural aspect of the economy clearly shows that the idea of reducing production to the primordial relation of man's *direct* action against nature must be rejected. This implies that neither labour is the ultimate cause of value nor productive technique can be reduced to a quantitative measure in terms of labour time alone. Marx's claim that only labour adds value to the commodity in the process of production is based on the notion that in the final analysis, labour is the only productive factor, which can only be established if commodity residue could be reduced to zero. For example, our equation system (6) solves for a finite positive rate

---

[31] Piero Sraffa, *Sraffa Papers* (Cambridge: Wren Library), D3/12/111: 132, letter to Eaton dated 12 February 1961.

of profits and positive prices and is compatible with either wages put equal to zero or labour input put equal to zero. The classical approach would suggest that when wages are put to zero, the rate of profits must become infinite and Marx's approach would suggest that when labour input is put to zero, then the rate of profits must become zero. Clearly, both these approaches are incorrect. Hence, the idea that the source of profits is surplus value or exploitation of labour must be abandoned.

So, how to understand class struggle?[32] In Marx's context, class struggle is understood to be the progenitor of surplus product—the struggle over the length of the working day between the workers and the capitalists, given a wage basket, is the source of the surplus and this happens prior to the activity of production. To understand the nature of the difference between Sraffa's notion of surplus and Marx's, we need to clarify some technical issues first. In classical economics as well as Marx, wages are treated as a part of capital, an amount of money advanced to the workers prior to production. In Sraffa's equations, wages are not a part of capital advanced by the capitalists, but are rather a share in in the total net output, which is appropriated on the basis of the quantity of labour provided by the workers in a similar way as profits are a share of net output appropriated by the capitalists on the basis of the quantity of capital provided by the capitalists—class struggle plays out directly or indirectly in determining the rates of profits and wages, but the question of the length of the working day remains unproblematized. Thus, in Sraffa's framework, if we reduce the size of the economy by half, which would also reduce the labour time worked by the workers by half, it will not make any difference to the solution of the system of equations. However, in Marx's context, since the wage basket per worker is already determined as the value of the labour-power, reduction in the labour time worked by the workers would amount to a rise in wages per hour of labour, which must lead to a fall in the rate of profits and changes in prices of production. So, from Marx's perspective, if we keep reducing the size of the economy, then we will hit upon a stage where all the net output is just equal

---

[32] This section is inspired by a comment to an earlier draft of this chapter by Professor Geoffrey Harcourt, who wrote: "I have now read your essay on Marx's Labour theory of value.... I think it is a very clear statement of your arguments. I agree with all except your last conclusion. I think the LTV is a qualitative argument in terms of unequal power between the classes which explains the origin of profits in the sphere of production, prior to their realisation (or not) in the sphere of distribution and exchange. I still find that this illuminates understanding of the essential nature of capitalist dynamics." See GCH with Prue Kerr, "Marx, Karl Heinrich (1818–83)," in *International Encyclopedia of Business and Management*, ed. Malcolm Warner (London: Routledge, 1996), 3388–95.

to the wage advances, which is compatible only with zero rate of profits. This, in Sraffa's context, translates into wage per hour of labour rising to absorb the whole of net output, and therefore is compatible only with zero rate of profits and labour-value price ratios. If we treat these wages as parts of necessary inputs in the production equations as fuel for the machines or feed for the horses, then we get back our subsistence economy.

Does this contradict our definition of economic production as conversion of free energy from nature to a form of energy that has economic value? The answer is: no. If labourers, or for that matter, even animals, are used in the production process, then one can calculate the energy consumed by the labourers and the energy contributed by the labourers in the production process. If the two energies are equal, then there must be surplus production in the system. Now, think of reducing the contribution of the energy from the labourers to the production process such that the total energy used in the production (including the free energy from nature) becomes equal to the total energy consumed in the production process, including the total consumption by the labourers. This will give us the subsistence economy. Marx's argument appears to be that the surplus production from here on can only consist of getting more energy out of the labourer in the production process, and this is made possible only because capitalists wield power over workers, which shows itself on the factory floor. But surplus could also be produced by making the production process more efficient in the sense that it is able to convert more naturally available free energy to economic goods without increasing the human labour input. From this perspective, the labourer can be made redundant and the surplus could be explained simply by the technique of production. These are the two fundamental nodes on which the whole of "surplus" discourse rests on. Thus the class struggle that Marx talks about is real in the sense that stretching the labour time beyond a point, given subsistence wages, does contribute to surplus production, but it is not the only means by which a surplus can be produced. Efficiency gains on the use of any input of production, for example, if a machine could contribute the same energy to production by consuming less fuel or if it reduces waste of raw materials, and so on, would also contribute to surplus production. This explains why within capitalism, there is a tendency to stretch the working day as long as possible on one hand and, on the other, also replace labour by machines once machines become cheaper or more efficient to employ.

Acknowledgements I take this opportunity to thank Professors Amit Bhaduri, Meghnad Desai, and Geoffrey Harcourt for their comments on an earlier draft of this chapter—the usual caveat applies.

BIBLIOGRAPHY

Böhm-Bawerk, Eugen von. *Capital and Interest.* 3 vols. Translated by George D. Huncke and Hans F. Sennholz. Illinois: Liberation Press, 1959.

Harcourt, G. C. and Prue Kerr. "Marx, Karl Heinrich (1818–83)." In *International Encyclopedia of Business and Management,* edited by Malcolm Warner, 3388–95. London: Routledge, 1996.

Jevons, W. S. *The Theory of Political Economy.* New York: Kelly & Millman, Inc, 1957.

Marx, Karl. *The Economic and Philosophic Manuscripts of 1844.* New York: International Publishers, 1964.

Marx, Karl. *Theories of Surplus Value, Part II.* Moscow: Progress Press, 1968.

Marx, Karl. *A Contribution to the Critique of Political Economy.* New York: International Publishers, 1970.

Marx, Karl. *Grundrisse.* Middlesex: Pelican Books, 1973.

Marx, Karl. *Capital.* Vol. I. New York: Vintage, 1977.

Marx, Karl. *Capital.* Vol. III. London: Penguin Classics, 1991.

Marx, Karl. *Capital.* Vol. II. London: Penguin Classics, 1992.

Marx, Karl and F. Engels. *The German Ideology.* New York: International Publishers, 1991.

Menger, Carl. *Principles of Economics.* Translated by J. Dingwall and B. F. Hoselitz. Auburn: Ludwig von Mises Institute, 2007.

Ricardo, David. *Principles of Political Economy and Taxation,* Cambridge: Cambridge University Press, 1951.

Ricardo, David. *Works and Correspondence of David Ricardo.* Vol. VIII. Edited by Piero Sraffa. Cambridge: Cambridge University Press, 1952.

Sinha, Ajit. *A Revolution in Economic Theory: The Economics of Piero Sraffa.* Cham: Palgrave Macmillan, 2016.

Sinha, Ajit. *Theories of Value from Adam Smith to Piero Sraffa.* 2nd ed. London: Routledge, 2018.

Sinha, Ajit. *Essays on Theories of Value in the Classical Tradition.* Cham: Palgrave Macmillan, 2019.

Smith, Adam. *An Inquiry into the Nature and Causes of the Wealth of Nations.* Vol. 1. Indianapolis: Library Fund, 1981.

Sraffa, Piero. "Introduction." In *Works and Correspondence of David Ricardo.* Vol. I. Cambridge: Cambridge University Press, 1951.

Sraffa, Piero. *Production of Commodities by Means of Commodities.* Cambridge: Cambridge University Press, 1960.

Sraffa, Piero. *Sraffa Papers.* Cambridge: Wren Library, Trinity College, n.d.

Wicksell, Knut. *Lectures on Political Economy.* Vol. I. London: George Routledge and Sons, Ltd., 1934.

Marx's Prescient Theory of Centralization of Capital: Crises and an Nkrumahist Response

Cynthia Lucas Hewitt

I. Introduction

This is a study of the dynamic of centralization of capital identified by Marx, and its applicability to the capitalist world-system of today. Marx theorized that the centralization of capital into the hands of ever fewer capitalists, completing the processes of accumulation and concentration, will lead eventually to the unemployment of the masses of the people and a crisis breakdown of the system of capitalism. This study asks the question— is there evidence that the abstract structure of processes underlying the system of capital, which Marx illuminated, is true and valid? Is it that his omissions on the side of social analysis are few, explainable, and, although maybe immense, do not invalidate the quality of his analysis of capital, and its import to the future of political and economic change in the "modern European world-system" of capitalism? This expression, drawn from the seminal work of Immanuel Wallerstein[1] (although the focus on the world-

---

[1] Immanuel Wallerstein, *The Modern World-System I: Capitalist Agriculture and the Origins of the European World-Economy in the Sixteenth Century* (Cambridge: Academic Press, 1976).

C. L. Hewitt (✉)
Faculty of the Sustainability Minor and the African American Studies Program, Morehouse College, Atlanta, GA, USA

319

S. Gupta et al. (eds.), *Karl Marx's Life, Ideas, and Influences*, Marx, Engels, and Marxisms, https://doi.org/10.1007/978-3-030-24815-4_15

system as a whole was pioneered by erudite African American sociologist Oliver C. Cox[2] as early as 1959) is perhaps the best designation of what Marx analysed. We are subsequently correctly encouraged not only to see the European world-system, but to recognize that there are positions outside looking in, as well as the possibility of seeing beyond it, to past mini-world systems and, hopefully, to a coming new "post-modern" world.

Marx analysed capitalism as a "progressive" system of social relationships with the potential for organizing ever more natural forces into production, and that once set into motion, must be continuous and expanding due to its nature, and thus would come to spread its tendrils and enact its "destructive/productive" relations everywhere around the globe. However, he also argued that the sheer force of the productivity which would develop would outstrip its social relationships that make possible the distribution and consumption of the output, leading to the collapse of the market system from not being able to sell everything, and eventual, and inevitable, revolutionary emergence of new relationships.[3] It is a system with fatal internal contradictions. A key driver in this is the centralization of capital—the progressive development of control over the accumulation of wealth of everyone and in everything, by a diminishing number of capitalists as competition leads to size efficiencies in big factories driving smaller capitals out of the market and taking control of their markets and production opportunities. Theoretically, once all people are in a relationship where they are either workers dependent for consumption on wages, or owners, the options for the owners to expand their sales will become much more limited, as the major source of expansion is new markets and dependencies of all kinds. How close have we come to reaching this "end-game"? How close are we to full incorporation of every area and every people into the capitalist world-system scenario of Marx's analysis?

---

[2] Oliver C. Cox, *The Foundations of Capitalism* (New York: Philosophical Library, 1959).

[3] Doubtless, the largest omission of Marx was the consideration of the final *coup de grace*, the environmental limits to endless production expansion, based on the degradation and exhaustion of resources. Of course, as stated by Herman Daly, *Beyond Growth, The Economics of Sustainable Development* (Boston: Beacon Press, 1997), the earth was "relatively" empty at that time, and neither use of materials or disposal of waste was understood widely to create irreparable destruction as it is understood today. Marx's conception of the degradation of human life through expanding production comes closest to this awareness. The environmental and population limits seen today over-determine the crisis potential of the system today.

Contemporary data on the presence of "access points" of various kinds where individuals and businesses are connected to banking and finance, that is, global capital, are presented as evidence of the expansion of centralization. The presence of these access points is argued to be reflective of the incorporation of peoples into the capitalist system (or proletarianization of them). The Financial Accessibility Survey (FAS) of the International Monetary Fund (IMF) reports access levels in core countries and "developing" countries. We look at the extent to which it could be argued that all people have come into a relationship with capital by comparing the density of engagement with the money systems. To what extent is there evidence that the majority, or a substantial segment of the population meets their consumption needs through engagement with finance institutions capable of centralizing money? Based on the reported level of financial access found in fully proletarianized nations, we compare the degree to which people outside of the Eurocentric core are also incorporated, that is, have come to rely on monetized lifestyles. Theoretically, it can be argued that only at the point where centralization of capital has reached a slowdown to global completion is it fully possible to see if Marx was wrong or right about what will occur next.

To the extent that any result of labour, any value, is deposited within the financial system, the maximum expansion will be enabled, and to the extent that some values are not deposited in the system—whether due to ownership under other principles, such as socialism, or an indigenous collective society, or the value is simply stored in one's mattress, the capitalist system has a reservoir which it could tap. Once it arrives on the border, it experiences any resistance as a blockage to be overcome in all the ways at its disposal: first, the destruction of communal land social structures and "freeing" the people from any ownership and any control. This process has also incorporated a cultural element of racism, which is used to legitimate the transfer of rights over land and resource, and denial of rights to justice as workers, to African and other Southern peoples. It is argued here that the completion of incorporation can now be vaguely glimpsed like a light at the end of a tunnel.[4] We are still, and again, hopeful.

To summarize, Marx theorized that the progressive accumulation and concentration of capital would lead to increasing centralization of capital in fewer and fewer hands, higher productivity, reduced need for labour and

---

[4] Although all bright lights in the future are not the dawn, some, like those of the Christian tradition, could be the result of the earth going up in conflagration.

expansion of surplus labour, and inevitable irreconcilable realization crises, and systemic change.[5] Analysis of the level of incorporation[6] of various areas of the world began with consideration of how to understand the relationship between the countries which Marx studied and experienced most closely, and the rest of the world's societies, which he hypothesized would basically follow the direction the European world-system core had taken.

Wallerstein's work, *The Modern World-System I*, served as a corrective to the over emphasis on country-bounded analyses by emphasizing that there is only one modern inter-connected capitalist world-system (w-s) containing both continuous centralizing accumulation of capital in politically and technologically best suited arenas—core states—which have been seen to shift in their relative prominence, and areas losing wealth—the periphery—in a process of incorporation of new areas over historic time.[7] It is also possible to see that capital has been centralized racially as the inheritance of endogenous European heritage families.[8] Both racial and cultural dimensions will come into play.

II. CENTRALIZATION OF CAPITAL

Marx's theory is unique in the extent of its dedication to modelling the social dynamics of change, that includes some statics—the capitalist cycle—but within a conceptual frame of a spiral with both reproduction and expansion/change. In "Wage Labour and Capital" and "Value, Price and Profit,"[9] Marx presents the spiral of the capitalist system, and

---

[5] Realization crisis refers to the inability to sell all the commodities produced, and as most profit or surplus value becomes available in the marginal final output of a production process, shrinking markets rapidly lead to an inability to sell all, and thus to "realize" the value put into the commodity through sale on the market, and a loss of profits.

[6] World-systems theory describes a society as "incorporated" when it is no longer self-sufficient in the production of the necessities of life, becoming reliant on the world-system, and thus taking "its place" within it.

[7] There has been lively debate among world-systems theorists whether the modern European world-system is the first and the only world-system ever existent. One wing of theorists, including Andre Gunder Frank and Barry Gills recently still considered this an open question for empirical exploration. See Andre Frank and Barry K. Gills, eds., *The World System, Five Hundred Years or Five Thousand?* (New York: Routledge, 1996).

[8] See Cynthia Lucas Hewitt, "Racial Accumulation on a World-Scale, Racial Inequality and Employment," *Review* XXV, no. 2 (2002): 137–71.

[9] Karl Marx, *Wage Labour and Capital*, in MECW (New York: International Publishers, 1977), 9; Karl Marx, "Value, Price and Profit," in MECW (New York: International Publishers, 1985), 20.

summarizes the analyses in clear and abbreviated form, presaging the concept of centralization of capital presented in Volume I of *Capital*. Growth in the available capital leads to capitalist production in more areas of consumption, increasing its concentration in industries, and more jobs. But soon, concentration leads to a struggle between the capitals for market share, and they now seek to reduce their cost of production through labour mechanization and heightened productivity, to reduce the need for labour and its quality, to win the market. This leads also to a relatively declining number of jobs, the bankruptcy of some enterprises, and centralization of capital. Once again, strong profits are made. However, Marx establishes that while "the rapid growth of capital is the most favourable condition for wage labour," that is, it creates more jobs, it is also the pathway to endless competitive struggle between them for relatively fewer positions in the new stage of production (Fig. 1).

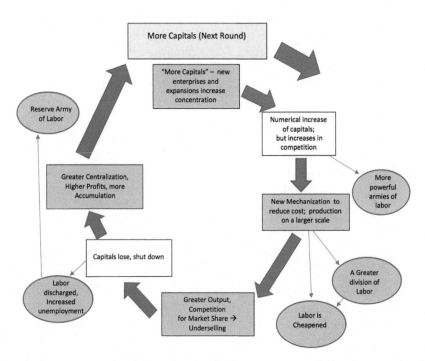

Fig. 1 The spiral of wage labour and capital

Here, we arrive at a major contradiction—the *realization crisis*: if a given amount of labour produces more products more cheaply, when they are sold in the market, the capitalist must sell more of them to attain the same or more *total mass* of surplus value. The entry of more, cheaper, products into the market generally assumes a market expansion. But with labour-saving mechanization in play, more people are surplus and less have earnings to buy the goods. The history of capitalism, therefore, on the one hand, is the history of the cheapening of labour and on the other, the struggle for markets. Generally, the acquisition of new markets is the safety valve that reduces the pressure by leading to new profits and new capital agglomerations in industries (capitals) already saturated by the production of commodities. The growth then of capitalist production at a more exten-sive scale and concentrated penetration of arenas of human needs is accompanied by new hiring and incorporating of labour.

However, likewise, these capitals come into competition with each other and seek to cheapen the product, undersell, and win market shares from each other. Winners accede to control over their market shares and resources, creating a now temporarily less competitive environment. Now, the capital formerly invested in failed companies will be reinvested in a company or industry that is producing surplus value for the owners. Capital is centralized in fewer and fewer hands. Marx writes:

> Capital grows in one place to a huge mass in a single hand, because it has in another place been lost by many. This is centralization proper, as distinct from accumulation and concentration... The battle of competition is fought by cheapening of commodities. The cheapness of commodities depends, *cæteris paribus*, on the productiveness of labour, and this again on the scale of production. Therefore, the larger capitals beat the smaller... The smaller capitals, therefore, crowd into spheres of production which Modern Industry [ignores]. Here competition rages in direct proportion to the number, and in inverse proportion to the magnitudes, of the antagonistic capitals. It always ends in the ruin of many small capitalists, whose capitals partly pass into the hands of their conquerors, partly vanish.[10]

This cycle of production is the most fundamental internal system-generated process of capitalism; however, Marx continues, "With capitalist production an altogether new force comes into play—the credit system, which in its first stages furtively creeps in as the humble assistant of accumulation, drawing into the hands of individual or associated capitalists,

[10] Karl Marx, *Capital*, Vol. I, in MECW (New York: International Publishers, 1996), 35: 626.

by invisible threads, the money resources which lie scattered, over the surface of society, in larger or smaller amounts; but it soon becomes a new and terrible weapon in the battle of competition and is finally transformed into an enormous social mechanism for the centralization of capitals."[11] This process is the focus of this chapter.

III. Centralization of Capital: Consideration of the Evidence

This analysis assesses the objective position of countries of the world today with respect to their citizens' involvement in, and their control over capital centralizing processes. Comparisons are made with respect to the level of concentration of "financialization" (a contemporary term)[12] to assess the degree to which centralization is taking place. Countries are grouped by w-s categories as core, periphery, or semi-periphery, derived theoretically from *The Modern World-System I* by Wallerstein. By definition, core countries have high capitalization in production and associated financialization. Periphery countries are the inverse, and constitute the "hinterland" where surplus value is extracted from low-cost workers, but little to no capital ownership is acquired by their citizens. The semi-periphery, on the other hand, are those countries with a mix of core-like and periphery-like conditions, often either moving upward towards core status or sliding downward, unable to retain core status. The semi-periphery is a somewhat grey area which, by analogy, tends to offer a safety valve for w-s theory, and has become the category into which over half the world's population is defined, including those in China, India, Indonesia, Brazil, and Nigeria. Fifty years ago, all would have been considered periphery.

The w-s position analysis is done for 188 countries. It is nuanced because it includes not only assessment of the strength of their capital (economic) position, but also of the state—the level of political strength (militarism) that serves that capital, and of the society—particularly the level of solidarity legitimating and strengthening that state. This analysis begins by evaluating foreign direct investment (FDI), a measure of capital transfer between countries when this funding constitutes basically a controlling share for the originating country capitalists in the foreign enterprises where it is invested—generally, approximately 20 per cent or more of the operating capital in a particular production enterprise. FDI is

---

[11] Ibid.
[12] See Cédric Durand, *Fictitious Capital* (New York: Verso, 2017).

money transferred as capital for investment, rather than for other reasons, such as for domestic consumption or for purchase of export goods, and so on. This record is provided by the IMF.[13] For analysis of centralization of capital, a five-year average of the level of stocks of FDI claimed by a country's nationals and the extent of annual outflow is used. This avoids too much emphasis on any given year, which may be anomalous for some reason. This analysis should identify the dominant and/or rising global centres of centralized capital, which we expect to be categorized as core or semi-periphery countries.[14]

Table 1 shows the 20 countries with the highest FDI flows, and their w-s status as core or semi-periphery, with the latter separated into two columns, the second of which separates out those countries conceivably

Table 1 Foreign direct investment (FDI), net outflows (in millions) five-year average, 2012–2016

	Country	Core	Semi-periphery	Chinese W-S
1	United States	346,321.2		
2	Netherlands	258,833.2		
3	Japan	143,461.2		
4	China			130,531.5
5	Germany	98,930.1		
6	Hong Kong SAR, China			93,282.1
7	Ireland	88,556.3		
8	Canada	65,984.0		
9	British Virgin Islands	62,952.2		
10	Switzerland	58,201.0		
11	Russian Federation	47,362.1		
12	France	45,786.4		
13	Luxemburg	41,907.7		
14	Spain	36,573.4		
15	Singapore			34,110.0
16	Korea, Rep. of		28,150.5	
17	Cayman Islands		20,974.8	
18	Norway	18,214.8		
19	Italy	15,763.1		
20	Brazil	14,504.7		

The World Bank, "Data Catalogue, Foreign Direct Investment, net outflows," 2018

[13] This process also corresponds roughly to what world-systems theory refers to as penetration.

[14] It is expected that the relative levels of FDI will also reflect early entry into the system because returns to capital involve a geometric expansion.

part of a new political economy phenomena. The United States, with a five-year average of $346,321.2 million of FDI is by far the first, followed by the Netherlands with $258,833.2 million, arguably the earliest territorial capitalist country, circa 1600. Japan, third, also reflects early entry. At about the same time as the United States was moving from the politics of a raw materials producing periphery economy to a contending core—the period of the Civil War in the United States—the Meiji Restoration, which launched Japanese industrialization, was taking place, circa 1865–75. As expected, there are no periphery countries on this list.[15]

IV. China

Most interesting is the occupation of the fourth position, with $130,351.5 million in FDI, by China. The third column lists nations which might be seen as part of a rising Chinese world-system. Given China's great domination in world commodity production, strong military capacity, and unified state, it is not clear if China is not a core nation. However, is it a core within the European world-system or an "attractor" in the formation of a successor system?

Table 2 shows that not only in terms of average annual flows over the last five years, but in terms of stocks of capital invested, China has risen rapidly to occupy the fifth position. The extent of Chinese FDI is not surprising, considering the Chinese need to organize the supply of all types of materials and services to facilitate their role as the manufacturing centre of the world. But it is very major: China's rise on this list seems to mark a world-historic systems shift. The rise of China is the single most challenging new aspect of global political economy and Marxist analysis of centralization of capital. China occupies a "semi-periphery" designation within the world-systems categories and a "developing nation" status in the Bretton Woods categorizations. Both of these, as will be seen, patently fail to take into consideration the full scope of the weight of the Chinese dynamic in global capital, to which this analysis, based on Marx's theorized centralization end-game, points.

In order to better assess the ranking of countries in terms of centralization of capital, in addition to FDI, the voting rights allocations of the IMF are considered because these reflect an internationally agreed-upon assessment of the size of a country's control over international trade—or in Marx's terms, international capital, whether it resides in the form of

---

[15] And none appear until the Philippines, number 39 in the list of 188.

Table 2 Foreign direct investment stocks, 2017 (2016) (in millions)

Rank	Country	FDI stock
1	United States	7,799,045.00
2	Netherlands	1,604,921.20
3	Germany	1,593,974.57
4	Great Britain	1,531,703.82
5	China	1,472,982.06
6	France	1,451,696.98
7	Japan	1,315,146.40
8	Canada	1,251,958.00
9	Switzerland	1,088,413.29
10	Ireland	899,499.88
11	Belgium	568,672.92
12	Spain	556,523.15
13	Italy	532,922.43
14	Australia	401,500.72
15	Sweden	384,817.86
16	Russia	382,278.00
17	Korea	296,641.00
18	Austria	248,271.77
19	Luxemburg	241,427.20
20	Brazil	201,767.00
21	Mexico	180,057.89
22	Norway	178,313.69
23	Denmark	175,999.89
24	South Africa	175,635.43
25	India	155,341.20

Source: Organization for Economic Co-operation and Development, 2016

commodities, wages for labour, machinery and infrastructure, or branding in markets. This ranking is also considered to help in adjudicating the W-S analysis of which countries are core, semi-periphery, or periphery. If the 2016 IMF voting shares of a country show them to be among the countries holding a dominant voting positions, it will help place them as core or semi-periphery in w-s status (See Table 3).

There has been significant change in the locations of capital concentration as measured by the voting shares, and a shift to China, over the last 35 years. The United States, with 16.52 per cent of the vote, holds a very dominant position, but also reflects a serious decline in hegemony, as it held 21.5 per cent of the vote in 1980.[16] Its share of the vote is more than

[16] James M. Broughton, *Silent Revolution, The International Monetary Fund, 1979–1989* (New York: International Monetary Fund, 2001), 856.

Table 3 World-systems status and IMF percentage of votes by country, Top 30

W-S status	Country	Economic power % IMF votes
C	United States	16.52
C	Japan	6.15
N	China	6.09
C	Germany	5.32
C	France	4.03
C	United Kingdom	4.03
C	Italy	3.02
S	India	2.64
C	Russian Federation	2.59
C	Canada	2.22
S	Brazil	2.22
S	Saudi Arabia	2.02
C	Spain	1.92
S	Mexico	1.80
C	Netherlands	1.77
S	Korea (Republic of)	1.73
C	Australia	1.34
C	Belgium	1.30
C	Switzerland	1.18
S	Indonesia	0.95
S	Turkey	0.95
C	Sweden	0.91
S	Poland	0.84
C	Austria	0.81
S	Singapore	0.80
C	Norway	0.78
S	Venezuela (Bolivarian Rep. of)	0.77
S	Malaysia	0.75
S	Iran (Islamic Republic of)	0.74
C	Denmark	0.71

International Monetary Fund, "IMF Member's Quotas and Voting power, and IMF Board of Governors," 2018

double the allocation of Japan (6.15), which is barely holding on to second place in the path of the rapidly rising China (6.09), in third place. The next four positions include core nations, theoretically anticipated: Germany (5.32), France (4.03), the United Kingdom (4.03), but also rising India (2.64) in position #7. The Russian Federation (2.59), and Canada now overrun by Brazil (tied at 2.22), complete the top 10 of the list of 188 nations. Historic holdings and country size matter, and China is joined by

India and Brazil, two other semi-periphery, large "BRIC" countries. Nigeria (.520) is the first periphery country to appear in the ranking, at position 35. In contrast, Kentor's 1980 world-system rankings, in a continuum from top core to least periphery status within the world-system, placed Brazil 17th, China 27th, and India 30th.[17]

For the first time, in 2016, the Chinese *renminbi* (RMB) was added to the currencies used to create the IMF "global currency,"[18] the globally convertible Special Drawing Rights (SDRs). To mark the launch of the new SDR basket, or mix of currencies, which define its value, Christine Lagarde, Managing Director of the IMF, stated: "The expansion of the SDR basket is an important and historic milestone for the SDR, the Fund, China and the international monetary system. It is a significant change for the Fund, because it is the first time since the adoption of the euro that a currency is added to the basket."[19] Unlike civil institutions, the IMF voting system is based strictly on economic power, not a democratic vote. Based on this review, countries were divided by w-s position for the analysis of the level of centralization of capital achieved and the anticipated rate of convergence across the system.

V. FINANCIAL ACCESS ANALYSIS

The relatively new IMF Financial Access Survey (FAS) data can arguably provide proxies for the level of incorporation of individuals into the capitalist economy. The FAS is data collected from central banks and financial regulators. It was motivated by the desire to assess the availability, use, and access to financial services by households and firms, in the context of Sustainable Development Goals (SDGs).[20] This study looks at the measures

[17] J. Kentor, "The Divergence of the Economic and Coercive Power in the World Economy 1960 to 2000, A Measure of Nation-State Position," IROWS Working Paper 46, 2009, accessed March 2019, https://irows.ucr.edu/papers/irows46/irows46.htm.

[18] The others are the U. S. dollar, the Japanese yen, the euro, and the British pound. In effect, these are the ruling currencies of the globe.

[19] See International Monetary Fund, "IMF Releases the 2016 Financial Access Survey, A Key Tool to Foster Financial Inclusion" (October 3, 2016), accessed March 2019, https://www.imf.org/en/News/Articles/2016/10/03/PR16441-IMF-Releases-the-2016-Financial-Access-Survey.

[20] Its emergence reflects gender equity concerns embedded in the sustainability and millennium development movement, reflected in the significant funding by Queen Maxima of the Netherlands (see Andre Mialou, "The IMF's Financial Access Survey (FAS)," Presentation

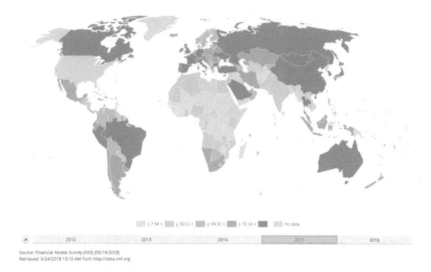

Source: Financial Access Survey (FAS) (05/19/2018)
Retrieved: 5/24/2018 10:10 AM from http://data.imf.org

Fig. 2   Automated teller machines (ATMs) per 100,000 adults, 2015

of ATM Machines per 1000 Persons (ATMs) and the Mobile Money Accounts Registered per 1000 Persons (MMAs) measures.

ATM machines are widely in use outside of African and some southwest Asian nations. (See Fig. 2). Considering the spread and concentration of ATM machines in regions of the global economy defined by world-systems, we see that the concentration is increasing relatively rapidly in periphery and semi-periphery nations, by 58.21 per cent and 31.29 per cent, from 2008 to 2016, respectively. See Tables 4 and 5. The most unincorporated area, Africa, is registering the fastest growth rate (69.9), with southwest Asia second (62.56), but these have very small base numbers. In contrast, the rates in core countries in 2016 were 103.91 per 1000 persons on average. Growth is very slight (2.64 per cent), and occasionally a downturn is recorded, which can be taken as a sign of having reached a saturation point in ATM concentration, or perhaps the impact of growth in online banking between 2009 and 2016.

to the IFC Workshop on Financial Inclusion Indicators (5–6 November 2012), accessed March 2019, https://www.bis.org/ifc/publ/ifcb38h.pdf), in addition to the Bill & Melinda Gates Foundation (see International Monetary Fund, "IMF Releases the 2016 Financial Access Survey") to launch its collection.

Table 4   ATM machines per 1000 persons by world-system position

World-system position	2008	2016	Per cent change
Core countries	101.24	103.91	2.64
Semi-periphery countries	54.57	71.64	31.29
Periphery countries	16.78	26.55	58.21

International Monetary Fund, Financial Access Survey (FAS)

Table 5   ATM machines per 1000 persons by region

Region	2008	2016	Per cent change
Africa	8.79	14.94	69.97
E. Asia	43.29	58.53	35.20
S.W. Asia	23.19	37.70	62.56
Europe	66.08	74.48	12.71
Latin America & Caribbean	36.06	49.73	37.90
North America	192.87	197.23	2.26

International Monetary Fund, Financial Access Survey (FAS)

The FAS also provides data on mobile money accounts registered per 1000 people (MMAR) by country. The innovation to utilize phones to create mobile banking is an interesting step in the de-materialization of money and seemingly a technological leapfrog for banking, which Africa has been theorized as likely to carry out in many arenas. The financial incorporation of the people in African countries registers a rapid penetration, with the entry of cell phones as mobile money access points. Kenya, where it seems to have started, and Tanzania, are in the lead in use of mobile money, as shown in the data for 2012 and 2015. These are followed by West Africa. See Figs. 3 and 4.

This form of penetration is now rapidly deepening in Africa in the countries where it is in use, with an 185 per cent rate of increase between 2012 and 2016, with some increase also in terms of number of countries. In 2012, 21 African countries in the periphery registered 206.41 MMAR per 1000 people, in comparison to zero usage reported in the core countries and many others (See Table 6). By 2016, the density had increased to 588.24 per 1000 people in 25 countries in Africa as a development region (See Table 7). There are a few cases where the data reported in the early years is no longer reported, hence whether a continued increase

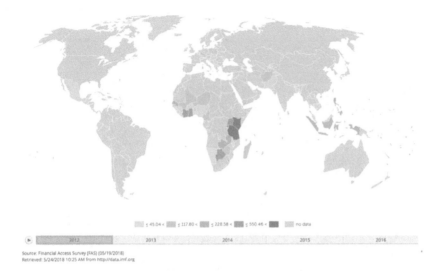

Source: Financial Access Survey (FAS) (05/19/2018)
Retrieved: 5/24/2018 10:25 AM from http://data.imf.org

Fig. 3 Mobile money accounts registered (MMAR) per 1000 adults, 2012

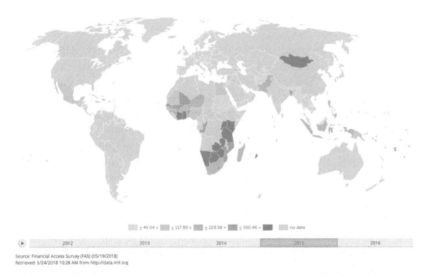

Source: Financial Access Survey (FAS) (05/19/2018)
Retrieved: 5/24/2018 10:28 AM from http://data.imf.org

Fig. 4 Mobile money accounts registered (MMAR) per 1000 adults, 2015

Table 6 Mobile money accounts registered (MMAR) per 1000 persons by world-system position

World-system position	2012	No.	2016	No.	Per cent change
Core countries	0	0	0.0	0	0
Semi-periphery countries	42.84	4	134.20	5	213.25
Periphery countries	174.05	29	487.70	40	180.21

International Monetary Fund, Financial Access Survey (FAS)

Table 7 Mobile money accounts registered (MMAR) per 1000 persons by region

Region	2012	No.	2016	No.	Per cent change
Africa	206.41	21	588.24	25	184.99
E. Asia	127.15	5	448.90	8	253.06
S.W. Asia	36.73	3	129.36	5	252.15
Europe	23.83	1	130.18	2	446.32
Latin America & Caribbean	38.16	3	194.95	5	410.93
North America	0	0	0	0	0

International Monetary Fund, Financial Access Survey (FAS)

occurred or it dropped off is not clear. Only one country, Afghanistan, reported major decline, and Malaysia reported slight decline between the two time points. The spread of MMAR is dependent upon enabling legislation and financial sector regulations, which may account for the lag in its appearance in some countries, or cessation, despite rapid growth elsewhere. In the few countries in other regions which have adopted the system, the increase in density was even more rapid, at 253 per cent to 446.32 per cent. Overall, this system shows viability as a method of increased consumer access to financial structures which have the potential to engage in centralizing capital processes in regions where other "access points" to financial services remained low.

VI. Absorption of the Periphery and China's Rise

The FAS data on ATM spread and mobile money emergence offer what appear to be good proxies for the rate at which the semi-periphery and periphery are bringing their population into the money economy and the global financial systems which centralize capital, and acculturate wage labour. Figure 5 shows a projection of the increase in concentration of

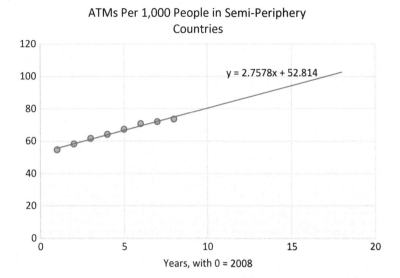

Fig. 5 Linear growth in density of ATMs annually, from 2008, in semi-periphery countries

ATMs based on the five-year data for semi-periphery countries. At its average rate of change, *in eight to ten years, the semi-periphery should catch up to the core in access of individuals* to financial systems as workers/consumers/proletarians. In approximately 15 years, so will the periphery. Figure 6 shows projections of the growth in density of ATMs for China alone. Depending upon whether one uses an exponential model of growth—which actually fits the data best—or a linear projection, *China would either be arriving at a density comparable to that of the UnitedStates (103 ATMs per 1000 persons) now or within three years.*

The innovation in mobile phone banking augers that the periphery will not take as long to reach comparable levels of financial access density as the semi-periphery did historically using the physical technology of the ATM and cash. The picture provided by the tremendous growth rates is complicated by lack of clarity about why it is emerging in some countries, particularly in Africa, and not in other.[21] However, given the very brief

---

[21] Jay Rosengard, "A Quantum Leap Over High Hurdles to Financial Inclusion: The Mobile Banking Revolution in Kenya," *John F. Kennedy School of Government*. RWP16-032. 2016, accessed June 2017, https://research.hks.harvard.edu/publications/workingpapers/Index.aspx.

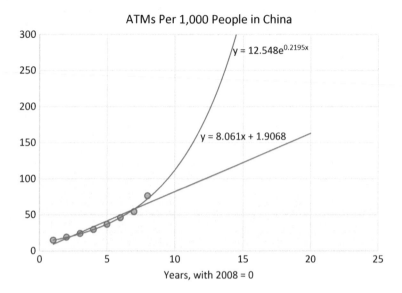

ATMs Per 1,000 People in China

$y = 12.548e^{0.2195x}$

$y = 8.061x + 1.9068$

Years, with 2008 = 0

Fig. 6 Growth in density of ATMs in year, linear and exponential projections from 2008, in China

time of its existence, it may also, in a short time, emerge in other countries as the cultural capital spreads. This spread may even affect the growth of ATMs, likely cancelling out and replacing some of the access they provided, so the growth of both these access points requires a more careful assessment of how they interact in any given population. But unquestionably, a calculation of the rate of increase that includes both will be higher than that of ATM alone; thus 15 years is an outside estimate of the completion of financialization of Africa. A much shorter estimate seems more appropriate. This augurs that the process of incorporating new areas of the globe into the world-system will essentially come to completion within 15 years, more likely 10. The expressed goal of the advocates of the Sustainable Development Goals of Women's Inclusion is full access by 2020.[22] Deepening of these processes should continue after this time, but the easy pickings of new markets for expansion will be, and probably even today is, over. Marx theorized that the *centralization* of capital is a process leading

---

[22] Mayra Buvinic, "The Clock is Ticking on Financial Inclusion and a Focus on Women Can Help," *Center for Global Development* (May 14, 2018), accessed May 2019, https://www.cgdev.org/blog/clock-ticking-financial-inclusion-and-focus-women-can-help.

to ever more global and massive crises, which ultimately will not be resolvable within the logic of capitalist production. These include the rising organic composition of capital and spread of surplus labour. Theoretically, now, and only in this period of emergence of some indication of full incorporation, can history prove Marx or his naysayers correct. The analysis here favours the continued relevance of Marx today.

The puzzle exposed in the pattern of findings is the world-historic emergence of a true bifurcation in the pattern of relationships within the world-system, as the Chinese centre with its "logic" of relationships, or nexus, of world-system processes emerges increasingly successful in competition with the European hegemony of the spiral of capitalism for approximately 300 years. China, and its logic of relationships, or relations of production, appears to be heading to become the dominant logic. To return to an Nkrumaist focus on the possibilities for African socio-economic rise, it can be seen that conditions under which the "freeing" of African culture/civilization would take place are now being revolutionized with the rise of China. It appears to be displacing the racist cultural hegemony of the European world-system. Assessment begins with several objective factors.

First, Chinese capital is not the product of slavery; it is the product of socialism. This is a fundamentally different foundation for concentration of wealth even if the wealth is being used in the capitalist global market under capitalist principles today. It was not stolen through slavery.

Second, China did not invade and occupy other peoples' land as settler-colonialists as did the Europeans (there are some border and expansion issues, such as with Tibet), not long-distance mass genocide and settler-colonialism.

Third, China is reaching a point of hegemony without predatory militarism as well.

These are the three hallmark features that gave the European people their lead in accumulating capital and wealth, *around which the principles that animate their social structure were formed*. But even their tremendous theft of life, land, and resources cannot shield them from being overtaken by a mass, united socialist system of political economy. China is arriving by a fundamentally different path to the position of hegemon of the world-economy[23]—it is a socialist path and that is already halfway there for Marx's

---

[23] A world-economy in distinction from a world-system implies economic integration without necessarily political domination/integration.

theory. On the other hand, no particular territory and people can be adjudged "socialist" from afar, yet many have withdrawn this designation from China. However, whether socialism is leading, contending, or just one orientation within a central coalition governing there, it is a factor. And, again, that makes China's pending dominance, and possibility of ascending to hegemony, arguably *an essentially revolutionary difference* from that of the previous countries whose succession can be traced under solid capitalist political control—up to and including the United States.

Evan A. Feigenbaum, on the Macropolo (Paulson Institute) website, expressed the "dis-ease" in the Eurocentric hegemon—the United States—that even the popular pronouncing of China as "post-communist" fails to alleviate. He wrote, "China accepts most *forms* but not necessarily our preferred *norms*. And that disconnect between forms and norms means that Beijing's revisionism and demands for change often play out *within* the existing international framework."[24] Feigenbaum argued that at the time of the Chinese revolution, the United States was fearful that China supported change from *without*, backing revolutionary movements to overthrow capitalist institutions and states around the world, the "domino effect" theory that led to the Vietnam war fiasco. Today, he argued, the danger comes not from China acting externally to overthrow capitalist institutions, but rather its strategic acting internally, to take over institutions. If Marx were alive today to read such Feigenbaum's points, maybe he would pronounce him a *Philistine* and laugh with mirthless glee at this classic solution: "if you cannot beat 'em, join 'em." A smile at this classic example of the unanticipated results of social actions is hard to resist!

With this perspective, that we are entering a period of struggle over norms and we need not necessarily privilege the plane of the material, objective structures—the states, banks, and international Bretton Woods institutions—as the sites of struggle. These institutions are still sitting there and there are no Chinese barricades in the streets in front of them!—yet they fear overthrow.

However, *alternatively, the argument that China is now capitalist could also be supported by Marx's theory of centralization as what we are observing may be resolved in a synthesis*, whereby former rivals in capitalist competition merge in the next phase, as previously occurred in the world-system.

[24] Feigenbaum, Evan A. Feigenbaum, "Reluctant Stakeholder: Why China's Highly Strategic Brand of Revisionism is more Challenging than Washington Thinks," *Macropolo* (Paulson Institute), accessed 2018, https://macropolo.org/author/evanfeigenbaum. See also by the same author, "China and the World," *Foreign Affairs*, January/February 2017.

Perhaps Chinese ascension augurs the completion of centralization, and not a bifurcation struggle? The Marxist expectation of subsequent revolutionary change being required due to capitalist crisis does not change, but it is a question of the way in which a transition to communism takes place.

Could a cultural shift take place that will change the nature of political struggles? Will it occur essentially through a people's demand for change in the name on the ledger for ownership of all the world's resources? Or through the people storming the Bastille and violent struggle until a mass insubordination among the military forces occurs? To some extent, it is fair to say that we are now observing the real-world transition to socialism, as China is now a part of the increasingly strong global forces that rule capital.

VII. The Nkrumahist Response

On the question of revolution, Marx describes a situation where people are operating under different principles in communist society, but he does not take this too far. According to Marx, capitalism is the latest iteration of systems of slavery attendant upon class society. At the core is the social relationship of slavery, the system of monopolization of the means of production through private property ownership. From within the European experience, it could be argued that this principle of social relationships overrides any other, and makes the emergence of socialism impossible. Today, the prophets of "development" are enshrining financial access as a goal for areas that have hither-to-fore escaped incorporation into this process—that is, organizing their existence through money exchange in markets, turning people into "free labour" dependent upon wages.[25] However, this appears to be a myopic outlook, or standpoint. As Marx points out, the worker becomes "free" in a two-fold manner: she or he is free of any compulsion by a communal or feudal organization to labour and to share, and also free of any claim over any means of production with which to labour on one's own behalf. The separation of people from their subsistence organizations of collective leads to entry into the "precariat"—the surplus labour proletariat underclass always at risk of perishing for lack of availability of employment. That, absent social revolution, this is now becoming a "lemming march to oblivion" for surplus labour, is perceptively analysed and illustrated by Samir Amin.[26] As Wallerstein so pithily related in the introduction to his seminal

[25] See UN DESA, "Sustainable Development Knowledge Platform," https://sustainabledevelopment.un.org/sdg8.

[26] "Forward: Rebuilding the 'Labour Front'," in *Labour and the Challenges of Globalization*, ed. Andreas Bieler et al. (Ann Arbor: University of KwaZulu-Natal Press, 2008), xiv–xxii.

work, *The Modern World-System I*, that, as a graduate student in Ghana during the independence struggle led by Kwame Nkrumsah, he "was bombarded by the onslaught of the colonial mentality of Europeans long resident in Africa" as well as "privy to the angry analyses and optimistic passions of the young militants of the African movements," and he learned that "not only were these two groups at odds on political issues, but that they approached the situation with entirely different sets of conceptual frameworks." Wallerstein concluded: "In general, in a deep conflict, the eyes of the downtrodden are more acute about the reality of the present, because it is in their interests to perceive correctly in order to expose the hypocrisies of the rulers."[27] The Africentric response is deep-rooted. Stokely Carmichael (later known as Kwame Ture), a key Nkrumahist theorist, wrote in 1974: "In Osagyefo's [the Teacher's in Akan, as Nkrumah is commonly called] classical philosophical work, *Consciencism*,[28] we can see that the theories of Marx and Lenin have their roots in communalism. Thus, as an African, I should study Nkrumahism, which knows communalism contains the very *foundation* of Marxism-Leninism. "It contains my history, African history, as it must be presented in order to 'become a pointer at the ideology which should guide and direct African reconstruction'."[29] An Nkrumahist response to Marxist theory begins with Nkrumah's theorization of the concept of neo-colonialism,[30] which emphasizes the struggle to end continued domination of African people after national liberation through imposition of cultural, social, and political control, and ultimately, military force, if necessary, to prevent accumulation of capital through ownership of resources, and profits in industrial production.

In *The Cultural Unity of Black Africa*,[31] renowned African social and physical scientist, Cheikh Anta Diop, of Senegal presents the African matriarchal social order as the most common cultural trait of African societies throughout history prior to colonialism and religious-based incursions, and the most fundamental underlying structural difference in the culture of Africa, and much of the Global South, in comparison with the

---

[27] Wallerstein, *The Modern World-System I*, 3.

[28] Stokely Carmichael, *Consciencism, Philosophy and Ideology for De-Colonization* (New York: Monthly Review, 1970).

[29] Stokely Carmichael, "Pan-Africanism—Land and Power," in *Robert Chrisman and Nathan Hare*, ed. Pan-Africanism (Ann Arbor: Bobbs-Merrill, 1974), 13.

[30] Kwame Nkrumah, *Neo-colonialism, The Last Stage of Imperialism* (New York: International Publishers, 1966).

[31] Cheikh Anta Diop, *The Cultural Unity of Black Africa* (London: Karnak, 1989).

patriarchal northern societies. Matriarchy involves inheritance through the female line and the presence of communal property in contrast to male lineage inheritance and private property. This cultural dichotomy cannot be explored fully here; however, Africa has been shown to have a deep store of communal principles based on this cultural heritage.

Feminist theorists, whose liberation struggle must also take them beyond economic questions, have theorized the rise of northern patriarchal class society based on a cultural clash with matriarchy. Riane Eisler explains the shift in human development by chaos theory. Small alternative systems—"peripheral isolates"—always exist in the interstices, or periphery, around even the most developed dominant systems, and at a time of systemic crisis, an isolate, if it can answer some, or many of the challenges faced by the dominant system, can grow, develop, and generalize rapidly, bringing about a new dominant system. The "revolutionary" shift from dominance of matriarchy to patriarchy, beginning around 4500 B.C.E., was theorized as occasioned by the expansion of northern patriarchal societies through exposure to and adoption of technologies developed in the matriarchal cultural south—metallurgy in particular—which led to their cultural solution to growth: predatory invasion of the south with new weapons and the wheel, and once introduced, the violence it engendered required defensive violence. The history of all southern hemisphere matriarchal societies attests to this. Chaos theory suggests that two different systems coming into contact will yield a revolutionary moment if the emergent system cannot be contained and co-opted by the old system, which happens when the new system rests on different *and superior* social principles. This is the essence of what Feigenbaum grasps. The structure of capitalism is being undermined from within, as well as from increasingly system-wide challenges from below.

The contemporary ethos and standpoints among Africans globally reflect both cultural disintegration under oppression, and cultural creativity, due to barriers to full acculturation into the European capitalist world-system social organization.[32] What we see is not only the resistance of African culture, but its *resilience* as expressions of African culture continue to achieve world prominence and to attract adherents. The scattering of the African people, both through the drawing of inane borders in Africa and transportation of millions to other people's lands, ensures a

---

[32] Amilcar Cabral provides a classic explanation in his presentation "National Liberation and Culture," *Return to the Source* (New York: Monthly Review, 1974), xx–xx.

cornucopia of "peripheral isolates" any of which might rise upon a successful principle, and attract and revolutionize human societies in a time of capitalist systemic crisis. Carmichael continued:

> If one is fighting for a revolution, one is talking about more than just changing governments and power, and that is changing the value system. What carries that value system is one's culture. What we have here is the beginning of people who are trying to grope for a real fight with the culture... Black people in America, Africans who live in America, especially must understand that and begin to alienate our people completely from the culture and values of Western society... It is very, very difficult, and we have to constantly try to understand the rejection of Western values... because once they are alienated there will be no influence over them. That is what we are seeking. We are seeking to stop all influence of Western culture on our people—completely... At the same time, there will be struggles inside the United States, always moving on different levels as black people keep trying to get a better way of life. Just as the Chinese or Indian diaspora play a huge role in consolidating their financial, human and social capital for the advancement of the nation, so African people must do.[33]

The struggle to engage in change making must come in the principles around which the system is organized and run. Revolution is ultimately a change in principle. It is analytically useful in the African people's struggle to align with, as well as go beyond, the feminist subsistence perspective and new sustainability resilience framings that include respect for indigenous socio-ecologies, to an Africentric *critique of the principles* of the northern hemispheric culture of capitalism. In the best tradition of the African southern hemisphere, by following the mathematical indicators to peep into the open cracks of ideologies in mortal combat, this analysis answers a call put forth by Queen mother of African philosophers, Marimba Ani: *Bolekaja!*[34] The primary and immense value of the work of Marx is the revelation of capitalism as an abstract system, that has internal contradictions that will inevitably grow in strength and disruptiveness until the social system is reorganized, and realigned with the productive forces. The analysis of FAS data shows rapid completion of levels of financial access

[33] Carmichael, "Pan-Africanism—Land and Power," 18.

[34] A Yoruba term meaning, "Come on Down, Let's Fight!" which she references in the introduction to her book, Marimba Ani, *Yurugu: An African-centered Critique of European Cultural Thought and Behavior* (Trenton, NJ: Africa World Press, Inc., 1994), 1, and learned from Chinweizu et al., *Toward the Decolonization of African Literature*.

saturation in populations in semi-periphery and periphery countries on par with that in core countries. By looking as this integration of access as the obverse side of integration of capitalist access to peasants and worker savings, it can be argued that completion of centralization of capital is occurring. It suggests that prior dismissal of Marx's theory was premature. Only now will Marx's prediction, based on his model of capitalism and its innate irreconcilable contradictions leading inevitably to revolution, be experienced as accurate or inaccurate.

BIBLIOGRAPHY

Amin, Samir. "Forward: Rebuilding the 'Labour Front'." In *Labour and the Challenges of Globalization*, edited by Andreas Bieler et al., xiv–xxii. Ann Arbor: University of KwaZulu-Natal Press, 2008.

Ani, Marimba. *Yurugu: An African-centered Critique of European Cultural Thought and Behavior*. Trenton, NJ: Africa World Press, Inc., 1994.

Broughton, James M. *Silent Revolution, The International Monetary Fund, 1979–1989*. New York: International Monetary Fund, 2001.

Buvinic, Mayra. "The Clock is Ticking on Financial Inclusion and a Focus on Women Can Help." Center for Global Development. Accessed May 2, 2019. https://www.cgdev.org/blog/clock-ticking-financial-inclusion-and-focus-women-can-help.

Cabral, Amilcar. "National Liberation and Culture." In *Return to the Source*. New York: Monthly Review, 1974.

Carmichael, Stokely. "Pan-Africanism—Land and Power." In *Robert Chrisman and Nathan Hare*, edited by Pan-Africanism, 9–19. Ann Arbor: Bobbs-Merrill, 1974.

Cox, Oliver C. *The Foundations of Capitalism*. New York: Philosophical Library, 1959.

Daly, Herman. *Beyond Growth, The Economics of Sustainable Development*. Boston: Beacon Press, 1997.

Diop, Cheikh Anta. *The Cultural Unity of Black Africa*. London: Karnak, 1989.

Durand, Cédric. *Fictitious Capital*. New York: Verso, 2017.

Feigenbaum, Evan A. "Reluctant Stakeholder: Why China's Highly Strategic Brand of Revisionism is More Challenging than Washington Thinks." *Macropolo* (Paulson Institute). https://macropolo.org/author/evanfeigenbaum/.

Frank, Andre Gunder and Barry K. Gills, eds. *The World System, Five Hundred Years or Five Thousand?* New York: Routledge, 1996.

Hewitt, Cynthia Lucas. Racial Accumulation on a World-Scale, Racial Inequality and Employment. *Review* XXV, no. 2 (2002): 137–71.

International Monetary Fund. "Financial Access Survey." Accessed June 2018. http://data.imf.org/?sk=E5DCAB7E-A5CA-4892-A6EA-598B5463A34C.

International Monetary Fund. "IMF Launches New SDR Basket Including Chinese Renminbi, Determines New Currency Amounts, September 30, 2016." Accessed March 2019. https://www.imf.org/en/News/Articles/2016/09/30/AM16-PR16440-IMF-Launches-New-SDR-Basket-Including-Chinese-Renminbi.

International Monetary Fund. "IMF Member's Quotas and Voting Power, and IMF Board of Governors." Last Updated: May 25, 2018. https://www.imf.org/external/np/sec/memdir/members.aspx.

Kentor, J. "The Divergence of the Economic and Coercive Power in the World Economy 1960 to 2000, A Measure of Nation-State Position". IROWS Working Paper 46, 2009. Accessed March 2019. https://irows.ucr.edu/papers/irows46/irows46.htm.

Marx, Karl. "Wage Labour and Capital." In MECW. Vol. 9, 197–228. New York: International Publishers, 1977.

Marx, Karl. *Capital.* Vol. I. In MECW. Vol. 35. New York: International Publishers, 1983.

Marx, Karl. "Value, Price and Profit. A Report to the General Council of the International." In MECW. Vol. 20, 101–49. New York: International Publishers, 1985.

Mialou, Andre. "The IMF's Financial Access Survey (FAS)." Presentation to the IFC Workshop on Financial Inclusion Indicators, 5–6 November 2012, Sasana Kijang, Kuala Lumpur. Accessed March 2019. https://www.bis.org/ifc/publ/ifcb38h.pdf.

Nkrumah, Kwame. *Neo-colonialism, The Last Stage of Imperialism.* New York: International Publishers, 1966.

Nkrumah, Kwame. *Consciencism, Philosophy and Ideology for De-Colonization.* New York: Monthly Review, 1970.

Organization for Economic Co-operation and Development. "OECD Data, FDI Stocks." Accessed May 2017. https://data.oecd.org/fdi/fdi-stocks.htm.

Rosengard, Jay. "A Quantum Leap Over High Hurdles to Financial Inclusion: The Mobile Banking Revolution in Kenya." John F. Kennedy School of Government. RWP16-032, 2016. Accessed June 2017. https://research.hks.harvard.edu/publications/workingpapers/Index.aspx.

Wallerstein, Immanuel. *The Modern World-System I: Capitalist Agriculture and the Origins of the European World-Economy in the Sixteenth Century.* Cambridge: Academic Press, 1976.

The World Bank. "Data Catalogue, "Foreign Direct Investment, Net Outflows (BoP, current $US)." Accessed March 2018. https://databank.worldbank.org/data/reports.aspx?source=2&series=BM.KLT.DINV.CD.WD#.

Petty Production and India's Development

Muhammad Ali Jan and Barbara Harriss-White

I. Introduction

Petty commodity production (PCP) has proved to be a remarkably persistent form of economic production. In much of the developing world even to this day, urban and rural small producers constitute the numerical majority of firms.[1] The preponderance of small-scale property within capitalist societies of the "south" has posed a theoretical quandary for orthodox Marxist conceptions of capitalist development, which had long predicted its end and the emergence of a polarized class structure with capital owners and property-less labour confronting one another. As capitalist social relations spread, most small-scale producers would be unable to compete and reduced to the status of property-less proletarians. However, even as most societies of the Global South have made the transition to capitalism, PCP has continued to be an important component of their socio-economic structure.

[1] Barbara Harriss-White, "Capitalism and the Common Man: Peasants and Petty Production in Africa and South Asia," *Agrarian South: Journal of Political Economy* 1, no. 2 (2012): 118.

M. A. Jan (✉) • B. Harriss-White
Wolfson College, University of Oxford, Oxford, UK

© The Author(s) 2019   345
S. Gupta et al. (eds.), *Karl Marx's Life, Ideas, and Influences*, Marx, Engels, and Marxisms, https://doi.org/10.1007/978-3-030-24815-4_16

The importance of PCP to the empirical realities of capitalism in developing countries is in inverse proportion to the importance given to it by Marxist scholars. To be sure, the classical view had been challenged early on by critical Marxist scholars. Disputes about PCP and the diverse forms it takes developed from the classical debates on the nature of the peasantry under capitalism.[2] More recently, debates about the nature of PCP under conditions of capitalist social relations have been revived.[3] Yet, despite its central importance in the political economy of the contemporary capitalist south, PCP remains marginalized within Marxism.

One of the reasons for this neglect is the apparent lack of attention paid to the concept by Marx himself. Marx focused on uncovering the "laws of motion" of contemporary capitalism, the class relations constitutive of it, the logic and dynamics through which the system reproduces itself, as well as how capital's inner logic causes it to experience systemic crises. As a result, Marx's analysis was systemic and the expansionary logic of capital that he unearthed meant that in his view, those forms of social reproduction that could not conform to the imperatives of capital accumulation would find themselves inevitably destroyed or thoroughly reconfigured under its pressure. Small-scale property was one such form.

While it seems that Marx's *oeuvre* is focused on large-scale industry, with petty production excluded, we argue here that this is only partially true. Marx did treat the theme of petty production extensively in his writings, but in an incoherent manner. First, his work on petty production is scattered. Second, the terms used in his writings on PCP are unstable, ranging from "peasants", "petty producers", "craftsmen" to "small holders" and "household producers". Third, the underlying meanings and contexts when any of these terms are used vary greatly and are not always clear.

However, a close reading of Marx's main texts on economics that pays attention to their contexts enables us to deduce three unifying themes. Here, we categorize them in terms of the problematics that underlie Marx's work on PCP. First, the *dissolution problematic*, dealing with the transformation of the peasantry into a landless working class under the impact of capitalist development, with the English transition as the paradigmatic case. Second, the *conservation problematic*, which allows for the incomplete separation of labour from its means of production under capital but views this as a form of disguised wage labour. Third, a hitherto underexplored aspect

---

[2] Karl Kautsky, *The Agrarian Question* (London: Zwan Publications, 1988), 168.
[3] Barbara Harriss-White, "From Analysing Filières Vivrières to Understanding Capital and Petty Production in Rural South India," *Journal of Agrarian Change* 16, no. 3 (2016): 485.

of Marx's writings on PCP posits the possibility of PCP's operating as a contradictory form under the logic of capital but with a degree of independence. We term this the *dialectic of exploitation and autonomy* and argue that it is here that the most fruitful developments of the concept of PCP can and do take place in India.

The chapter is divided into two parts. In part one, we present an overview of the three problematics we have identified in Marx's writings pertaining to PCP, emphasizing the tensions and contradictions they generate. In the second part, we assess the extent to which Marx's ideas are relevant to actually existing capitalism in the Indian case. We argue that while all three problematics can be found in the Indian social formation, it is important to recognize that the diversity and internal logics of PCP are more complex than accounted for in Marx's writings. Hence the best way to conceptualize PCP is to understand it as being internal to Indian capitalism, rather than a form that will be eventually be transcended.

II. The "Dissolution Problematic": Large-Scale Industry and Primitive Accumulation

Marx considered forms of PCP, particularly the peasantry and craftsmen, to be the most widespread form of social reproduction in pre-capitalist epochs. It was through the transformation of the key social groups representing these epochs that the social relations of capitalist production first emerged.[4] While discussing usurer's capital in his important chapter on "Pre-capitalist Relations" in Volume III of *Capital*, he observes that usurers earn money by financing both the "extravagant landed magnates" as well as "small producers who possess their own conditions of labour, including artisans but especially peasants, since wherever pre-capitalist conditions permit small autonomous individual producers, the peasant class must form their great majority".[5]

Though Marx identified other epochs of production such as the "Asiatic", "Classical" and "Germanic",[6] it was European "Feudalism" which first produced a successful transition to capitalism. In Marx's view, feudalism was itself an outgrowth of the "Germanic" system of individual

---

[4] Karl Marx, *Pre-Capitalist Economic Formations* (New York: International Publishers, 1964), 82.

[5] Karl Marx, *Capital*, Vol. III (London: Penguin Books, 1981), 729.

[6] Karl Marx, *Grundrisse: Foundations of the Critique of Political Economy* (London: Penguin Books, 1973), 471–9.

peasant proprietors who formed the base of the social formation. The Germanic system only transforms into "feudal" relations once towns and a landlord class emerged above the "village communities" to live off the latter's surplus. Though scholars have disputed Marx's account of the evolution of pre-capitalist Western Europe, it is clear that he was not interested in the intricacies of feudalism itself but in highlighting how far the changes within it could explain the genesis of capitalist social relations.

For our purposes, his account is important because it forms the basis for the orthodox and the dominant Marxist position on PCP as a form destined to be overcome or destroyed during the transition towards capitalism, that we call the "dissolution problematic". This dissolution problematic has two dimensions: (i) an economic one where the destruction of PCP is attained mainly through the "dull compulsions of economic life" emanating from the logic of capital accumulation; (ii) a political-economic dimension where the destruction of PCP is instituted by state and class power as a pre-condition for capital accumulation, most famously described through Marx's analysis of "primitive accumulation".

The economic dimension of the "dissolution problematic" emanates mainly from the expansion of capitalist social relations, particularly in the form of large-scale industry, which exploits wage labour and economies of scale, against which petty production is unable to compete and entirely dissolved. There are numerous yet scattered references to the "destructive" impact of capitalism on the economy of independent petty production. In Volume I of *Capital*, for one example, Marx refers to the revolutionary effect of large-scale industry in agriculture through the "annihilation of the bulwark of the old society, the peasant" and its "substitution" by the "wage-labourer".[7]

A similar argument is made for non-landed forms of PCP. For example, in *The German Ideology*, Marx emphasizes how, where large-scale industry penetrated, it "destroyed the crafts and all earlier stages of industry".[8] The guild structure of many crafts became a fetter for the further development of the "automatic system" and as a result, it had to be overcome and dissolved under the onslaught of propertied capitalist manufacturing. Here, Marx's point was the unstoppable march of the logic of capital and the destruction of all prior forms that could not conform to, or compete with, the imperative of capital accumulation.

---

[7] Karl Marx, *Capital*, Vol. I (London: Penguin Books, 1976), 637.
[8] Karl Marx, *The German Ideology* (London: Lawrence and Wishart, 1970), 78.

But perhaps the most widely known manifestation of the "dissolution problematic" was Marx's dramatic analysis of the transformation of peasant producers into landless proletarians in the chapter on "primitive accumulation" in Volume I of *Capital*. Here, Marx describes, in vivid detail the transition to capitalist farming through the destruction of the till then comparatively free and relatively prosperous yeoman peasantry. This process begins in the sixteenth century through the forcible "removal of the peasantry from the land" as well as the "coercive usurpation of commons".[9] Moreover, this is no longer brought about by the logic of capital accumulation but by the political and legal power of a Parliament dominated by "the landlord and capitalist appropriators of surplus-value", which passed the infamous Enclosure of the Commons Act, furthering the process of primitive accumulation.[10]

Primitive accumulation for Marx is, therefore, nothing more than the process whereby pre-capitalist petty producers are forcibly separated from their means of subsistence and production and "hurled into the labour market as free, unprotected and right-less proletarians".[11] This process then results in the formation of a capitalist landlord class, a class of capitalist tenant farmers as well as a class of property-less agricultural workers: Marx's classic agrarian transition. A similar process of uprooting and separation is experienced by independent craftsmen under the impact of modern industry as highlighted earlier, and through this process, a modern industrial proletariat, as well as the industrial "reserve army" of labour, are created. This political-economic process of the transformation of peasants into proletarians is the "dissolution problematic".

Given the central role played by the imperatives of capital accumulation resulting in both greater concentration of units of capital alongside an ever-increasing mass of humanity being reduced to the status of property-less wage labour, it is no surprise that the "dissolution problematic" has become the Marxist orthodoxy. A further reason for its status is that the polarized class contradiction between capital and labour also prepares the way for the inevitable overcoming of the capitalist mode of production by socialism, whose leadership is assumed by the proletariat. Hence the idea of an ever-increasing mass of property-less wage labourer is central to classical Marxist theory and political practice.

[9] Marx, *Capital*, Vol. I, 878.
[10] Ibid., 886.
[11] Ibid., 876.

Yet, closer scrutiny of Marx's writings enables us to appreciate Marx's alternative visions of the transition to capitalism and, through them, the multiple ways and reasons why PCP may not only continue to survive the transition to capitalism, but be constantly recreated within it. This is what we term the "conservation problematic".

III. The "Conservation Problematic" and Its Logics: Resilience and Recreation

The view that forms of small-scale production persist during the transition to capitalist agriculture and that the complete separation between the labourer and his means of production is but one of the many forms that capitalist social relations can take has preoccupied critical Marxist scholarship.[12] Marx recognized that the history of the separation of petty producers from their means of production was a historically varied process, assuming different forms in different countries and running through its various phases in different orders of succession, and at different historical epochs.

As opposed to the "dissolution problematic", in this narrative, Marx allowed for the possibility of capitalist control over the labour process and the production of surplus value, even as producers retained some assets. But while the form was preserved and petty producers retained control over their means of production, their reproduction was now subsumed under the logic of capital accumulation. The best-known analysis of the "conservation problematic" occurs in the Appendix to *Capital*, Volume I, on the formal and real subsumption of labour, and in the analysis of merchant capital in Volume III.[13]

Critical Marxist scholarship has long distinguished the formal from the real subsumption of labour as representing two historic stages in the process of subordination of petty producers to capital.[14] In the former, capital begins to take hold of the overall conditions of reproduction of petty producers so that they become dependent on markets dominated by capital while still retaining formal control over their land, tools and so on. Capital is appropriating the producer's labour as surplus value, which means it is already part of capital but the form of production remains that of the small producer.

---

[12] Jairus Banaji, "Capitalist Domination and the Small Peasantry: Deccan Districts in the Late Nineteenth Century." *Economic and Political Weekly* 12, no. 33/34 (1977): 1375–404.

[13] Marx, *Capital*, Vol. I, 1075; Marx, *Capital*, Vol. III, 379.

[14] Banaji, *Capitalist Domination*, 1376.

Formal subsumption arises because, unlike the English case, where peasants were forcibly removed from their lands and transformed into wage labourers, Marx admits that in most cases, capital finds the labour process that it seeks to dominate at hand without the need to separate the producer from his means of production. In a striking paragraph, he writes:

> *The fact is that capital subsumes the labour process as it finds it, that is to say, it takes over an existing labour process, developed by different and more archaic modes of production. And since that is the case it is evident that capital took over an available, established labour process....If changes occur in these traditional, established labour processes after their takeover by capital, these are nothing but the gradual consequences of that subsumption.*[15]

So, in cases where capital takes hold of petty production and subsumes it, the process of transformation from formal to real subsumption occurs slowly. But there is a tension between the critical Marxist concept of PCP and Marx's analysis of the formal subsumption of labour and it is this. For Marx, formal subsumption already implies that the surplus appropriated from the direct producer takes the form of absolute surplus value, which can be increased or decreased through the intensity of work. While the external form may be that of an independent producer, it is merely an appearance (or disguise) behind which he has, in essence, already been transformed into a wage worker for capital.[16] The contradictory, dialectical existence of PCP as both subsumed under capital but retaining a degree of actual not merely formal control, is missing from his analysis.

Marx contrasts formal subsumption by (agro) industrial capital to situations where capital is to be found in "certain specific, subordinate functions but where it has not emerged as the immediate owner of the process of production", most notably usurer's and merchant's capital, where the peasant or petty producer is made advances in the form of money and raw materials in exchange for which they sell their products through him. For example, in Volume III, he argues that a possible transition from feudalism to capitalism takes the form of the "merchant taking direct control of production himself"[17] or, in Volume II, he refers to the putting out system with respect to the cottage industries of Russia being "pressed more and more under the service of capitalism".[18]

---

[15] Marx, *Capital*, Vol. I, 1021.
[16] Marx, *Pre-Capitalist Economic Formations*, 767.
[17] Marx, *Capital*, Vol. III, 452.
[18] Marx, *Capital*, Vol. II (London: Penguin Books, 1978), 318.

Marx also acknowledges, but does not develop, the important idea that under certain circumstances, capital itself may generate PCP in order to fulfil key functions for capital accumulation. For example, in his chapter on primitive accumulation, he refers to periods in English history where capital alternates between destroying handicrafts and rural industry in certain forms and particular branches, while it "*resurrects* them again elsewhere because it *needs* them to some extent for the preparation of raw materials", which is why peasants and craftsmen continue to appear throughout the period of capitalist development in English history, "but always in diminished strength".[19]

It is important to note that for Marx, this is a phenomenon of transition, with merchant's capital as an antediluvian form. Its exploitation of petty production is not even part of the formal subsumption of labour to capital and the process comes to a halt once large-scale industry begins to dominate production, tears apart rural domestic industry and paves the way for capitalist agriculture. The main reason for this, as Marx puts it, is that:

> *The immediate producer still performs the functions of selling his wares and making use of his own labour. But the transition is more strongly marked here than in the case of the usurer. We shall return later to these forms, both of which survive and reproduce themselves as transitional subforms within the framework of capitalist production.*[20]

For Marx, the fact that the immediate producer retains a degree of autonomy over decisions about his output precludes the possibility of his being subsumed even formally under capital. Marx consistently contrasts a situation where the direct producer retains some independence to that of the formal subsumption of labour to capital where independence is merely an illusion behind which capital is already appropriating surplus as absolute surplus value. A further example of what is now often called "disguised wage labour" (DWL) is from the *Grundrisse*, where he describes the formal subsumption of hitherto independent weavers and spinners to the control of the merchant who transforms the property of the former into "sham property" and reduces them to the status of wage labourer.[21]

---

[19] Marx, *Capital*, Vol. I, 911–12.
[20] Ibid., 1023.
[21] Marx, *Grundrisse*, 510.

To sum up, Marx allows for the preservation of previous forms of petty production and even their recreation for the benefit of capital in certain circumstances. We term this the "conservation problematic". However, the inherent contradiction of PCP as combining the class places of both capital and labour sits uneasily with other arguments by Marx. First, while recognizing that capital can dominate the conditions of reproduction without entirely separating the producer from the means of production, he nonetheless disallows any autonomy which is important for the concept of PCP. Instead, he posits that the formally subsumed labourer is only outwardly independent and has, in essence, been reduced to the status of a wage labourer from whom absolute surplus value is appropriated.

Second, he also assumes that money or input advances by merchants and the consequent exploitation—in the form of interest rates or through lower prices for commodities—signify an antediluvian form of capital, which is best theorized as a transition to capitalism prior to the stage of formal subsumption. As capitalism's hold over the labour process intensifies, PCP is transformed into a disguised form of wage. Thus, the "conservation problematic" is primarily about the conservation of the form of petty production behind which its autonomous existence has been circumscribed.

By contrast, PCP has been theorized as a form of production which exists within the circuits of capital but which has a relatively autonomous existence.[22] First, even while it is exploited by capital, exploitation takes place through markets other than labour. Second, most PCP reproduces through multiplication of economic units rather than accumulation.[23] Finally, since the form combines the class places of capital as well, there remains in certain circumstances, the possibility of accumulation. Thus, the dialectic is one where both exploitation and accumulation can occur, and thus, PCP is both subsumed under the imperatives of capital accumulation but also retains a certain degree of autonomy.

This brings us to Marx's third view of PCP where in Marx's writings its contradictory existence is acknowledged and the question whether PCP can retain its autonomy as a subform within the framework of capitalist production is posed.

---

[22] Henry Bernstein, "Capitalism and Petty-Bourgeois Production : Class Relations and Divisions of Labour," *Journal of Peasant Studies* 15, no. 2 (1988): 260.

[23] Harriss-White, *From Analysing Filieres Vivrieres*, 479.

IV. THE DIALECTIC OF AUTONOMY AND EXPLOITATION

In an important section titled "The labour of handicraftsmen and peasants in capitalist society" in his *Theories of Surplus Value*, Marx gives what is perhaps the closest approximation of the critical Marxist view of PCP as a contradictory form of production under the circuits of capital accumulation. He writes:

> *It is possible that these producers, working with their own means of production, not only reproduce their labour-power but create surplus-value, while their position enables them to appropriate for themselves their own surplus-labour or a part of it (since a part of it is taken away from them in the form of taxes, etc.). And here we come up against a peculiarity that is characteristic of a society in which one definite mode of production predominates, even though not all productive relations have been subordinated to it….the independent peasant or handicraftsman is cut up into two persons. As owner of the means of production he is a capitalist; as labourer he is his own wage labourer. As capitalist he therefore pays himself his wages and draws his profit on his capital; that is to say, he exploits himself as wage labourer and pays to himself in the surplus-value, the tribute that labour owes to capital.*[24]

What is remarkable about this passage is that, unlike in the rest of his writings on the theme, Marx for the first time acknowledges that forms of petty production can not only exist under capital, but that they can exist as precisely a contradictory mode without being fully subsumed under the logic of capital accumulation, which reduces the independent producer to the status of wage labour, either outright or in disguise. This also opens up the theoretical possibility that PCP may not only be able to hold its own (contradictory position) under capital, but that in certain circumstances, it may be able to reproduce itself even at the expense of capital. The latter scenario is demonstrated empirically by Marx through his important section on the development of capitalism in the American colonies in Volume I of *Capital*.

Here, Marx writes how despite the plans of the European colonizers to implant large-scale industrial capital, the conditions found in the American colonies prevented this from happening. The would-be colonial capitalists possessed large quantities of "money, means of subsistence, machinery

---

[24] Karl Marx, *Theories of Surplus Value*, Vol. I (London: Lawrence & Wishart, 1969), 452–3.

and other means of production" but were unable to secure that most important condition for the development of capitalist industry—a mass of dispossessed wage workers.[25] The abundance of land in the colonies meant that poor Europeans found it more profitable to own a piece of land and use their own means of production, however primitive, to become independent producers.

According to Marx, this frustration is reflected in the writings of the English colonialist Edward Gibbon Wakefield who notices how, despite the constant arrival of new immigrants from Europe alongside the possession of money by a handful of capitalists, "the labour market is always understocked. The law of the supply and demand of labour consistently collapses." Indeed, as Marx writes, "despite throwing capital and thirsting after exploitation", the process in the colonies seems to be the reverse of the mother country; "today's wage-labourer becomes tomorrow's independent peasant or artisan, working for himself."[26]

Moreover, wage labourers continue to vanish from the labour market to become independent producers, and are able to enrich themselves at the expense of the "capitalist gentlemen". This not only has a further negative impact on the position of the labour market but crucially demonstrates to the producers that they can accumulate even at the expense of capitalists, thereby reducing what Marx terms "the relation of dependence and the feeling of dependence on the abstemious capitalist".[27]

Despite Marx's inability to see independent producers as operating under the logic of capital with a degree of autonomy (unlike in the quote at the beginning of the section), this brilliant analysis nonetheless anticipates some of the most important themes which subsequent scholars of PCP have explored in detail: the advantage that PCP possess in certain realms of production, its ability to deprive capital of labour power and undercut it, the possibility of accumulation from PCP, and most importantly, the desire for autonomy and independence which motivates PCP to reject wage labour.

So, since the first two problematics are unable to conceptualize petty production's playing an important role in the transition to capitalism (apart from either being destroyed completely or being so thoroughly dominated by it that it loses any independent existence), they are not useful in explaining why

---

[25] Marx, *Capital*, Vol. I, 932.
[26] Ibid.
[27] Ibid., 933.

PCP has been such a prevalent and persistent form of production under capitalist social relations. It is only the third problematic where Marx recognizes the contradictory existence of PCP as simultaneously embodying the possibility of accumulation while being exploited by capital that can provide some clues as to why small producers of various kinds have managed to reproduce themselves so remarkably even while social formations have been entirely dominated by the logic of commodity production.

In the next part, we see how far Marx's problematics of dissolution, conservation, autonomy and exploitation help us understand the actual experience of capitalist transition in the second most populous nation on earth—India.

V. PETTY COMMODITY PRODUCTION AND CIRCULATION IN THE DEVELOPMENT OF CAPITALISM IN INDIA

India's capitalist transition and ongoing transformations have created a complex, uneven and heterogeneous social formation. Rampant differentiation has occurred and advanced forms of corporate capital have been created with family dynasties, often grafted onto former colonial managing agencies, now wielding global power, confronting a substantial organized wage workforce, and putting sustained pressure on it to casualtie. However, the remaining 90 per cent of India's workforce is unregistered un-unionized and, except for a tiny minority, deprived of rights at work.[28]

Despite the growth of polar classes of capital and labour, it is still possible that the total capital controlled by family firms outweighs that of corporate capital. The most common form of livelihood is still self-employment. Out of the discursive Tower of Babel through which petty production is construed, "self-employment" is the least unstable category. In the 2013–14 Economic Census, 71.7 per cent of firms were self-employed in own-account enterprises. In terms of agricultural land in 2013, more than 80 per cent was operated by people declaring themselves self-employed.[29] In terms of livelihoods, PCP provides the robust core not only of agrarian and manufacturing production, but also services, commercial and even financial capital (which, because value could not be created in

---

[28] A. Srijia and Srinivas V. Shirke, *An Analysis of the Informal Labour Market in India* (New Delhi: Confederation of Indian Industry, 2014), 1.

[29] Government of India, *Economic Statistics* (New Delhi: Ministry of Statistics, 2014).

realization, were considered non-productive and even insignificant by Marx). Yet, due to the low purchasing power associated with PCP, self-employment is considered a constraint on the development of India's national market.

In India, PCP is unevenly distributed, rarely dominating or even populating a whole state territory. It co-exists with other forms of production, for some of which it may be functionally necessary for accumulation, while elsewhere it occupies niches in ways that are not directly exploited. Three types of co-existence can be distinguished. The first is "process-sequential", in which PCP and wage work are deployed at different *stages* in a system of commodity production (as in the smelting and crafting of metal); the second is "process-segregated" in which certain *sectors* of the informal economy are populated by PCP and others by firms with wage workers (e.g. local informal retail versus wholesale trade); and the third is "process-integrated" in which PCP and factory production using wage labour are *combined at all stages* of a commodity supply chain (e.g. garments).[30]

The research literature has generated no consensus about the forces driving the persistence of PCP. Since capital and labour are fused in PCP, it is not dynamized by contradiction—at most through "tensions" which are specific to particular historical contexts. Over a span of several decades, characterizations such as "blocked transition"[31] and "blocked differentiation"[32] have drawn attention to the roles of non-corporate capital in maintaining small-scale (often fragmented) production. There is much debate over how dependent this process of maintenance forces PCP to be.

Manifestations of all three of Marx's problematics—dissolution, conservation and the dialectic of exploitation and autonomy—are found. However, the evidence that would enable the analyst to gauge their relative numerical preponderance or political-economic significance is conspicuous by its absence, or it consists of national surveys that ignore context and process, or is created in local surveys and case studies from which generalization is not possible.

[30] Alessandra Mezzadri, "Globalisation, Informalisation and the State in the Indian Garment Industry," *International Review of Sociology* 20, no. 3 (2010): 492.

[31] John Harriss, *Capitalism and Peasant Farming: Agrarian Structure and Ideology in Northern Tamil Nadu* (New Delhi: Oxford University Press, 1982).

[32] Muhammad Ali Jan, "Rural-Commercial Capital: Accumulation, Class and Power in Pakistani Punjab" (PhD dissertation, University of Oxford, 2017).

Dissolution

Differentiation

The diversification and complexity of India's rural non-farm economy are qualifiers for evidence for inequality (and by implication, differentiation) that is based on land alone. While a small capitalist elite (0.24 per cent of rural households in 2013) operates over 10 ha of land, average land ownership declined from 1.1 ha in 1992 through 0.7 ha in 2003 to 0.6 ha in 2013. Agriculture remains a labour sponge of last resort. Yet, despite significant regional variations, at the all-India level, entirely landless rural households form only 7.4 per cent. While agriculture has declined dramatically in its relative contribution to GDP from over 30 per cent in 1990–91 to 14 per cent by 2010–11, its labour force increased in absolute terms from 210 m to 270 m[33]—and remains some 43 per cent of India's total.[34]

Incomplete Primitive Accumulation

The dual separation of wage labour from its means of production and the consolidation of property compatible with capitalist investment takes place through both market exchange and physical force. Pauperization as a result of the loan market (demand for which is provoked by needs as varied as occupation-related accidents and diseases or dowry demands) provokes migration, land sales and micro-property ownership. The deployment of force—in inadequately compensated state land seizures for SEZs and development-induced displacement for infrastructure, dams and irrigation, mines, power-plants and factories—has displaced between 30 and 60 million since Independence.[35] In fact, India's paradox of jobless growth is resolved by dispossession under primitive accumulation (PA) being incomplete: "dispossession without proletarianization", in what Adnan has argued is a diverse repertoire of processes in which the state is active in both preserving and creating PCP while it also both initiates and arrests PA.[36]

---

[33] No doubt, some who present agriculture as their main occupation are combining work in agriculture with work in non-agriculture.

[34] Venkatesh et al., "Trends in Agriculture, Non-Farm Sector and Rural Employment in India: An Insight from State Level Analysis," *Indian Journal of Agricultural Sciences* 85, no. 5 (2017).

[35] Walter Fernandes, "Singur and the Displacement Scenario," *Economic and Political Weekly* 42, no. 3 (January 2007): 204.

[36] Shapan Adnan, "Primitive Accumulation and the 'Transition to Capitalism,' in Neoliberal India: Mechanisms, Resistance and the Persistence of 'Self-Employed' Labour," in *Indian Capitalism in Development*, ed. Barbara Harriss-White and Judith Heyer (London: Routledge, 2015), 33.

So, under PCP, it is not that dissolution and differentiation are impossible. Some households are able to invest in assets and expand by employing wage labour, while others slither into ever-greater dependence on wages. But the theoretically remarkable characteristic of the Indian case is how comparatively rare this is, and how much more common is its tendency to expand through multiplication rather than through the concentration and centralization of capital. PCP exists and expands alongside other forms of capitalist production relations.

Conservation

The (Re)creation of PCP

The era of "liberalization" has seen much continuity in the unregistered economy with self-employment, a significant component of India's economic growth, driving workforce expansion. In agriculture, petty production is being miniaturized. Complex micro portfolios of production, trade and (migrant) labour proliferate throughout India. The interests of merchant's and commercial capital in not entirely dispossessing petty producers, but allowing the persistence and proliferation of micro-property which exploits its under- or un-paid family labour has long been recognized. Outside agriculture, between 1990 and 2011, own-account firms doubled in number. The average wage labour force per firm in India dropped from three workers to just two, while 95 per cent of firms in India employ fewer than five people.[37]

Formal Subsumption and Disguised Wage Labour

In India, forms of production such as subcontracting, outsourcing, insourcing, home-working and smallholder production are widely interpreted not as independent forms, but as structurally no different from wage work, merely differentiated by precarity, dependence and the scale of assets, or even regarded as "disguised *un*employment".[38] While in its official report of 2007, the National Council for Enterprises in the Unorganized Sector (NCEUS) concluded that PCP is DWL, in fact their conclusion is based on

---

[37] Harriss-White, *Capitalism and the Common Man*, 117.
[38] Deepankar Basu, "An Approach to the Problem of Employment in India," *UMass Amherst Economics Working Papers* 239 (2018).

the example of home-working[39] and, with qualifications, of "a good proportion" of a "mixed bag" of case studies of non-agricultural self-employment.[40] While there is no doubt that DWL proliferates in India, NCEUS subsequently concludes that self-employed economic units have a dual character of enterprises and workers. In NCEUS 2007, to the extent that PCP is treated as DWL, without making this explicit, the NCEUS recommends supporting a transition from DWL to PCP and from PCP to petty capital.

If PCP is a transitional stage of formal subsumption of labour to capital, it looks likely to be an indefinitely long one.

The Dialectic of Exploitation and Autonomy

PCP has also developed as a form of independent activity for the market in the spheres of manufacturing, trade and services—production and circulation: productive activity, necessary but unproductive activity, and activity which for some commentators is neither productive nor necessary.

Yet, where petty production has been compared with wage work, it is found, just as Marx argued, that returns are greater to the former than the latter.[41] However, it does not follow, as it does in Marx, that supply and demand for wage labour collapses. Nor, where it has been studied, does wage labour always develop to petty capital. Rather, self-employment and wage labour have been found to develop separately, structured through relations of social status.

In India, the form of PCP cannot be deduced in any pure and simple way from the social and cultural relations in which it is embedded. Marx called these "patriarchal, political or even religious admixtures".[42] Accumulation is both supported and constrained by micro-political relations of gender (in which men are allowed to save and invest while women are normatively—and even forcibly—prevented from saving) and by caste: occupational choices are still mostly restricted for Dalits and Adivasis, the hours of toil are set customarily, and the returns to effort can and do differ on caste-discriminating lines.

---

[39] NCEUS, *Reports on the Financing of Enterprises in the Unorganised Sector and Creation of a National Fund for the Unorganised Sector* (New Delhi: Government of India, 2007), 50.

[40] Ibid., 66–73.

[41] Olsen et al., "Multiple Shocks and Slum Household Economies in South India," *Economy and Society* 42, no. 3 (2013): 412.

[42] Karl Marx, *Economic Manuscript of 1861–63*, in MECW (London: Lawrence & Wishart, 1994), 34: 102.

Accumulation, involving graduating from PCP to petty capital employing wage labour, may be constrained by consumption-investment balances. While decisions on these balances may change over time, a household's needs for consumption expenditure and for spending on protection against risk (including health) are not considered separately from decisions about investments and working capital in those households which combine production and consumption.

Constraints on class differentiation are also found in the exchange relations in non-labour markets in which PCP is embedded. The persistence of tied contracts in several of the markets in which exchange takes place in both agriculture and non-agriculture (above all, in the "labour-intensive" textiles and garments sectors) has generated a large literature.[43] The social terms and conditions of tied labour reduce returns below the levels they might otherwise be expected to reach. Less well acknowledged is the common addition to operating costs that happens when payments for what petty producers sell are delayed, while payments for what they need to buy are not.[44] These combine to reduce the investible surplus.

Yet, despite the risk of adverse domestic balances and exchange relations, small social surpluses are accumulated and play a key part in the multiplication of small firms through savings, borrowing, small profits and partnerships, through the transfer of assets between and within families at marriages, and through inheritance. As early as 1978, Moser, from a comprehensive global review of urban informality, concluded PCP to be a permanent feature of capitalism in developing countries.[45]

Therefore, while all three problematics are to be found in India, it is nonetheless safe to say that PCP in its diverse forms has been an enduring feature of Indian capitalism. Not only have forms of petty production survived the onslaught of capitalist social relations (while being thoroughly reconfigured by its logic), but Indian capitalism constantly recreates PCP anew in diverse forms in order to exploit it through input, credit and output markets. But the reproduction of PCP is also the outcome of the strategies of survival and desire for autonomy of petty producers themselves,

---

[43] Mezzadri, *Globalization, Informalization and the State*, 496.

[44] Barbara Harriss-White, "Debt, Credit and Contractual Synchrony in a South Indian Market Town," in *Microfinance, Debt and Over Indebtedness: Juggling with Money*, ed. Isabelle Guerin, Solene Morvant-Roux, and Villarealm Magdalena (New York: Routledge, 2014).

[45] Caroline Moser, "Informal Sector or Petty Commodity Production: Dualism or Dependence in Urban Development," *World Development* 6, no. 9/10 (1978): 1056–60.

which need to be understood in a dialectical relationship with their exploitation through different markets controlled by capital.

The tension between capital's need to exploit PCP and the latter's strategies for autonomy and possibilities of accumulation are always mediated through an institutional environment, not simply informal regulation by capitalists and PCP, but the formal regulation of the state. In many ways, the Indian state itself has been a crucial player in the constant reproduction of PCP, even as it has simultaneously been involved in its destruction through strategies of primitive accumulation. This is achieved through interventions in markets for land, labour, credit, inputs and outputs, which are never free of the contradictory goals of policy makers and the struggles by social groups themselves, often resulting in outcomes that are the opposite of what was intended.

So scholars, policy makers and activists who categorize PCP as a "transitional" form which will eventually be bypassed are bound to be disappointed. PCP is central not only to Indian capitalism but to capitalism in much of the Global South. The diverse forms through which PCP reproduces, the diverse logics underlying PCP, and their relations to labour exploitation all need urgent and systematic mapping. So too do the political struggles that PCP engenders.

VI. PCP: What Is to Be Done?

Do the forms taken by PCP politics accord to the forms identified by Marx?

Despite its economic significance, PCP has never generated a political party. Considered as labour, the politics of PCP suffers from *not* being labour. Labour politics focuses on struggles to improve the terms of exploitation in, and vanquish oppression on, labour markets. But if PCP is labour, then it requires an expansion of the concept of exploitation to markets other than labour: those for premises, land and machines, money and the supply of raw materials and finished commodities. Power struggles on these markets are not recognized as labour politics by unions, by labour policy makers or by scholars of labour. Insofar as PCP are owners of capital, farmers' movements and business associations admit them to join mobilizations (such as for price support).[46] But while

---

[46] Christine Lutringer, "A Movement of Subsidized Capitalists? The Multilevel Influence of the Bharatiya Kisan Union in India," *International Review of Sociology* 20, no. 3 (2010): 518.

these forms of collective action are often termed "populist", they rarely allow for the political aspirations and interests of PCP to be represented if they differ from those of local capitalist elites.

As for the mobilization of PCP for itself, the Self-employed Women's Association, which spread from Gujarat to cover 2 per cent of India's workforce, is regarded as an important political model for what may be achieved in the fight for work security, income security, food security and social security. But it is not generally replicable. Its unique attributes include the vast, complex range of activities it comprises (over 80 trades, and other activities ranging from housing and childcare to banks, education and eco-tourism), its capacity to cross-subsidize them until enterprises make profits, its engagement with the state rather than directly with employers, and a scale attracting international funding and engagement.

So, PCP has no coherent politics. The strategic questions for PCP and India's development are whether to try to remove the constraints to accumulation and to try to destroy PCP and DWL and accelerate the creation of a formal proletariat; or whether to try to transcend such forms by collectivized, cooperative and/or socialized forms of production or whether to accept and support it. And how.

Such questions have been rarely asked or answered. The Indian state's response to PCP has been incoherent and often self-defeating. When the state engages in city beautification, when it invokes the law of eminent domain to seize land for public infrastructure or for corporate capital, it actively destroys PCP commonly with little or no compensation.[47] PCP is also disenfranchised under Indian labour law, because for cases to be brought to court an individual employer must be identified, which has proved impossible to do. The labour laws not only disenfranchise, they also de-class petty capital, PCP and labour alike, because employers of up to five wage workers (recall this is 95 per cent of total firms) are themselves legally classified as "labour" on grounds of their relatively small size and lack of access to social security.

Yet, when the state seeks to develop small-farmer agricultural technology and extension services, implement land reforms, build micro-industrial estates and expand micro finance, it promotes PCP. During 2005–09, for example, the NCEUS, despite its lack of consensus over self-employment,

---

[47] Michael Lieven, *Dispossession without Development: Land Grabs in Neoliberal India* (New Delhi: Oxford University Press, 2018).

treated it as a form of entrepreneurial capital, advocating credit, skills-training and secure sites as elements of "pro-poor development".[48] And when the state establishes safety nets of social protection, it protects PCP along with wage labour. PCP is also both sustained and disadvantaged through unintended outcomes—as when the rural employment guarantee scheme incentivizes PCP by raising the formal wage floor, under which PCP competes, or disadvantages it by expanding and formalizing credit for which PCP has no acceptable collateral.

Despite threats from the expansion of export agriculture, from contract production for supermarkets and corporate capital, from stricter attempts at phytosanitary regulation and rising hedonic standards, from speculation in food markets by finance capital and from the commodification of applied life sciences, such is its armoury of resistance that there is little evidence for anything but a continuing proliferation of PCP as a constitutive form of Indian capitalism. While PCP may undergo further transformations, it seems all but proof against differentiation. In any case, since India's corporate sector does not absorb wage labour, any attempt by corporate capital and/or the Indian state to crush PCP in the informal economy would be nothing short of a disaster for livelihoods.

Finally, it is important to note that PCP is increasing not only in India and the Global South, but also in the Global North. As new technologies emerge and entities like the "gig economy" establish themselves, we observe a shift in the "world of work" away from wage labour to increased "self-employment". In the UK, for example, the last decade has seen the number of "self-employed" people increase by 24 per cent—from 3.9 million to 4.7 million.[49] This is by no means an isolated trend: all across Europe and North America, stable waged employment is unravelling in favour of short-term, casual forms of work where employers are difficult to identify and labour and capital are combined in complex ways within the same person.

If this is true, then Marx's famous dictum that "the country that is more developed industrially only shows, to the less developed, the image of its future" needs to be inverted.[50] It seems more likely that labour forms

---

[48] NCEUS, *Reports on the Financing of Enterprises in the Unorganised Sector and Creation of a National Fund for the Unorganised Sector* (New Delhi: Government of India, 2007).

[49] Sunny Sidhu, *Trends in Self-employment in the UK: Analyzing the Characteristics, Income and Wealth of the Self-employed* (London: Office for National Statistics, 2018).

[50] Marx, *Capital*, Vol. I, 91.

in the Global South are the future of capitalism in the Global North, and for this reason alone, serious attention needs paying to PCP and its development.

VII. Conclusion

This chapter has attempted to answer why despite their centrality to the capitalist social formations of the Global South, petty commodity producers remain neglected in Marxian political economy. It has argued that the main reason for this neglect is the scattered and often contradictory manner in which petty production was understood by Marx himself. Through an excavation of his writings on the subject we demonstrate that while much of Marx's writings view petty production as a hangover from the past destined for oblivion under the logic of capital, a more complicated picture emerges from a deeper reading of his texts where Marx does allow for petty production as form of disguised wage labour and where he even allows for its existence as a contradictory combination of capital and labour within the framework of capitalism.

In the second part, this chapter illuminates these contradictory aspects of Marx's thought on PCP through a brief overview of capitalist transformations in India. While all three aspects of Marx's views on PCP (i.e. dissolution, conservation and the dialectic of exploitation and autonomy) can be found, it is in the third sense of being a contradictory form that is simultaneously subsumed under the logic of capital and exploited by it while retaining a degree of autonomy, that PCP can be most fruitfully conceptualized for contemporary conditions. In paying homage to the power of Marx's thought, we also recognize its historical limitations and the constant need to both benefit from it but also develop it.

Bibliography

Adnan, Shapan. "Primitive Accumulation and the 'Transition to Capitalism' in Neoliberal India: Mechanisms, Resistance and the Persistence of 'Self-Employed' Labour." In *Indian Capitalism in Development*, edited by Barbara Harriss-White and Judith Heyer, 23–45. London: Routledge, 2015.

Banaji, Jairus. "Capitalist Domination and the Small Peasantry: Deccan Districts in the Late Nineteenth Century." *Economic And Political Weekly* 12, no. 33/34 (1977): 1375–404.

Basu, Deepankar. "An Approach to the Problem of Employment in India." UMass Amherst Economics Working Papers 239, 2018. Retrieved from https://scholarworks.umass.edu/econ_workingpaper/239.

Bernstein, Henry. "Capitalism and Petty-Bourgeois Production: Class Relations and Divisions of Labour." *Journal of Peasant Studies* 15, no. 2 (1988): 258–71.

Centre for Equity Studies. *India Exclusion Report 2013–14.* Bangalore: Books for Change, 2013.

Fernandes, Walter. "Singur and the Displacement Scenario." *Economic and Political Weekly* 42, no. 3 (January 2007): 203–6.

Government of India. *Economic Statistics.* New Delhi: Ministry of Statistics, 2014.

Harriss, John. *Capitalism and Peasant Farming: Agrarian Structure and Ideology in Northern Tamil Nadu.* New Delhi: Oxford University Press, 1982.

Harriss-White, Barbara. "Capitalism and the Common Man: Peasants and Petty Production in Africa and South Asia." *Agrarian South: Journal of Political Economy* 1, no. 2 (August 1, 2012): 109–60.

Harriss-White, Barbara. "Debt, Credit and Contractual Synchrony in a South Indian Market Town." In *Microfinance, Debt and Over Indebtedness: Juggling with Money,* edited by Isabelle Guerin, Solene Morvant-Roux, and Villarealm Magdalena, 103–24. New York: Routledge, 2014.

Harriss-White, Barbara. "From Analysing Filieres Vivrieres to Understanding Capital and Petty Production in Rural South India." *Journal of Agrarian Change* 16, no. 3 (2016): 478–500.

Jan, Muhammad Ali. *Rural-Commercial Capital: Accumulation, Class and Power in Pakistani Punjab.* PhD Dissertation, Oxford University, 2017.

Kautsky, Karl. *The Agrarian Question.* London: Zwan Publications, 1988.

Lieven, Michael. *Dispossession without Development: Land Grabs in Neoliberal India.* New Delhi: Oxford University Press, 2018.

Lutringer, Caroline. "A Movement of Subsidised Capitalists? The Multilevel Influence of the Bharatiya Kisan Union in India." *International Review of Sociology* 20, no. 3 (2010): 513–31.

Marx, Karl. *Pre-Capitalist Economic Formations.* Translated by E. J. Hobsbawm. New York: International Publishers, 1964.

Marx, Karl. *Theories of Surplus Value.* Vol. I. London: Lawrence & Wishart, 1969.

Marx, Karl. *The German Ideology.* London: Lawrence & Wishart, 1970.

Marx, Karl. *Grundrisse: Foundations of the Critique of Political Economy.* London: Penguin Books, 1973.

Marx, Karl. *Capital.* Vol. I. London: Penguin Books, 1976.

Marx, Karl. *Capital.* Vol. II. London: Penguin Books, 1978.

Marx, Karl. *Capital.* Vol. III. London: Penguin Books, 1981.

Marx, Karl. *Economic Manuscript of 1861–63.* In MECW, Vol. 34. London: Lawrence & Wishart, 1994.

Mezzadri, Alessandra. "Globalisation, Informalisation and the State in the Indian Garment Industry." *International Review of Sociology* 20, no. 3 (2010): 491–511.

Moser Caroline. "Informal Sector or Petty Commodity Production: Dualism or Dependence in Urban Development." *World Development* 6, no. 9/10 (1978): 1041–64.

National Commission on Enterprises in the Unorganised Sector. *Reports on the Financing of Enterprises in the Unorganised Sector and Creation of a National Fund for the Unorganised Sector.* New Delhi: Government of India, 2007.

Olsen, Wendy, Penny Vera Sanso and V. Suresh "Multiple Shocks and Slum Household Economies in South India." *Economy and Society* 42, no. 3 (2013): 400–31.

Sidhu, Sunny. *Trends in Self-Employment in the UK: Analyzing the Characteristics, Income and Wealth of the Self-Employed.* London: Office for National Statistics, 2018. https://www.ons.gov.uk/employmentandlabourmarket/peopleinwork/employmentandemployeetypes/articles/trendsinselfemploymentintheuk/2018-02-07.

Srija, A. and Shrinivas V. Shirke. *An Analysis of the Informal Labour Market in India.* New Delhi: Confederation of Indian Industry, 2014. http://www.ies.gov.in/pdfs/CII per cent20EM-october-2014.pdf.

Venkatesh, P., M. L. Nithyashree, V. Sangeetha, and Suresh Pal. "Trends in Agriculture, Non-Farm Sector and Rural Employment in India: An Insight from State Level Analysis." *Indian Journal of Agricultural Sciences* 85, no. 5 (2017): 671–7.

Index[1]

---

[1] Note: Page numbers followed by 'n' refer to notes.

© The Author(s) 2019   369
S. Gupta et al. (eds.), *Karl Marx's Life, Ideas, and Influences*, Marx,
Engels, and Marxisms, https://doi.org/10.1007/978-3-030-24815-4